How Racism
Takes Place

George Lipsitz

How Racism Takes Place

TEMPLE UNIVERSITY PRESS
Philadelphia

TEMPLE UNIVERSITY PRESS
Philadelphia, Pennsylvania 19122
www.temple.edu/tempress

Permission to revise and reprint selections from three of the author's earlier publications is hereby acknowledged:

"The Silence of the Rams: How St. Louis School Children Subsidize the Super Bowl Champs," in John Bloom and Michael Nevin Willard, eds., *Sports Matters: Race, Recreation and Culture* (New York: New York University Press, 2002), 225–245. Copyright 2002 New York University Press.

"The Racialization of Space and the Spatialization of Race: Theorizing the Hidden Architecture of Landscape," *Landscape Journal* 26, no. 1 (March 2007), 10–23. Copyright University of Wisconsin Press.

"New Orleans in the World and the World in New Orleans," *Black Music Research Journal* 31, no. 2 (2011). Copyright 2011 by the Board of Trustees of the University of Illinois. Used with permission of the University of Illinois Press.

Library of Congress Cataloging-in-Publication Data

Lipsitz, George.
  How racism takes place / George Lipsitz.
     p. cm.
  Includes bibliographical references and index.
  ISBN 978-1-4399-0255-4 (cloth : alk. paper) — ISBN 978-1-4399-0256-1 (pbk. : alk. paper) — ISBN 978-1-4399-0257-8 (e-book)
  1. United States—Race relations. 2. United States—Social conditions. 3. Racism—Economic aspects—United States. 4. Income distribution—United States. 5. African Americans—Social conditions. 6. African Americans—Economic conditions. 7. Human geography—United States. I. Title.
  E185.615.L5765 2011
  305.800973—dc22

                                                                                          2010045079

Printed in the United States of America

15 14 13 12 11 10

Contents

SECTION IV Invisible Archives

SECTION V Race and Place Today

How Racism
Takes Place

Introduction

Race, Place, and Power

It is an aspect of their sense of superiority that
the white people of America believe they have
so little to learn.
—Martin Luther King, Jr.

What happened to the hopes of the civil rights movement? What has become of Dr. King's dream? How can it be that decades after the adoption of comprehensive civil rights laws, racial identity remains the key variable in shaping opportunities and life chances for individuals and groups in the United States? Why does race still matter so much? The most popular answers to these questions lead us in exactly the wrong directions. Since the 1970s, politicians, pundits, and publicists have argued that Black people have shown themselves to be simply unfit for freedom. They argue that in a time when civil rights laws clearly ban discrimination, the persistence of racial inequality demonstrates that Blacks have been unable to take advantage of the opportunities afforded them. Equal opportunity exists, they contend, so unequal outcomes have to be attributed to what they perceive to be the deficient values, beliefs, and behaviors of Black people themselves. At times those who adhere to these positions concede that past generations of Blacks had legitimate grievances about slavery, segregation, vigilante violence, and disenfranchisement, but they argue that the problems that Black people confront today are of their own making. What was once done to them by white racists, this line of argument contends, Blacks are now doing to themselves. Inequality between races today, they claim, exists because Blacks allegedly commit more crimes, have lower rates of marriage, and higher rates of children born out of wedlock. They contend that Black students perform poorly on standardized tests because they and their parents do not value education, and that they are disproportionately poor because their parents either refuse to work or because they foolishly purchase expensive and flashy consumer goods while refusing to save money. Some of these critics even blame these conditions on civil rights laws themselves, arguing that efforts to desegregate schools, to promote fair hiring, and to end housing discrimination have led Blacks to expect special preferences and privileges simply because they are Black. At the same time, these critics complain that society practices reverse racism by punishing hardworking whites and giving unearned rewards to unqualified Blacks.

In my book *The Possessive Investment in Whiteness*, I showed how focusing on Black disadvantages deflects attention away from the unearned advantages that whites possess. It is not so much that Blacks are disadvantaged, but rather that they are taken advantage of by discrimination in employment, education, and housing, by the ways in which the health care system, the criminal justice system, and the banking system skew opportunities and life chances along racial lines. Moral panics about alleged Black misbehavior, I argued, are designed to obscure the special privileges that whites receive from collective, cumulative, and continuing forms of discrimination.[1]

A large and unrefuted body of research reveals how the economic standing of millions of white families today stems directly from the unfair gains and unjust enrichments made possible by past and present forms of racial discrimination. A wide range of public and private actions protect the assets and advantages that whites have inherited from their ancestors, wealth originally accumulated during eras when direct and overt discrimination in government policies, home sales, mortgage lending, education, and employment systematically channeled assets to whites. For example, at least forty-six million white adults today can trace the origins of their family wealth to the Homestead Act of 1862. This bill gave away valuable acres of land for free to white families, but expressly precluded participation by Blacks.[2] Seventy years later, the 1934 Federal Housing Act distributed federally insured home mortgages to whites in overtly and directly discriminatory fashion, building additional equity in the estates of some thirty-five million white families between 1934 and 1978 while systematically excluding Black families from those opportunities.[3] Moreover, because money is passed down across generations through inheritance, the patterns of the past still shape opportunities in the present. Whites not only inherit the riches that flow across generations because of these policies, but new provisions in the tax code consistently add new forms of favored treatment to inherited wealth while increasing taxes on earned income.

Segregated housing leads to segregated schools that give white people privileged treatment, better facilities and better trained teachers. School and neighborhood networks give them access to insider information which enables them to receive preferential treatment when seeking the 80 to 90 percent of jobs in U.S. society that are never openly advertised to the general public. Over time, these uncompetitive processes shape wealth accumulation. They produce cumulative disadvantages for African Americans, but provide "locked in" advantages for whites. As Daria Roithmayr explains in her innovative work on whiteness as an efficiently functioning racial cartel, whites used restrictive covenants, racial zoning, redlining, steering, blockbusting, and mob violence between 1866 and 1948 to monopolize advantages for themselves and their descendants. They acted collectively as a group to gain favored access to homeownership, employment, education, and political power. The Federal Housing Administration and other government agencies translated aspirations for racial power into public policy, channeling home loans to whites while denying them to Blacks. Although many of the practices that secured these gains initially were outlawed by the civil rights laws of the 1960s, the gains whites received for them were already locked in place. Even more important, nearly every significant decision made since then about urban planning, education, employment, transportation, taxes, housing, and health care has served to protect the preferences, privileges, and property that whites first acquired from an expressly and overtly discriminatory market.[4]

Blacks and whites with similar incomes, work histories, and family alignments have very different relationships to wealth. Blacks currently possess merely seven to ten cents for every dollar of net worth that whites possess.[5] Largely because of racialized space, whiteness in this society is not so much a color as a condition. It is a structured advantage that channels unfair gains and unjust enrichments to whites while imposing unearned and unjust obstacles in the way of Blacks. Of course, not all whites benefit equally from the possessive investment in whiteness, but even the poorest of the poor among whites do not face the degree of concentration in impoverished neighborhoods and schools or the levels of exposure to environmental hazards that routinely confront middle-income Blacks.

The wealth that present-day whites acquire from expressly discriminatory and racist land use practices makes a huge difference in their lives. Middle-class whites have between 3 and 5 times as much wealth as equally achieving blacks. Disproportionately large inheritances provide them with transformative assets that enable whites to make down payments on homes, start businesses, and pay for college educations. Inherited wealth is the main reason why whites and Blacks earning exactly the same incomes have widely divergent wealth portfolios.[6] Sociologist Thomas Shapiro shows that between 1990 and 2020, some seven to nine trillion dollars will be inherited by the "baby boom" generation. Almost all of that money is rooted in profits made by whites from overtly discriminatory housing markets before 1968. Adult white wage earners routinely inherit money *from* parents, while adult nonwhite wage earners routinely send out money *to* their parents to compensate for the low wages and lack of assets they possess because of racial discrimination. Shapiro's research reveals that white inheritance is seven times larger than Black inheritance. One out of three "baby boom" generation whites in 1989 could count on bequests, but only one in twenty Blacks could have similar expectations. In addition, even among those who do inherit wealth, whites are four times as likely as Blacks to receive a sizably significant inheritance. On the average, whites inherit $102,167 more than Blacks. White families are 2.4 times as likely as Blacks to have parents who can provide help with down payments or closing costs. Largely because of assets inherited from the past, Blacks get $2.10 in net worth for every dollar earned, whites get $3.23. Cuts in inheritance and capital gains taxes disproportionately benefit whites and make property income more valuable compared to wage income. The homes that whites do acquire in largely white neighborhoods cost them less than comparable homes purchased by Blacks, but they appreciate in value much more than homes in Black neighborhoods. Only 26 percent of white children grow up in asset-poor households, but 52 percent of blacks and 54 percent of Latinos grow up in these economically fragile households. According to Shapiro, inheritance is more important in determining life chances than college degrees, number of children in the family, marital status, full-time employment, or household composition.[7]

Because these inequalities started with discrimination in the past, one might expect that they would become less important over time, that improvements in race relations would gradually narrow the racial wealth gap. Yet precisely the opposite is the case. Assets that appreciate in value and are transferred across generations *increase* in value over time, especially when their privileged beneficiaries skew public policy to make the fruits and rewards of past discrimination even more valuable in the present. A 2010 study conducted by Shapiro and his colleagues at the Institute on Assets and Social Policy at Brandeis University revealed that the wealth gap between Blacks and whites quadrupled between 1984 and 2007. More than a quarter of African American families have no assets at all. Even *high-income* Blacks average assets of only $18,000 compared to the $74,000 in assets held by *middle-income* whites. These differences are not due to market forces, personal attributes, or family composition, but rather are the consequence of both direct discrimination and the indirect effects of the racial dimensions of state policies designed to provide incentives and subsidies for asset-building activities like homeownership. Seemingly race-neutral changes in public policies have also played an important role in widening the racial wealth gap. Cuts in inheritance and capital gains taxes over the past three decades have augmented the value of past discrimination, increasing the fortunes of the white beneficiaries of past and present housing discrimination. At the same time, deductions allowable for local property taxes produce massive federal subsidies for school taxes in largely white suburbs.[8] Shapiro and his colleagues conclude that present-day job achievements do not predict family wealth holdings adequately, reiterating that people with similar incomes and work histories have vastly different levels of wealth because of past and present racial discrimination.[9]

Privatization of public institutions, cuts in government services, and capital flight to low-wage countries decreases opportunities for upward mobility for most Americans. Under these circumstances, inherited wealth becomes even more important for those positioned to receive it. A 2002 study found that parental income had become a more reliable predictor of children's eventual earnings than it had been in the 1980s.[10] The damaging effects of this racial wealth gap are exacerbated by the massive refusal in our society to desegregate schools or enforce civil rights laws banning discrimination in employment and education. Having civil rights laws on the books is not an effective way of protecting Black rights when white lawlessness is routinely condoned and encouraged by the major institutions in our society. The words that Dr. King wrote about this dynamic in 1967 still hold true today,

> Throughout our history, laws affirming Negro rights have consistently been circumvented by ingenious evasions which render them void in practice. Laws that affect the whole population—draft laws, income-tax laws, traffic laws—manage to work even though they may be unpopular; but laws passed for the Negro's benefit are so widely unenforced that it is a mockery to call them laws. There is a tragic gulf between civil rights laws passed and civil rights laws implemented. There is a double standard in the enforcement of law and a double standard in the respect for particular laws.

How Racism Takes Place challenges the people blaming Blacks for the persistence of unequal racial outcomes in U.S. society today to come to grips with the fatal couplings of place and race in our society. When I say that racism "takes place" I mean it figuratively, in the way that historians do, to describe things that happen in history. But I also use the term as cultural geographers do, to describe how social relations take on their full force and meaning when they are enacted physically in actual places. By examining residential and school segregation, mortgage and insurance redlining, taxation and transportation policies, or the location of environmental amenities and toxic hazards, we learn that race is produced by space, that it takes places for racism to take place.

Relations between races are relations between places, as the work of geographer Laura Pulido demonstrates.[11] White identity in the United States is place bound. It exists and persists because segregated neighborhoods and segregated schools are nodes in a network of practices that skew opportunities and life chances along racial lines. Because of practices that racialize space and spatialize race, whiteness is learned and legitimated, perceived as natural, necessary, and inevitable. Racialized space gives whites privileged access to opportunities for social inclusion and upward mobility. At the same time, it imposes unfair and unjust forms of exploitation and exclusion on aggrieved communities of color. Racialized space shapes nearly every aspect of urban life. The racial imagination that relegates people of different races to different spaces produces grossly unequal access to education, employment, transportation, and shelter. It exposes communities of color disproportionately to environmental hazards and social nuisances while offering whites privileged access to economic opportunities, social amenities, and valuable personal networks. The lived experience of race takes place in actual spaces, while the lived experience of place draws its determinate logic from overt and covert understandings of race. Yet as I attempt to demonstrate in this book, the actual long-term interests of whites are often damaged by spatial relations that purportedly benefit them, while Black negotiations with the constraints and confinements of racialized space often produce ways of envisioning and enacting more decent, dignified, humane, and egalitarian social relations for everyone.

People of different races do not inhabit different places by choice. Housing and lending discrimination, the design of school district boundaries, zoning regulations, policing strategies, the location of highways and transit systems, and a host of tax subsidies do disastrous work by making places synonymous with races. The racial meaning of place makes American whiteness one of the most systematically subsidized identities in the world. It enables whites to own homes that appreciate in value and generate assets passed down to subsequent generations. At the same time, Blacks confront an artificially constricted housing market that often forces them to remain renters unable to take advantage of the subsidies that homeowners receive from the tax code. When they do manage to own homes, Blacks are forced to do so on terms that compel them to pay more for dwellings that are worth less and appreciate in value more slowly than comparable homes inhabited by whites. Housing and school segregation function to channel white children into well equipped classrooms with experienced teachers while crowding Black children into ill-equipped buildings where they are taught by inexperienced teachers and surrounded by impoverished classmates many of whom suffer from lead poisoning, malnutrition, and a variety of undiagnosed and untreated disabilities. The estimated four million violations of federal fair-housing law that take place every year offer whites privileged access to parks, playgrounds, fresh food, and other amenities while relegating Blacks to areas that suffer disproportionate exposure to polluted air, water, food, and land.

Living in segregated inner-city neighborhoods imposes the equivalent of a racial tax on people of color. One important way in which this "tax" is imposed is on the health and well being of Black bodies. The racial wealth gap is also a racial health gap. Michael Marmot, chairman of the World Health Organization's Commission on Social Determinants of Health, offers a vivid illustration of the health consequences of racialized space. "If you catch the metro train in downtown Washington, D.C. to suburbs in Maryland," Marmot observes, "life expectancy is 55 years at the beginning of the journey. At the end of the journey, it is 77 years. This means that there is a 20-year life expectancy gap in the nation's capital, between the poor and predominately African American people who live downtown, and the richer and predominantly non–African American people who live in the suburbs."[12]

Researchers have long established how racial discrimination in housing impacts health as well as wealth. Relegating people of different races to different places artificially skews exposure to toxic hazards. The neighborhoods of people of color become prime sites for the location of garbage and toxic-waste dumps, incinerators, lead-based paint on playground equipment and interior walls, metal-plating shops, and concentrated pollutants from freeways and factories. Segregation-related educational inequality, racialized policing strategies, mismatches between the location of jobs and the residences of communities of color, siting of supermarkets and fast-food outlets, and the constant emergence of new forms of racially targeted exploitation like predatory lending, insurance redlining, foreclosure abandonment, and underbounding (discussed in Chapter 10) combine to undermine the health of ghetto and *barrio* residents.

Research indicates that discrimination itself is a health hazard, that the panoply of racially tinged everyday experiences that people of color confront can injure their cardiovascular, endocrine, immunologic, and metabolic systems, contributing to increased chances for hypertension, obesity, diabetes, depression, asthma, and infections.[13] Nancy Krieger notes that anticipating and/or receiving racial discrimination "provokes fear and anger: the physiology of fear . . . mobilizes lipids and glucose to increase energy supplies and sensory vigilance and also produces transient elevations in blood pressure; chronic triggering of these physiologic pathways leads to sustained hypertension."[14] A U.S. Department of Agriculture study found that the inner-city poor pay on average 4 percent more for food than suburban dwellers pay.[15] In addition, many inner city areas are "food deserts," filled with fast-food outlets, convenience markets, and liquor stores but void of stores selling fresh fruits and vegetables. One study conducted in New Orleans found that neighborhoods that were predominately Black housed an average of 2.4 fast-food restaurants per square mile, while the number in predominately white neighborhoods was only 1.5 fast-food establishments per square mile.[16]

The cumulative vulnerabilities crafted by centuries of anti-Black racism leave African Americans facing multiple and overlapping economic obstacles. Direct discrimination by insurance agents and mortgage loan officers compounds the already difficult economic situation facing working-class and poor people of color as can be seen from the ways in which segregation into different neighborhoods channels people of different races to different sectors of the banking industry. Banks locate branches disproportionately in suburban neighborhoods, forcing inner-city residents to turn to nonbanking institutions for banking services. Thus they are compelled to pay exorbitant fees for simple needs like cashing checks.[17] Residents of white neighborhoods can expect to do business with mainstream financial service providers. Their neighborhood banks offer them savings and checking accounts, certificates of deposit, prime rate mortgages, individual retirement accounts, and automobile and home improvement loans. People who live in Black neighborhoods, in contrast, find only low-end service providers. They transact business with payday lenders, pawn shops, check-cashing establishments, rent-to-own shops, and subprime mortgage lenders who charge them exorbitant fees and rates of interest because they do not have access to the top end of the banking industry. A North Carolina study found that Black neighborhoods house three times as many payday lenders as white neighborhoods.[18] The number of check-cashing businesses in the nation jumped from 2,151 in 1986 to 5,500 in 1997 and 22,000 in 2003.[19] Fees charged on payday loans can amount to an annual rate of as much as 400 to 1,000 percent.[20]

Among workers with incomes under $83,000 per year, the percentage of families without bank accounts rose from 9.5 percent to 13.5 percent between 1977 and 1989. But among families with an average annual income below $11,970—nearly one-fifth of the population—the percentage of families without bank accounts went from 30 percent to 41 percent.[21] Increases in deposit fees, branch bank closings, increased levels of personal debt, and the stagnation of real wages hurt all middle- and low-income workers during this time period, but members of aggrieved racial groups suffered the most. In nearly every aspect of life, from the frequency and duration of layoffs to the locations of branch bank closings, race proved to be a more decisive variable than class.[22] Yet the same banks that discriminate against minority applicants for standard home loans profit tremendously from the subprime loans that became the basis of the national economic meltdown in 2008 (see Chapter 4). All too often, race rather than class or creditworthiness determines who gets subprime loans. The Center for Responsible Lending calculated that in 2002 high-income African Americans were three times more likely to be subjected to subprime terms than low-income whites.[23] A study by the Reinvestment Fund of mortgage lending in ten cities discovered that the amount of subprime lending in an area rose in proportion to the number of elderly and Black residents, even after accounting for credit risks and the condition of housing stock.[24] More than half of the Blacks refinancing loans in Philadelphia and its suburbs received subprime loans, but only 11 percent of whites needed to turn to the subprime sector for refinancing purposes.[25] Another Philadelphia study found only 2 percent of white borrowers in that city used subprime lenders for home purchases, compared to 20 percent of Blacks. In middle-income neighborhoods in Chicago, subprime refinance loans constituted 48 percent of lending in predominately Black neighborhoods but only 8 percent in comparable white areas.[26] Researchers for the Department of Housing and Urban Development found that African American neighborhoods nationwide were five times more likely to see subprime purchases than white neighborhoods.[27]

The home loan industry often attributes Black reliance on subprime lenders to inadequate consumer sophistication rather than admitting to the pervasive nature of discrimination that drives minority consumers to subprime lenders. The current crisis is a direct result, however, of laws that freed the banking industry from regulation, from the 1980 law passed by Congress that removed interest-rate caps on first-lien mortgages to the Banking Reform Act of 1999 and its attendant securitization of the mortgage industry that enabled individuals to make enormous profits by making unsecured loans in a largely unregulated market. Credit-starved Blacks trapped in artificially constrained housing markets proved to be ideal targets for unscrupulous and unregulated lenders.

Spatial isolation from employment opportunities and municipal facilities also raises transportation costs, while expenses for health care increase because of augmented exposure to environmental hazards and decreased access to primary care physicians and preventive medical services.[28] The predominately Black and Latino neighborhoods of South Central Los Angeles have one primary care physician for every 12,993 residents, but there is one primary care physician for every 214 residents in the largely white area of Bel Air. Suburban and largely white Bethesda, Maryland, boasts one pediatrician for every 400 children, but the Black neighborhoods in southeast Washington, D.C., have one pediatrician for every 3,700 children.[29]

Redlining by insurance companies plays an important if often invisible role in imposing impediments to asset accumulation. Insurance rates are higher in inner-city areas than in suburbs, even when loss ratios are higher in the suburbs. In his excellent study of urban decline in twentieth-century St. Louis, Colin Gordon demonstrates that residents of Black neighborhoods had difficulty finding insurance companies willing to sell them policies. They paid more for the policies that they did purchase than residents of comparable white neighborhoods in the suburbs, often losing their coverage as soon as they made a claim.[30] A study of insurance redlining in Chicago by the U.S. Commission on Civil Rights and one on insurance redlining in Milwaukee by researchers from the University of Wisconsin's branch campus in that city revealed that the number of insurance policies written per owner-occupied dwelling in any given area depended more on race than on any other variable including neighborhood poverty rate, age or condition of buildings, homeowner income, population turnover, frequency of fires, or levels of crime.[31] A federal audit of twenty-four cities found that 53 percent of Black insurance seekers experienced some form of discrimination. These acts ranged from insurance agents not returning phone calls about insuring property in minority neighborhoods to agents withholding information about insurance options from Black customers, from charging Blacks more money for less coverage to charging white customers less money for more coverage. In Chicago, Black insurance seekers faced discrimination 83 percent of the time. Blacks in Memphis experienced the fewest instances of discrimination in this study, but they still faced discrimination 32 percent of the time. White applicants, in contrast, found that their race increased their options and their coverage while providing them with lower rates.[32]

A study by the Commissioner of Insurance for the state of Missouri found that residents of low-income Black neighborhoods in St. Louis paid $6.15 for every thousand dollars of coverage, while residents of poor white neighborhoods paid only $4.70 for every thousand dollars of coverage. In addition, the loss ratio was higher in the white areas. The Shelter Group insured many homeowners in the St. Louis area, but in the city of St. Louis and the suburban zip codes with the largest minority populations that firm had virtually no customers. In the predominantly white suburban zip code 63026, Shelter had one agent and 501 policies in force. In zip code 63132, however, where 40 percent of the residents were Black, the company had no agents and only sixty-two policies. Yet zip code 63132 had a median income of $34,695, higher than that in the mostly white 63026 where earnings averaged $31,336.[33] An investigation conducted by the Missouri Insurance Department in 1991 discovered a map of the city of St. Louis in an office of the Farm Bureau Town and Country Insurance Company with a circle drawn around the inner city with the words "ineligible property" written inside the circle.[34] One mid-1990s study discovered that the loss ratio for insurance companies in the predominately Black neighborhoods of central Atlanta was 79 percent while annual premiums were $705. In the mostly white areas of north Fulton and northwest DeKalb counties, however, loss ratios were 92 percent while premiums averaged only $349.[35] The competitive economic position of whites benefits tremendously from these unfair gains and unjust enrichments.

Along with discrimination in insurance coverage and home rentals and sales, discriminatory practices by mortgage lenders play a central role in skewing housing opportunities and life chances in U.S. cities along racial lines. Along with Native Americans, Asian Americans, and Latinos, African Americans pay higher rates for home mortgage loans than whites, even after controlling for borrower credit history, debt levels, and income.[36] Lenders subject Black applicants to more credit checks than white applicants. They require more documentation from them even before meeting to discuss the terms of a loan. Whites face less restrictive qualification standards, receive more advice than Blacks about creative financing options, and routinely secure loans with lower escrow and reserve account contributions.[37] Minority applicants also face more obstacles to securing loans for improving existing dwellings. These loans have even greater value for minorities than they do for whites, because systematic discrimination leaves minority homeowners facing an artificially constricted housing market that makes it harder for them to move to new dwellings. An Atlanta study showed that nearly 33 percent of Black applicants and 30 percent of Latino applicants were rejected for home improvement loans—compared to 15.4 percent of whites.[38]

The patterns of the past continue to impede progress in the present in many ways. A 2008 study by sociologist Jesus Hernandez revealed that the physical locations of foreclosures of homes owned by Blacks and Latinos in Sacramento between 1998 and 2008 could be predicted precisely by finding the areas in Sacramento in 1939 that were redlined for whites but that were not secured by restrictive covenants. Even though the individuals who shaped and profited from the patterns of 1939 were long gone, their actions determined that the home foreclosure crisis of the turn of the twenty-first century would have disproportionate impact on minority borrowers.[39] Moreover, housing discrimination holds a direct and reciprocal relationship to employment discrimination. Disinvestment in an area's housing frequently causes an exodus of shopping centers, food stores, restaurants, full-service banks, and other institutions capable of providing employment, career training, and economic growth.[40] When minority workers are confined to neighborhoods far from the places of highest job growth, they suffer a competitive disadvantage with other job seekers.[41] Job discrimination can produce subsequent new forms of housing discrimination. One reason why banks and mortgage lenders discriminate so systematically is because their work forces are segregated as a result of their discriminatory policies as employers. A recent study of five metropolitan areas showed that an increase in Black administrators and officers in banks led to higher approval rates for Black loan applicants.[42] Similarly, bringing more minorities into the industry workforce would be one of the most effective ways of addressing the many different manifestations of insurance redlining.[43]

Of course, racialized space is not simply a matter of Black and white. In many of my previous publications I have described and analyzed the construction of physical places and discursive spaces by Latinos, Asian Americans, and Native Americans.[44] I have written about Chicano poster art and low riders, Asian American music and musicians, and Native American poetry, about interethnic antiracist organizing by the Asian Pacific Environmental Network, Asian Immigrant Women Advocates, the Labor Community Strategy Center, and the Midwest Treaty Network. I have long maintained that race in the United States and around the world is a complex and polylateral phenomenon, that different aggrieved communities have widely varying relations with each other as well as with whites, that the histories they share entail both coalitions and conflicts. The first racial zoning ordinance in the nation was intended to clear Chinese residents of San Francisco out of desirable neighborhoods downtown and confine them to slum neighborhoods adjacent to polluting factories and noxious waste dumps.[45] The restrictive covenants used everywhere to deny housing opportunities to Blacks also blocked Asian Americans, Latinos, and Native Americans from neighborhood choices and homeownership opportunities. Highway construction and attendant urban renewal programs destroyed some sixteen hundred Black communities in the twentieth century, but they devastated many Latino and Asian American neighborhoods as well.[46] During the first eight years of federally funded urban renewal, more than 75 percent of those displaced were Black or Latino.[47] The harsh realities of racialized space confront Native Americans in border towns and urban ghettos, while all communities of color suffer from disproportionate proximity to environmental hazards.[48] I focus on the Black/white binary in *How Racism Takes Place* not because I believe it exhausts the racial geography of our society, but because a focus on Black spaces reveals particular dynamics that have been central to the general construction of racialized space for everyone. The particular history of anti-Black racism focuses our attention on urgent choices that need to be made now. I view the evidence and arguments that I present here about the Black spatial imaginary as contributive to rather than competitive with the substantial, substantive, and superb work done by scholars of all races about racialized space and Latinos, Asian Americans, and Native Americans.[49] Because racial projects are flexible, fluid, and relational, the contours of anti-Black spaces are relevant to all communities of color. They are crucibles where other kinds of cruelty are learned and legitimated. When discrimination succeeds, it does not stop with one group but rather becomes generalized as a social principle and practice. Yet resistance to racialized spaces by Blacks can also have important generalizable implications for other aggrieved groups.

How Racism Takes Place argues for the importance of acknowledging the degree to which our society is structured by a white spatial imaginary and for confronting the serious moral, political, and social challenges mounted against it by a black spatial imaginary. The white spatial imaginary portrays the properly gendered prosperous suburban home as the privileged moral geography of the nation. Widespread, costly, and often counterproductive practices of surveillance, regulation, and incarceration become justified as forms of frontier defense against demonized people of color. Works of popular film and fiction often revolve around phobic representations of Black people unfit for freedom. These cultural commitments have political consequences. They emerge from public policies that place the acquisitive consumer at the center of the social world, that promote hostile privatism and defensive localism as suburban structures of feeling. They encourage homeowners to band together to capture amenities and advantages for themselves while outsourcing responsibilities and burdens to less powerful communities.

The first section of How Race Takes Place identifies the white spatial imaginary as a problem. It delineates the ways in which seemingly race-neutral urban sites contain deeply embedded racial assumptions and imperatives. As Martin Luther King argued decades ago, "To find the origins of the Negro problem we must turn to the white man's problem."[50] In Chapter 1, I explore the white spatial imaginary to explain how and why the racially propelled logic of hostile privatism and defensive localism has come to dominate decisions about both private investment and public policy. In Chapter 2, I explain how the necessity of turning segregation into congregation has produced a distinct Black spatial imaginary that counters hostile privatism and defensive localism with democratic and inclusive ideals. The white spatial imaginary often relies on misdirection, on creating spectacles that attract attention—yet detract our gaze from the links that connect urban place and race. In Chapters 3 and 4, I examine how municipal subsidies for a football stadium in St. Louis and the emergence of the television series The Wire promoted subject positions that encouraged spectators not to see things that were right in front of their eyes: urban poverty and educational inequality in St. Louis and predatory lending and community-based resistance in Baltimore. Stadium building in St. Louis and sensationalized depictions of ghetto life in Baltimore reveal that urban sites and urban sights work together to produce and sustain racial meanings. They enact a public pedagogy about who belongs where that has disastrous consequences for our shared social life.

Understanding the causes and consequences of the white spatial imaginary holds the key to understanding what happened to the dreams of the civil rights movement. Of course, the democratic and egalitarian insurgencies of the 1960s won some significant victories. It matters that the Supreme Court decided that segregated schools violated the constitutional rights of Black children in the 1954 *Brown* case. Opportunities have been opened up for millions of people of all races, genders, sexual identities, and degrees of ability and disability because the 1964 Civil Rights Act banned discrimination in employment. Our democracy is stronger because the 1965 Voting Rights Act prohibited practices designed to deny the franchise to members of aggrieved groups. In the face of the structural weaknesses written into the 1968 Fair Housing Act, activist citizen groups forced to function as private attorneys general have established a body of case law and administrative rulings that now make it possible for previously excluded individuals and groups to accumulate assets that appreciate in value and can be passed down to future generations. The election of Barack Obama in 2008 as the first African American president was a product of many forces, but prominent among them were the changes in the national racial order created by decades of legislation, litigation, education, and agitation.[51]

Yet these victories have been partial, incomplete, and even ephemeral. Racial justice remains elusive. Passing laws that proclaim equality does not produce practices that instantiate that equality in everyday life. In a characteristically brilliant discussion, critical race theorist Kimberle Crenshaw explains how this inversion of priorities has come about. She shows that a determined and deliberate repudiation of the aims and ideals of the civil rights movement has become the dominant force in U.S. culture and politics. Fueled initially by massive white resistance to school desegregation in the North and South, the era of repudiation took shape through an extended series of Supreme Court decisions, legislative initiatives, and actions by the executive branch of government. Supported by leaders of both political parties and cooperative judges, these actions dismantled or undermined many of the key policies created during the civil rights era, such as school desegregation and affirmative action. At the same time, municipalities, states, and the federal government routinely refuse to enforce fair-employment and fair-housing laws. In order to protect and preserve the traditional privileges of whiteness, leaders across the political spectrum have increasingly embraced the cynical strategy of "color blindness." They argue that recognizing race for the purposes of redressing racial injustices violates law and morality as much as the explicitly race-based discrimination that made it necessary to pass civil rights laws in the first place. In all areas of U.S. life, we now confront the presumption that color-bound injustices require color-blind remedies, that race-based problems should be solved by race-blind remedies.[52] As a result, more than four decades after the civil rights activism of the 1960s, and nearly one hundred and fifty years after the abolition of slavery, race remains the most important single variable determining opportunities and life chances in the United States.

Nowhere is this more evident than in the racialization of space. Seemingly race-neutral urban sites contain hidden racial assumptions and imperatives. The design, construction, administration, financing, and policing of shopping malls, sports arenas, schools, highways, and transportation corridors follow the racial logics of hostile privatism and defensive localism. They loot public resources for private gain, channeling massive subsidies and tax breaks toward wealthy corporations and investors while diminishing city services and imposing new burdens on renters and owners of inexpensive property. These spaces make racial segregation seem desirable, natural, necessary, and inevitable. Even more important, these sites serve to produce and sustain racial meanings; they enact a public pedagogy about who belongs where and about what makes certain spaces desirable.

Perhaps the most destructive effect of the white spatial imaginary is its role as a crucible for the arguments I referenced at the beginning of this introduction, the idea that Black people have shown themselves unfit for freedom by failing to take advantage of the opportunities afforded by civil rights laws. Today's segregated schools, neighborhoods, and workplaces produce white people who know very little about Blacks and even less about themselves. They certainly know next to nothing about the actual history of the civil rights movement or the beliefs of Dr. King. Today, people who profit tremendously from the privileges that accrue to them because of their color piously cite Dr. King's dream that one day his children would be judged by the content of their character rather than by the color of their skin. They cite this phrase in everyday conversation, public policy debates, and even Supreme Court decisions as justification for opposition to affirmative action, school desegregation, fair housing, fair hiring, and fair lending. They tell us that the way to get beyond race is to stop mentioning that racism exists. They do not know that Dr. King argued that "giving a man his due may often mean giving him special treatment," that he wrote that "a society that has done something special *against* the Negro for hundreds of years must do something special *for* him, in order to equip him to compete on a just and equal basis."[53] They do not know that by 1967 Dr. King talked less about his dream and more about how important it was for white America to wake up.[54] The people who congratulate their country and themselves on the passage of civil rights laws in the 1960s have created a rhetorical Martin Luther King to serve their interests who bears little resemblance to the actual historical Martin Luther King. They imagine that white benevolence in the 1960s enabled Dr. King and his followers to attain their goals. They do not know that in his last book, published the year before he was murdered, Dr. King charged that "White America was ready to demand that the Negro should be spared the lash of brutality and coarse degradation but had never truly been committed to helping him out of poverty, exploitation or all forms of discrimination."[55] Focusing directly on the content of their character, Dr. King found white Americans wanting. "They are uneasy with injustice," he observed, "but unwilling yet to pay a significant price to eradicate it."[56] Dr. King did not view the passage of civil rights laws as the fulfillment of his dream. Instead, he saw in them a colossal failure of will, of nerve, of integrity. He charged that "after writing piecemeal and incomplete legislation and proclaiming its historic importance in magnificent prose, the American government left the Negro to make the unworkable work."[57] King saw the laws passed by Congress as fatally flawed, designed deliberately to be inadequate and destined never to be fully enforced. Rather than resolving racial inequalities responsibly, these laws enabled whites to pretend that the problem had been solved. They catered to white vanity but did little to protect Black humanity. As King complained in 1967,

> Every civil rights law is still substantially more dishonored than honored. School desegregation is 90 percent unimplemented across the land; the free exercise of the franchise is the exception rather than the rule in the South; open occupancy laws theoretically apply to population centers embracing tens of millions, but grim ghettos contradict the fine language of the legislation. Despite the mandates of law, equal employment still remains a distant dream.[58]

The conditions we face today are eerily similar to the realities Dr. King described more than four decades ago. Civil rights laws remain largely unenforced. Affirmative obligations to promote fair housing are consistently evaded by cities, counties, and states.

School segregation is reverting to the levels of the 1970s. Voting rights are routinely compromised by gerrymandering, by requirements for photo identification at polling places, by purging people who move frequently from voting rolls, and by disenfranchising ex-offenders. Moreover, judges assiduously protect white privilege by treating civil rights remedies as more egregious violations of individual rights than the forms of direct discrimination that made them necessary in the first place. Yet Dr. King was not only a critic of the white spatial imaginary; he was also a champion of the Black spatial imaginary. He believed that it contained important tools for building a more decent, humane, and just society, not just for Black people but for everyone. In the course of sustained struggle, Dr. King came to understand that white supremacy was not an aberrant practice in an otherwise just society, but rather one node in a larger network of misplaced priorities. Like his ancestors who emerged from slavery to forge Abolition Democracy in the nineteenth century, Dr. King believed that it was not enough merely to remove negative racist obstacles in the way of Blacks, but instead that it was necessary to create new democratic practices and institutions. Calling for "a radical restructuring of the architecture of American society," King specifically rejected the idea that the purpose of the civil rights movement was to make Blacks exactly like whites.[59] Instead, the goal was to transform both Blacks and whites (and everyone else) into new kinds of humans, into people capable of creating new racial and spatial relations. "Let us, therefore, not think of our movement," he urged, "as one that seeks to integrate the Negro into the existing values of American society." Instead, King asked his followers to "be those creative dissenters who will call our beloved nation to a higher destiny, to a new plateau of compassion, to a more noble expression of humaneness."[60]

King perceived part of the race problem and its solution as spatial. "The suburbs are white nooses around the Black necks of the cities," he wrote. "Housing deteriorates in central cities; urban renewal has been Negro removal and has benefited big merchants and real estate interests; and suburbs expand with little regard for what happens to the rest of America."[61] King complained that "the federal government subsidizes the nonpoor twice as much as the poor when we include various forms of subsidies such as middle-income public housing, tax deductions for mortgage interest and real estate taxes."[62] He called for the creation and enforcement of fair-housing laws, desegregation of neighborhoods, an end to homelessness, and a guarantee that all housing would meet minimum standards of adequacy.[63]

Yet King believed that the nation's racial and spatial problems had already started to produce racial and spatial solutions. He saw ideas and actions emanating from Black spaces as tremendously valuable to the nation at large. In Montgomery in 1955 and 1956, Black people boycotted the buses and walked to work on the sidewalks. They conducted lengthy public mass meetings that turned churches into sites for deliberative talk, face-to-face decision making, and collective mobilization. Masses in motion on the streets of Birmingham, students staging sit-ins a lunch counters throughout the South, freedom riders transforming buses and bus stations into new democratic spaces, marchers protesting racist violence on rural highways in Mississippi or pushing for voting rights on the road from Selma to Montgomery expressed new spatial and racial imaginaries. King recognized the importance of the fact that these actions took place in actual places, that they enacted in real time the social relations that dreamers could only envision. "By taking to the streets, and there giving practical lessons in democracy and its defaults," King asserted, "Negroes have decisively influenced white thought."[64] More than any individual reform, the great achievement of the civil rights movement was the creation of Blacks as an aggrieved and insurgent people dedicated to the democratic transformation of the nation and the world. Up to the day he died, King kept insisting on the need for direct action. For him, action mattered precisely because it did not depend solely on moral suasion, but instead strengthened ethical appeals by supporting them with what Dr. King called "constructive coercive power."[65] Consistent with his oft-repeated injunction that in order to comfort the afflicted it was often necessary to afflict the comfortable, King also believed that collective action in public contained powerful potential for expanding democracy. Mass participation required critiques and demands capable of involving the broadest possible range of participants, countered tendencies toward autocracy and bureaucracy by generating the development of new leaders among the rank and file, and kept leaders accountable to their constituents. King believed in participatory democracy as both a means and an end. As he explained, "No great victories are won in a war for the transformation of a whole people without total participation. Less than this will not create a new society; it will only evoke more sophisticated token amelioration."[66]

I have dealt with the ideas of Dr. King at length in this introduction because his good name is often invoked to support and justify policies he certainly would have opposed. The statements that he made on these subjects are a matter of public record. If we do not know his ideas, it is because time and time again we have been lied to about them. But there is more at stake here than the personal reputation of one national icon, even one as brilliant and visionary as Dr. King. The ideas that King championed were not his alone. They emerged from and spoke for a Black spatial imaginary created in dispersed and diffuse sites by a broad range of activists, artists, intellectuals, and ordinary citizens.

The second part of *How Racism Takes Place* looks at some of the sources of the spatial, racial, and social imaginary that King deployed so deftly. In the wake of the civil rights movement, music by Horace Tapscott, visual art by Betye Saar and John Biggers, and writing by Paule Marshall and Lorraine Hansberry explored the creative and generative dynamics of the Black spatial imaginary. These artists and Dr. King himself came out of a tradition. They owed much to the people largely unknown to history described by Charles Mills as thinkers and creators who "under the most difficult circumstances, often self-educated, denied access to formal training and the resources of the academy, the object of scorn and contempt from hegemonic white theory, nevertheless managed to forge the concepts necessary to trace the contours of the system oppressing them, defying the massive weight of a white scholarship that either morally justified this oppression or denied its existence."[67] The archives created by these artists, activists, and intellectuals continue to inform the Black spatial imaginary in the present as I argue in my discussions in this book of the activities of the World Stage Performance Gallery in Los Angeles, Project Row Houses in Houston, Students at the Center in New Orleans, and fair-housing councils all across the nation. I focus on practices and products of expressive culture to examine how Blacks have consistently drawn a distinct spatial imaginary to oppose the land use philosophy that privileges profits over people and instead to create new "use values" in places that have little "exchange value." Many of these works of expressive culture contested the oppressions of race by imagining strategic realignments of place, by presenting strategies for altering the scale, scope, and stakes of space—for burrowing in, building up, and branching out. They proceed from a philosophy that sees art as a vital part of the life of a community, that finds value in devalued spaces, and that offers alternatives to possessive individualism and competitive consumer citizenship. These strategies and sensibilities permeate the Black spatial imaginary today in many different ways. They guide diverse efforts to turn segregation into congregation, to transform divisiveness into solidarity, to change dehumanization into rehumanization. In Chapter 10, I explore how participating in contemporary challenges to the hostile privatism and defensive localism of the white spatial imaginary can help us understand and advance the democratic and egalitarian ethos of the Black spatial imaginary.

I turn to works of expressive culture that emerged from the Black spatial imaginary in the mid-twentieth century not out of nostalgia for a lost golden age, but rather because these works constitute a living archive of oppositional consciousness and thought, because their prophetic power predicted the problems we confront today, and because their ideas and aspirations continue to guide struggles for democratic and egalitarian social change in the present. Just as *Where Do We Go from Here: Chaos or Community?*—the book that Dr. King published the year before he died—contains crucial insight about the importance of continuing to struggle today for affirmative action, school desegregation, fair hiring, fair housing, and environmental justice, the music, art, and literature of the mid-twentieth century provides us with continuing insights about the White spatial imaginary and how to contest it.

Although reflecting the individual aesthetic choices and personal preoccupations of their creators, the artistic practices and products I discuss in this book also offer evidence about the central role played by place in the cognitive mapping and structural economy of race from the mid-twentieth century through the present. The innovative, imaginative, and even eccentric character of many of these works of art stems from an unusual ambition to blend aesthetic and political goals into a unified totality. Like other artists, intellectuals, and activists from aggrieved communities, they engage in what literary critic Raymond Williams called "a long march to alternative institutions which have to be raised from the resources of surviving and potential in-place communities."[68] Black artists show how racialized space produces *both* solidarities of sameness and dynamics of difference. No one spatial strategy suffices to solve the diverse and plural problems that white supremacy poses for Black communities. Yet changing the scale, scope, and stakes of space—burrowing in, building up, and branching out—can serve different purposes at different times, functioning as parts of a reticulated web that accomplishes more collectively than any one tactic might achieve individually. Although these strategies were ostensibly designed to reorder space, it would be more accurate to say that they work within time and space to advance new understandings of ancestry, inheritance, association, affiliation, and action.

When history takes place, it does so in actual places. Among aggrieved groups, history also takes places away, leaving some people, as David Roediger reminds us, displaced, disinherited, dispossessed, and just plain dissed. In the United States, racial subordination has manifested its full force and fury through physical segregation and spatial subordination. African American expressive culture has functioned as both a symptom and a critique of the nexus that links race and space. Its compelling qualities testify to the shameful duration, depth, and dimension of the racialization of space and the spatialization of race. Yet works of expressive culture from this tradition also offer evidence about what Raymond Williams identifies as the "intransigent attachments to human diversity and recreation" that survive as long as people "keep living and looking beyond the routines which attempt to control and reduce them."[69] Now more than ever, we need to understand the full force and pernicious power of the white spatial imaginary. Yet we also need to learn lessons that the Black spatial imaginary can teach.

I believe that understanding the causes and consequences of racialized space can advance the cause of racial justice. It can help address and redress the injuries that Black people experience from living in a society where not just white property but even white vanity is valued more highly than Black humanity. But the problems produced by racialized space should not be simply the particular and parochial concerns of Blacks. Although the system through which race takes place delivers short-term advantages and benefits to whites, racialized space ultimately hurts everyone. It creates expensive and dangerous concentrations of poverty, pollution, disease, and crime.

It misallocates resources by squandering the talents and abilities of deserving Blacks while moving less talented whites into positions they do not deserve. It encourages environmentally unsound patterns of development and transportation, disperses populations inefficiently. It helps produce much of the antisocial behavior that it purports to prevent. It deprives cities, counties, and states of tax revenues by depressing property values artificially. It promotes a suburban culture of contempt and fear that fuels opposition to sensible economies of scale, that encourages each subunit of government to try to win gains against every other subunit. Perhaps most important, it undermines democracy by isolating Black people and the spatial and social imaginaries they have developed over time from potential white allies who would derive great benefit from them—if they could only overcome their allegiances to racial privilege.

Malcolm X used to say that racism was like a Cadillac because they make a new model every year. The names change, he charged, but the game's the same. The achievements of the civil rights revolution of the 1960s changed many of the names. It is no longer permissible to maintain overtly segregated school systems and public accommodations. Racial discrimination in employment and housing now clearly violates the law. Yet changing the names did not change the game. Race still exists because racism persists. Ending the fatal links that connect place and race would do much for social justice. In the conclusion of *How Racism Takes Place*, I outline measures that need to be taken to end the skewing of opportunities and life chances in our society along racial lines. We need to change the game, not just the names by which it is called. To understand how to accomplish this task, we need to turn in Chapter 1 to an examination of the white spatial imaginary and to ask the questions that Dr. King posed at a key point in *Where Do We Go from Here: Chaos or Community?* He asked, "Why does white America delude itself, and how does it rationalize the evil it retains?"[70] These are questions well worth answering. The rest of this book will attempt to answer them.

SECTION I

Social Imaginaries
and Social Relations

The White Spatial Imaginary

To be born white in this country is to be born to an
inheritance of privileges, to hold in your hands the keys
that open before you the doors of every occupation,
advantage, opportunity, and achievement.
—FRANCES E. W. HARPER

A manual published in 1943 instructed real estate brokers about recommended best practices in their profession. The book advised against the sale of homes that might bring some form of blight to an otherwise respectable area. The publication enumerated the types of buyers who should not be allowed into a neighborhood. Understandably enough, it advised that people seeking to purchase private homes to be used as houses of prostitution or distribution points for bootleg liquor would "cause considerable annoyance" to neighbors. In the same passage, however, it listed another potential menace: "a colored man of means who was giving his children a college education and thought they were entitled to live among whites."[1]

The equation of a Black father sending his children to college with bootleggers, madams, and pimps says a great deal about the white spatial imaginary. Black desires for upward mobility and intergenerational advancement are not honored here as exemplary components of the American dream, but are condemned instead as a kind of criminal incursion on white privilege. This correlation between criminality and Black occupancy of a home in a white neighborhood did not come from the lips of an isolated, aberrant, hate-filled snarling bigot. It appeared in a matter-of-fact passage in an instruction manual for white professionals. It corresponded fully with prevailing land use practices of that era, with the racially specific restrictive covenants that real estate brokers promoted, that states enforced, and that federal loan agencies required. It conformed to the predominant commitment among developers, appraisers, and planners to promote coordinated racial exclusion of Blacks as a mechanism for inflating the value of properties owned by whites. Of course, Black real estate agents might have viewed this upwardly mobile Black father differently, but whites would not allow them to conduct business in white areas. In the years before fair-housing laws were passed, Black real estate brokers faced death threats, assaults, and bombings of their residences by angry whites intent on policing the color line.[2] Even worse, the understanding in the manual of potential Black neighbors as criminals stealing wealth that somehow should be reserved only for whites helped fuel and excuse wave upon wave of violent white vigilante attacks on Black people seeking to move into white neighborhoods or use recreational facilities reserved for whites in the years that followed.

These attacks reached a crescendo in the 1940s and 1950s as documented thoroughly in research by urban historians Thomas Sugrue, Arnold Hirsch, Clarence Lang, Colin Gordon, Josh Sides, and many others. Attacks on Blacks seeking to enter spaces reserved for whites constituted actual rather than imagined criminal behavior.[3] Yet because it was criminality exercised on behalf of whiteness, its perpetrators knew that ultimately they would be protected and supported by legally constituted authorities. This shameful history of white violence in northern cities in defense of white neighborhoods remains a protected secret in our society. In city after city, whites "defended" their neighborhoods by throwing rocks, bricks, and bottles at Black families, by vandalizing homes occupied by Blacks, by burning crosses on front lawns to let their new neighbors know they were not welcome. Even public facilities funded by tax money collected from everyone remained reserved for whites. When the city of St. Louis announced the desegregation of its municipally owned and operated swimming pool in Fairgrounds Park in 1949, thirty Black children showed up for a swim. More than two hundred whites brandishing weapons and shouting racist epithets surrounded the pool to drive them out. Police officers escorted the Black youths to safety, but whites began attacking Blacks they encountered in and around the park. By nightfall, five thousand whites assembled at the site. They cornered Black pedestrians, attacking them with lead pipes, baseball bats, and knives. Two white men advised the crowd to "get bricks and smash their heads." Police officers restored order temporarily, but in response to the upheaval the city rescinded the desegregation order and closed its pools entirely.[4] Similar white violence in the Trumbull Park area of Chicago starting in 1953 succeeded in intimidating the Chicago Housing Authority from placing any new housing projects in mixed neighborhoods for a generation, a decision that contributed significantly to future Black segregation and concentrated poverty in that city.[5] Los Angeles antiracist activist Johnny Otis wrote in 1960 that he had seen so many crosses burned on homes newly occupied by Blacks in that city that it made him wonder if the original bearer of that cross had not died in vain.[6] White citizens mobbed a fair-housing march led by Martin Luther King, Jr., in Marquette Park in Chicago in 1966. White residents of Pontiac, Michigan, used dynamite to blow up thirteen school buses to try to prevent school desegregation in that city in 1971. White adults held Black students hostage inside a South Boston high school and smashed windows and doors of the federal building in Boston in 1974 in defiance of a federal court order desegregating local schools. All these people knew that ultimately the executive, judicial, and legislative branches of government would side with them against the desegregation of neighborhoods and schools. Their resort to violence won them important concessions. It guaranteed that federal fair-housing laws would be written with virtually no meaningful enforcement positions, that Congress would pass antibusing legislation, that presidents would promise to appoint antibusing judges to the federal bench, and that ultimately the Supreme Court itself would back away from the desegregation mandates it enunciated in the *Brown* decision.

Yet while this history of white criminality has been ignored and all but expunged from popular memory and official history, the idea that Blacks moving into white neighborhoods constitutes a criminal transgression of its own still looms large in the white spatial imaginary. As David Freund shows in his carefully documented history of state policy and white racial politics in the suburbs, whites benefited tremendously from the privileged access they enjoyed to the expressly discriminatory government-supported mortgages that enabled them to move to white suburbs in the 1940s and 1950s. Blacks shut out of the housing market by private and public discrimination were left with access only to inadequate and substandard means-tested public housing that deprived them of the assets that whites secured from homeownership. Yet instead of recognizing themselves accurately as recipients of collective public largesse, whites came to see themselves as individuals whose wealth grew out of their personal and individual success in acquiring property on the "free market." At the same time, whites viewed inner-city residents not as fellow citizens denied the subsidies freely offered to whites, but as people whose alleged failures to save, invest, and take care of their homes forced the government to intervene on their behalf, to build housing projects that were then ruined by alleged Black neglect. White suburbanites ignored how the artificially constricted housing market available to Blacks deflated home values, stripped homeowners of equity, reduced tax revenue for city services, created unhealthy conditions, led to overcrowding, and promoted crime. They did not acknowledge how federal funding formulas deprived housing projects of the capital reserves needed for maintenance and upkeep or how discrimination in the private sector made housing projects dwellings of last resort for the poor rather than the mixed-income communities they were initially designed to be.[7] Instead, as Freund demonstrates, whites attributed urban decay and poverty to the behavior of Black people, not to discrimination and ill-conceived public policy. At the same time, they viewed the relative prosperity of the suburb as a reflection of the moral worth of white people.[8] They fought to keep Black people out of their neighborhoods because they associated them with the ghettos that whites created and from which they profited. Concentrated residential segregation enacted in concrete spatial form the core ideology of white supremacy—that Black people "belonged" somewhere else. In a deft paraphrase, Charles Mills represents the moral geography of whiteness as "saying" to Blacks that "you are what you are in part because you originate from a certain kind of space, and that space has those properties in part because it is inhabited by creatures like yourself."[9]

Decades and centuries of segregation have taught well-off communities to hoard amenities and resources, to exclude allegedly undesirable populations, and to seek to maximize their own property values in competition with other communities. These nearly universal strategies for class advantage follow a distinct racial pattern in the United States. They subsidize segregation and produce rewards for whiteness. A white spatial imaginary based on exclusivity and augmented exchange value forms the foundational logic behind prevailing spatial and social policies in cities and suburbs today. This imaginary does not emerge simply or directly from the embodied identities of people who are white. It is inscribed in the physical contours of the places where we live, work, and play, and it is bolstered by financial rewards for whiteness. Not all whites endorse the white spatial imaginary, and some Blacks embrace it and profit from it. Yet every white person benefits from the association of white places with privilege, from the neighborhood race effects that create unequal and unjust geographies of opportunity. The white spatial imaginary is grounded in a long history of housing discrimination, but it has been augmented and extended considerably in recent years by new tax and zoning policies that favor construction of planned-unit developments, condominiums, cooperative apartment houses, subdivisions, and other forms of mass-produced and corporate-sponsored common-interest housing. The white spatial imaginary deploys contract law and deed restrictions to channel amenities and advantages to places designated as white. It makes the augmentation and concentration of private wealth the central purpose of public association. It promotes policies that produce sprawl, waste resources, and generate enormous social costs in order to enable some property owners to become wealthier than others. It produces a society saturated with hostile privatism and defensive localism through secret subsidies for exclusive and homogeneous housing developments premised on promoting the security and profitability of private property regardless of the larger social costs to society.

The white spatial imaginary has cultural as well as social consequences. It structures feelings as well as social institutions. The white spatial imaginary idealizes "pure" and homogeneous spaces, controlled environments, and predictable patterns of design and behavior. It seeks to hide social problems rather than solve them. The white spatial imaginary promotes the quest for individual escape rather than encouraging democratic deliberations about the social problems and contradictory social relations that affect us all. The suburb is not only an engine of self-interest, but also a place that has come to be imbued with a particular moral value consistent with deeply rooted historical ideals and illusions. Among dominant groups in the United States, socially shared moral geographies have long infused places with implicit ethical assumptions about the proper forms of social connection and separation.[10] Historian David W. Noble identifies a spatial imaginary at the heart of European conquest and settlement of North America in the seventeenth century. Republican theorists in the Renaissance juxtaposed virtuous and timeless nature with corrupt and time-bound human society. They believed that free nations had to be composed of homogeneous populations with ties to the national landscape, to "timeless spaces" where citizens lived in complete harmony with one another. Starting in the seventeenth century, European settler colonialists imagined that American space might offer a refuge from the corruptions of European time. Coalescing around what Noble calls "the metaphor of two worlds"—the idea of America as an island of virtue in a global sea of corruption—these ideals became institutionalized within the national culture of the United States through the writings of transcendentalists, the visual art of the Hudson River School, evocations by historians of the frontier as a unique source of regeneration, and ultimately, in the ideal of the private properly ordered suburban home and homogeneous community.[11]

Yet in order to have pure and homogeneous spaces, "impure" populations have to be removed and marginalized. The putatively empty and timeless North American space that settlers wanted to serve as the refuge from the corruptions of European time was actually occupied by indigenous people with histories of their own. Rather than sharing North American space with Indians as common ground, the moral geography of the colonists required conquest, genocide, and Indian removal to produce the sacred ground that the Europeans felt would be pleasing to God as a City on a Hill. The creation of homogeneous polities living in "free" spaces required the exclusion of others deemed different, deficient, and nonnormative. Noble shows that belief in a redemptive American landscape as a refuge from the corruptions of European "time" performed important cultural work necessary for the construction of the United States as an imagined community. As "civilization" penetrated the West, however, it became more and more difficult for Americans to believe that they inhabited such a landscape. In response, the properly ordered and prosperous domestic dwelling eclipsed the frontier as the privileged moral geography of U.S. society, as the nation's key symbol of freedom, harmony, and virtue.

The association of freedom with pure spaces outlived the frontier, shaping ideals about the properly ordered prosperous private dwelling. In the late nineteenth and early twentieth centuries, this ideal coalesced around racial zoning, restrictive covenants, mortgage redlining, blockbusting, steering, and a host of attendant practices responsible for racially segregating residential areas in the United States. Today, racially exclusive neighborhoods, segregated suburbs, and guarded and gated communities comprise the privileged moral geography of the contemporary national landscape. These sites draw their privileged relationship to freedom less from harmony with the natural landscape than from their exclusion of nonnormative others and the maximization of the exchange value of their houses. The privileged moral geography of the properly ordered prosperous private dwelling depends upon systematic exclusion. It produces a racially marked form of consumer citizenship that seeks to secure services for oneself at the cheapest possible price and to pass the costs of remedying complex social problems on to less powerful and less wealthy populations. This stance places every unit of government in competition with every other unit, strengthening the hand of wealthy individuals and corporations while defunding the democratic civic institutions established to regulate them. These practices serve the interests of owners and investors twice over: increasing public spending in well-off districts increases their property values, while reducing spending in poorer communities makes residences in them worth even less to their inhabitants. The effect of this social warrant is to add to white competitive and comparative advantage in accumulating assets that appreciate in value and that can be passed down across generations.

The white spatial imaginary views space primarily as a locus for the generation of exchange value. Houses are investments that appreciate in value over time. Assets accumulated or increased through real estate transactions receive favored treatment from the tax code, making them worth more than other kinds of income. Subsidies like the homeowners' mortgage deduction serve homeowners doubly. In this case it underwrites the costs of owning a home and inflates property values. In turn, the mortgage interest deduction increases income for school districts in wealthy suburbs because tax rates are pegged to assessments. Perhaps most importantly, the neighborhood race effects of segregated housing give white homeowners advantages and amenities unavailable to most minority home seekers: access to superior schools, protection from environmental hazards, proximity to sources of employment, inclusion in word-of-mouth networks about jobs and business opportunities, and the use of better services than those that can be secured from the under-funded public sphere after three decades of suburban tax rebellions. These insurgencies do not so much lower taxes as shift them regressively—away from income taxes, property taxes, inheritance taxes, and capital gains taxes, and toward sales taxes, payroll taxes, and user fees. For residents of these spaces, dwellings are fungible assets that can increase in value as their own-ers "trade up" or "flip" their properties, aided by the tax breaks given for capi-tal gains and the propensity for upscale neighborhoods to insulate themselves from the social costs incurred by high-risk populations.

Preferences for private dwellings, private developments, and privatization of municipal services may appear to be market choices, but in reality they reflect the coordinated manipulation of market forces by wealthy corpora-tions and their allies in government. During the 1960s, the Federal Hous-ing Administration helped developers adjust to increases in land prices by encouraging the construction of condominiums and planned unit develop-ments. FHA officials smoothed access to federal mortgage insurance for sub-divisions with commonly owned open spaces rather than large private yards. These developments offered choice amenities to the wealthy residents who could afford them, promoting their sense of separation from services and amenities paid for from general tax revenues.[12] Perhaps most important, the FHA promoted private recreational spaces and amenities as an alternative to publicly owned and universally accessible facilities. The FHA recommended a plan in 1964 (at the peak of the civil rights movement's mobilizations) that favored control by private homeowner associations over recreation centers and park land in planned developments. The effect of this plan was to pro-mote segregation. At a time when Black activists and their allies of all races were being arrested, mobbed, and beaten for trying to desegregate swimming pools and other venues purportedly open to the public, the FHA argued that public ownership of pools, parks, and playgrounds near new planned unit developments would have to be open to the public at large if general tax reve-nues paid for them. The agency expressed doubt about the "suitability" of this arrangement. The plan also stipulated that homeowners and renters should not govern these spaces as members of the same association because home-owners and renters "have different interests and do not mix well in associa-tion."[13] Positing homeowners and renters as rivals with diametrically opposed interests rather than as neighbors or fellow citizens promoted what econo-mist Robert Reich describes as "the secession of the successful" from civic life, providing them with material incentives for directing investment away from the public interest and toward their own pecuniary gain. As he explains, "In many cities and towns, the wealthy have in effect withdrawn their dollars from the support of public services and institutions shared by all and dedicated the savings to their own private services."[14]

Contemporary critics clearly recognized that the expansion of planned unit developments under these terms would make existing residential segregation permanent, that it would replace decision making about land use by local governments answerable to the public with decisions made by private homeowners' associations answerable only to their own economic desires and interests. There were fewer than five hundred homeowner associations in the United States in 1964. Today there are nearly 250,000. More than thirty million people now live in common-interest developments. Private security guards now outnumber police officers. Coupled with weak and largely unenforced fair-housing laws, these institutions enshrine the racial demography of the past in perpetuity. They treat the homogeneity and isolation of neighborhoods as a moral good, and create social spaces premised upon hostile privatism and defensive localism. In common-interest developments, private homeowners' associations exercise degrees of governing power routinely denied to duly elected public officials. Residents of these developments exercise the powers of government through their associations, pay fees for amenities and services that only they (and other members of the associations) can use, and consequently resist the provision of general services by local government as a form of double taxation. They still want to use the public roads and public utilities that make their subdivisions possible and that are paid for by taxpayers, but they do not want to pay taxes to support them. Instead, they treat their association dues and fees as a form of taxation because they pay for private security guards and landscaping of common areas. Yet they insist on reserving access to these areas to those who own them. By imagining that investments in their own property are actually a form of taxation, they then oppose paying taxes that serve the general interest, viewing other neighborhoods not as parts of a shared polity, but rather as economic competitors.

Homeowner associations exist for the sole aim of improving property values in competition with other neighborhoods.[15] Like their predecessors throughout the long history of suburban development, common-interest developments promise prosperity, predictability, and security. Yet in actual practice, they only exacerbate residential inequalities, increase urban problems, and promote wasteful and environmentally destructive growth. They privilege speculation over savings. They fragment communities and provoke ruinous competition between neighborhoods. As each group of homeowners seeks to maximize rewards and minimize obligations at the expense of

other groups of homeowners, they defund the economic and social infrastructure required to produce the very prosperity, stability, and security they seek.
Incorporation and tax policies encourage each subunit of government (city,
county, state, federal) to try to pass on obligations to every other subunit. This
zero-sum game leads inevitability to disappointment. Disappointment promotes resentment that often grows into rage and righteous indignation. These
affective states function as modal structures of feeling among people active
in homeowners' associations and tax limitation groups, and the participants
in right-wing talk radio programs. They have helped create what is surely the
most sullen, surly, embittered, and disgruntled group of "haves" in the history of the world. The affective rewards of recreational hate become a kind
of reparation for the gradual disintegration of the social fabric. Unwilling to
face the consequences of how three decades of tax cuts for corporations and
wealthy individuals have undermined the material and moral well-being of
this society, white property owners vent their rage against immigrants and
inner-city residents, supporting policies that punish the poor and reward the
rich, and in the process exacerbate the very problems they purport to address.
As Black revolutionary George Jackson noted decades ago, our society promotes contempt for the oppressed. "Accrual of contempt is its fundamental
survival technique," Jackson wrote about U.S. society, adding, "This leads to
the excesses and destroys any hope of peace eventually being worked out between the two antagonistic classes, the haves and the have-nots. Coexistence
is impossible, contempt breeds resistance, and resistance breeds brutality, the
whole growing in spirals that must either end in the uneconomic destruction
of the oppressed or the termination of oppression"[16]

Today's homeowner and condominium associations give the appearance
of democracy without the substance. Homeowners with direct financial interests in association activities do participate in governance activities. Yet the
burden of work usually falls to self-selected, untrained, and unregulated individuals with spare time who then find themselves completely dependent on
property managers, lawyers, and accountants for guidance and advice. These
professionals have a financial stake in continuing to work with the associations. For both volunteers and professionals, maximizing property values
becomes the one sure sign of success. These dynamics create a kind of participatory plutocracy, a system that elevates the illusion of private advantage
over the genuine well-being of individuals and communities.[17]

Even though they need low-wage workers to landscape their grounds,
build their houses, repair their streets, clean their homes, and take care of
their children, suburban property owners seek to avoid paying taxes that
might contribute to the shelter, health, education, or transportation needs of
their employees. They do so in order to have more money spent on services

and amenities for themselves. Private deed restrictions and fees to homeowners' associations enable them to be fiscal liberals for themselves but fiscal conservatives toward others. Conservative scholar Charles Murray celebrates this organized abandonment of aggrieved communities of color as a harbinger of the eventual demise of the state itself, as a necessary step toward the end of all government regulation and control of private property. Bringing the spatial imaginary of the national landscape full circle, Murray predicts that the wealthiest fifth of the population will soon control sufficient privatized services and political power to simply ignore inner cities, to view them with the same detachment that urban and suburban dwellers now have for "Indian reservations," an ignorance and indifference that Murray evidently believes to be worthy of praise.[18]

Enabled by support and subsidies from municipal, state, and federal government agencies in the forms of subsidized loans, tax breaks, and zoning regulations, the inequalities at the heart of racialized space in the United States in fact violate the letter and spirit of laws that have been on the books for years. The 1968 federal Fair Housing Act outlawed racial discrimination by real estate brokers, mortgage lenders, insurance agents, and homeowners, identified integrating neighborhoods as an important national goal, and ordered cities, counties, and states to take actions to affirmatively advance fair housing. But the original law contained no meaningful enforcement provisions, allowed for only minimal financial penalties, and placed the burden of investigation, exposure, and adjudication on private citizens rather than on the departments of Justice or Housing and Urban Development. Decades of tireless activism by fair-housing advocates has made the most of what the law allows, and amendments to it in 1988 strengthened their efforts, but housing experts agree that minority home seekers today are virtually powerless in the face of the more than four million incidents of housing discrimination that take place every year.[19]

Whites generally endorse the spatial arrangements that provide them with unfair gains and unjust enrichments. A survey in Atlanta found that 90 percent of whites in that city proclaimed willingness to move into a neighborhood with one Black household. Yet only 26 percent affirmed that they would move into a neighborhood with as many as eight Black households.[20] The pervasiveness of housing discrimination and mortgage redlining sets in motion a range of practices that decapitalize Black communities. Redlining leads to disinvestment. Impediments to homeownership make it harder to accumulate capital for business start-ups. Money made from businesses in the Black community flows to other neighborhoods. A study by sociologist John Yinger in 1997 estimated that housing discrimination imposed a "racial tax" on Black households amounting to an aggregate three billion dollars per year.[21]

It is not that suburban whites are innately racist and consequently favor land use policies that increase the racial gap, but rather that prevailing land use policies produce a certain kind of whiteness that offers extraordinary inducements and incentives for a system of privatization that has drastic racial consequences. In his excellent study of the origins and evolution of the mobilizations for property tax limitation that emerged during the 1970s, Clarence Lo notes how antitax and antibusing activists drew upon their experiences as suburban dwellers who benefited from racial discrimination in housing to fashion a common notion of consumer citizenship. "Whites joined antibusing movements," Lo observes, "because they sought to maintain advantages for their racial or ethnic group in the consumption of government services."[22] Even the use of the term "forced busing" by white activists as the way to describe desegregation plans copied the example of opponents of fair-housing laws, who in the 1964 campaign to repeal California's Rumford Act declared themselves opponents of "forced housing." The defenders of segregated housing became the defenders of segregated schools. The segregated neighborhoods and social circles that resulted served as the main sources of mobilizations for tax limitation, defunding the public sector, and denying social services to minorities and immigrants. Philip J. Ethington's empirically rich and theoretically sophisticated studies of race and space in Los Angeles show that the white neighborhoods most physically isolated from black communities provided the most enthusiastic support for California's unconstitutional 1964 repeal of fair-housing legislation, 1978's Proposition 13 tax limitation initiative, and 1994's unconstitutional Proposition 187 denying state-supported education and health care to undocumented immigrants.[23] As Daniel HoSang establishes in his brilliant book *Racial Propositions*, these measures reflected and shaped a political whiteness that remains the dominant force in the state's politics to this day.[24] Racialized space enables the advocates of expressly racist policies to disavow any racial intent. They speak on behalf of whiteness and its accumulated privileges and immunities, but rather than having to speak *as* whites, they present themselves as racially unmarked homeowners, citizens, and taxpayers whose preferred policies just happen to sustain white privilege and power. One of the privileges of whiteness, as Richard Dyer reminds us, is never having to speak its name.[25]

Even poor people who are white live in better neighborhoods, attend better schools, and face less exposure to environmental hazards than many middle-class people who are Black. In Washington, D.C., more than a quarter of the metropolitan area's impoverished Blacks live in high-poverty inner-city neighborhoods, but a mere 2 percent of the non-Black poor live in areas with concentrated poverty.[26] When poor whites deal with landlords, police officers, merchants, social workers, and elected officials, they know that they will be treated more respectfully than their Black counterparts. Whiteness also has an enormous cash value. It is worth a lot of money to be white. As a systemic structured advantage, whiteness concerns interests as well as attitudes, property as well as pigment. White supremacy does not exist or persist because whites foolishly fear people with a different skin color. It survives and thrives because whiteness delivers unfair gains and unjust enrichments to people who participate in and profit from the existence of a racial cartel that skews opportunities and life chances for their own benefit. It externalizes the worst social conditions onto communities of color and provides whites with a floor below which they cannot fall.[27] A sociological study published in 2001 discovered that whites viewed the racial composition of a neighborhood as more important than property values, school quality, frequency of crime, or the class standing of residents. Whites indicated they would not buy a home in a neighborhood that was more than 15 percent Black under any circumstances. They did not express this preference because they desired living among their fellow whites, but rather because they did not want to live among people who were Black.[28]

Yet the white spatial imaginary produces many of the problems it purports to bemoan. For example, when wealthy white communities use neighborhood race effects to monopolize services and amenities for themselves, they concentrate nuisances and hazards in minority areas. Less powerful and less cohesive neighborhoods bear the burdens of pathogenic exposures exported from more cohesive and powerful communities. People of color do not use drugs with greater frequency than whites, but they are much more likely than whites to be arrested and incarcerated for drug use.[29] Drug enforcement efforts target minority neighborhoods because the lack of political and economic power of people in these neighborhoods means that drug dealers find it easier to serve their diverse clientele who come from areas throughout the region by setting up shop on the street in minority neighborhoods. These neighborhoods are forced to tolerate drug dealing in the same ways that they have to endure toxic hazards, polluting businesses, and other criminal enterprises that wealthier and whiter neighborhoods would find intolerable. The selective policing that allows illegal activities to be shifted to interzones and ghettos inhabited by people of color extends to the policing of individual drug users. Moral panics about drug use in the suburbs lead not to mass arrests of suburban drug purchasers and users but rather to sweeps and arrests in inner-city neighborhoods where drug users are more likely to be on the streets than in private homes, less likely to be represented by attorneys, and more likely to plead guilty than incur the expenses of a trial. These neighborhood race effects can have calamitous consequences that go beyond disproportionate arrest and incarceration rates. Surveillance and aggressive policing in minority neighborhoods make possession of clean syringes risky, for example, leading drug users to create underground "shooting" galleries where they share syringes, thus increasing risks of HIV/AIDS. Those arrested in these galleries get sent to prisons where they are subjected to another place of unsafe sex and sharing of needles. The higher HIV infection rates that result from these racialized practices of policing and punishment increase the spread of HIV to sexual partners when prisoners return home.[30] The resulting health crises devastate the social and emotional ecosystems of neighborhoods and families, leading to enormous social costs for all.

Condemning whiteness is not the same as condemning white people. Whiteness is a structured advantage subsidized by segregation. It is not so much a color as a condition. Yet because whiteness rarely speaks its names or admits to its advantages, it requires the construction of a devalued and even demonized Blackness to be credible and legitimate. Although the white spatial imaginary originates mainly in appeals to the financial interests of whites rather than to simple fears of otherness, over time it produces a fearful relationship to the specter of Blackness. The possessive investment in whiteness guarantees whites that the "not free" is "not me."[31] Just as Asian American identity has long been treated as the master sign of the "forever foreign," Blackness in U.S. national culture has become the master sign of fear of the social aggregate, of the phobia of being engulfed and overrun by some monstrous collectivity. In fearing a linked fate with other people, the white spatial imaginary is innately antidemocratic. The lack of democracy in our society is both cause and consequence of the possessive investment in whiteness. For example, residents of wealthy white neighborhoods frequently believe that suburban segregation protects them from urban crime. Yet as the drug example shows, segregation does not prevent crime, but rather concentrates and exacerbates it. Concentrated poverty is one of the main causes of crime, and residential segregation is the single most important cause of concentrated poverty.[32] Failure to enforce fair-housing laws between 1970 and 1995 made the number of census tracts with a population that was at least 40 percent poor increase from 1,500 to more than 3,400. The numbers of people living in those tracts rose from 4.1 million in 1970 to more than 8 million in 1990.[33] Segregation and poverty produce what Craig Haney calls "criminogenic" conditions. Overcrowding, differential policing, abandoned buildings, lack of legitimate employment opportunities, and the high stress caused by poverty, low wages, and social fragmentation create conditions conducive to criminal activity.[34] Chronic poverty creates family disruption and personal distress along with constant frustration and humiliation. Authorities also treat ghetto residents in ways that promote nonnormative behaviors and attitudes. Black children routinely encounter hostility from child welfare workers, teachers,

and police officers. For example, Black students are not innately more dis-
ruptive than white students, yet a survey of 9,000 middle schools published
by the Southern Poverty Law Center in 2010 revealed that 28.3 percent of
Black male students were suspended at least once during the school year
compared to a 10 percent rate for white males. Eighteen percent of Black
girls in middle schools received suspensions, more than 4 times as often as
the 4 percent of white girls who faced suspensions.[35] Black children are less
likely than white children to secure needed mental health care or in-home
social services, but are more likely to be institutionalized for emotional problems. School authorities single them out for disciplinary punishments, for
subjective offenses such as "disrespect" or "excessive noise." Black students
are three times more likely than white students to be labeled as developmen-
tally disabled and twice as likely to be deemed emotionally disturbed. Yet
once diagnosed, they are less likely to be in mainstream classrooms and more
likely to be in programs that leave them with minimal job skills and marginal
educations. High rates of incarceration also subject Black young people to the
kinds of confinement and treatment that increase violent behavior and make
recidivism more likely.[36]

Yet the fact is that the enormous increase in incarceration of people of
color starting in the 1970s did not emerge in response to any rise in criminal
activity. The crime rate had already been falling for decades when the prison
boom began. Ruth Wilson Gilmore shows how bond traders and rural real
estate interests envisioned prisons as solutions to problems that had nothing
to do with the kinds of crimes for which most inmates are incarcerated. Jordan Camp and Naomi Murakawa explain that it was the inability of ruling
groups to meet the increasingly radical demands for social changes raised in
communities of color that led to prison building. As Murakawa argues, the
nation "did not confront a crime problem that was then racialized, it confronted a race problem that was then criminalized."[37]

Because spokespersons for groups invested in the white spatial imaginary
cannot admit that segregation causes these problems, they advocate mass
incarceration as a way of punishing putatively deviant individuals. Politically
inspired policing targets ghetto areas because its inhabitants can be incarcerated more easily than other offenders. These practices also protect white suburban lawbreakers from the consequences of their own use of illegal drugs.
One national survey released in 2000 revealed that white youngsters between
the ages of twelve and seventeen were more than a third more likely to have
sold illegal drugs as Black youths from the same age cohort.[38] Another study
published the same year showed that white students used heroin at seven
times the rate of Black students, used crack cocaine at eight times the rate
of Black students, and used powder cocaine at seven times the rate of Black

students.[39] Yet more than 75 percent of people imprisoned for drug use were Blacks or Latinos. In seven states, Blacks made up 80 to 90 percent of drug offenders sent to prison. In at least fifteen states, Blacks were twenty to fifty-seven times more likely to be imprisoned on drug charges than whites.[40] A 2009 report by Human Rights Watch on disparities in drug arrests revealed that Blacks are arrested for drug offenses at rates two to eleven times the rate for whites.[41] Police officers routinely detain Blacks and Latinos more often than whites. People of color make up slightly more than half the population in New York City, but 80 percent of police "stops" are of Blacks and Latinos. Only 8 percent of the whites in New York who are stopped by police officers are frisked, but 85 percent of Blacks and Latinos are frisked.[42]

Whites receive a racial and spatial exemption from accountability for illegal drug use. As Michelle Alexander observes,

> From the outset, the drug war could have been waged primarily in overwhelmingly white suburbs or on college campuses. SWAT teams could have rappelled from helicopters in gated suburban communities and raided the homes of high school lacrosse players known for hosting coke and ecstasy parties after their games. The police could have seized televisions, furniture, and cash from fraternity houses based on an anonymous tip that a few joints or a stash of cocaine could be found hidden in someone's dresser drawer. Suburban homemakers could have been placed under surveillance and subjected to undercover operations designed to catch them violating laws regulating the use and sale of prescription "uppers." All of this could have happened as a matter of routine in white communities, but it did not.[43]

The United States now has one of the highest incarceration rates in the world, somewhere between five to eight times greater than other industrialized nations. Blacks and Latinos account for nearly three-fifths of the prison population. A survey conducted in 2001 found that 16.6 percent of Black males had experience with incarceration. Yet rather than reducing crime, mass incarceration increases it. Removing so many people from communities disrupts social networks, diminishes adult authority and control over young people, lowers productivity and income, and pressures families to find legal or illegal ways to get money to pay exorbitant fees for fines and bail bonds.[44] Incarceration undermines marital stability and child rearing, debilitates the physical and mental health of inmates, interrupts their work histories, and subverts acquisition of employable skills. In several states, previous felony convictions make it impossible to obtain government jobs or employment in licensed occupations.[45] Carceral institutions oriented toward punishment rather than rehabilitation produce people without career prospects other than crime, creating new generations of criminals. Nonviolent drug offenders convicted of possession of small amounts of marijuana for recreational use leave prison as ex-felons. Because they have been convicted of crimes, they cannot be licensed in many trades and professions, are barred from living in public housing or from receiving food stamps, and face systematic discrimination by employers and landlords. After having been locked up in jail, they find themselves locked out of mainstream society. A system more likely to produce the criminality it purports to prevent can hardly be imagined.[46]

Moral panics about crime produce costly mass incarceration practices paid for by suburban whites who resist having their tax dollars spent on inner-city education, transportation, health care, and infrastructure, yet foolishly allow enormous sums to be spent locking up inner-city residents.[47] At the same time, urban and suburban whites reduce their own political power because inmates housed in rural prisons count as part of those areas' populations for representation purposes. Yet the prisoners cannot vote, giving rural residents the kinds of augmented voting power that residents of slave states secured from the three-fifths clause. These augmented votes influence state and national politics to the detriment of people in urban and suburban areas whose embrace of mass incarceration undermines their own political power to a degree not seen since the Supreme Court's "one man, one vote" ruling in *Baker v. Carr* in the 1960s.

Those who argue that unequal racial outcomes in the aftermath of the civil rights movement prove that Blacks are unfit for freedom fail to see how the white spatial imaginary has created the conditions it condemns. Those people who complain about Blacks "playing the race card" refuse to admit that white people own the whole deck, and even worse, that deck is stacked. As George Jackson argued in the 1970s, "When the white self-congratulatory racist complains that blacks are uncouth, unlettered; that our areas are run-down, not maintained; that we dress with loud tastelessness (a thing they now also say about their own children), he forgets that he governs. He forgets that he built the schools that are inadequate, that he has abused his responsibility to use taxes paid by blacks to improve their living conditions, that he manufactured the loud pants and pointed shoes that destroy and deform the feet. If we are not enough like him to suit his tastes, it's because he planned it that way. We were never intended to be part of his world."[48]

Of course, many well-intentioned people of all races have struggled for racial justice, and they continue to do so today. Every ethnic, racial, and religious group has a precious and honorable tradition of social justice. People of all races work together every day on antiracist projects. Some observers take solace in these facts and in the surveys that show that Americans disapprove of prejudice in ever increasing numbers. Yet by placing the emphasis on preju-dice rather than on power, we lose the ability to see how race does its work in our society, how it systematically skews opportunities and life chances along racial lines, how it literally as well as figuratively "takes place." The preju-dice model presumes that racism entails isolated acts by aberrant individuals motivated by hatreds they cannot control. Although racist individuals have long existed and many more of them than we like to admit remain among us today, race has not become an issue in American law or social policy because some people dislike others because of their color. Whether we like each other or not, racism does its deadly work because it makes the lives and property of some people worth more than the lives and property of others. Racism is not incidental, aberrant, or individual, but rather collective, cumulative, and continuing. It is not simply a behavior that leaves people with hurt feelings. It is, as Ruth Wilson Gilmore argues, "the state-sanctioned and/or extralegal production and exploitation of group-differentiated vulnerability to prema-ture death."[49]

Analyzing racism from the perspective of power rather than prejudice leads logically to the study of racial projects as articulated by Michael Omi and Howard Winant in their indispensible book, *Racial Formation in the United States*.[50] Race has no innate psychological or transhistorical mean-ing for Omi and Winant, but is instead the product of conscious and histor-ically specific racial projects that imbue racial identities with determinant social meanings. The history of the United States has been a history of suc-cessive and cumulative racial projects. From the start of European settle-ment in North America, whites acted in concert to gain collective privileges. As Edmund Morgan explains in his classic work *American Slavery, Ameri-can Freedom*, white settlers solved the labor problem at Jamestown by import-ing Black slaves and relegating them to a subordinate status, so that even the poorest whites had the security of a floor through which they could not fall.[51] White communities deeply divided by class tensions found they could unite by waging war on Native Americans and seizing their lands.[52] The Con-stitution did not merely allow white individuals to hold Blacks as slaves as they wished, but instead created an elaborate federal system designed to pro-tect the power of slaveholders. White people who did not hate Blacks were policed by their peers and driven back inside the boundaries of whiteness by laws that banned intermarriage, limited the rights and freedoms of even those Blacks who were not slaves, and mandated racial zoning and other coer-cive approaches to space. Vigilante violence disciplined whites viewed as too favorable to Blacks. The restrictive covenants that obligated white homeown-ers to sell their homes only to other whites were not the product of individual preferences or market forces, but rather emerged out of coordinated collective

actions by white homeowners, real estate brokers, and elected officials. Whatever their psychological dimensions may have been, these actions systematically and collectively functioned to secure unfair gains for whites as a group.
They are not the sum total of actions by individuals, but rather manifestations
of a remarkably consistent and remarkably durable preference for whiteness, a
system that functions as a racial cartel guiding the nation's social, economic,
and political life.[53]

Sociologist Herbert Blumer argued in the 1950s that race prejudice is not
primarily a matter of private, personal, and individual attitudes, but rather a
matter of group position. The essence of racial categorization is to connect
individuals with a group, and then treat them all according to that group
membership. By lumping together Blacks as a subordinate group, all whites
became part of a superior group. They use that group position to craft public,
political, and institutional measures that give them privileges and advantages.
Blumer concedes that members of dominant groups often express personal
prejudice and disdain for those they view as different, but he argues that
they do so largely because they fear that humanizing the subordinated group
would threaten the dominant group's entitlements, privileges, and preroga-
tives. Group position cannot be simply affirmed in the abstract, however; it
has to be made and remade every day through institutional actions. Racialized space is one of the important ways in which the idea of a superior group
position for whites finds tangible expression.

In analyzing how race gets used as the basis for group position, actions by
prominent citizens and government officials loom large for Blumer because
they possess the power to "manufacture events to attract public attention and
to set lines of issue in such a way as to predetermine interpretations favorable to their interests."[54] Blumer worried that elites would use race to manipulate the masses and pervert democratic rule, that elites would manufacture
and manipulate events to promote the protection of whiteness as group position. Blumer's prediction perfectly describes the politics of this nation from
the 1960s through the present. Elite whites with standing, prestige, authority, and power have repeatedly chosen to portray judicial efforts to implement
desegregation mandates as cataclysmic occurrences, as events more threatening to the nation than the segregation and discrimination that caused the
courts to act in the first place. Moral panics about affirmative action, immigration, inner-city drug use, and nonnormative sexuality divert attention away
from the progressively declining economic status of ordinary citizens, from
the radical redistribution of wealth upward that three decades of neoliberal
and neoconservative policies have produced. Thus racism takes place in the
United States not because of the irredeemably racist character of whites as
individuals, but because the racial project of whiteness is so useful to elites

as a mechanism for preserving hierarchy, exploitation, and inequality in society at large. Poor whites with compelling grievances against class exploitation can be mobilized to support their white skin privileges instead of advancing their class interests.

These practices have a long history. In the years immediately following the Civil War, an alliance between newly emancipated Blacks and poor whites raised radical challenges to the privileges of white male propertied power. That alliance produced free public schools, internal improvements, broader access to the ballot and service on juries, and other new democratic institutions. But elites used race-baiting to break up that alliance, to win whites over to anti-Black laws and policies that led to the excesses of the Gilded Age largely in the form of public policies that subsidized the rich at the expense of the majority of the population. Conservative courts used the specter of excessive concessions to Blacks and imagined attendant injuries to whites to invert the meaning of antisubjugation measures like the Thirteenth, Fourteenth, and Fifteenth Amendments. Starting in the 1870s, judges invalidated measures designed to protect the civil rights of Blacks, but then extended new freedoms to corporations. Collaborating with the revival of racist rule in the South enabled northern business interests to get southern support for restrictive tariffs. The removal of northern troops cemented the restored political power of wealthy southern whites in national affairs. Denying rights to Black people injured African Americans as a group, but as W. E. B. Du Bois argued so effectively in his classic book *Black Reconstruction in America*, it hurt the nation as a whole by demolishing the democratic institutions and practices that Black people played a central role in creating. "Democracy died," Du Bois wrote, "save in the hearts of Black folk," where it still resides today.[55]

In our time, the actions of the Supreme Court in protecting the white spatial imaginary in school desegregation cases since the 1970s offers an exemplary model of exactly what Blumer feared. Shifts in principles and positions that otherwise contain no consistency or logic at all become legible and understandable when seen as protection of white space. In 1954 and 1955, the Supreme Court declared that segregated education violated the constitutional rights of Black children, yet it left the pace of desegregation up to the whims and convenience of those who had been discriminating against them. Massive resistance by whites guaranteed that almost no progress was made during the first decade after the court's order. The 1964 Civil Rights Act even contained "sweeteners" offering incentives to school districts to help persuade them to follow what had been the law of the land for ten years. When school districts in both the North and South continued to defy the courts, frustrated judges ordered desegregation plans that entailed transporting students to integrated schools by bus. Before *Brown v. Board*, and up through the court rulings mandating desegregation in 1971 and 1973, sending students to schools on buses had been one of the mainstays of segregation. No white parents objected to Black students being sent miles away from their homes to attend all-Black schools, nor did they protest the bus rides used to send white students to white schools in the era of mandatory segregation. In the 1971 *Swann* decision, Supreme Court Chief Justice Warren Burger noted that eighteen million children—39 percent of the total population of K–12 students—already rode buses to school during the 1969–1970 academic year.[56] Yet when federal courts responded to nearly two decades of white lawbreaking by ordering busing for the purposes of desegregation, leaders of all three branches of government conspired to make the decision an event of monumental importance by depicting it as a threat to the sanctity of white schools and homes. No technological changes had been made in the nature of the bus. The same buses that had served as routine instruments for segregation were viewed as affronts to liberty when assigned to take students to integrated schools. Suddenly, the school bus became a threat to the well-being of children, a monstrous entity because it traversed and challenged racialized space.

Whites in Pontiac, Michigan, and Boston, Massachusetts, used violence to try to prevent implementation of federal court orders desegregating schools. Presidents Nixon, Ford, and Carter expressed support not for the authority of the courts, but for the opponents of desegregation. President Ford criticized the judge who issued the Boston school desegregation order, not the parents who used violence to defy it. White political leaders in California placed a proposition on the ballot in 1979 to prevent state judges from ordering busing. The proposition passed with nearly 70 percent of the vote.[57]

At the federal level, Congress passed new laws reining in the ability of the courts to enforce desegregation orders. Finally, the Supreme Court abandoned the precedent it set in the 1971 Charlotte case with a series of rulings starting with its decision in the *Milliken v. Bradley* Detroit School segregation case in 1974. Lower courts had ruled that city, county, and state officials had designed school district boundaries in Detroit to provide white students with access to superior schools in the city and its suburbs. They found that segregation in Detroit city schools stemmed from deliberate decisions by school officials including building new schools in the center of neighborhoods known to be largely white or largely Black, and permitting white students to transfer out of majority Black schools, while at the same time denying requests by Black students to transfer to majority white schools. The courts ordered a redrawing of district lines to send children in the Detroit area by bus to integrated educational settings. Nearly three hundred thousand children in the three-county area covered by the case already rode buses to school. Yet a public outcry against this decision depicted busing as outlandish and cruel, as an unnatural act separating young children from their parents. These protests attracted support from political leaders of both major parties, and eventually persuaded the Supreme Court to overturn the lower court ruling.[58] The majority of the Court stated that the basis for their decision was the sanctity of the principle of local control over schools. "No single tradition in public education is more deeply rooted than local control over the operation of schools," the majority opinion held, noting "local autonomy has long been thought essential both to the maintenance of community concern and support for public schools and to quality of the educational process."[59] Yet in fact, there was no system of local control in force in Detroit in 1974. The Supreme Court of Michigan had ruled repeatedly that education in the state "is not a matter of local concern but belongs to the state at large."[60] The fiction of local control, however, proved useful in defending privileged access to favored schools for whites. It was used to deny claims for equal justice by children of color and their parents.

Thirty years later, however, conservative Supreme Court judges who had declared themselves strict constructionists who would be bound by previous decisions threw out the principle of local control in fully activist fashion when it suited their purposes. The Supreme Court ruled in 2007 that modest school desegregation programs in Seattle and Louisville violated the rights of white children. When confronted with actions by local school boards in Louisville and Seattle that actually helped minority children, the Court simply jettisoned the principle of local control. Chief Justice Roberts's opinion went so far as to claim that deference to local school boards "is fundamentally at odds with our equal protection jurisprudence."[61] Just as the school bus had been fine when used for segregation but an affront to decency when deployed for the purpose of desegregation, local control had been a core principle of constitutional law when it was used as a justification for segregated schools, but became at odds with the Constitution when used to desegregate schools.

The Supreme Court's about-face in respect to neighborhood schools in the Louisville and Seattle school desegregation cases follows a disgracefully dishonest and dishonorable legacy of bending the law so that whiteness always wins. The members of the Roberts Court who voted to outlaw the Seattle and Louisville desegregation plans did not present themselves openly as opponents of Black people. They were, they claimed, defenders of limited government who want to protect the original intent of the authors of the Constitution. Yet they knew full well that the authors of the Constitution enthusiastically supported extensive government power when it served the interests of white supremacy, just as the Roberts Court did. As Nathan Newman and J. J. Gass explain in their generative work on the forgotten history of the Thirteenth, Fourteenth, and Fifteenth Amendments, aggressive federal

power was established in the first place to defend slavery and the group privileges of whites. Constitutional provisions including the three-fifths clause
giving slave states extra representation in Congress, the permission granted
to continue the slave trade until at least 1808, and the Electoral College all
emerged as part of efforts to protect slavery. Along with subsequent legislation and court decisions, the Constitution did not simply give individuals who
wanted to own slaves the right to do so. It put the full power and force of the
federal government behind requiring citizens to help slave catchers return
fugitive slaves to their owners. The 1850 Fugitive Slave Act authorized federal
commissioners to compel private citizens to help them catch runaway slaves
and to arrest and imprison anyone who interfered with efforts. Even the Confederate Constitution refused to recognize state sovereignty when it came to
the central government's protection of the slaveocracy.[62]

The "threat" of federal power only became an issue for white jurists and
legislators once slavery had been abolished. This is the form of federal power
that the Roberts Court seeks to rein in today. When newly freed Blacks and
their white allies tried to inscribe in the Constitution the same protections
for Black freedom that had been previously been given to white slave-owning,
cries against excessive government power became dominant in white supremacist circles. The end of slavery witnessed collective white mobilization to
restore slavery under a different name. Even after the adoption of the Thirteenth Amendment and its authorization to enact "appropriate legislation" to
wipe out all vestiges and badges of the slave system, southern states enacted
Black codes to constrain freed people and gave the green light to vigilante
violence in order to maintain white rule. In response, Congress passed the
Civil Rights Act of 1866, a law that applied specifically to Blacks, guaranteeing them the right to conduct business and enjoy the rights, immunities,
and privileges of whites (identified expressly by race in the law) in every state.
Supporters of the Fourteenth Amendment in Congress argued that it not only
required the states to enforce the Bill of Rights, but also gave Congress the
power to criminalize private conduct by individuals attempting to deny constitutional rights to Blacks. They gave the Freedman's Bureau express authority to provide economic assistance to Blacks (even those who had not been
enslaved) and they passed the Civil Rights Act of 1875 banning segregation
in public accommodations and transportation.

Honest believers in original intent would embrace the color-conscious
"new birth constitution" created in the 1860s and 1870s. The same power
that had been used to deny rights was now being use to provide them. Laws
had now been passed empowering the state to punish private discrimination and to recognize race in order to remedy the wrongs of racism. The
original support for slavery written into the Constitution had at last been

addressed and redressed. Yet the present-day conservatives who claim to honor original intent ignore this whole history. Instead, they interpret civil rights laws of the 1860s and 1870s and the Thirteenth, Fourteenth, and Fifteenth Amendments from the perspective of the enemies of these laws, the whites who transformed the antisubjugation principles of Abolition Democracy into anti-racial-recognition principles that enabled the reestablishment of white supremacy as the law of the land. Conservative jurists in the nineteenth century refused to punish acts of violence by whites against nonviolent Black citizens attempting to exercise their rights. They turned logic and reason upside down in order to come to conclusions that supported the group position of whites. Before the Civil War, the courts said the federal government could prosecute private individuals who interfered with the capture of runaway slaves, but after the war they barred the government from prosecuting individual whites who shot and killed Blacks attempting to vote. In 1878, the Supreme Court declared unconstitutional a Louisiana law that *banned* segregation on trains as an illegal state infringement on interstate commerce, yet upheld the constitutionality of a Mississippi law *requiring* segregation on trains.[63] Perhaps most egregiously, the expressly color-conscious and antisubjugation principles of the Thirteenth, Fourteenth, and Fifteenth Amendments and the 1866 Civil Rights Act were transformed into their opposites by judges who pretended that the purpose of these laws was to prevent the state from recognizing race. A century later, conservative judges would perform the same alchemy on *Brown v. Board* and the 1964 Civil Rights Act.

This checkered history of tailoring decisions to elevate the convenience of whites over the constitutional rights of Blacks provided the background and overarching logic for the Supreme Court between 1986 and 2005 when William Rehnquist served as Chief Justice. The Rehnquist Court argued for the necessity of reigning in federal power and respecting traditions of local governance when it terminated a Kansas City school desegregation plan, but took the opposite position in deploying federal power to overturn the minority set-aside program for city contracts approved by the Richmond, Virginia, city council in the *Croson* case and in voiding the North Carolina legislature's decision to create a congressional district with a slight majority of black residents in *Shaw v. Reno*. The Rehnquist Court did not mind intervening in local matters when white firefighters complained about a court-approved affirmative action hiring program in Birmingham in *Martin v. Wilks*, or when white teachers litigated against a voluntary collective bargaining agreement between the teachers' union and the school board in Jackson, Michigan, in the *Wygant* case. Yet it presented itself as an impassioned defender of local control when local decisions protected the property and privileges of whites.

Like the majorities on the Roberts and Rehnquist courts, people with public platforms in our society often laud the promises of the civil rights movement. They celebrate the court decisions and civil rights laws that call for desegregated schools, neighborhoods, and workplaces. But since the early 1970s, the leaders of our nation have been largely uninterested in supporting the concrete practices, policies, and programs that are necessary to achieve those ends, especially school desegregation, enforcement of fair-housing laws, implementation of affirmative action policies, and programs of targeted investments to communities abandoned because of their neighborhood race effects. Even worse, when the leaders of our society do talk about civil rights, they worry more about the rights of those who profit from racism than the rights of those who are deprived because of it. For most of the past four decades, our political culture has focused enormous attention on the minor (and sometimes actually only imagined) injuries that whites experience from civil rights remedies like school desegregation and affirmative action. Whites believe that so-called reverse discrimination against them is a more serious social problem than the very real and deadly skewing of opportunities and life chances along racial lines that actually takes place in our society through inequalities in education, employment, and asset accumulation.[64] From the Supreme Court's decision in the 1978 Bakke case through its ruling in the Ricci case in 2009, federal judges display consistent and extravagant empathy for whites purportedly injured by civil rights remedies, but little concern for Blacks blocked by pervasive racial discrimination.

The white spatial imaginary recruits white people to act against their own best interests and to ignore their better selves. Martin Luther King, Jr., later recalled his conversations with the white guards and wardens he encountered in Birmingham in 1963 when he was jailed for conducting nonviolent direct action protests against segregation. These whites were eager to talk to Dr. King, to explain to him exactly why he was wrong to challenge white supremacy. One day King asked them about their work, about the places where they lived, about how much they got paid. When they answered his questions, King replied, "You know what? You ought to be marching with us. You're just as poor as Negroes." King went on to tell them that his jailers were themselves imprisoned in their whiteness, that they put themselves in the position of supporting their oppressors "because through prejudice and blindness you fail to see that the same forces that oppress Negroes in American society oppress poor white people. And all you are living on is the satisfaction of your skin being white, and the drum major instinct of thinking that you are somebody big because you are white. And you're so poor you can't send your children to school. You ought to be out here marching with every one of us every time we have a march."[65]

Some whites *have* responded to the democratic impulses of the Black spatial imaginary, and not just poor whites. The citizens who brought the initial suit to desegregate Detroit's schools that led to the *Milliken v. Bradley* decision included white parents who believed that their children were harmed by school policies that deprived them of an integrated education.[66] The precedent setting *Trafficante* fair-housing case in 1972 included complaints by whites that the managers of their apartment complex injured them by excluding Blacks because that discrimination deprived them of living in an integrated community, inhibited their ability to make business and professional contacts with members of minority groups, and left them stigmatized among their friends as people too parochial and prejudiced to live in a diverse area.[67] These whites were willing to challenge the racial and spatial logics of society in hopes of helping to craft a more democratic future for all. They recognized the harm that the white spatial imaginary inflicts on both society and themselves. In that respect, they followed in the footsteps of an interesting and enlightening (albeit virtually unknown) precursor, a nine-year-old girl from Delaware whose words have much to teach us. As the school desegregation cases that eventually led to the *Brown v. Board* decision made their way through the courts, the National Association for the Advancement of Colored People's Legal Defense and Education Fund hired social psychologists to study the effects of school segregation on children. As Gabriel Mendes's fine scholarship reveals, the Wilmington, Delaware, branch of the NAACP arranged for eight Black and five white students from that city to travel to New York for interviews with psychologist Frederic Wertham. The nine-year-old white girl remained silent during most of the sessions. Wertham asked her why she had not spoken, suggesting that perhaps the topic did not interest her, but she answered, "I care a lot about it myself." She related that the boys in her class at school claimed that "colored children" should be tied up and be forced to work while white children played. Explaining that she often played with the daughter of a Black woman who worked for her family, the girl expressed her frustration with the white boys. "People don't care," she proclaimed, "They don't think about others, they just think about themselves, so they think they are better than the Negro."[68]

Like the white plaintiffs in *Milliken* and *Trafficante*, this precocious and insightful nine-year-old girl from Wilmington, Delaware, has not been well served by the leaders of her community. Her ideas have not received the sustained subsidies and structural supports given to the white vigilantes who rioted against Black incursions into white neighborhoods and schools, to the violators of federal fair-housing laws, to the school districts evading desegregation mandates or the businesses subverting fair-employment opportunities. Yet she recognized a crucial truth that those of us who are white (like me) need to recognize and rectify. As I have argued elsewhere, we cannot attribute our investment in whiteness to the color of our skin. Sadly, it is a chilling reflection on the content of our character. If 1 percent of the energy currently expended on denying the enduring significance of race in our society were channeled toward disavowing the white spatial imaginary, it would enable us to take an important first step toward a more decent, dignified, and democratic existence. But disavowing whiteness will not be enough. Merely removing negative obstacles in the way of democracy will not produce a democratic society. We need to envision and enact new democratic practices and new democratic institutions. To do so, we need to understand the Black spatial imaginary.

2

The Black Spatial Imaginary

A geographical imperative lies at the heart of every struggle
for social justice.
—RUTH WILSON GILMORE

In the painting *Inkwell Beach* that graces the cover of the paperback edition of this book, Juan Logan calls attention to the racialization of space and the spatialization of race. Part of a series titled Leisure Space, and directly related to the representations that make up the artist's equally brilliant Unintended Relations series, *Inkwell Beach* memorializes the ways in which Black people turned segregation into congregation during the Jim Crow era. In those days, whites attempted to inscribe on the landscape the artificial divisions between the races that the pathologies of white supremacy instantiated in social life. Assuming that beaches and the oceans that touched them belonged to whites unless otherwise specified, whites took favored swimming spots for themselves and relegated Blacks to less desirable roped-off portions of sand and surf. Whites ridiculed and demonized these spaces that white supremacy created, derisively describing them as inkwells, as if the color of Black people might wash away in the water and pollute it. Yet as Logan's brilliantly colored bold images clearly convey, Black people transformed these resorts of last resort into wonderfully festive and celebratory spaces of mutuality, community, and solidarity.[1] Like the escaped slave known to the world as Harriet Jacobs hiding in a tiny garret room above her grandmother's house for six years and eleven months who transformed that tiny space into a spot where she watched and judged the white world, like the first generation of free Blacks who combated hunger and malnutrition by taking the fatbacks and intestines of pigs discarded by whites and blending them with collard greens to make savory and nutritious meals, and like the many unheralded conjurers in twentieth-century Black communities who provided health care for impoverished people by turning the roots of plants into medicines, the patrons of these beaches turned humiliating and dehumanizing segregation into exhilarating and rehumanizing congregation. As art historian Laurel Fredrickson astutely observes, many of Logan's paintings and installations revolve around African understandings of land as shared social space rather than as disposable private property, and of identity as the product of interpersonal connections rather than individual differences.[2]

One reason racialized space goes largely unnoticed is that it has been produced by the long history evoked so powerfully in Juan Logan's art. Racialized space has come to be seen as natural in this nation. Spatial control, displacement, dispossession, and exclusion have been linked to racial subordination and exploitation in decisive ways. From the theft of Native American and Mexican lands in the nineteenth century to the confiscation of Black and Latino property for urban renewal projects in the twentieth century, from the Trail of Tears to the Japanese Internment, from the creation of ghettos, barrios, reservations, and "Chinatowns" to the disproportionate placement of toxic hazards in minority neighborhoods, the racial projects of U.S. society have always been spatial projects as well. Although all communities of color have experienced social subordination in the form of spatial regulation, the particular contours of slavery, sharecropping, and segregation in the United States have inflected the African American encounter with the racialization of space and the spatialization of race in unique ways.[3]

The plantation, the prison, the sharecropper's cabin, and the ghetto have been the most visible and obvious manifestations of white supremacist uses of space. Perhaps less visible and obvious, but no less racist, have been the spaces that reflect and shape the white spatial imaginary—the segregated neighborhood and the segregated school, the all-white work place, the exclusive country club, or the prosperous properly gendered white suburban home massively subsidized with services, amenities, tax breaks, and transportation opportunities unavailable to inner-city residents. African American battles for resources, rights, and recognition not only have "taken place," but also have required blacks literally to "take places." The famous battles of the mid-twentieth-century civil rights movement took place in stores, at lunch counters, on trains and buses, and in schools. These battles emerged from centuries of struggle over spaces, from fights to secure freedom of movement in public and to enter, inhabit, use, control, and own physical places. This long legacy helps account for the power of the Black spatial imaginary and its socially shared understanding of the importance of public space as well as its power to create new opportunities and life chances.

Enslaved Africans in America quickly recognized the connections between race and place. Because they had been mostly free in Africa but enslaved in America, because racialized permanent hereditary chattel slavery differed in every respect from the nature of the slavery they knew in their native continent, slaves sought to keep alive memories of the motherland through a broad range of spatial practices. They buried their dead in African ways, decorating graves with household items, breaking plates, cups, and utensils to symbolize the ruptures between the living and the dead, between their North American present and their African past. They placed jars of water outside their homes and nailed mirrors onto their walls to capture "the flash of the spirit," alluding to streams and rivers as metaphors about flow, continuity, and connection between worlds.[4]

Africans in America constantly found themselves forced to negotiate spaces of containment and confinement in the land of their captivity. One New England slave named Caesar displayed a special commitment to movement across space when he made a remarkable escape from bondage in 1769. It was neither unusual nor unexpected for some slaves to flee to freedom, but Caesar's flight was especially dramatic. An accident made him lose both of his legs, yet somehow, he still "ran" away.[5] This was a man who really wanted to be free. Henry "Box" Brown executed a particularly imaginative escape from slavery in Richmond, Virginia, in 1848. Disconsolate because his wife and children were sold to a North Carolina slave owner, Brown decided to flee to freedom. Packing his body into a box three feet long and two feet deep, he "mailed" himself by Adams Package Express to freedom in Philadelphia, some twenty-seven hours away by wagon travel.[6] Some antebellum fugitives from slavery found they could even hide themselves in plain sight of their oppressors. In the Deep South especially, where large plantations were plentiful, escapees made their way north by moving from plantation to plantation. They secured food and shelter in the slave quarters at night, but mixed freely among the field slaves at work during the day. Although they could be seen, they remained unnoticed by the masters and overseers on large plantations who often could not really distinguish one slave from another.[7] These enslaved Africans in America found it necessary to address the injuries of race by fashioning new understandings of space.

Caesar and Henry Brown expanded the *scope* of space, moving outside the terrains controlled by the slave masters. They branched out. The underground "outliers" and field-laboring runaways reduced the *scale* of space, carving out limited zones of freedom too small and too hidden to be vulnerable to their enemies. They burrowed in. Other freedom seekers changed the *stakes of space* through schemes that turned sites of containment and confinement into spaces of creativity and community making. Slave women who served food and worked as maids or slave men working as drivers and butlers could eavesdrop on conversations and report important information back to their communities.[8] Religious ceremonies, songs, and conjuring rituals in isolated "brush arbors" enabled worshippers to summon into their presence the God of the oppressed, not as a figure to console them in their oppression, but rather as a real living force whose commitment to their emancipation was clear and unambiguous.[9] They turned the coping religion handed to them by their oppressors into an enabling religion of their own design. While others branched out or burrowed in, they built up.

Many former slaves who fled to freedom maintained contact with the spaces of slavery. Harriet Tubman lived as a slave for twenty-eight years. Her personal escape to free territory brought her freedom, but she did not sever her ties to the South completely. Thinking constantly about Southern bondage even while living in apparent freedom in the North, she concluded that neither she nor the land in which she lived could be free unless slavery ended. Tubman returned surreptitiously to the slave South nineteen times, leading more than three hundred slaves to freedom. During the Civil War she conducted reconnaissance missions for the Union army in Confederate-controlled territory in South Carolina and helped lead the Combahee River Expedition which blew up enemy supplies.[10] Other free Blacks joined the abolitionist cause, putting perpetual political pressure on their former owners.

Over time, these spatial relations produced particular understandings of racial identities. Those understandings did not simply reflect the existence of racialized space in society; they come to function as a part of it. Urban historians and sociologists have done excellent work revealing how decisions about zoning, taxation, social welfare, and urban renewal have had racial causes and consequences, but they have been less sensitive to the ways in which prevailing cultural norms and assumptions, what I call the dominant social warrant of the white spatial imaginary, have functioned to make the racialization of space ideologically legitimate and politically impregnable. Under these conditions, struggles for racial justice require more than mere inclusion into previously excluded places. They also necessitate creation of a counter social warrant with fundamentally different assumptions about place than the white spatial imaginary allows. Race-based social movements that have often seemed to social-movement theorists as expressions of unthinking racial essentialism, nationalism, and parochialism, as evidence of immature and unreflective allegiance to shared skin color and phenotype, in reality owe much of their existence to the ways in which those skin colors and phenotypes become meaningful in the United States largely through shared experiences with racialized places.

Black people pay an enormous price for the couplings of race and place that permeate society. Pervasive racial segregation creates a geographically organized vulnerability for Blacks. Not only are they concentrated demographically, but the processes that turn white privilege and power into property, into the accumulation of assets that appreciate in value and can be passed down across generations, also leave Black people with little control over the economic decisions that shape their lives. Discriminatory lending and investment practices mean that outsiders own most of the businesses in Black communities. As Malcolm X used to rhyme, "When the sun goes down, our money goes to another part of town." Banks and business establishments take more money out of Black communities than they put in. "Middlemen" entrepreneurs unable to open businesses in white neighborhoods can secure loans to open businesses in Black neighborhoods, but Blacks cannot. Blacks who do own businesses experience impediments to selling their products to people who are not Black. Millions of dollars are made by businesses in Black communities, but the profits made from them are invested elsewhere.[11]

The trajectory from these unequal spatial relations to place-based and race-based social movements emerges clearly in the insightful scholarship of John Logan and Harvey Molotch. They explain that without control over the exchange value of the neighborhoods in which they live, Blacks are largely denied access to the forms of place-based political mobilization based on protecting property values that enable other groups access to and influence in the political system. Inner-city Blacks may inhabit a neighborhood, but they are generally not owners of it or investors in it. Their powerlessness produces profits for others. They must move more often than homeowners do, depriving them of stable social networks and long-term attachments to place. Yet segregation also promotes new forms of congregation, what Logan and Molotch describe as "an extraordinary coping system built upon mutual exchange and reciprocity."[12] This system goes beyond hostile privatism and defensive localism to envision and enact broader affiliations and alliances. Race-based mobilization enables dispersed groups to find common ground, to inhabit the same politics even though they do not inhabit the same neighborhood. They make broad social demands on behalf of not only all Blacks in the region, but also on behalf of other deprived places and the people who live in them. As Logan and Molotch argue, these demands require "a more profound ideology than that behind the immediate and concrete interests of protecting one's property values or daily round."[13]

Spatial imaginaries honed in inner cities persist when Blacks move to suburbs, and for good reasons. The division between cities and suburbs does not conform exactly to the demographic concentration of whites and Blacks. Since the 1970s, Blacks have gradually started moving to suburbs. Yet Black

suburbanization is largely concentrated in areas with falling rents and declining property values, most often in older inner ring suburbs. For example, census tracts that had more than 25 percent Black populations in St.
Louis County in 1990 were concentrated in one corridor adjacent to the city's
north side. Suburbs with Black populations above 60 percent (Bel Ridge,
Berkeley, Beverly Hills, Hillsdale, Kinloch, Northwoods, Norwood Court,
Pagedale, Pine Lawn, Uplands Park, and Wellston) lay in contiguous territory outside the city limits. Seven of these 9 municipalities reported median
household incomes of $27,000 or less compared to the county median income
of $38,000.[14]

African Americans and members of other aggrieved communities of color
have been largely unable to control the exchange value of their neighborhoods
because of the power of the white spatial imaginary and the policies that flow
from it. Yet in response, they have developed innovative ways of augmenting
the use values of the spaces they inhabit. They pool resources, exchange services, and appropriate private and public spaces for novel purposes. These
practices have been vital to the survival of Black people and Black communities, but they also offer a model of democratic citizenship to everyone. Relegated to neighborhoods where zoning, policing, and investment practices
make it impossible for them to control the exchange value of their property,
ghetto residents have learned how to turn segregation into congregation. They
have augmented the use value of their neighborhoods by relying on each other
for bartered services and goods, by mobilizing collectively for better city services, by establishing businesses geared to a local ethnic clientele, and by
using the commonalities of race and class as a basis for building pan-neigh-
borhood alliances with residents of similar neighborhoods to increase the
responsibility, power, and accountability of local government. Black neighborhoods generate a spatial imaginary that favors public cooperation in solving public problems.

The radical solidarity at the heart of the Black spatial imaginary stems
not so much from an abstract idealism as from necessity. Pervasive housing
discrimination and the segregation it consolidates leave Blacks with a clearly
recognizable linked fate. Because it is difficult to move away from other members of their group, they struggle to turn the radical divisiveness created by
overcrowding and competition for scarce resources into mutual recognition
and respect. Cross-class affinities are an important outcome of these practices. According to sociologist Lincoln Quillian, a majority of Blacks, but only
10 percent of whites, at some time in any given decade will live in a poor
neighborhood.[15] African Americans in households headed by males whose
income places them above the poverty line are more likely to live in an area
of concentrated poverty than poor whites in female-headed households.[16] The

average white family earning less than $30,000 a year lives in a neighborhood with higher educational achievement and a lower rate of poverty than a Black family that earns more than $60,000 annually.[17] As a consequence, cross-class alliances mean something different in Black communities than they do in white residential areas.

The ideology that emerged from these spatial realties accounts for much of the radicalism championed by Dr. King and the civil rights movement (see Introduction). In his famous "Letter from Birmingham City Jail" and on many other occasions throughout his life, King proclaimed, "Injustice anywhere is a threat to justice everywhere. We are caught in an inescapable network of mutuality, tied in a single garment of destiny. Whatever affects one directly, affects all indirectly."[18] Of course, King drew on a broad range of sources for these ideas, ranging from the Bible to the philosophy of Immanuel Kant. But his words resonated with the masses because they spoke to the conscious-ness they had learned in racialized spaces. This was the consciousness that responded to the radical divisiveness of racialized capitalism with radical sol-idarity, that united the chitlin' eaters with the chicken eaters, that cared as much about the town drunk as the town doctor, that motivated Ella Baker to urge educated entrepreneurs steeped in the culture of uplift to work with bootleggers and pool hall hustlers immersed in the culture of the blues.[19]

These ideas directly contradict the political logic produced by the white spatial imaginary. As Logan and Molotch explain, simple self-interest should lead members of aggrieved groups in another direction, to reject radical democracy in favor of hierarchical plutocracy. to disidentify with the non-normative and powerless people in their own ranks. A system of triage might enable well-off and moderately wealthy members of aggrieved communities to secure significant concessions from the system in return for buying into it. When confronted with egalitarian and democratic social movements, people in power always hold out the lure of individual escape for selected individu-als. The logic of the system encourages potential rebels to instead seek posi-tions as administrators of austerity, apologists for corporate power and white privilege, or political shills for redevelopment schemes certain to exacerbate the very problems they purport to solve. There is never a shortage of Black people auditioning for these roles. Yet given the enormous rewards potentially available to those who identify with whiteness, the enduring popularity and power of Black radical democracy needs explaining. The explanation is not so much a matter of race as a matter of place.

Because Black people have different relations to places than whites, the Black spatial imaginary continuously generates new democratic imaginations and aspirations. On the one hand, embracing the ideals of the white spatial imaginary does not work as well for Blacks as it does for whites, because the whole system is premised on their subordination. A study of Black homeowners in the one hundred largest metropolitan areas, for example, discovered that they received on average 18 percent less return on their housing investment than whites obtained.[20] Research by Chenoa Flippen reveals that even when Blacks obtain assets that appreciate in value and can be passed down across generations, they obtain them on terms that impede wealth creation. It is not just that homes owned by Blacks are worth substantially less than homes owned by whites, and that homes in Black neighborhoods appreciate in value more slowly than homes in white neighborhoods, but that mature Black homeowners actually experience depreciation of home values more than appreciation. Because of residential segregation, mortgage redlining, direct discrimination, and a whole host of neighborhood race effects, decisions that make economic sense for whites do not make sense for Blacks.[21] Similarly, research by Camille Zubrinsky Charles demonstrates that directly contrary to the experience of whites, homeownership actually has a negative effect on Black residential outcomes. Black renters can inhabit less segregated and more affluent neighborhoods than Black homeowners. In fact, because of segregation and its attendant social consequences, Blacks are the only group who find themselves economically *penalized* for homeownership.[22]

At the same time that systematic residential segregation inhibits Black access to the prosperous private home, it augments the public value of some seemingly private spaces. In Black neighborhoods where most businesses are owned and controlled by outsiders, those that Blacks do own can become important sites of solidarity and mutuality. In his research on the origins of the civil rights movement, Aldon D. Morris explains that beauty parlors sometimes served unexpected purposes. As sites owned by Blacks and almost never patronized by whites, beauty parlors could host freedom schools and function as meeting places for strategic discussions. Recent scholarship by Melissa Harris-Lacewell, Vorris Nunley, Ingrid Banks, and Adia Harvey Wingfield (among others) further elaborates the uncommon roles played by these seemingly common sites up to the present day precisely because of the politics of place and race.[23]

This imagination has not been confined to the hair salon. Faced with uncertain access to public meeting halls, vexed by aggressive police surveillance, and deprived of spaces they controlled themselves because of systematic impediments to asset accumulation, Blacks had to learn to recognize the public possibilities of privately owned places, to perceive potential new uses for any arena open to them. During the 1950s, St. Louis politician Jordan Chambers turned the back room of a nightclub he owned into his unofficial ward headquarters. When Malcolm X visited the city to deliver a public address in 1963, he spoke at a roller rink on Finney Avenue. In 1970, St. Louis activist Ivory

Perry coordinated activities by doctors, nurses, and medical students screening and treating children poisoned by toxic lead from a command post that he set up in a neighborhood tavern, Maurice's Gold Coast Lounge.[24]

The white disdain for Blacks that extended even to the dead meant that funeral homes operated by whites generally refused to serve Black customers. Even as corpses, Blacks were unwanted by whites. Yet this discrimination created openings for Black entrepreneurship in the mortuary industry. Suzanne Smith's fascinating history of African American funeral directors reveals that these businesses served the living in many creative and unexpected ways. The Detroit Memorial Park Cemetery raised sufficient capital for its Black owners to enable them to offer home mortgage loans to Blacks at a time when white lenders would not. The building housing the offices of the Metropolitan Funeral System Association's burial insurance business in Chicago also featured the Parkway Ballroom that enabled Blacks to attend dances and concerts free from the indignities of Jim Crow segregation that prevailed elsewhere in the city. Preston Taylor, a Black undertaker in Nashville, opened a private recreation park for Blacks featuring a skating rink, clubhouse, picnic grounds, and an amusement hall adjacent to the cemetery he owned. During the 1950s some Black funeral directors aided the emerging civil rights movement by placing voter registration information on the back of funeral fans.[25]

Although nearly every aggrieved immigrant, ethnic, and racial group has drawn on the resources of fraternal orders and mutual aid societies, these organizations have been even more important to Blacks because of the many obstacles to capital accumulation they have faced. By the 1920s Black fraternal organizations owned $20 million worth of property that housed banks, hospitals, and social welfare agencies.[26] The Knights of Tabor and the Daughters of Tabernacle attracted fifty thousand members to nearly one thousand lodges in the 1940s and 1950s largely because those groups operated a hospital in Mound Bayou, Mississippi, at a time when most hospitals in the south refused to treat Black patients.[27] For many years Martin Luther King's Southern Christian Leadership Conference housed its national headquarters in The Prince Hall Grand Lodge of Georgia building in Atlanta.[28]

The Black spatial imaginary turned sites for performance and prayer into venues for public political mobilization. Scholars have long recognized how religion and music play central roles in African American culture, but for the most part they have been insufficiently attentive to the ways in which these cultural practices have loomed so large because they take place in spaces over which Blacks exercise some control. Places designed for prayer and performance frequently become sites for politics, while political gatherings signal their legitimacy by incorporating elements of prayer and performance inside them. Civil rights groups in the 1960s staged fund-raisers at entertainment venues, including the Village Gate nightclub in New York's Greenwich Village and the Comiskey Park baseball stadium in Chicago.[29] In the 1970s, Jesse Jackson's Operation Breadbasket organization staged weekly meetings on Saturday mornings in a six-thousand-seat motion picture theater in Chicago that featured performances by choirs and orchestras, sermons by Reverend Jackson, and display tables advertising merchandise for sale by Black-owned businesses.[30]

People who do not control physical places often construct discursive spaces as sites of agency, affiliation, and imagination. One of the most important yet least known dimensions of Black expressive culture is its consistent preoccupation with place and power. Both canonized works of art and a variety of vernacular expressive practices in Black communities speak to the spatial aspects of racial identity. These works of expressive culture function as repositories of collective memory, sources of moral instruction, and mechanisms for transforming places and calling communities into being through display, dialogue, and decoration. Like activists, artists committed to Black freedom proceed by promoting new understandings of the scale, scope, and stakes of place and space, by burrowing in, branching out, and building up.

African American artists and intellectuals have created a distinct spatial imaginary in a broad range of cultural expressions, from the migration narrative that Farah Jasmine Griffin identifies as the core trope within Black literature, music, and art, to the celebration of city streets in the imagery and iconography of hip-hop where streets become performance spaces for graffiti writing, mural art, and break dancing. Photographs by Roy DeCarava and Teenie "One Shot" Harris lovingly delineated the contours of Black urban life while works of fiction by Ann Petry and Toni Cade Bambara memorialized women's negotiations with both domestic and public spaces. Geographer Clyde Woods shows how that the expressive culture of blues music grew directly out of the politics of place in the Mississippi Delta, that the blues constitute a key component of a distinct African American ethno-racial epistemology. His evidence and argument brilliantly demonstrate that this *ethno-racial* epistemology is also an *ethno-spatial* epistemology.[31]

Understanding racialized space requires us to stage a confrontation between the moral geography of pure space expressed by the hostile privatism and defensive localism of the white spatial imaginary that permeate segregated spaces in the United States on the one hand, and the moral geography of differentiated space as it has developed in the Black spatial imaginary on the other. This conversation will show that the national spatial imaginary is racially marked, that segregation serves as a key crucible for creating the emphasis on exclusion and augmented exchange value that guides the contemporary ideal of the properly gendered prosperous private home. Changing the racialized nature of opportunities and life chances in the United States requires policies, practices, and institutions that reject the white spatial imaginary and constitute a new social charter along the lines embodied in the Black spatial imaginary. Our primary goal should be to disassemble the fatal links that connect race, place, and power. This requires a two-part strategy that entails a frontal attack on all the mechanisms that prevent people of color from equal opportunities to accumulate assets that appreciate in value and can be passed down across generations, as well as a concomitant embrace of the Black spatial imaginary based on privileging use value over exchange value, sociality over selfishness, and inclusion over exclusion.

Black expressive culture has long been one of the sites where a counter warrant against the white spatial imaginary can be found. For example, street parades held a powerful allure for the young Louis Armstrong in segregated New Orleans at the start of the twentieth century. Later in life, the trumpeter's unparalleled virtuosity would enable Armstrong to travel across countries and continents, but as a child he needed the street parade merely to move freely across town. Most of the time it was dangerous for a Black child to venture out into unknown areas. White thugs and police officers routinely attacked Blacks who wandered out of the ghetto and into places where whites lived. Armstrong discovered, however, that by volunteering to tag along with brass bands helping Bunk Johnson or Joe Oliver carry their horns when they got tired, he could see the rest of the city safely. Recalling those excursions fondly in his later years, Armstrong noted that marching along with the brass bands granted him "safe passage throughout the city." When he grew up and assumed a role as a full-fledged member of one of those bands, it meant that, at least on parade days, "I could go into any part of New Orleans without being bothered."[32]

More than four decades years after the end of slavery, Blacks like the young Louis Armstrong still did not have freedom of movement. Chains no longer bound them to plantations. Fugitive slave laws no longer put the full force of the federal government behind tracking them down. Yet a whole new set of practices and rules constrained their mobility. The names had changed, but the game was the same. The sharecropping system tied Black workers to the land. Laws against loitering and vagrancy made every Black person subject to arrest on the whim of whites. These "criminals" found themselves incarcerated inside newly created prisons that replicated the social relations of slavery. Legally constituted authorities winked at vigilante violence designed to keep Blacks "in their place," figuratively and literally. Jim Crow segregation shaped the spaces African Americans could occupy in stores or on streetcars. Even cemeteries were segregated. White policing of public space forced Blacks to step off of sidewalks and into the streets to make room for whites when they passed. Racial zoning and restrictive covenants relegated Black people to crowded, dirty, and dangerous slums. Politically motivated policing prevented African Americans from leaving the spaces to which they had been assigned, yet rendered them powerless to protect their neighborhoods from outside assaults, attacks, and rampages.

Blacks prevented from traveling freely through space on their own accord, however, often found themselves forced to move quickly to flee from white oppression and violence. The downtown Black neighborhood in New Orleans where Armstrong was raised was populated by refugees from waves of anti-Black violence in the Louisiana countryside during the late nineteenth century. When the white supremacist counterrevolution against Abolition Democracy succeeded in restoring the social relations of slavery in the Louisiana countryside after 1880 through sharecropping and Ku Klux Klan terrorism, tens of thousands of Blacks left the hinterlands, gathering together for mutual protection in New Orleans.[33] The 2007 film *Banished* by Marco Williams documents the well-known practice of "whitecapping," through which jealous whites used violence to force Blacks from homes and farms that whites wanted to own. The cities of Harrison, Arkansas, and Pierce City, Missouri, as well as most of Forsyth County, Georgia, became locales inhabited only by whites once Blacks were forced out. Whites then used the legal fiction of "adverse possession" to claim title to lands they had never purchased, to occupy and own them, to pass on the unfair gains and unjust rewards they secured in this way to future generations. Black families, however, lost control of their assets and the ability to transfer their wealth to their descendants. Yet even when Black property was not stolen as overtly as it was in Pierce City, Harrison, and Forsyth County, Black communities suffered continuously from displacement, dispossession, and decapitalization. White mob violence destroyed Black homes and businesses in East St. Louis, Illinois, in 1917, in Chicago in 1919, and in Tulsa in 1921. Highway building and urban renewal in the mid-twentieth century destroyed some sixteen hundred Black communities.[34]

For the young Louis Armstrong, street parades served as his first introduction to Black peoples' struggles over space. They functioned as one small part of a broader cultural and political negotiation with couplings of race and place. Participants in street parades used the spaces of the city to create new social relations among themselves. Musicians, dancers, and spectators learned to communicate effectively with one another in public, to anticipate each other's moves and energies. Musical patterns of antiphony featured "call and response" between lead instruments and the rest of the band. "Second line" dancers and drummers joined the processions in answer to the invitations, challenges, and calls of the marching bands. Going out into the city alone without being harassed or constrained by whites was practically an impossible achievement for a Black man in turn-of-the-century New Orleans, but going together as members of a band provided protective cover and mutual support.

Parades provided Black people with opportunities to enter new spaces. Even more important, however, inside the space of the parade itself musicians and their followers could bring the spatial imaginary of their neighborhoods out into the rest of the city as they marched along. Their music, marching, sartorial styles, and speech displayed the local neighborhood inflections and accents that they applied to mass-produced music, clothing, and culture. The dialogues they created among musicians and between musicians and marchers brought performances of African antiphony (call and response) and sanctified church heterophony (multiple versions of the same melody) into public places previously marked as white spaces. Musicians in street parades engaged in dialogic and democratic relations with audiences and spectators. These practices differed sharply from the monologic displays of virtuosity that dominated the conservatory and the concert hall. As Thomas Brothers observes in his splendid book on Armstrong's youth in the Crescent City, "Parades thus offered disenfranchised Negroes a chance to assertively move their culture throughout the city's public spaces, the very spaces where African Americans were expected to confirm social inferiority by sitting in the rear of trolley cars and by stepping aside on sidewalks to allow whites to pass."[35]

Street parades reversed the maps of inclusion and exclusion in New Orleans. Musicians who would have been shunned as unwelcome outsiders on any other day were welcomed and celebrated as guests of honor on the days when parades were held. Parades changed the meanings of inside and outside space. Music played inside concert halls or nightclubs entailed high overhead costs, necessitating admission fees. Music played for commercial consumption in clubs needed the approval of those who owned the property. But music played outside at parades, picnics, and lawn parties created democratic spaces for cultural production, distribution, and reception. The music was free. Outside music proved especially effective in rearranging cognitive mappings of place in New Orleans because the city's humid air, low altitude, and low-rise development allowed music to be heard over great distances, sometimes as much as a mile and half to three miles.[36] Street music also encouraged openness and improvisation. Bands responded to sounds they encountered accidentally, to the rattles of junk collectors' wagons and streetcars, to the sounds of street musicians playing on tin horns, to church bells, and to music emanating from storefront churches, dance halls, and taverns.[37] Because they did not control the neighborhoods in which they lived, and because traversing putatively public space could be dangerous for them, marching in the streets took on different meaning for Blacks than it did for whites. Taking to the streets was a quintessentially political act that deployed performance as a means of calling a community into being and voicing its values and beliefs. Of course, whites paraded too, but because they controlled private spaces and had routine access to public places, they did not develop the same kind of collective and communal cultural politics of the street that emerged from the Black spatial imaginary.

Not every Black community enjoyed the relationship with street parades that prevailed historically in New Orleans, but Blacks in every city, town, and hamlet created cultural forms that celebrated movement in defiance of segregationist constraints and confinement. As Herman Gray notes, a street and road aesthetic organized around travel and adapting to new experiences served vital purposes in establishing jazz music as both a local and national practice among Blacks in the twentieth century.[38] Even Blacks who stayed at home nonetheless incorporated movement into their lives. Household decorations and yard art transforming refuse into treasure utilized discarded tires, hubcaps, and wheels as raw materials that evoked mobility and power symbolically. Sometimes these objects even produced the movement they seem to merely evoke. In East Detroit during the summer of 1998, Tyree Guyton was bothered by crack cocaine dealers using abandoned houses on his block as their place of business. The drug traffickers conducted transactions during all hours of the day and night. The stream of people coming to their doors disrupted the neighborhood and frightened its inhabitants. Guyton wished that the abandoned houses would just go away. He nailed tires and hubcaps to the walls of these houses to suggest movement. "Curved space spins," he proclaimed, adding "I put something round on a square, on a house, and make it go."[39] Of course, the laws of physics being what they are, Guyton's alchemy did not work in the way he intended, at least not directly. The houses did not move anywhere. Yet he succeeded anyway. As Guyton nailed more and more tires and hubcaps to the houses, they attracted attention. Neighborhood children and pedestrians came to view the decorations. Word spread across town. People in cars drove by to see Guyton's art. Panicked by so much public scrutiny, the drug dealers moved their business elsewhere.[40]

In the early 1970s, when the energy crisis made big gas-guzzling automobiles seem outdated, Black sculptor Jim Gary in Farmingdale, New Jersey, transformed the skeletons of abandoned cars into statuesque dinosaurs, some of which were 60 feet long and 20 feet high. Gary would use of hundreds of parts from as many as ten vehicles in a single work. He turned brake "shoes" into dinosaur feet and transformed oil pans into dinosaur jaws. Generator fans served as lash-ringed eyes, and leaf springs functioned as rib cages in his creations. In Gary's opinion, old Chryslers made the best dinosaurs. When transporting his work to galleries and collectors, Gary placed them on a huge flatbed trailer which he created out of salvaged automobile parts. As he traveled he provoked impromptu parades on the highway as drivers followed him for miles to take in the spectacle he had created.[41]

In many Black communities, the ability to travel to far-off places gave merchant seamen and railroad workers (especially Pullman porters) special prestige. As a youth in Birmingham in the1920s, Lionel Hampton remembers groups of Blacks sitting by the railroad tracks on summer afternoons to watch the trains go by. Hundreds of people went to the railroad station every evening at six o'clock to watch "The Special" depart for Atlanta. As the train pulled away slowly from the depot, workers put on a show for the crowd assembled outside. Dining car waiters unfurled big white table cloths and draped them over tables. They tossed vases with roses in them to one another for placement on ledges and tables, moving quickly and artfully to put plates and utensils in their proper places. Pullman porters waved sheets and blankets as they made up berths for the night. Firemen shoveled coal furiously, and their helpers tossed stray lumps of coal to the crowd to use for heating their homes. When the train pulled away from the station, spectators cheered and applauded as porters and waiters looked out the windows and waved. The Black fireman rang the bell, and the white engineer blew the train whistle long and loud.[42]

Movement also provided the guiding aesthetic for Dr. Billy Taylor in Harlem in 1964. A pianist, composer of the song "I Wish I Knew How It Would Feel to Be Free," and host of jazz radio and television programs in New York City, Taylor turned the streets of Harlem into a performance space by placing jazz ensembles on flatbed trucks. These "jazzmobiles" cruised through neighborhoods as Taylor invited pedestrians to dance.[43] Mobility also guided the work of preachers who fashioned ways of making their ministries mobile by marching through the streets with their parishioners to bodies of water where they could conduct outdoor baptism ceremonies, staging revivals in tents, and broadcasting services on the radio. Reverend C. L. Franklin moved his ministry from Buffalo to Detroit in 1946 precisely because "I wanted to be in a city where there were crossroads of transportation. Trains, buses, planes, where people are coming and going, conventions of all kinds, and migrations."[44] The New Bethel Baptist Church invited him to be their pastor in 1945, but when Franklin arrived he discovered that the congregation met in a converted bowling alley that needed extensive repairs. He set out to construct a new sanctuary on Detroit's main Black boulevard, Hastings Street, but conducted services outdoors on sunny days and in a housing project community center when it rained. Broadcasting services on the radio helped Franklin build a following. A local record store owner taped the preacher's sermons and played them on loudspeakers outside his Hastings Street store near Franklin's church. The sermons almost always attracted crowds, which alerted record distributors and radio stations to Franklin's potential commercial viability. He became a national celebrity in Black communities through some seventy recorded sermons that sold well. Yet even fame and fortune were not sufficient in the face of the power of racialized space. A federally funded urban renewal program demolished Franklin's Hastings Street church and much of the neighborhood surrounding it.[45]

The strong desire to move freely across space formed an important part of the Black spatial imaginary, but it has rarely been easy to translate hopes of moving freely into the ability actually to do so for African Americans. All forms of transportation have entailed vexed confrontations with the dynamics of racialized space. Railroad trains, streetcars, and buses became special sites of contestation during the civil rights movement. It is not mere coincidence that *Plessy v. Ferguson*, the key Supreme Court case legitimizing segregation, concerned seating arrangements on passenger trains, or that it was the bus boycott in Montgomery that launched the career of Dr. King and the modern freedom movement, or that freedom riders in the 1960s tested the limits of Jim Crow by seeking service at segregated bus station lunch counters. Transit systems became more important to Blacks than they were to whites because of the dynamics of racialized space. In the mid-twentieth century, federally funded highway construction destroyed Black neighborhoods in city after city while subsidies for the automobile-oriented suburb further secured the spatial privileges of whiteness. Dr. King identified transit racism as an important element in skewing opportunities and life chances along racial lines in a 1968 essay. "Urban transit systems in most American cities . . . ," King wrote, "have become a genuine civil rights issue—and a valid one—because the layout of rapid-transit systems determines the accessibility of jobs to the black community."[46]

These problems persist today. Contemporary antiracist activists in Atlanta, Los Angeles, San Francisco, and New York view "transit racism" as a major factor skewing opportunities and life chances along racial lines. Public transportation vehicles are not more segregated than neighborhoods, jobs, or schools, but in a society where race is coterminous with space, transit vehicles are sites where segregated worlds collide.[47] Transit racism channels subsidies to mostly white suburban commuters while making commuting difficult for people of color. Blacks and Latinos make up 62 percent of urban bus riders and 35 percent of subway riders. They are twice as likely as whites to get to work by riding public transit, walking, or biking. Overfunding of highways and underfunding of nonautomotive means of transportation result in public transit commutes taking twice as long as travel by car.[48] Inadequate public transportation, residential segregation, and automobile-centered development also endanger Black lives. When the construction of the I-10 Freeway subsidized white migration to suburban St. Tammany Parish outside New Orleans, housing opportunities opened for Blacks in New Orleans East. But they found themselves living without cars and without public transit in an automobile-centered locale. Fatal accidents took the lives of several pedestrians trying to cross the I-10 service road to reach shopping centers.[49]

The American Broadcasting Corporation's program *Nightline* examined a similar situation in the 1999 episode "The Color Line and the Bus Line." It detailed the death of Cynthia Wiggins, a seventeen-year-old African American single mother in Buffalo, New York, run over by a ten-ton dump truck on her way to work as she attempted to cross a crowded seven-lane highway to get to her job at a fast-food counter in the Walden Galleria shopping mall. Her death was an accident, yet she would not have been on the spot where she died had it not been for transit racism. City officials, bus company managers, and shopping mall owners conspired to make sure that buses traveling from Black neighborhoods could not stop at the mall in the nearly all-white suburb of Cheektowaga in an effort to cater to the fears and prejudices of suburban whites by keeping down Black patronage of the mall's establishments. Wiggins had to take the bus because there were no jobs available in her neighborhood and she did not own a car. The spatial mismatch between jobs and employment confronting her reveals a local manifestation of a national problem. Close to 50 percent of low-skill jobs are unavailable to Blacks because the jobs are located in white suburbs inaccessible by public transportation.[50] Residential segregation leaves Blacks more physically isolated from available jobs than any other racial group.[51]

Engaged to be married and hoping one day to study to become a doctor, the ambitious Wiggins rode the Number 6 bus for fifty minutes each day to her job as a cashier at Arthur Treacher's Fish and Chips restaurant. "Welfare reform" policies passed by a Republican Congress and signed into law by a Democratic president required her to hold down a job in order to receive benefits necessary for the survival of her child. With no employment available in her decapitalized neighborhood, Wiggins travelled to the suburbs to work. Although charter buses routinely transported passengers to the mall, city buses were not allowed on the property. Wiggins had disembarked at a bus stop three hundred yards from the mall and had to cross seven lanes of traffic on Walden Avenue, a highway with no sidewalk. She had almost completed her journey across the street on December 14, 1995, on a snowy Buffalo winter day, when the traffic light changed and the truck driver (who probably did not see her) started his vehicle.[52] Had Wiggins been less determined to work to support herself and her child, she might not have been killed. Yet her death was not entirely an accident. Nationwide, Blacks have a higher likelihood than whites of dying in pedestrian-vehicle accidents, in part because they walk more and drive less, but also because transit racism places them in situations of jeopardy.[53]

Yet compared to other potential sites for fights about segregation, public transportation has offered Blacks some tactical advantages. Because a transit system takes people to work, white employers have a direct interest in its smooth and timely operation. Disruptions in service affect everyone, not just Blacks. The Montgomery bus boycott divided whites because resolute defenders of segregation of the buses had to confront the displeasure of wealthy whites who expected their maids and cooks to arrive to work on time. Fare-paying Black passengers might be able to make demands on a transit line as customers that they could not make to their own employers as workers. Yet for those very reasons, public transit sites often have enormous tactical and symbolic meanings for defenders of white space, as the trajectory from *Plessy v. Ferguson* to *Milliken v. Bradley* indicates. In his important research on infrapolitics and the Black working class, Robin Kelley demonstrates how Blacks in Birmingham during the 1940s waged constant struggles over racialized space on city buses. They battled with bus drivers who shortchanged them or who attacked them for allegedly not following instructions, who sometimes made them pay fares in the front of the bus then directed them to enter by the side and drove off without letting them board. The main goal of these Blacks was not to sit next to whites, but rather to be treated with respect and dignity, to receive the services for which they paid, and to get to their destinations on time. In St. Louis, Black passengers even resisted desegregation of the buses in the 1960s when the newly constituted Bi-State Transit Agency reneged on promises to hire Black drivers and insisted on the termination of service by the private Service Car company that had previously provided inexpensive and efficient jitney service in Black neighborhoods.[54] Vehicles moving across spaces came to mean something different to Blacks than they did to whites. Living in segregated neighborhoods posed enormous problems, but traversing their boundaries also brought new challenges every day.

Making unexpected use of public spaces has been a persistent theme for Black visual artists including Juan Logan and Betye Saar (see Chapter 7). David Hammons creates installations out of perishable materials like human hair, grease, powder, and snowballs to make his work unavailable for permanent exhibition in galleries or museums. He forages on the streets for materials and exhibits much of his work outdoors. Hammons solicits feedback about his installations from homeless men and women rather than from patrons of museums and galleries, whom he describes as the "worst audience in the world" because he views them as people "out to criticize not to understand" and as a group that "never has any fun."[55] Hammons adorns trees on inner-city streets with empty bottles that were once filled with alcohol consumed by homeless people, asserting, "Black lips have touched each of these bottles."[56] One time Hammons dragged a cotton bale through the streets of Harlem to evoke the history of migration from the plantation to the ghetto and to signify on the title of one of Chester Himes's books, *Cotton Comes to Harlem*. The provocation caused Black people to tell Hammons stories about memories of picking cotton but also to urge him to drag the bale away. One person told him, "I don't ever want to see that stuff again."[57]

The Black spatial imaginary that emerges from complex couplings of race and space promotes solidarities within, between, and across spaces. Like the white spatial imaginary, it is not reducible to embodied identity. Some antiracist whites have played important roles in advancing the Black spatial imaginary. Some Blacks have opposed it bitterly. Every Black person, however, suffers in some way from the neighborhood race effects associated with Black residential and commercial districts. Yet while it has been created by terrible and inexcusable injustices, the Black spatial imaginary has vitally important creative and constructive things to offer to this society and to its potential for democracy. The Black spatial imaginary views place as valuable and finite, as a public responsibility for which all must take stewardship. Privileging the public good over private interests, this spatial imaginary understands the costs of environmental protection, efficient transportation, affordable housing, public education, and universal medical care as common responsibilities to be shared, rather than as onerous burdens to be palmed off onto the least able and most vulnerable among us.

For most of the past half century, suburban property owners have mobilized politically to cut property taxes, resist school desegregation, and fight equal spending on education across district lines. In response, Black residents of the differentiated spaces of cities and inner-ring suburbs have emerged as the most fervent advocates for fair and affordable housing, for measures to combat childhood lead poisoning and other public health menaces, for the creation and maintenance of efficient and safe transportation systems, and for equitable educational opportunities. Journalists, politicians, scholars, and land-use professionals have long been cognizant that these views represent the experiences and opinions of different *races*, but they have been less discerning about the degree to which these differences in views stem from the experiences and opinions generated by life in different *places*.

Chapters 3 and 4 demonstrate links between social structure and culture in the white spatial imaginary. Chapter 3 examines the spatial and racial logic behind city and state subsidies for a sports stadium in St. Louis, while Chapter 4 explores the limits of the liberalism enunciated in the HBO cable television production *The Wire*. Both projects reveal the workings of the white spatial imaginary and the need for a counter to it, which I will present in Chapters 5 through 10.

SECTION II

Spectatorship and Citizenship

3

Space, Sports, and
Spectatorship in St. Louis

There is a spatial dimension to discrimination.
—JOE FEAGIN

When the St. Louis Rams defeated the Tennessee Titans on January 23, 2000, to win the National Football League's Super Bowl championship, the team's players, coaches, and management deserved only part of the credit. Sports journalists covering the game cited the passing of Kurt Warner and the running of Marshall Faulk as the key factors in the Rams victory. Others acknowledged the game plan designed by head coach Dick Vermeil and the player personnel moves made by general manager John Shaw. But no one publicly recognized the contributions made by 45,473 children enrolled in the St. Louis city school system to the Rams victory. Eighty-five percent of these students were so poor that they qualified for federally subsidized lunches. Eighty percent of them were African American. They did not score touchdowns, make tackles, kick field goals, or intercept passes for the team. But revenue diverted from the St. Louis school system through tax abatements and other subsidies to the Rams made a crucial difference in giving the football team the resources to win the Super Bowl.

In the home city of the 2000 Super Bowl champions, children attended underfunded public schools staffed by underpaid and inexperienced teachers. In the year when the Rams won the Super Bowl, beginning teachers in the local school district received annual salaries of $26,501 with a B.A. degree, $26,511 with an M.A., and $29,443 with an Ed.D. or Ph.D. The average salary for teachers in the district in 2000 was $33,269 per year.[1] Compensation was so meager in St. Louis that teachers' union president Sheryl Davenport reported that the district could not even attract qualified *substi-*

tute teachers in competition with neighboring school systems. Consequently, teacher assistants frequently staffed classrooms when the primary instructor was absent. Out of 104 school districts in the region, the pay scale for teachers in St. Louis was the seventy-third lowest.

The problems facing the school system were of long standing. During the 1990–1991 academic year, more Black students dropped out of the city's high schools (1,421) than graduated from them (966).[2] By 1999, for every hundred students who began the ninth grade in St. Louis schools, only thirty graduated.[3] The total dropout rate from the city schools in 1998–1999 was 18.7 percent, the highest in Missouri and more than three times the state average of 5.5 percent.[4] During the 1999 Missouri School Improvement Program Review, the city's schools met only three of the state's eleven performance standards. Yet at the same time, tax abatements for profitable businesses including the Rams football team deprived St. Louis children of seventeen million dollars annually in educational funding.[5]

St. Louis's school-age children suffered a distinct class injury because of the subsidies received by the Rams. Students from low-income families lost access to educational dollars so that they could be spent subsidizing the profits of the millionaire owner of the Rams. The injury in this case was also a racial one, and not merely because most of the students in the city school system were Black. The starkly unequal educational opportunities offered to students in different districts within the St. Louis metropolitan area stemmed directly from carefully designed and deliberate discrimination against African Americans. The diversion of funds to the Rams was only the latest in a series of measures designed to prevent Blacks in St. Louis from competing fairly with whites, to relegate them to separate and unequal segments of the area's housing, labor, and educational infrastructure.

In St. Louis, a deliberate and irretrievably racial logic has long guided local decisions about redevelopment, planning, taxation, transportation, and zoning.[6] In the late nineteenth and early twentieth centuries, whites in St. Louis developed, honed, and refined many different mechanisms designed to segregate the city by race. A racial zoning ordinance mandated that Black home buyers and renters could move into a new residence only if a majority of the residents already living on the block were Black. Restrictive covenants promoted by real estate brokers, lenders, and government agencies placed requirements in deeds obligating their holders never to sell the property to anyone who was Black. As Colin Gordon observes in his excellent book *Mapping Decline*, market forces did not create housing segregation in the St. Louis region. On the contrary, public policies protected antimarket collaboration among whites by regulating, restricting, and rigging private economic exchanges to preserve and augment the possessive investment in whiteness.[7]

The Supreme Court ultimately declared racial zoning to be unconstitutional in the *Buchanan v. Warley* case in 1917, and the Court ruled that states could not enforce restrictive covenants in the 1948 *Shelley v. Kraemer* case. Yet even after being ruled illegal and illegitimate, these practices remained important in shaping the contours of racialized space in the city. Subsequent policies about land use, development, and taxation sought to protect the cumulative benefits and underlying spatial and racial logics of the outlawed forms of overt discrimination. Gordon notes that the racial prejudice of real estate brokers became the "ethical and effective foundation of local incorporation, zoning, taxation, and redevelopment policies in St. Louis and its suburbs."[8] In the 1950s and 1960s, the federal government subsidized home mortgage loans and funded transportation and infrastructure projects that augmented the economic value of racially exclusive suburbs while locating means-tested public housing projects in inner-city Black neighborhoods. Even after direct references to race disappeared from federal appraisers' manuals, race remained the crucial factor in determining whether borrowers received federally supported mortgage loans. Only 3.3 percent of the 400,000 FHA mortgages in the greater St. Louis area went to Blacks between 1962 and 1967, most of them in the central city. Only 56 mortgages (less than 1 percent) went to Blacks in the suburbs of St. Louis County.[9] Three savings and loan companies with assets of more than a billion dollars worked together to redline the city effectively, lending less than $100,000 on residential property inside the city limits in 1975.[10] The local savings and loan institutions made loans totaling $500 million in the greater St. Louis area in 1977, but just $25 million of that total (less than 6 percent) went to the city, almost all of it to the two mostly white zip codes at the municipality's southern border.[11] Depreciation provisions added to federal tax laws in the mid-1950s encouraged capital flight to the suburbs and discouraged reinvestment in inner cities. These policies imposed particular and inordinate costs and liabilities on Blacks, but they hurt the entire region as well. They misallocated resources, depressed property values, increased inner-city taxes, concentrated poverty, promoted suburban sprawl and drained resources away from needed expenditures on housing, health care, and education.

The residential patterns and racial hierarchies that were created initially by restrictive covenants, racial zoning, redlining, and mob violence between 1880 and 1960 continued to shape the contours of all of the important planning policies that governed the city and its suburbs afterward. Downtown redevelopment for the Rams stadium followed clear precedents established previously by a variety of slum-clearance, highway-building, and urban-renewal policies in the mid-twentieth century, as well as by neoliberal public-private partnerships in subsequent decades. Protection of white property and privilege guided nearly all decisions about laws and policies that promoted the establishment of new small and exclusive suburban municipalities with restrictive zoning codes, that concentrated public housing in inner-city areas, that offered tax incentives for industrial and commercial establishments to move to the suburbs, and that established separate school districts with vastly unequal resources. Suburban governments used zoning and other land-use controls to promote homogeneity, isolation, and defensive localism. When circumstances created the possibility of integration, whites acted quickly and decisively against it. State and county policies about municipal incorporation enabled white residents of Kinloch to break away from their Black neighbors in 1937 and form the city of Berkeley as an all-white well-funded municipality while leaving Kinloch without a viable tax base.[12] When residents of the all-white suburb of Black Jack learned in 1970 that a church group planned to build apartments that would be open to Black renters, the city dissolved itself and drew up new incorporation papers prohibiting multifamily dwellings in order to prevent their community from being integrated.[13]

In a city where direct discrimination confined Blacks to an artificially constricted housing market, landlords and real estate brokers were free to charge them high costs for inferior and unhealthy dwellings in overcrowded areas. Slum-clearance, urban-renewal, and redevelopment programs made a bad situation worse by bulldozing houses inhabited by Blacks without providing adequate replacement housing. The majestic Gateway Arch on the riverfront, the corridor of municipal buildings and parks near City Hall and Union Station, the midtown redevelopment area near St. Louis University, and the downtown baseball and football stadia all stand on land formerly occupied by housing available to Blacks. Seventy-five percent of the people displaced by construction of new federal highway interchanges in the downtown area were Blacks.[14] Redevelopment in the Mill Creek Valley area alone displaced some twenty thousand Black residents, creating new overcrowded slums in the few areas into which they were able to relocate. Urban renewal dispersed Black social and business networks to far-flung locations, decreased the value of Black-owned property, and created higher tax burdens for those who remained by eliminating tax-paying properties while granting tax abatements to new projects in the redevelopment zones.[15]

The patterns needed to maintain marginal advantages for individual whites produced calamitous social conditions for the region as a whole. But in St. Louis, nothing succeeds like failure. When urban renewal created new slums in other parts of the city, these areas were then targeted for new redevelopment schemes that repeated the errors and compounded the consequences of the earlier ones. Public money spent in support of private for-profit schemes that could not be sustained by sound market practices created programs ostensibly aimed at eliminating urban blight, promoting reinvestment in the city, and enhancing the region's well-being. Yet these initiatives wound up exacerbating the very problems they purported to solve. They failed to face the expressly racial causes and the collective social consequences of urban decay in St. Louis. The white spatial imaginary led people to believe that people with problems *are* problems, that the conditions inside the ghetto are created by ghetto residents themselves, that rather than investing in people of color and their communities, civic problems should be solved by displacing Black people and creating new homogeneous, pure, and prosperous spaces for whites. Thus in the white spatial imaginary, creating and maintaining a domed stadium erected largely for the amusement, pleasure, and comfort of white suburban spectators came to seem like a more legitimate expenditure of public funds than education for Black children.

As a federal judge ruled in the 1981 *Liddell* case, Black students in city schools had seen their constitutional rights violated systematically by the city of St. Louis, by St. Louis County, by the state of Missouri, and by the federal government itself. The concentration of Black students in city schools with high-poverty populations stemmed from the cumulative effects of the ways in which school district lines were drawn, from the placement of low-income housing projects in Black neighborhoods, from the county's use of zoning to reject public housing projects and integrated mixed-income private developments, from the actions by real estate brokers and landlords that confined Black people with vouchers for subsidized housing to Black neighborhoods, from mortgage and insurance redlining, from the subsidies for "white flight" created by the Federal Housing Administration's home mortgage loan policies, and from the refusal by the state's housing development corporation to publicize, promote, or even adhere to federal fair-housing regulations even after having been ordered to do by a federal court.[16] Housing segregation not only concentrated Black children in Black schools, but also into the school districts with the least resources. The subsidies to the Rams not only augmented the power of rich people over poor people; they are also an illustrative example of the depths, dimensions, and duration of the possessive investment in whiteness.[17]

The Rams were not the only St. Louis corporation to receive tax abatements or other subsidies. Some of the money that the city lost through tax abatements was recouped from increased municipal revenue from sales and earnings taxes paid by the Rams, their employees, and their fans. School funding, however, is almost completely tied to property taxes, and as a result, the recouped revenues could not be spent on education. According to one conservative estimate, for every dollar the city abated in property taxes, the schools lost fifty-seven cents.[18] In addition, despite extravagant claims that tax abatements and other subsidies would increase the general wealth of cities, the St. Louis case shows clearly that subsidies for professional sports teams and other corporations do not "trickle down" to the majority of the population, but instead function largely as a means for transferring wealth and resources from the poor and the middle class to the rich.

In order to attract a National Football League team to play in St. Louis after the owners of the Cardinals moved that franchise to Phoenix, the region's business and political leadership conducted a well-funded public relations campaign that secured approval from taxpayers to spend $270 million of public money (actually more than $700 million counting interest payments over thirty years) to build a domed stadium as an addition to the city's downtown convention center.[19] The facility, constructed completely with public funds, stands 21 stories high and contains 800,000 square feet of concrete block, a 500,000-square-foot roof covering 12 acres, 595 miles of wire and cable, 32 escalators, and 12 passenger and freight elevators. They undertook this project even though the city at that time had no team. The high costs involved in building such a lavish stadium made it necessary to spend even more money to attract a team, or else the entire investment would have been wasted. After being denied a franchise by the National Football League's expansion committee, civic leaders turned their efforts toward convincing the Rams to move to St. Louis from Los Angeles. As part of their inducements to the team, St. Louis officials simply gave forty-five million dollars of tax revenues raised in St. Louis to Rams owner Georgia Frontiere so she could pay off debts incurred by the Rams in Los Angeles and build a new practice site for the team in St. Louis. To pay off the mortgage on the domed stadium, city, county, and state officials committed twenty-four million dollars a year or fifty-five thousand dollars per day for thirty years from tax revenues.[20] St. Louis County imposed a new hotel tax to pay its share of the debt, but the city of St. Louis and the state of Missouri identified general fund revenues as the source of their contributions.[21]

The state of Missouri's contribution to the domed stadium was especially offensive because state agencies and officials had played a primary role in undermining educational opportunities for Black students in the city of St. Louis. In the 1990s, Missouri had the lowest per capita taxation of all fifty states and ranked forty-third in educational spending per pupil.[22] Consequently Missouri's schools depend more than schools in other states on local funding from property taxes—the source that most reflects the inequalities shaped by housing discrimination.[23] By minimizing the state's contribution to education, Missouri's government increased the value of segregated housing in suburban communities where the presence of shopping centers and the high value of property allow for large expenditures on education despite low property tax rates. At the same time, these taxation policies decreased the value of housing in inner cities and the largely Black inner-ring suburbs of north St. Louis County where low property values and unmet infrastructure needs required higher tax rates.[24]

The specifically racist malice of state officials toward St. Louis's Black children became starkly evident when federal courts required them to take remedial action after having been found guilty of de jure segregation in the St. Louis school desegregation case. Ruling that the city, county, state, and federal governments had violated St. Louis students' constitutional rights by collaborating to maintain an illegally segregated school system, the courts mandated the creation of a voluntary cross-district busing program that included the establishment of new magnet schools in the city of St. Louis. Judges also ordered the state of Missouri to encourage local governments to enforce fair-housing laws and to promote integrated housing. Yet rather than complying with the law, state attorney general (and later governor, senator, and U.S. attorney general) John Ashcroft used the powers of his office to promote massive resistance to the court's orders at every turn. Ashcroft delayed implementation of court orders, appealed even minor rulings to higher courts, and opposed every magnet school proposal. Ashcroft demonstrated an unusual understanding of the concepts he often touted in other contexts like personal responsibility and respect for the law. When it came to school desegregation, he maintained that the state should take no responsibility for the harm done to Black children by the segregated educational system that the state had created and condoned. Ashcroft railed against sending students by bus to new schools to produce desegregated learning environments, without acknowledging that St. Louis County and the state of Missouri felt that busing was fine when it was used for the purpose of segregation. Before the *Brown v. Board* decision, St. Louis County and the state of Missouri routinely used buses to transport *all* Black students in the county to segregated Black schools in the city. Most egregiously, Ashcroft lied repeatedly to the people of Missouri, claiming that the state had never been found guilty of any wrongdoing. In fact, the clear finding of the federal judiciary was that the state of Missouri was obliged to pay most of the costs of the St. Louis desegregation program precisely because it was guilty of violating the *Brown v. Board* ruling.

Under Ashcroft's demagogic and racist leadership, the state of Missouri spent nearly four million dollars fighting desegregation and resisting accountability for the damage done to Black children by the state's own illegal actions.[25] Ashcroft's Missouri Housing Development Commission even refused the token step of drawing up a plan to enforce fair-housing laws as the court had ordered it to do. Instead, the agency acquiesced to white resistance to integrated housing so thoroughly that it did not even encourage local governments to enforce the fair-housing laws already on the books.[26] Thus a state unwilling to spend money on educating Black children showed itself to be quite willing to spend money to fight federal court orders mandating desegregation. A state led by politicians who proclaimed themselves proponents of small government found it reasonable to obligate taxpayers to pay millions of dollars in subsidies to the Rams football team for thirty years.

Government spending and state subsidies made the domed stadium project possible. If huge sports arenas made money, private investors would pool their funds and build them with their own resources. In order for a domed stadium to be profitable, it must host an enormous number of events. Economists estimate that every million dollars of debt for stadium construction necessitates two dates with large crowds every year. A hundred million dollar stadium requires two hundred football or baseball games, concerts, and religious revivals per year. A 270 million dollar project like the domed stadium in St. Louis needs 540 such dates for every 365-day year—a practical impossibility.[27] The Convention Center adjacent to the domed stadium did manage to schedule some 240 events per year, but the size of the conventions and car shows at that venue were too small to make a dent in the overall project's debt obligation. In fact, there would be no need for the domed stadium at all if not for the Rams who play only eight regular season games at home each year. These eight dates and the sporadic exhibition or playoff games that sometimes supplement them actually lose the stadium money because they do not produce enough revenue to offset costs.[28] The team paid only $25,000 in rent per game, an amount aptly characterized by one local journalist as barely enough to cover the cost of turning on the lights.[29]

Yet while squandering colossal amounts of public revenue, the domed stadium in St. Louis offered lavish amenities to select patrons, especially to the wealthy individuals and corporations who purchased the 122 luxury boxes that circled the building. League regulations require home teams to split ticket revenues on a 60–40 basis with visiting teams, but these rules do not apply to luxury suites. The Rams kept all that money. The team thus played its games in a publicly funded stadium on a virtually cost-free and extremely profitable basis. The Rams received all revenue from ticket sales, concessions, and luxury seating. The lease was structured to obligate government to pay even more to the Rams in the future. One provision held that if attendance drops below 85 percent of capacity, the city of St. Louis's Convention and Visitors' Commission pledged to purchase all unsold luxury suites and club seats, ranging in price from $700 to $110,000 per year per ticket. Another provision said that if other teams built facilities for other teams on a basis more lucrative than the Rams' arrangement with St. Louis, the city would supply the team with more revenue. The Rams kept for themselves more than $24 million of the $36.7 million paid by Trans World Airlines to have the stadium named the "Trans World Dome" when it first opened, and it continued to profit disproportionately from the naming rights when the Edward Jones brokerage replaced TWA as the stadium's main sponsor. The Rams also retained 75 percent of all other advertising revenue up to $6 million, and 90 percent of revenues from advertising above that figure. Business experts estimated that the value of advertising revenues alone to the Rams approached $15–20 million per year.[30]

While the Rams and their fans in the expensive luxury suites are housed lavishly inside the dome, Black children in St. Louis face the consequences of a segregated housing market. The shortage of affordable housing for all people in the St. Louis metropolitan area is exacerbated by racially discriminatory practices by real estate brokers, lenders, landlords, and insurance agents that confine African Americans to an artificially constricted housing market.[31] A 1990 survey of housing segregation found that St. Louis ranked as the eleventh most segregated city among the 232 largest metropolitan areas in the nation.[32] Poverty and a disastrous shortage of adequate dwellings forced some children to have to move and change schools so often that they were never exposed to any one single teacher, pedagogy, or curriculum for very long. St. Louis school administrators and teachers estimated that about half of their students in the 1990s moved to a new residence during any given school year.[33]

Many African American children in St. Louis also lived in dwellings with lead-based paint on the interior and exterior walls, exposing them to a strong likelihood of developing toxic amounts of lead in their bloodstreams. One out of every four children tested in St. Louis in 1998 was found to be lead poisoned. Medical authorities discovered 1,833 *new* cases of lead poisoning in that year alone. Moreover, the full dimensions of lead poisoning in St. Louis remained unknown because the city had only enough funds to test 40 percent of preschool-age children.[34] National studies showed that lead poisoning is even more of a racial injury than a class injury. Among the poorest families Black children were almost twice as likely as white children to contract lead poisoning. Among the working poor, Black youths were three times as likely to develop lead poisoning as their white counterparts.[35]

The domed stadium was not the first gigantic structure in St. Louis built with public funds. A 630-foot-high stainless steel arch on the banks of the Mississippi River celebrates Thomas Jefferson's purchase of the Louisiana Territory and the westward expansion that followed it. Local residents ruefully note that it cost the U.S. government more to build the arch commemorating the Louisiana Purchase than it cost Jefferson to purchase the territory itself in the first place. But the construction and management of the domed stadium are more than a matter of local excess. Properly understood, the history of this stadium can help us understand some of the central dynamics of contemporary urban economics and politics in cities all across the nation.

Why would the political and business leadership of a city faced with crises in public education and public health extend such lavish subsidies to a spectator sport? What happens to a city or a society that neglects the education of its children in order to build sports arenas? Why is the racial injury done to Black children in St. Louis not just their problem, but also a manifestation of how racial inequality in our society encourages a misallocation of resources with ruinous consequences for the majority of the population?

Despite their high public profile, professional sports are not a significant sector of the U.S. economy. As southern politician Sam Ervin once noted, as a locus of economic activity and a generator of profit, the national sports industry is no larger than the pork and beans industry.[36] A study commissioned by the mayor of Houston found that the local sports industry in that city (including all nonsporting events held at the local domed stadium) had a smaller economic impact on the locality than the Houston Medical Center. Sports spending amounted to less than 1 percent of the local economy.[37] Yet professional sports teams play a privileged role in public-private partnerships for urban redevelopment everywhere, and their utility for such projects tells a great deal about the general priorities and practices of our society.

Justifications for projects like the domed stadium in St. Louis generally revolve around two related claims about the benefit of professional sports to the economic and social health of the city and the need to protect the competitive position of the local team in relation to wealthier franchises. These claims are worth investigating, not because they are true, but rather because their blatant and obvious mendacity serves to occlude the actual role played by subsidies for sport within the urban economy in particular, and within consumer culture more generally. Discretionary spending on sports and other forms of entertainment is limited. Subsidies for new arenas and entertainment districts tend to shift spending from one part of a city to another, but they rarely generate new wealth. The subsidies supplied to sports entrepreneurs create artificial advantages for some profit-making firms over others. They misallocate resources away from more productive and more socially beneficial investments. They impose direct and indirect burdens on small business owners and on middle-income and lower-income taxpayers.

The experience of the Rams in St. Louis exemplifies the economic advantages available to team owners. Sports franchises generate a flow of cash that can be invested in many ways. They provide long-term appreciation as well. The anticompetitive cartel qualities of sports leagues insure a shortage of franchises, inflating the value of all teams so that owners always make a profit when they sell the team. Sometimes they make money by selling the team to themselves, forming a separate corporation that now "owns" the club. This enables the owners to loan money to the team and receive the principal and interest back in return payments from it. The payments appear as a debit on the club's financial records as they provide the owners with a flow of cash from the operation. In addition, owners can provide themselves with large salaries and expense accounts as team executives.[38] The most significant economic benefits that accrue to professional team owners, however, come from tax benefits. The tax advantages available to owners of sports teams provide secret subsidies to professional franchises and impose secret burdens on taxpayers unable to take advantage of the favored treatment afforded team owners.

Financial institutions capable of selling thirty-year bonds for stadium construction profit directly from the municipal subsidies that make it economically feasible to create new sporting venues. Corporate executives of all kinds can take their clients and coworkers to football games and even deduct a large part of that expense from their taxes by claiming it as business-related entertainment. Nearly half of the gate receipts of most National Football League franchises come from sales to corporations.[39] In addition, returns to investors on the kinds of municipal bonds used to create sports arenas are not taxed by the federal government, a subsidy that costs the federal treasury more than two million dollars a year for a project the size of the domed stadium in St. Louis.[40] As a writer in *Fortune* magazine concluded, "Professional sports teams qualify for so many tax benefits as to render their 'book' profit or loss figures meaningless."[41] Yet owners neglect to mention these tax advantages when they lament their paper losses in public in order to extract even more subsidies. Taxpayers doubly subsidize sports franchises by producing the revenue needed to build stadia and arenas in the first place, but then also paying higher taxes and receiving fewer government services to make up for the revenue lost from tax breaks extended to sports team owners.

Owners of teams can also claim players' salaries as depreciable assets for five years after buying a franchise, even though the cartel-like nature of professional football guarantees that the value of players on the roster will not actually depreciate. Depreciation credits can be extended even more by forming a new corporation and transferring ownership of the team to it, even when franchise ownership remains essentially in the same hands.[42] At the domed stadium in St. Louis, nearly two million dollars a year of the cost of luxury boxes and club seats are written off as business-entertainment deductions.[43]

Claims about the value of sports franchises to cities are often articulated, but rarely investigated. The studies that have been conducted provide ample room for skepticism about the economic value of sports to the average worker, consumer, or business owner. One study of seventeen cities during the 1994 baseball players' strike found that sales of nondurable goods actually *increased* in thirteen of the cities without the revenue usually brought in by major league baseball. Another longitudinal study examined nine cities between 1965 and 1983 and found no significant correlation between building a stadium and economic growth. In all but two of these cities, the opposite took place—the municipal share of regional income actually declined after the opening of a new stadium or the relocation of a team. Another study of fourteen cities hosting professional sports franchises could find no positive economic gain attributable to sports in most cases.[44]

Economist Robert Sorenson of the University of Missouri–St. Louis pointed out that no one has done a thorough study on the revenues generated by the St. Louis stadium. "I don't think the city really wants to," he noted, observing, "They'd be embarrassed by what they'd find."[45] Seven hundred and twenty million dollars invested over thirty years could make an enormous difference in the economy of a city the size of St. Louis. Loans for housing renovation and acquisition could stabilize neighborhoods and offer individuals opportunities to accumulate assets that appreciate in value that could be passed along to future generations. Throughout the 1990s, for example, the city of St. Louis lacked funds for assisting middle-income families interested in buying houses inside the city limits.[46] Loans to small businesses could increase employment opportunities and stimulate the local economy by generating wage earnings and profits almost certain to be spent in local stores, invested in local banks, spent on local goods and services, and used to increase municipal revenues.

A massive domed stadium, however, does none of this. It occupies a huge amount of tax-abated land surrounded by freeways and parking garages that inhibit rather than encourage the development of new businesses. It drains resources from the rest of the city while creating increased needs for police protection, traffic control, fire safety, and the construction and maintenance of new electrical power, water, and sewer systems. It provides windfall profits for millionaire athletes, investors, and owners, almost none of whom live in, or even invest in, the city. Because most owners and players live outside the cities where they make their money, tax subsidies for sports franchises produce less tax revenue for cities than would be true of businesses with local managers and employees.[47] Moreover, the hidden subsidies for luxury boxes and revenue bonds shift tax burdens away from the wealthy, thereby imposing new (albeit unacknowledged) tax burdens on local middle- and low-income workers.

In the past, stadium construction in St. Louis has repeatedly failed to generate the revenues promised by city boosters. The Civic Center Redevelopment Corporation justified spending twenty million dollars of public money (80 percent of the total cost) to build Busch Stadium for the St. Louis Cardinals baseball team in 1966. They promised that tax abatements for the stadium would enable the Cardinals to give the city $540,000 in payments in lieu of taxes within ten years. But the team paid only $269,324 to the city in lieu of taxes in 1976, while downtown retail establishments discovered no increase in business because of the stadium. By 1981, the Anheuser Busch brewery, which owned the Cardinals (and which enjoyed the free publicity that came from having a stadium with the same name as one of their brands of beer), threatened to move the team out of St. Louis unless the Civic Center Redevelopment Corporation gave them full ownership of the stadium along with control over parking, concessions, adjacent offices, and hotels. Waging what he later boasted of as "a skillful public relations campaign," the brewery's president claimed that the increased holdings would enable the team to compete for better players. But he knew what the public did not, that concerns about the competitive position of the Cardinals were only a smoke screen, that the heart of the matter was "essentially a real estate deal, a very big real estate deal. And, for Anheuser Busch . . . a very good deal."[48]

The brewery offered a ridiculously low bid of $30.2 million for the entire package, which was valued at somewhere between $75 million and $90 million. When a competitor offered a bid of $58.9 million, the brewery broke off negotiations and used its influence behind closed doors, eventually succeeding in gaining a controlling interest over the properties in question. The brewery paid $3 million to purchase the team in 1953, added $5 million toward the cost of the new stadium in 1976, and may have paid as little as $53 million in 1981, to emerge in control of most of the real estate in the southern part of downtown St. Louis in return.[49]

In the mid-1990s, Anheuser Busch sold the Cardinals to a new group of investors that included the corporation that owned the city's only daily newspaper, the St. Louis Post-Dispatch. Pointing to the revenues available to the Rams, the new ownership group immediately began to complain about "antiquated" Busch Stadium (then only thirty years old) and started using their influence to get the state of Missouri to pass enabling legislation for a new baseball stadium to be financed with $120 million in cash and real estate contributions from the Cardinals and $250 million in public money. The state contributed $45 million to build the new stadium. St. Louis County contributed through a bond issue that obligates taxpayers to provide $108 million. The city exempted the new stadium from property tax obligations for twenty-five years—a tax abatement that will cost the city and its public schools an additional $600,000 every year.[50] For good measure, the city of St. Louis repealed its 5 percent tax on tickets, resulting in a decrease in municipal revenues by at least another $5 million per year.[51] Armed with the surplus profits the new stadium produced from public monies, William DeWitt and other members of the Cardinals ownership group then donated large sums of money to the electoral campaigns of conservative candidates who trumpeted their opposition to government spending on education, housing, highways, and health care.

The subsidies that St. Louis channels to the owners of sports teams while neglecting the educational and health needs of its children may seem like the product of the particular problems of one especially troubled city, a metropolis devastated by capital flight, deindustrialization, and economic restructuring, a municipality left with few other feasible options for urban renewal and redevelopment. Certainly, distinctly local factors can be found inflecting every aspect of the stadium deal given to the Rams. But the significance of the ways in which African American St. Louis schoolchildren and some of their poor white and Latino/a classmates have been forced to subsidize the professional football franchise in their city lies less in local factors than in larger transformations that have taken place in the United States over the past thirty years that have decisively altered the meanings of local place, politics, and property. However extreme, the St. Louis experience is a representative part of a larger pattern.

Twenty-nine new sports facilities were constructed in U.S. cities between 1999 and 2003 at a total cost of nearly nine billion dollars. Sixty-four percent of the funds to build those arenas—approximately $5.7 billion—came directly from taxpayers.[52] In Philadelphia, construction of a new baseball stadium for the Phillies and a new football stadium for the Eagles cost $1.1 billion. City funds supplied $394 million, and state tax revenue contributed an additional $180 million.[53]

In their generative study of urban economics, John Logan and Harvey Molotch argue that urban investors try to trap capital in the areas they own in order to win advantages against competitors elsewhere. Downtown real estate investors and owners try to enhance the value of their property by making their part of town the locus of profitable activity. They increase their profits considerably when they secure public assistance for land acquisition, development, and construction, and when they acquire tax abatements and tax increment financing for their projects.[54] In addition, inequalities among—as well as within—cities force small local units to compete with one another for capital to such a degree that few can afford to withhold subsidies from developers.

During the late industrial era, when Keynesian economics prevailed (1933–1976), urban redevelopment in North America coalesced around progrowth coalitions led by business leaders and managed by elected officials and supported largely by urban voters. These coalitions often pursued disastrous policies that destroyed inner-city homes in order to build highways, office buildings, and cultural attractions oriented toward the interests of suburban commuters.[55] In order to secure better spaces for large corporate headquarters and in order to build the kinds of cultural institutions required to recruit top-rank executives (symphony halls, art museums, and theaters), local elites felt they had to offer compensatory concessions to a broader population. Banks with money tied up in conventional mortgages and industrialists in need of a healthy and educated work force made charitable contributions to social service agencies. Politicians in need of voter approval for the bond issues that financed new developments made sure that their constituents received services from the city. Bankers, business leaders, and politicians all found themselves (for different reasons) attentive to "place" in the local region that made their well-being possible.

The postindustrial era, however, helped "delocalize" capital. Mergers made large local corporations small entities inside transnational conglomerates. Deregulation made it easier for banks to neglect local investment. Computer-generated automation allowed for "outsourcing," turning high-wage skilled jobs that had to be performed by educated workers in urban areas into low-wage unskilled tasks that could be done virtually by anyone in virtually any place. Containerization and capital flight enabled management to ship industrial production overseas. Forty-four thousand manufacturing workers in St. Louis alone lost their jobs between 1979 and 1982. Even before the presidency of Ronald Reagan, government programs established to aid urban areas were restructured to begin funneling benefits away from inner cities and toward the suburbs, especially funds to develop infrastructures for new (often racially segregated) developments.[56] An astounding increase in the use of industrial development bonds and tax increment financing treated private for-profit developments as if they were public services, shifting resources away from taxpayers and toward businesses that found themselves strapped for capital. State and local governments sold only $6.2 billion of bonds for commercial projects in 1975, but that total climbed to $44 billion by 1982. These tax-exempt bonds cost the federal treasury $7.4 billion in 1983. At the same time, regular bond sales for the construction of schools, hospitals, housing, sewer and water mains, and other public works projects in cities tapered off.[57] Direct federal aid to urban areas fell by 60 percent between 1981 and 1992.[58]

After Reagan's election to the presidency in 1980, the nation's business and political leadership expanded on themes developed during the terms of Richard Nixon, Gerald Ford, and Jimmy Carter to advocate policies cutting federal expenditures on cities in order to "return" money to state and local governments. This "new federalism" emphasized "revenue sharing" and

block grants rather than direct federal spending or administration of programs targeting particular needs. Revenue sharing enabled municipalities
to take money originally intended for the sick, the old, the very young, and
the poor, and instead use it to cut property taxes for the wealthy, subsidize
corporate development projects, and increase security and police protection
in the new zones of wealth surrounded by blocks and blocks of desperately
poor people.

Federal funds for water, sewage treatment, and garbage disposal declined
by more than $50 billion per year during the 1980s. State aid to cities dropped
from 62.5 percent of local urban revenues to 54.3 percent during the decade.
The corporate share of local property tax burdens counted for 45 percent of
such revenues in 1957 but fell to 16 percent by 1987.[59] These changes help
redistribute wealth upward while fracturing the fabric of local life in urban
areas, pitting each governmental unit against every other unit, and creating
the preconditions for the kinds of subsidies secured by the Rams in St. Louis.

Proponents of the new federalism proclaimed their intention to return
power to the people at the local level. But in reality, these policies were
designed to remove local obstacles to capital investment and to break the
power of inner-city social movements and political coalitions. First, the new
federalism transferred resources and decision-making authority away from
cities and toward county, suburban, and rural governments. Second, it left
the "public" represented by a plethora of administrative units too small to
resist the demands of capital by themselves. Suburban growth, for example,
strengthens the hand of big investors by enabling them to play off one small
suburb against another.

While purporting to make local connections to place more meaningful,
the new federalism and revenue sharing did the opposite, creating deadly
competition between places for scarce resources and diminishing the power
of those most dependent on local places for residence, work, and community. It also increased the power of those approaching local places as sites for
speculation and profit. In short, it delocalized decision making about urban
life in order to create new circuits for investment capable of generating massive returns. This pattern not only requires an end to concessions granted to
urban residents like those made by the progrowth coalitions in the Keynesian era, but even discourages philanthropy and civic-minded reinvestment
of profits back into the sites that produced them. Rather than giving back to
urban areas to show themselves good citizens, today's transnational investors
expect cities to supply them with subsidies for the privilege of profiting from
local sites and resources. In fact, business coalitions like Civic Progress in St.
Louis that often speak in support of local subsidies for public-private development are usually dominated by the very local firms most responsible for dis-

investment in the local economy and most responsible for the flight of capital to more profitable places.

Tax cuts for the wealthy and transferring programs like Aid to Families with Dependent Children and General Assistance to the states have exacerbated the delocalization of decision making in urban areas. Every time a unit of government cuts necessary services, it increases the pressure on the unit just below. Cuts in federal spending on infrastructure and social welfare put pressure on the states. State cutbacks impose new demands on counties, in turn squeezing the resources of cities. As Sidney Plotkin and William Scheuerman point out, under these conditions "every unit in the sub-national government system must preserve, protect, and expand its tax base at the expense of every other unit."[60] Municipalities within a region compete for low-risk wealthy populations and high-yield establishments like shopping centers. They seek to avoid responsibility for high-risk poor and disabled populations or low-yield high-cost institutions like hospitals and schools. But this competition only produces new inequalities that can be used in a race to the bottom by capital, promoting bidding wars between government bodies that reduce property taxes and other obligations while increasing subsidies and the provision of free services to corporations.

The subsidies offered to sports structures like the domed stadium in St. Louis proceed from this general pattern. In the Keynesian era, St. Louis financial institutions invested in their own region. But since the 1980s they have been shifting investments elsewhere, exporting locally generated wealth to sites around the world with greater potential for rich and rapid returns. Building the domed stadium offered them an opportunity to create a potential source of high profit for outside investors in their region. Large projects like these generate some new short-term local spending on construction, financing, and services. They clear out large blocks of underutilized land for future development. But because they are so heavily subsidized, projects like the domed stadium wind up costing the local economy more than they bring in while they funnel windfall profits toward wealthy investors from other cities.[61]

Although claiming to base their actions on capitalist principles of profit making and risk, investors in the St. Louis domed stadium actually counted on the government to eliminate any risk on their part by passing along debt obligations to the city, county, and state governments. Potential profits projected to result from the project lay not in new consumer spending or the ripple effect it might have on the local economy, but rather on profits derived from real estate speculation by knowing insiders. Here again, federal tax policies make an enormous difference because they encourage speculation and discourage broad-based investment in the local economy. Income gained from investment is treated more favorably in the federal tax code than income generated from the production of actual goods and services. In addition, mortgage interest payments can be deducted from income, depreciation allowances can be taken on newly built property, and in abatement zones property taxes can be waived completely.[62] The tax structure makes developments that are unprofitable for the local region quite profitable for individual speculators and investors.

Business leaders often claim that professional sports franchises have intangible values, that they give a city a "big league" image that makes it easier to attract capital and corporate relocations. But no evidence supports this claim. It is true that individual corporations find it easier to recruit top-flight executives when they can offer them the use of tax-subsidized luxury boxes at sporting events, but nothing indicates that this is a wise investment for the entire area, that it means more to fiscal health of the region than adequate housing, medical care, or schools.

At least twenty-four million dollars a year in city, county, and state tax dollars will continue to be spent on the St. Louis stadium project through the year 2022. That sum could increase, however, because a clause in the stadium contract frees the football team to flee to another city if the money the team receives from the building does not place the Rams among the top eight NFL franchises in municipal subsidies. Yet even if it somehow eventually becomes an economic success for someone, the domed stadium has already been a disaster for the residents of St. Louis. The Rams can always move again. After all, they were the Cleveland Rams before they were the Los Angeles Rams. Even inside Los Angeles, the team moved from the Los Angeles Coliseum to Anaheim Stadium after officials in that suburban city expanded the size of their facility from 43,250 to 70,000 seats, constructed new executive offices for the team's use, and built 100 luxury boxes for use by Rams fans. But when Georgia Frontiere found a better deal somewhere else, the Rams left Anaheim too.[63] The team's lease in St. Louis contains a provision stipulating that the Rams can move to another city or demand a whole new round of upgrades on the stadium if it does not remain among the best in the NFL for ten years.[64]

Subsidies to previous franchises did not prevent St. Louis from losing the basketball Hawks to Atlanta or the football Cardinals to Phoenix. In fact, by using subsidies to provide the Rams with more profit in a metropolitan area with three million people than they could get in one with more than nine million, the backers of the stadium have unwittingly increased the number of their potential competitors. With subsidies like these, professional football franchises can move virtually anywhere and make a profit. The Tennessee Titans, defeated by the Rams in the 2000 Super Bowl, previously played in Houston as the Oilers, until a subsidized stadium in Nashville persuaded team owner Bud Adams to move his operations there. He could make more money in a smaller city because of government subsidies.

The National Football League will make sure that franchises are limited, that teams will always have leverage with the cities in which they play simply by threatening to move somewhere else. As long as the tax system encourages speculative investment over the production of goods and services, resources will be misallocated into projects like the domed stadium. As long as the federal government abdicates its responsibilities to states and cities, capital will have a free hand, and the public interest will be represented by fragmented government bodies too weak to resist the concessions demanded by corporate interests. As long as urban political coalitions and social movements remain more poorly organized than the representatives of corporate and suburban interests, poor children will continue to pay for projects like the sports stadium in St. Louis out of funds originally intended for education, medical care, and transportation.

Shortly after the domed stadium was constructed and opened, the shopping mall adjacent to it failed and closed. The city's prize convention hotel directly across the street from the stadium filed for bankruptcy protection. Shortly after the new baseball stadium opened, the city of St. Louis raised taxes three times, increased fees for water service, curtailed trash collections, laid off municipal employees, and leased part of Forest Park to private interests to raise funds for park maintenance.[65] Yet even if the convention center and stadium somehow serve as focal points for new business, even if the Rams remain in St. Louis, even if the Super Bowl championship they won in 2000 is the first of many, and even if new stores, restaurants, and hotels are established near the stadium, the vast majority of people in St. Louis will be no better off. Recreational discretionary spending will just shift from one part of town to another, and entrepreneurs in the newly marginalized areas will then demand the same kinds of concessions and subsidies supplied to their competitors. As long as urban real estate investment projects are dominated by global investors, local political leaders will simply be administrators of austerity and supervisors of the subsidies sought mostly by out-of-town investors. Inequalities between cities and within them make it possible to play off one part of town against another, to provoke political leaders from different jurisdictions into bidding wars to obtain high-profile projects. But rather than reducing inequality, urban developments like the domed stadium in St. Louis exacerbate it. They not only take money out of education and health care to service debts incurred by speculators, but they also drain resources away from the precisely targeted "demand side" expenditures (loans for housing and small business, public works projects) that might lessen inequality and increase opportunities and life chances for inner-city populations.

The delocalization of decision making about urban spatial relations leaves residents with little stake in the cities in which they live. It fractures the social fabric, encouraging individuals and communities to monopolize high-yield and low-risk economic activities in areas they control while dumping low-yield and high-risk obligations onto others. Inequality generates poverty and its attendant costs: underutilization of human resources, increased expenditures for health care, impediments to local investment, and the diversion of resources toward increased policing and incarceration. Such practices are not only unjust; they are also inefficient. Cities with the least amounts of economic and social polarization have less crime and experience faster growth. They utilize human resources more efficiently and provide a better quality of life for more people.[66]

At a time when cities should be imposing *more* taxes on profitable ventures like the Rams, when sports arenas should come with long-term leases with large penalties for moves to other cities, the opposite seems to be the case. Whether it is the sports business or the pork and beans business, it has become increasingly difficult to "trap" capital and secure a fair share of the tax burden from business enterprises. But the costs of inaction are far greater than the risks of action on these matters. Efforts to lessen the leverage of the NFL by asking Congress to remove the limited antitrust exemption it enjoys, a revision of the tax code to discourage speculation and encourage more productive spending, and measures to reverse the new federalism's fracturing of political authority by displacing decision making on to small units that are powerless to resist the demands of concentrated capital are measures that would all help residents of St. Louis and other cities resist the plundering that is now taking place in the name of development.

Yet we need to understand as well the role that culture plays in the politics of stadium subsidies. Relentless attacks on public schools, libraries, parks, gyms, transportation systems, and other services over the past thirty years have left people with few public spaces that promote mutuality and commonality in urban areas. The delocalization of decision making has undermined local political organizations and leaders, while the mobility of capital has undercut the critical force of trade unions and other community organizations. The creation of new specialized markets and the emergence of new "lifestyle" differences based on seemingly trivial consumer preferences divide families and communities into incommensurable consumer market segments.

Under these conditions, professional sports fill a void. They provide a limited sense of place for contemporary urban dwellers, offering them a rooting interest that promises at least the illusion of inclusion and connection with others. This illusion is not diminished by contrary evidence, by the fact that every St. Louis Ram would become a Tennessee Titan and every Tennessee Titan would become a St. Louis Ram tomorrow if they could make more money by doing so, by the fact that team owners preach the virtues of unbridled capitalism while enjoying subsidies that free them from the rigors of competition and risk, by the fact that impoverished and often ill school-children are called upon to subsidize the recreation of some of their society's wealthiest and healthiest citizens.

Entire communities pay the price for the profits secured by speculators and investors from subsidized sports developments. But the aggrieved racial minorities who need public services the most because of rampant discrimination in the private sector suffer most of all. Cruelly enough, the success of Black athletes in St. Louis on the football field every Sunday helps build public identification with a project that systematically deprives Black children of needed educational resources. Nearly two-thirds of NFL players are Black, a demographic imbalance shaped by the very inequalities the stadium project exacerbates. By offering lavish salaries to successful athletes but only a discount education to nonathletes, our society tells poor people that their value as gladiators far outweighs their worth as students or citizens.

The denial of educational resources to Black children in St. Louis because of the domed stadium is not a peculiar aberration in an otherwise just society. It represents just one of the many forms of systematic inequality and injustice that underwrite "business as usual" in our society. Despite claims that the 1964 Civil Rights Act "ended" racism, our society continually devises new ways of rewarding racism and subsidizing segregation. St. Louis students receive meager resources for their educations, but even that small amount is too much for the team owners, developers, and business leaders who use their power to divert resources away from the schools in pursuit of even more wealth for themselves.

For her skill at securing public funds for private purposes, Rams owner Georgia Frontiere was rewarded with a Super Bowl trophy. For his efforts in blocking the implementation of a federal court order and refusing to take responsibility for the obligations that the law imposed on the state of Missouri, John Ashcroft became the attorney general of the United States. Black students and parents in St. Louis, however, who have broken no laws, who instead turned to the federal courts to secure the educational opportunities guaranteed to them by the Fourteenth Amendment have not received the kinds of rewards reaped by the Frontiere and Ashcroft families. In fact, their victimization played an essential part in Frontiere's and Ashcroft's success.

Every Ram victory will be celebrated loudly, but the despair of students deprived of decent educations will be kept quiet. People speaking the language of democracy will continue to broadcast the illusions of "trickle-down" economics to us at high volume, but ever so quietly, they produce not democracy but plutocracy. They sacrifice the rights of citizens in order to subsidize the profits of speculators. In the case of the St. Louis domed stadium, "trickle-down" economics sends a clear message that our society values entertainment more than education, that the pursuit of unlimited profits for the wealthy counts for more than the basic needs of the poor. The exploits of the Rams on the football field make their fans cheer and fill the dome with joyous and high-decibel noise. But quiet as it's kept, the echoes of educational inequality will be heard long after the fans' cheers have died down.

4

The Crime *The Wire* Couldn't Name

*Social Decay and
Cynical Detachment in Baltimore*

We have to bring the cat out of hiding, and where he is
hiding is in the bank.
—JAMES BALDWIN

The *Wire* may well be the best program ever to appear on television. In sixty episodes broadcast on the HBO cable network from 2002 through 2008, David Simon's drama about police officers and drug dealers in Baltimore displays a unique understanding of race and place. On this show, criminals, crime fighters, and ordinary citizens are trapped in spaces they cannot control. Urban life is a constant series of small interpersonal meetings, negotiations, and confrontations. Breaking with decades of crime dramas that pit virtuous guardians of law and order against monstrous outlaws, *The Wire* emphasizes similarities between drug dealers and police officers. The criminals and the cops both come from working-class backgrounds. Both have been shaped by the social relations and social codes of the neighborhoods where they were raised. Both view the work they do as "just business," as they fight to survive and long to move up in their respective organizations. Corruption is taken for granted, not only inside the police department and the hierarchy of organized crime, but in every other major urban institution as well: in government, the school system, trade unions, the media, and businesses. Recognizing that the "war on drugs" relies on police practices that produce the very criminality they purport to prevent, *The Wire* demonstrates that individual villainy has systemic causes, that corrupt police officers and criminal sociopaths are the logical and inevitable products of dominant approaches to drug interdiction and incarceration.

Part of *The Wire*'s unusual achievement comes from its approaches to physical place and urban space. The show displays a ferocious attachment to the specificities of space in Baltimore, shooting on location in devalued unglamorous neighborhoods. Long lingering shots of red brick row houses, housing project yards, and portside cranes display knowledge of—and affection for—quotidian local places. Producers instruct camera operators to "shoot in the wide," placing individual characters in a broader social habitat. When the plot for Season 2 required ambient noise from the local port, the program's producers refused to employ stock recordings and insisted instead on making their own recordings of the sounds of boat whistles and cranes in the local harbor. They insisted that port sounds from New York or Los Angeles would not be the same as those heard in Baltimore. Rather than establishing the show's Baltimore location with depictions of official welcoming signs or recognizable tourist sites, the opening montage for each season deploys quick cuts to depict a jumble of mostly ghetto spaces including a wall with graffiti wryly signifying on the name of the city as "Bodymore, Murdaland."

Local affiliations and memories loom large in the lives of the show's key characters. Police officer Bunk Moreland went to high school with some of the drug dealers he now seeks to arrest. He recalls Black athletes who excelled in playing lacrosse, surely an experience unique to Baltimore. Crime syndicate operator Proposition Joe can afford to live in an affluent suburb but he prefers to remain in the modest house that his grandfather purchased when he became the first Black person to own a home in previously segregated Johnson Square. Frank Sobotka of the stevedores' union fights to keep the port a viable source of employment because he cherishes the social world that workers inhabited in the era before containerization and capital flight. Looking at a closed manufacturing plant, he laments that a country that used to make things now relies on speculation. Now we subsist, he opines acidly, by putting "our hand in the other guy's pocket." Nostalgia for lost worlds poignantly punctuates the diminished social wage and augmented corruption of a present that appears as the end product of a historical shift that is never named or explained.

In the television medium, interiors of apartments and homes are generally spaces of intimacy, affection, and affluence. On family dramas and situation comedies, domestic sets become virtual shopping catalogs featuring fashionable furnishings and accoutrements. On *The Wire*, however, inhabitants of affluent homes frequently seem to be trying too hard, decorating their dwellings with questionable taste. These homes of middle-class professionals and affluent business executives are sites of awkward and anxious conversations. Dwellings inhabited by the working class are cramped and conspicuously spare, while the homes of the poor are clearly dwellings of last resort, sometimes even squatter's spaces in abandoned buildings. Streets and offices are routinely more interesting and intimate than homes, while public gatherings in taverns, on street corners, at basketball courts, in union halls, and in churches display a lively sociality that seems absent from the tense home lives of the program's characters. In direct contradiction to nearly everything else that appears on television, *The Wire* is relentlessly critical of both the family and business, depicting both institutions as traps that constrain individuals and cultivate greed and envy rather than promote initiative or affection.

Like many of its most memorable characters, *The Wire* does its work through misdirection. The format of traditional crime dramas encourages viewers to speculate about the identity of the criminal. Yet the work of *The Wire* is not so much to identify the criminal as it is to name the crime. At first, this seems like an easy task. The show is filled with picturesque villains who perpetrate violent and cruel criminal acts. Yet it soon becomes clear that these characters are not so much the instigators of crime as its functionaries. Like the police officers assigned to investigate and arrest them, the crooks in *The Wire* are mostly soldiers caught up in a larger system, workers with guns carrying out orders inside an irrational bureaucracy. Low-level drug runners and dealers try to quit the game, but the absence of alternatives and the lingering effects of their criminal records and street reputations leave them with nowhere to go. Mid-level dealer D'Angelo Barksdale envisions a world where drug dealing can be separated from killing, but when he limits his cooperation with his uncle's drug empire, the uncle's aide-de-camp orders D'Angelo's murder. High-level dealer Stringer Bell notices that drug dealing is a lot like legitimate businesses only with more risks. He tries to transition into a role as a real estate speculator and developer. He finds to his dismay, however, that legitimate business is even more corrupt and ruthless than drug dealing. He gets cheated by people who know the new game better than he does.

The Wire also presents the police differently from the traditional crime drama. These police officers harbor no hopes of ending the drug trade or cleaning up the city. Drug dealing is too pervasive and too profitable to be stopped. Yet funding for law enforcement depends upon the appearance of progress. As a result, officers are pressured by their superiors in the department to make arrests that lead to convictions. The easiest arrests to make are of street-level dealers and soldiers who are likely to plead guilty and serve out their sentences to prove their loyalty to the drug syndicate for which they work. Police officers know that these practices do not make a dent in the drug trade, that they produce large numbers of ex-inmates with virtually no chance for gainful employment outside of crime. Yet the officers cannot escape this system any more than the drug dealers can. In Season 3, Major Bunny Colvin attempts to clean up street corners and make the ghetto safer for its inhabitants by cordoning off the entire drug trade into one decriminalized area.

Yet in a city without adequate social support services for addicts and with no viable opportunities for lives lived without crime and drugs, he simply moves the criminal activity from one site to another. Moreover, politicians and law enforcement officials recognize Colvin's experiment as a direct challenge to the logic of drug interdiction and incarceration they have followed for decades and upon which their funding depends. Even though this logic produces more crime than it prevents, they cannot change course because their whole reason for being and their ability to tap public funds now rests upon an unquestioning allegiance to the "war on drugs" paradigm.

It is not just cops and criminals who are trapped in *The Wire*. Every significant institution in the city has its own form of corruption that contributes to Baltimore's urban nightmare. The same kinds of conundrums that confront police officers and drug dealers vex union officials and business executives, elected officials and their appointees, teachers and journalists. Institutional pressures inside bureaucracies encourage people to prefer the appearance of solving problems to actually solving them. Just as police officers "juke" statistics to make it look like they are making the city safer, teachers are told to produce student test results that give the appearance of educational progress. In Season 5, we see how the city's major newspaper follows this same logic, looking for stories with cheap, easy, and simplistic solutions to complex social problems rather than informing the public about their full contours and dimensions. It is easier and more immediately gratifying for journalists, educators, and law enforcement officials to pretend that problems are being solved than it is to take the steps that actually would be necessary to solve them.

Perhaps the most innovative feature of *The Wire* is its insistence that social problems are knowledge problems, that social ills persist because we have been encouraged to look at them in the wrong ways. The program is especially suspicious of the staples of other crime-fighting shows: new technologies, clues, and confessions. As its name indicates, *The Wire* revolves around electronic surveillance, about the efforts of one special investigations unit to eavesdrop on telephone conversations by drug dealers. Like data mining, security cameras, drug testing, data bases of sexual predators, and other technological fixes for social problems favored by neoliberal regimes of security, electronic eavesdropping asks us to accept a reduction in privacy in exchange for promises of safety and security. Supported by a seemingly endless stream of films, books, and television programs, the dominant political imagination of our country presumes that all this equipment works perfectly all the time, that it intimidates criminals and empowers law enforcement officials with the tools they need to maintain public safety. *The Wire*, however, reveals the practical limits of these fantasies. Surveillance equipment is costly to purchase and difficult to maintain. The people who operate the equipment and

interpret its findings are not always adequately trained or appropriately attentive. Criminals quickly learn the best ways to disable surveillance devices, to
evade their range, and even to use them to mislead the people watching and
listening to them. The police operatives on *The Wire* work together skillfully
to make ingenious and effective use of wiretap evidence, although they increasingly violate legal and moral standards to do so. Yet the key to their cases
is not the evidence they obtain, but their ability to interpret it.

Unlike most crime dramas and detective stories where provoked confessions or discoveries of key evidence bring legal and narrative closure to open
cases, *The Wire* presents criminal investigation as more of a journey than
a destination. Detectives learn to perceive significance in small things, to
see with "soft eyes," lingering over pebbles or scraps of paper to discern how
they might contain clues to a larger reality. Yet even evidence needs to be
viewed with skepticism in *The Wire*. In the fifth season, series protagonist
Jimmy McNulty fabricates evidence about murders of homeless men in order
to secure resources, legal backing, and publicity that he intends to use for a
long-delayed and underfunded drug investigation. He has become as dishonest and corrupt as any of the drug dealers he is investigating. To its credit,
The Wire does not offer us the usual excuse for police malfeasance—that it
is being done for a noble purpose. Jimmy McNulty's aims in this instance
are purely personal. He wants to reinforce his image of himself as always
the smartest person in the room, as a someone who does not let the system hold him back. Like his criminal antagonists, like the high-ranking but
petty police officer Stanislaus Valchek who wastes massive amounts of scarce
police resources to settle a personal feud, like the police chiefs and educators who want better statistics so that they can get promoted, like the journalists who see the suffering of others as a way to sell more newspapers and win
prizes, McNulty has become a cog in a machine that entices individuals to
exercise authority without accountability or integrity.

What it asks of its detectives, the program also asks of its viewers. *The
Wire* avoids direct explanations. It defers narrative resolution. It lets dramatic
tensions fester over episodes and seasons. Because it allows its characters to
display forms of complex personhood, we are recruited to like unlikable people, are betrayed by characters we have come to trust, and get surprised by
dishonorable people who unexpectedly commit honorable acts. Yet we are
also humbled by the limits of individual morality in the face of fundamentally
immoral systems and structures. For producer David Simon and his many
skilled associates and collaborators on *The Wire*, the problems the program
depicts in inner-city Baltimore stem primarily from the war on drugs and the
ways in which that crusade has misallocated resources and misordered priorities. For all of its picturesque villains on both sides of the law, the true villain

of *The Wire* is the war on drugs, a public policy that produces and perpetuates the very behaviors it purports to prevent.[1]

Presenting an extended critique of the war on drugs on a widely watched cable network as *The Wire* did between 2002 and 2008 is no small accomplishment. *The Wire* also offered an important alternative to the relentless demonization of Black inner-city residents that has gone virtually unchallenged for decades in popular culture and public policy.[2] Instead of presenting one more incarnation of what Esther Lezra has aptly named "monstrous mistranslations of Blackness," *The Wire* displays a range of Black experiences, identities, and characters rarely seen in commercial culture. Magnificent roles assigned to talented Black actors reveal the existence of a reserve army of Black acting talent previously untapped by the culture industry. Complex plots and compelling characterizations prove the ability of at least one part of the public to embrace narratives more complicated than standard crime-fighting fare usually allows.

The program also ultimately intervened in the actual life of some of the neighborhoods it depicted. Cast member Sonja Sohn, who played the role of Detective Kima Greggs on the show, was initially troubled by many of the conditions the program depicted because of their similarity to what she had experienced growing up in subsidized housing in the south end of Newport News, Virginia. The scenes reminded her of home, but the principled behavior that her police officer character displayed did not ring true. Sohn explained that growing up she viewed the police as an oppressive force "who never brought order . . . who I never saw help anybody."[3] Grateful for the first real break she received as an actor and impressed by the program's quality, Sohn still worried about the dynamics that turned some people's tragedies into raw material for other people's amusement. "This stuff needs to be divulged," she conceded, "but it still ends up being entertainment, and that bothers me."[4] In response, Sohn attempted to reverse the process, to turn an entertainment commodity into part of a program for social change. She started a nonprofit organization named Rewired for Change aimed at young people from east and west Baltimore. Using episodes of *The Wire* as the basis for conversations about life chances and choices, Sohn's initiative serves a core group of twelve participants referred to it by courts and social service agencies. The group meets twice a week in a room provided by the University of Maryland School of Social Work in downtown Baltimore where students view episodes of the show, relate them to their lives, write and perform their own poetry, and meet with counselors and advisers individually. "I want this program to be in Baltimore," Sohn insists. "It's natural. There are other cities where I could take this, but I believe here is the place."[5]

Other cast members followed a similar path. The seemingly unlikely pair of Felicia "Snoop" Pearson and Jamie Hector jointly runs the organization Moving Mountains, a youth drama group located in Baltimore and New York designed to draw young people out of violent activities by teaching them skills in performing arts. Pearson and Hector both play villains on *The Wire* (Hector as Marlo Stanfield and Felicia as a dramatized version of herself). They came to these roles, however, from very different paths. Hector was raised by his Haitian immigrant parents in Brooklyn and studied acting at the Lee Strasberg Theater and Film Institute. Pearson's parents were incarcerated drug addicts. She was born prematurely, raised in a foster home in east Baltimore, dealt drugs at an early age, and was convicted of second-degree murder at the age of fourteen. Actor Michael K. Williams, who plays the charismatic gay outlaw Omar Little (the same last name as Malcolm Little, aka Malcolm X), "discovered" Pearson in a Baltimore nightclub. She explained that she had just lost her job and did not want to go back to prison. Williams suggested that she visit the set to see if she could get work as an assistant to one of the producers. Struck by her unique appearance and demeanor, the producers auditioned her for a part in the drama, basing her character largely on her actual life and using her actual nickname, Snoop. Thrown together because of their roles, Hector and Pearson discovered to their dismay that some of the young people they encountered had a misplaced admiration for the villainous characters they played on screen. The two actors started Moving Mountains as a way to reach out to these youths, to channel their enthusiasm and engagement into performance. "Sometimes they get confused about the acting and real life, you know?" Pearson confides. "So [I say] that's acting. I tell 'em all the time. That's acting, man, acting."[6]

There is no gainsaying the remarkable accomplishments of *The Wire*. It spawned art-based educational activism by some of its key actors, displayed a unique attentiveness to the poetics of place in Baltimore, and challenged the reigning logic of the war on drugs and its simultaneous punishments and abandonments of inner-city populations. There was one crime, however, that *The Wire* could not find and the program's producers did not even mention. This crime makes its presence felt obliquely during Season 4 when Snoop Pearson purchases a powerful nail gun at a hardware store. The clerk chats with her about the tool and its utility for home improvement projects, unaware that Snoop is purchasing the nail gun so that she can hide the bodies of people she killed inside abandoned buildings and board them up effectively. Dead bodies inside abandoned buildings disappear from the homicide statistics because without corpses the people slain might merely be missing. The detectives, however, gradually come to understand that the abandoned and boarded up buildings hide heinous crimes, that Marlo Stanfield's seemingly bloodless takeover of the drug trade from the Barksdale family and Proposition Joe entailed murder after murder. The detectives uncover this crime in the boarded-up buildings, but they miss the more serious one that preceded it.

Boarded-up abandoned buildings on inner-city streets in Baltimore are evidence of a crime that took place long before Snoop Pearson came along: the discriminatory land use policies dating back to the days of Jim Crow seg-regation that were honed and refined throughout the twentieth century and continue today in the form of reverse redlining that targets Black neighbor-hoods for predatory loans. Like St. Louis, Baltimore has been both a southern city stained by Jim Crow segregation and a border-state metropolis charac-terized by the patterns of racial exclusion and racial violence in the North. On three separate occasions before World War I, the Baltimore City Coun-cil enacted racial zoning ordinances that banned Blacks from moving onto majority white blocks.[7] Although invalidated along with similar racial zoning ordinances in cities across the nation (including St. Louis) by the Supreme Court's verdict in the 1917 *Buchanan v. Warley* case, these ordinances estab-lished a precedent for future forms of segregation in Baltimore, especially restrictive covenants and mortgage redlining. By the 1920s, Blacks made up 20 percent of the city's population but were crowded into approximately 2 percent of its residential areas. Overcrowding and the dearth of medical facil-ities willing to treat African Americans produced a tuberculosis mortality rate among Blacks of 450.9 per 100,000 population in 1918 compared to a rate of 156.1 per 100,000 population among whites. Segregation produced these dis-parities, but the white spatial imaginary led whites to disavow their responsi-bility for these conditions and instead blame the incidence of tuberculosis on the "immorality" of Blacks, providing yet another justification for segregation. As historian Samuel Kelton Roberts demonstrates, whites in Baltimore came to view Blacks with "infectious fear," and they justified segregated neighbor-hoods as a way to protect themselves from contagion. All subsequent "slum clearance" and urban renewal plans in Baltimore proceeded from the pat-terns established during the years when tuberculosis was not yet curable by medicine. As Roberts explains, "The metaphorical language of blight contain-ment employed after 1940 by white property owners and makers of housing policy—describing the movement of crime, vice, and social pathology—was not far removed from the uses of house infection that also had little basis in science."[8]

Early in the twentieth century, the city's segregated Jim Crow schools spent three times as much on the education of white students as they did on Blacks. Local whites were organized in one of the largest chapters of the Ku

Klux Klan in the nation.[9] Housing discrimination created an artificially constrained housing market for Blacks, compelling them to pay inflated prices for dwellings in the oldest and poorest sections of the city. By the 1930s, Baltimore had the third worst housing stock of any city in the nation.[10] During World War II, southern Black migrants seeking jobs in defense plants produced a 25 percent increase in the Black population of Baltimore, but the boundaries of segregation hardly moved at all. By 1946, Baltimore had the largest percentage of dilapidated housing among any of the seven largest cities in the United States.[11]

Trapped in costly but substandard and overcrowded neighborhoods, Blacks strongly desired to expand the areas of settlement open to them. The local branch of the NAACP, one of the largest in the country, filed suit in state court in 1938 challenging the legitimacy of restrictive covenants, but its claims were rejected by the Maryland Court of Appeals. Even after the Supreme Court ruled in the 1948 *Shelley v. Kraemer* case that states could no longer enforce restrictive covenants, white homeowners in Baltimore continued to sign them, and several federal agencies actually required them as a condition for federal mortgage assistance. White vigilante violence did the rest. In one representative case, an African American family moved into a house on a previously all-white block on West Fayette Street on the west side in 1948. Vandals broke many of the home's windows and scrawled KKK on the outside walls.[12]

During the 1950s, an already scarce supply of housing available to Blacks grew smaller as a result of urban renewal and highway construction projects. More than three thousand Black families lost homes to the wrecking ball in west Baltimore neighborhoods. The city built 15,000 units of public housing between 1951 and 1971, but urban renewal and highway building projects displaced more than seventy-five thousand people. When new developments reserved exclusively for whites opened up in the outer-ring suburbs of the region during the 1950s, the stage was set for unscrupulous speculators and real estate brokers to reap exorbitant profits through blockbusting.

Blockbusting requires racialized space. Blacks desperate for better housing become willing to pay high prices for the limited amount of housing stock available to them. Whites frightened by what they think the presence of blacks in the neighborhood will do to property values become persuaded to sell their homes at low prices. The blockbusters promote panic-selling among whites by whipping up fears about racial change in the neighborhood, and then profit by reselling the homes they purchased at low prices from whites to eager Black home buyers at high prices. Between 1955 and 1965, Baltimore became one of the prime examples of how blockbusting can skew opportunities and life chances along racial lines.

For many years, University of Maryland, Baltimore County, American Studies Professor Edward Orser conducted a thought experiment with his students. He asked them to imagine a community with twenty thousand inhabitants. Ten years later, the population would still be twenty thousand, but composed of almost no one who had lived there ten years earlier. He asks what could cause this total turnover in population. The students struggle with the problem and eventually fail to come up with any explanation of how a change like this could happen. Environmental catastrophe would make it hard to rebuild and surely some previous residents would want to return if rebuilding took place. Economic reverses affecting twenty thousand different people would undermine the economy so thoroughly that new residents would not move in, even if everyone present wanted to leave. Orser then explains to the students that the scenario is not made up, that it happened in Baltimore's Edmonson Village when blockbusting changed the neighborhood's population from white to Black. He explains that collective behavior based on race achieved a transformation greater than the ones that might be produced by environmental or economic disaster. Yet this powerful force can be very hard to see, even when it is inscribed on urban space. "Such social dynamite," Orser argues, is "so much a part of our cultural surround that we simply accept it as a given, as something that we presume we understand, whether consciously or at some other level of our psyche, and whether we really do or not."[13]

Blockbusting and white flight from Edmonson Village and other Baltimore neighborhoods during the 1950s and 1960s helped set up the conditions that are taken for granted in *The Wire*. The program shows us poor whites who embrace hip-hop music, clothing, and speech, white police officers who work with Blacks in an atmosphere remarkably free of racial tension, and an interracial romance between police lieutenant Cedric Daniels and state's attorney Rhonda Pearlman. Yet the white officers who work productively with Blacks on the program return home to all-white neighborhoods. With the exception of Lieutenant Daniels (who we are told lives in the relatively affluent Ashburton area of northwest Baltimore), Black officers who outrank whites live in lesser dwellings in Black areas. We see white businessmen and professionals at work in the city, but for the most part we do not see the wealthy neighborhoods of north Baltimore or the favored zones of white flight in the outer suburbs.

When race does come up, however, whites are portrayed as innocent victims. Especially in the programs about electoral politics, *The Wire* tells us that the city's Black population and its attendant racial solidarity make it impossible for worthy whites to become police commissioners and difficult for a white politician to become mayor (although one succeeds in the show and several have in real life). Yet we do not learn how or why this came about. *The Wire* cannot tell us how white and Black spaces in the city became separated, how white speculators and blockbusters made money because they were financed by large banks whose officers were unwilling to make loans to creditworthy Black home seekers, how Blacks paid premium prices to move to better neighborhoods that immediately were abandoned by investors and city governments once they arrived, how most churches in white neighborhoods resisted desegregation while those that welcomed newly arrived Blacks into congregations soon lost their white members, how white parents kept their children at home and picketed schools when Black students broke the color barrier in them. If Blacks in Baltimore (and elsewhere) use their linked fate as Blacks to seek access to jobs and city services, it is because they have been denied the degree of control over the use and exchange values of their neighborhoods that has routinely been enjoyed by whites[14] (see Chapter 2). If Blacks vote as a block in Baltimore (and elsewhere), it is because they have learned through hard experience that no one else will care as much about their survival as they do.

The Wire will not tell us that 45,000 Black families signed up for the waiting list for public housing in Baltimore in 1989, that in that year a majority of renters paid more than half of their incomes for rent, that 79,000 of the city's housing units were substandard and another 5,000 abandoned, that lenders routinely denied credit for homes in Black areas while funneling funds into neighborhoods undergoing gentrification by whites.[15] By the time *The Wire* completed its run in 2008, the number of abandoned units in Baltimore had increased to between 40,000 and 50,000 out of a total housing stock of slightly more than 300,000 dwellings.[16] *The Wire* has no room for a confrontation like the one that Barbara "Bobby" McKinney staged in 1993 when she invited city officials to a "sleepover" in her housing project apartment so they could "wake up the same we do"—to no hot water service, clanging pipes, water leakages and flooding, exposed electrical wiring, children infected by fungus, rat infestations, and multiple unanswered maintenance requests.[17]

For all of their attentiveness to local circumstances in Baltimore, the producers of *The Wire* evidently did not notice that in the middle of the show's run (in 2005) a federal judge presiding over the *Thompson v. HUD* case found the U.S. Department of Housing and Urban Development guilty of creating, promoting, and exacerbating racial segregation in Baltimore in violation of the 1968 Fair Housing Act. Five of the six leading plaintiffs in this suit were Black women, veterans of decades of struggle for dignity and decency in public housing. For nearly four decades, HUD pursued policies that restricted low-income Blacks to central-city segregated neighborhoods despite clear legal obligations to create housing opportunities throughout the metropolitan area. HUD's actions in Baltimore (as in other cities) privileged the exclusionary desires and preferences of suburban whites over the agency's legal obligations to take affirmative steps to decrease segregation.[18] A thorough report by court-appointed expert john anthony powell proposed significant remedies for the Black people injured by HUD's policies in Baltimore over the years, remedies that included targeted investment and support for moving to communities of opportunity outside the central city. While full remedies have not yet been implemented, some two thousand families so far have been awarded vouchers to move to low-poverty nonsegregated neighborhoods.[19] These are crime-fighting policies, but they would never appear as such on *The Wire* or anywhere else in commercial culture.

Early in 2008, the city of Baltimore filed a lawsuit against the Wells Fargo Bank in United States District Court. Similar to actions taken by municipalities and private citizens in Buffalo, Cleveland, and Memphis, this lawsuit responded to the crisis created in Baltimore by foreclosures on thirty-three thousand homes since the year 2000. The suit contended that the foreclosure actions hurt the city by reducing revenues from property taxes and real estate transfer fees while increasing the costs of police and fire protection. This wave of foreclosures left the city with large numbers of abandoned and vacant homes that became prime sites for drug use and drug dealing, prostitution, and other illegal activities. The city of Baltimore's lawsuit cited a survey in Chicago that found that a foreclosed home lowered the property values of each single-family home within a quarter of a mile by approximately 1 percent. Another study conducted in Chicago found that each foreclosure cost municipal government as much as $34,199. Even citizens whose homes were not foreclosed lost money simply because they lived in neighborhoods with large numbers of foreclosed homes. Research conducted in Cleveland discovered that home prices fell $778 per home for each 1 percent increase in property tax delinquencies in the neighborhood.[20] Another study conducted in Philadelphia discovered that homes within 150 feet of an abandoned house lost an average of $7,627 in value, that homes located 150 to 199 feet from a foreclosed dwelling experienced a decline of $6,810, and houses between 300 and 499 feet from a foreclosed home lost $3,542 in value.

The key to the complaint filed against Wells Fargo revolved around the issue of racialized space. Attorneys representing the city of Baltimore introduced evidence that revealed a concentration of foreclosures in majority Black areas. Between 2000 and 2004, nearly half of Wells Fargo's foreclosures were concentrated in census tracts with African American populations exceeding 80 percent. Nearly two-thirds were in tracts that were at least 60 percent African American. Yet fewer than 15 percent of Wells Fargo's foreclosures were in areas that had a Black population of 20 percent or less. These patterns continued and even increased slightly between 2005 and 2007.[21] The complaint revealed that Wells Fargo's foreclosed homes were concentrated in neighborhoods with a population at least 75 percent Black, including Belair Edison, East Baltimore, Pimlico/Arlington/Hilltop, Dorchester/Ashburton, Southern Park Heights, Greater Rosemont, Sandtown-Winchester/Harlem Park, Greater Govans, and Waverly.

The lawsuit attributed the concentration of foreclosures in Black neighborhoods to "reverse redlining." It accused the bank and its officers of targeting these areas for deceptive, predatory, and otherwise unfair loans. Other lenders foreclosed on loans in Baltimore during this time period, but Wells Fargo accounted for more foreclosures than any other lender. Its pace of foreclosures was increasing when the suit was filed. In Black neighborhoods, more than 8 percent of the bank's loans ended in foreclosure, but in white neighborhoods only 2.1 percent of the loans were foreclosed. Wells Fargo's rate of foreclosures in Black neighborhoods was four times its rate in white neighborhoods and twice as high as the city's overall foreclosure rate. The city charged the bank with using home costs as a proxy for race by targeting homes more likely to be in African American neighborhoods for interest rate increases, while lowering rates for homes likely to be in white neighborhoods. Even the average time to foreclosure differed by race: 2.06 years in Black areas as opposed to 2.45 years (19 percent longer) in white sections of the city.

Many of the loans to Blacks that led to foreclosures were fixed-rate loans whose soundness is relatively easy to predict using automated underwriting models. If the bank followed the same procedures for judging the creditworthiness of loans in Black areas as it did in white areas, there should have been no difference in the foreclosure rate. Yet the city charged that Wells Fargo did not use the same standards for Black and white borrowers because it stood to gain financially from discriminatory treatment. Directing applicants who qualified for prime rates to the subprime market provided additional profits for lenders and brokers. Wells Fargo made loans at least 3 percentage points above the federally established benchmark to 65 percent of its Black mortgage customers in Baltimore but to only 15 percent of white borrowers. Many of the high-cost loans made by Wells Fargo in Black neighborhoods were refinance loans, which often entice borrowers to pay excessive costs with few benefits. According to the city's complaint, Wells Fargo did not impose higher rates and costs on Blacks to guarantee creditworthiness of risky borrowers, but instead resorted to unsound practices that could have been predicted to produce foreclosures simply as a means of making short-term profits. The city asked for declaratory and injunctive relief for the harm done to Baltimore by an unprecedented wave of mortgage foreclosures that it attributed to "unlawful, irresponsible, unfair, deceptive, and discriminatory lending practices" by the bank.

Attorneys for Wells Fargo responded to the Baltimore suit with a blanket denial that its loan policies had any racial intent or effect. Like mortgage lenders facing similar charges in other cities across the country, the bank's position was that it had been victimized by irresponsible and unworthy borrowers who took on debts they could not afford in the hope that home values would continue to rise indefinitely. When the housing market crashed, they found themselves without adequate funds to pay their loans, the defense alleged. The bank made no mention of how the 1999 banking reform act contributed to the securitization of the home lending industry, reducing needed regulatory safeguards and creating vast new opportunities for short-term profits by speculators. The bank was most emphatic in arguing that its loan officers were color-blind, that creditworthiness rather than race accounted for the pattern of foreclosures in Baltimore.

In early summer of 2009, however, two former Wells Fargo loan officers stepped forward to challenge that description. Tony Paschal alleged that when he worked in the Baltimore offices of Wells Fargo, loan officers referred to Blacks as "mud people" and described subprime loans as "ghetto loans." He reported that his supervisor characterized minority customers as "people who don't pay their bills," who "have bad credit," and who live in "slums and hoods."[22] Yet rather than avoiding these putatively unworthy customers, Paschal claimed that "the company put 'bounties' on minority borrowers" as a way to encourage aggressive marketing of subprime loans in minority communities. Another former loan officer, Beth Jacobson, described her work at the bank as riding "the stagecoach from hell," because she and her colleagues routinely pushed people who qualified for prime loans into the subprime market. "We went right after them," she recalled. Jacobson reported watching other loan officers copy and paste credit reports from qualified applicants onto the applications of less worthy borrowers.[23]

On December 30, 2009, attorneys for the city of Memphis and for Shelby County, Tennessee, filed suit against Wells Fargo in the U.S. District Court for the Western District of Tennessee that offered evidence of actions by Wells Fargo in Memphis similar to the allegations of reverse redlining that had been raised in Baltimore. The complaint pointed out that in Black neighborhoods in the Memphis area, Wells Fargo's loans went into foreclosure eight times more frequently than its loans in white areas. The filing included testimony by former loan officers at the bank affirming that Wells Fargo executives encouraged them to target areas inhabited by Blacks for deceptive high-priced loans.[24] The city's lawsuit alleged that more than half of the loans made by Wells Fargo to Blacks in Shelby County were subprime loans, while the rate for whites was only 17 percent. A study conducted by researchers at the University of Memphis found that the city lost 7,000 home owners between 2005 and 2008, two-thirds of them through foreclosure.[25]

Early in 2010, the trial judge dismissed the city of Baltimore's suit against Wells Fargo, arguing that it did not seem plausible to blame one bank for actions that others also committed. The judge did not make this ruling based on the city's actual complaint or even on evidence gathered through discovery, but rather on the basis of the vague new "plausibility" standard that the Supreme Court established in its 2009 ruling on the *Iqbal v. Ashcroft* case. Crafted by a conservative Supreme Court expressly to limit the ability of individuals to make civil rights complaints against powerful institutions, the new plausibility standard allowed the judge to use "common sense" and personal perceptions about the context of the case to make his ruling. The judge did leave open the door for the city to refile the case with a complaint more carefully tailored to the specific harm done to the city by specific foreclosures, and the city's lawyers announced they would do just that.

Why did *The Wire* miss the drama of the fight for fair housing in Baltimore? Although suffused with nostalgia for the history of Baltimore's white working-class neighborhoods and the politicians who represented them, *The Wire*'s long memory does not include the long history of successful organizing, like the campaigns undertaken by Black women in Baltimore's public housing projects delineated in rich detail by historian Rhonda Y. Williams in her indispensible book *The Politics of Public Housing: Black Women's Struggles against Urban Inequality*.[26] *The Wire* presents housing projects as desolate dwellings of last resort without acknowledging the decades during which tenants led by grassroots women leaders struggled for decent living conditions in them.[27] It would be unrealistic, of course, to expect one television program, even one that stretches over sixty episodes, to cover everything that happens in a city. However, the absence of fair-housing issues from *The Wire* is not incidental, but rather constitutive of the show's grounding in the white spatial imaginary. When the writers and producers of *The Wire* think about the key institutions structuring urban life in Baltimore, they focus on the police department, containerization of the port, the school system, the press, the political system, and private charities. The program displays a maturity and sophistication about these institutions rarely seen in popular entertainment, in part because so many of *The Wire*'s creators had firsthand experience with them. The show's creator, producer, and chief writer David Simon covered the police department as a journalist for the *Baltimore Sun*. Writer Ed Burns worked as a police officer and as a seventh grade teacher in city schools. *The Wire* is relentlessly on target in exposing the bureaucratic imperatives and dysfunctional contradictions of police work, teaching, and journalism.

Yet the firsthand experience that enables the creators of *The Wire* to critique these institutions so effectively does not enable them to step back and see how these institutions are the products of racialized space and possess racial and spatial imaginaries. The demise of the daily newspaper and its important role in the public sphere, for example, appears as a simple consequence of corporate greed and media mergers. Yet the demise of the daily newspaper stems in significant ways from the subsidies for white flight that promoted suburban growth in Baltimore and other cities. When city commuters rode buses and trolleys, they purchased morning and afternoon papers to read as they rode. Massive subsidies for suburbanization led to the city losing more than 200,000 residents in the postwar period.[28] When automobile-based commuting from the suburbs became the norm, radio and television news eclipsed the daily paper, especially newspapers published in the afternoon. Newspaper circulation in Baltimore and other cities remained stable until the 1970s, when it began a decline that has accelerated in recent years for many of the reasons that *The Wire* identifies. Yet suburban growth also changed the content of newspapers as well. Unable to rely on high-volume sales among city residents, newspapers became more dependent on advertising aimed at wealthy suburban commuters. As a result, coverage of municipal news declined and features about suburban lifestyles proliferated.[29] Newspapers have long pandered to the consciousness that places private consumption at the center of the social world and makes shared social problems seem like forces of nature incapable of being addressed by principled political action. In this respect, *The Wire*'s pessimism about solving urban problems is a *symptom* of prevailing power relations, not a *critique* of them. *The Wire* treats the demise of the newspaper and the decline of public schools as distinctly urban problems unconnected to the suburbs. Yet *The Wire* misses completely that the suburb and the ghetto are mutually constitutive, that unfair gains and unjust enrichments primarily available to whites have created undeserved impediments to upward mobility for communities of color. Like the newspaper and the school system, the ghetto is itself an institution, one created and maintained deliberately by systematic residential segregation.

In one insightful sequence, *The Wire* does show how wealth accumulated through the drug trade gets channeled into downtown urban renewal. But the show does not have the vision capable of perceiving that urban renewal itself has been as deadly to Baltimore's Black communities as the drug trade. Urban renewal has long been accompanied by planned shrinkage, a policy that systematically removes city services from areas targeted for renewal. Planned shrinkage saves cities money by withholding municipal services, but it also drives down land costs to make urban renewal projects more profitable. It also creates the kinds of contagious housing destruction that resulted in the abandoned boarded-up buildings that Snoop Pearson uses to dispose of bodies. As Mindy Thompson Fullilove notes, "Under the right circumstances, contagious housing destruction can destroy miles of urban habitat. It is easily stopped by effective fire service, garbage pickup, and building code enforcement, but, sadly, civic redlining—that is, the withdrawal of key municipal services—is part of the redlining process."[30]

Even the most sympathetic white police officer, journalist, or teacher depicted in *The Wire* goes home at night to a very different reality than the one that Black characters and Black people confront every day in their neighborhoods. People who inherit assets originally secured in an expressly discriminatory housing market do not think of themselves as the beneficiaries of unfair gains and unjust enrichments. They do not realize that they profit from a system that leaves Blacks with an artificially constrained housing market. They do not know what it is like to struggle for decency, dignity, and respect without being able to control the use or exchange value of a neighborhood. As a result, for all its good intentions and valuable knowledge, *The Wire* can only tell the story of the ghetto by analogy. Ed Burns described teaching in city schools as like serving in the war in Vietnam. David Simon describes the crime story as a key national archetype, asserting that "the labyrinth of the inner city has largely replaced the spare, unforgiving landscape of the American west as the central stage of our morality plays."[31] A crucial shootout involving Omar Little replicates a memorable scene in *The Wild Bunch*. These are understandable analogies and cinematic choices, but Baltimore schools are not like the Vietnam War. Ghetto gun battles are not like *The Wild Bunch*. Black people do not control the morality plays and national archetypes created about them. The images and actions transmitted on *The Wire* are designed to appeal to outsiders eager for titillation, enraptured by spectacle and horror. They do not represent the perspectives of people who face the consequences of racialized space every day in the way that the Black women activists portrayed by Rhonda Williams do.[32] This is no small omission. By not availing itself of the knowledge of inner-city residents about their own conditions, *The Wire* uncritically accepts the neoliberal and neoconservative verdict on the civil rights movement and the war on poverty, what Williams correctly describes as "the inaccurate and simplistic belief that these programs were dismal failures and that poor people's plight is incurable unless they are morally rehabilitated."[33]

In fact, the expansion of social programs cut the poverty rate in half between 1960 and 1973. It was the abandonment of these programs that produced the desperate conditions depicted on *The Wire*. During the presidencies of Ronald Reagan and George H. W. Bush, the systematic dismantling of social programs made poverty increase steadily while imposing the

harshest costs of economic restructuring and deindustrialization on communities of color in order to preserve political support from whites. By 1992, the
poverty rate had gone back up to where it had been in the 1960s, but its impact was concentrated on communities of color.[34] Between 1970 and 1995,
poverty rose only slightly in suburbs, from 7 percent of the population to 9
percent. It surged in cities, however, rising from less than 13 percent in 1970
to 20 percent in 1995.[35] In these areas, Black workers are twice as likely to be
unemployed as white workers. Black children are twice as likely as white children to die as infants.[36]

Yet people trained to view the world from the vantage point of the white
spatial imaginary attribute these changes not to the effects of increasingly
deadly forms of structural racism, but to the conduct of Black people themselves. They likely view *The Wire* as a record of increasing Black criminality
that explains the poverty of Black communities. It is true that the disparity
between Blacks and whites in unwed childbearing is three to one and the
disparity in regard to incarceration is eight to one. Yet these are more *consequences* of racialized and spatialized poverty than *causes* of it. The rate of
Black criminal behavior has not changed, either in absolute numbers or in
comparison to white criminal behavior. What *has* changed are the degrees of
prosecution and punishment meted out to Blacks, largely for nonviolent drug
offenses.[37] *The Wire* captures some of these dynamics, but it does not recognize the full dimensions of the subsidy for whiteness that they entail. The
drug war removes large numbers of Black low-wage workers from the labor
market. It hides their chronic unemployment and abandonment. It protects
white workers by eliminating large numbers of potential Black competitors.
It disguises declines in wages paid to Blacks as modest gains because those
likely to earn the lowest wages are taken out of the labor force.[38]

Without a systemic analysis of how housing discrimination creates the
ghetto, *The Wire* is left with the default positions inscribed in the white spatial imaginary: that people who *have* problems *are* problems, that social welfare programs produce only "poverty pimps" and hustlers who take advantage
of the poor, and that social disintegration has gone so far it simply cannot be
stopped. These values "hail" certain kinds of viewers: knowing cynics who
enjoy having their worst fears confirmed, passive voyeurs who think of themselves as noble because they feel sorry for others from the safety of their living
rooms, and self-satisfied suburbanites who use portrayals of Black criminality to absolve themselves of any responsibility for the inequalities that provide
them with unfair gains and unjust enrichments. Precisely because residential segregation has been so pervasive for so long, it now appears to be a
part of the natural environment, a reality that has always been and that will
always be. By evading the structure that created and sustained the ghetto in

the first place, *The Wire* leaves us with nothing to do but be disturbed and challenged, yet ultimately numbed by depictions of our own destruction. We seem to have reached the stage that Walter Benjamin predicted decades ago where society experiences its own destruction as a pleasure of the first order. Yet Black people living in ghettos may not have the luxury of that kind of resignation. As the tenant mobilizations that led to the *Thompson v. HUD* and the *Baltimore v. Wells Fargo* cases demonstrate, Black people continue to mobilize and organize, to educate and agitate. Without access to HBO or any other powerful media outlet, they continue to insist along with Baltimore welfare rights organizer Bobby Cheeks that "no matter what system a person is influenced by, they have certain rights and they can affect the way they are treated."[39] Cheeks and other activists hold this belief because of what they have done as individuals, but also because they share a Black spatial imaginary that sees and hears everything that the surveillance devices on *The Wire* cannot seem to find.

A Bridge for This Book

Weapons of the Weak and Weapons of the Strong

The fact that today's citizens are powerless at the center
of their lives creates frenzies at the boundaries. The most
tortured boundary in American society for the last 300
years, has been the line that separates whites from blacks.
—MARSHALL BERMAN

Many popular songs contain a component that musicians call the
bridge. The bridge is a turning point, a place where a song marks
what came before and what is to follow, usually through an interlude
of eight bars in a different key. This section of *How Racism Takes Place* is the
bridge, the middle eight, the intermezzo that connects the origins, evolution,
and impact of the white spatial imaginary with the ways in which works of
expressive culture steeped in a Black spatial imaginary have envisioned and
enacted alternative ways of knowing and ways of being. This bridge offers arguments about why place matters, about why culture counts, and about how
history takes place. It seeks to take stock of the obstacles to democracy, dignity, and decency posed by the white spatial imaginary discussed in Chapters 1 through 4, and to prefigure the importance of the generative ideas and
actions emanating from aggrieved Black communities that are discussed in
Chapters 5 through 10.

The white spatial imaginary encapsulated in stadium construction in St.
Louis augmented the visibility of a few Black athletes. It did so, however, by
hurting the well-being of Black children. Funds that should have flowed to
city schools to create new democratic opportunities were funneled instead
to pump up the profits of a privately owned football team. The white spatial imaginary manifested in representations of inner-city life in Baltimore in
The Wire increased the visibility of a few Black actors. Yet it did so by strate-
gically evading the history of predatory lending, redlining, blockbusting, and
urban renewal in Baltimore. In both cases, the hypervisibility of a few Black

performers enabled and excused the erasure of the needs and aspirations of larger Black communities. These contradictions are not merely coincidences. Spectacular Blackness often serves white interests. White supremacy renders Black identity socially peripheral. Yet as Peter Stallybrass and Allon White explain, the socially peripheral is often symbolically central.[1] Because whites learn who they *are* through demeaning portrayals of who they *are not*, they need images of Blackness to stabilize an otherwise ungrounded white identity. Whites become reliant on representations of race because it promises them fixity and stability. Whatever else changes in their lives, they remain not-Black. They crave spectacular images of Blackness to confirm this fact. Cedric Robinson argues that the incessant racial representations that permeate our culture are often forgeries of memory and meaning designed to justify the unjustifiable. They are unrelentingly hostile to their exposure *as* racial regimes but unrelentingly eager to exhibit race as proof that identities and social relations are static, stable, and secure. Yet actual racial regimes are inherently unstable systems, constantly in need of revision and reconfiguration.[2] As Malcolm X asserted, racism is like a Cadillac; they make a new model every year.[3]

The domed sports stadium in St. Louis and *The Wire*'s depictions of ghetto crime in Baltimore both promoted forms of citizenship and social membership based on spectacle and spectatorship. Proponents of the stadium project justified their initiative as an endeavor that could unite a polarized city. They claimed that people of different races living in different places could be brought together through shared identification as fans (and customers) of a sports franchise. They did not explain, of course, why the site of unity should be a sport played and watched mostly by men, why the ends of unity would be served best through subsidies to a business owned by wealthy whites and supported largely by wealthy white customers, or why there was no mechanism inserted into the plans for the stadium complex to insure that the contracts, jobs, and investment opportunities attendant to the project would flow to members of all races. The reconciliation envisioned in this project was limited to the sphere of shared spectatorship, and even there it was assumed that the sharing would be done from different vantage points. The affective pleasures of reconciliation rely on leaving in place the real differences and inequalities that are fictively reconciled through culture. The power of football games to bring diverse people together on Sunday afternoons depends on their being divided every other day of the week. The domed stadium not only failed to make those differences disappear; it reinforced them by reproducing stratification and inequality in its core practices. People from diverse backgrounds may root for the local football team, but only wealthy individuals and corporate executives can afford the tickets. The domed stadium offers a different experience to the fans watching from luxury boxes than it does to fans sitting at home and viewing the games on television.

If the object of the expenditure of massive amounts of public funds on the stadium truly was reconciliation of antagonistic social groups, many other projects could have accomplished those ends more effectively and efficiently. The money could have been spent on playing fields and playgrounds to be used by men and women, by adults and children, by Blacks and whites, by rich and poor. The money could have been spent on supporting the creation of integrated neighborhoods where members of different races could encounter each other not merely as fellow sports fans but as neighbors, friends, and citizens with mutual responsibilities and obligations. The money could have been spent on supporting small business start-ups and home-improvement loans in undercapitalized areas. It could have addressed the dearth of affordable quality health care. Yet sensible projects like these can rarely even be discussed in our society while money-losing stadium projects are funded in city after city. Projects, policies, and programs that would be cost-effective, enhance the general welfare, and genuinely reconcile divided social groups do not even become subjects for debate because they do not conform to the imperatives of the white spatial imaginary.

The fact that the promise of reconciliation is fraudulent does not mean that it is insignificant. The fiction that building sports facilities helps the economy of cities and their residents enables the consumer desires of sports fans to be portrayed as a worthy social ends. Self-interest becomes figured as service to the public interest. We do not really need to fund education, housing, transportation, and health care, the stadium subsidy teaches us; what we need is to spend more on our own amusement. Anxieties about racial inequality can similarly be made to disappear in this formulation. The masses of Black people may be poor, but Black football players receive millions of dollars in salaries. Their success is seen as proof that anyone who wants to can succeed in America, not that a completely imbalanced set of priorities teaches young Blacks that they are worth next to nothing as teachers, accountants, electricians, or nurses but are worth millions as gladiators risking their bodies for the viewing pleasure of wealthy whites. Affection for Black athletes convinces suburban whites that they are not racists, that they would approve of Black people if only they were the right kind of Black people. If inner-city Blacks fail to make the money white spectatorship brings to a few athletes, it must be their own fault. Of course, the love shown for these athletes is contingent. It does not extend to thinking that the players should be allowed to sell their services freely to the highest bidder, negotiate for a larger share of advertising and television revenues, or remain on the sidelines when they are injured. The subsidized spectatorship that subsidized stadiums promote also invites fans to view football from the perspective of the team owners. Televised games routinely feature reaction shots from the owners' boxes. Fans who subsidize the profits of owners who never have to open their books to the public are convinced that the players are greedy, that they make too much money, that ticket prices are too high because players are making more money than they deserve.

In a sport like professional football—where more than half the players are Black yet most of the fans in the teams' target audiences are white— race matters a great deal. Whites are still the overwhelming majority of team owners, general managers, and coaches. White management of Black athletes reassures fans that whites are still in control, that demographic diversity is something that needs to be managed by whites. Black and white players hugging each other after victories exude a utopian aura precisely because Blacks and whites are so segregated from each other in the rest of society. In sports, racial difference becomes the basis for an affective spectacle that justifies the prevailing relations of power.

The creators of *The Wire* most likely saw themselves as engaged in a project that was much more serious and much more socially conscious than the stadium initiative in St. Louis. They did not celebrate civic boosterism. They condemned capitalist greed. They did not try to hide the problems of the ghetto, but instead placed them center stage. The St. Louis stadium initiative sought to address urban problems by hiding them, to "revive" downtown by driving out its residents and creating a new commercial destination for suburban residents and tourists. *The Wire* followed what appears to be an opposite course, turning the inner city into a spectacle that seemed to honor the appealing creativity and dynamism of the culture of inner-city residents. Yet like the stadium project, *The Wire* located spectacle and spectatorship at the center of our shared social life. Both projects took advantage of the cumulative vulnerabilities of Black communities to produce profits for investors. Both the television show and the stadium were "other-directed" spectacles that offered viewers opportunities to witness different forms of Blackness from safe and distant vantage points. Certainly the decisions made by most viewers of *The Wire* about where they live, about what schools their children attend, about where tax money is spent, and about where capital is invested, effectively guarantee that these viewers will never encounter in person the kinds of people they enjoy "meeting" when they watch the show. There are, of course, some constructive possibilities latent in the desires of these viewers to know more about a world that is generally hidden from them. Their interest in the kind of inner city portrayed on the program, where Blacks and whites work together with minimal racial divisiveness, may speak to utopian desires for more dignified and decent social relations. Their seeming acceptance of (and even enthusiasm for) portrayals of ghetto residents as complex people contains the potential for resistance against the idea that people who *have* problems *are* problems. Yet the spectacle of rehumanization that *The Wire* stages still ignores the history of dehumanization resulting from the organized abandonment of Black communities enacted by predatory lending, redlining, blockbusting, real estate steering, urban renewal, environmental racism, and differential policing. The "otherness" portrayed in *The Wire* still remains fully enclosed within a white spatial imaginary. A show dedicated to the value of noticing evidence, of following clues to their logical conclusion, of deromanticizing and demythologizing the criminal justice system, still naturalizes the relegation of different races to different places. No matter how much or how nobly its inhabitants struggle against ghetto conditions, the ghetto remains the seemingly natural habitat of Black people in *The Wire*, rather than the calculated and self-interested creation of white supremacy. Our problem is not just that our society needs better images and better imaginations; it is that the images and imaginations that dominate are inflected with the premises and presumptions of the white spatial imaginary. They function perniciously as social forces with disastrous consequences.

In interviews and appearances designed to promote the program, *The Wire*'s creator and producer David Simon referred to the show as a "visual novel." Simon deployed this description to explain why everything is not explained to viewers, why characters do not engage in dialogue that establishes their identities or recapitulates actions depicted earlier, why each episode does not wrap up all of the stories it introduces. This complexity challenges viewers but also provides them with pleasures of discovery stretched out over time. Yet the program follows the logic of the novel in other ways as well. As literary scholar Nancy Armstrong explains, the novel played a key role in *producing* rather than merely *reflecting* the modern subject. It encouraged people to define themselves through fear-inducing threatening representations of debased others. Once established convincingly in literature, this subject began to dominate law, medicine, philosophy, and history. Readers learned to recognize true individuals as subjects battling what Armstrong calls "an engulfing otherness, or mass, that obliterated individuality."[4] This absolute opposition between the individual and the group precludes other understandings of social relations. If the mob always threatens to engulf the individual, if society is made up of monstrous and less-than-human others, freedom becomes a zero-sum game in which one person's freedom can only come at the expense of others. Freedom from the group becomes a legible goal, but freedom within the group seems like an impossibility. The reading subject created by the novel is an individual, but not a rugged one. The form's emphasis on interiority, on pity for the masses but fear

of them, leads to a submissive individualism rooted in the voyeuristic titillation of the spectator.

The Wire blends the traditional subject-making project of the novel with
the needs of the contemporary managerial and professional class. As Ryan
Brooks notes in an astute analysis, the program advances both a theory of
knowledge and a theory of action. True and useful knowledge in The Wire is
obtained only by observers (including viewers) who watch others but remain
invisible themselves. Effective action in the show depends upon "expert intervention at the level of the institutional structures shaping people's lives."[5]
While of course anyone from any walk of life can watch and enjoy The Wire,
the maximally competent and receptive implied and inscribed spectator is
a member of the professional and managerial class. Just as rodeos "hail"
cowboys to assess how well others do ranch work and soap operas recruit
housewives to become surrogate supervisors of the intimate lives of family
members, The Wire recruits viewers to inhabit subject positions as analysts
and managers of urban life, not as interactive participants in it.

In a thoughtful piece about his experiences writing about the inner city,
crime novelist and Wire script writer George Pelecanos explores the moral
quandary that his work poses for him. While researching his novels or shooting scenes of The Wire on location in Baltimore ghetto neighborhoods, Pelecanos encounters young people whose lives are very different from his own.
They treat him like a celebrity, and it makes him feel generous and benign
to give them attention or to let them play with the television equipment for
a while. When their work together is over, however, the writer drives home
in an expensive high-performance vehicle to a house in a beautiful neighborhood where he sleeps comfortably with his family. Pelecanos routinely tells
interviewers that he seeks to dignify inner city young people to audiences
that know next to nothing about them and their lives. Yet in this piece he con-
fesses to a gnawing feeling that he is really just exploiting them for his own
personal gain. "At the end of the day," he observes, "we go back to our lives
and they go back to theirs. For them, nothing has changed."[6]

The unease that Pelecanos expresses could lead him to many different
kinds of actions. He could research and write about redlining, restrictive covenants, segregation, and contagious destruction. He could chronicle mobilizations for fair housing that have a long history in Baltimore and are still taking
place today. He could use his public visibility to campaign for better urban
policies. He could donate a small part of his earnings to organizations struggling for social change. He could research the reasons why relations between
races are relations between places. But he does none of this. Instead, Pelecanos insists that his role as a writer is simply to do "good, honest work," not
to perform "some sort of public service." "At best," he argues, "a viewer might

watch our show and be inspired to become the kind of extraordinary person—teacher, coach, foster parent, mentor—that I can only conjure up as a fictional character in my head. The kind of person, that is to say, who is far better than me."[7] Pelecanos notes that he gradually forgets the people whose lives provide the raw material for his fiction. Mentioning one youth in particular, the novelist admits, "Occasionally I wonder what became of him, but then the moment passes. I have my own family to dream about and worry over, and they occupy most of my thoughts. Them, and the books I have yet to write."[8]

What appears to be self-criticism in Pelecanos' rumination is an illusion. While he raises the issue of his own guilt, he does so only to dismiss it. Sure that his job is not to perform "a public service," he does himself and the public a disservice. Pelecanos' expressions of concern about ghetto youth promote his credentials as a thoughtful caring person with a sufficiently interesting interiority to make his novels worth reading. Yet his knowing cynicism, his weary resignation to his belief that it has to be this way, his conviction that caring about others means neglecting the private needs of his own family and distracting him from his true calling as an artist—all are forms of collaboration and submission. Pelecanos does not see that the wealthy suburb where he sleeps is not simply a neutral site where he happens to live, but rather a place that produces a racial and spatial imaginary that has shaped him and constrained him in ways imposing inescapable limits on both his art and his social imagination. Confronted with a collective, continuing, and cumulative social problem, his only solution is to imagine new individual characters: heroic teachers, coaches, foster parents, and mentors who will touch us and inspire our admiration. His work as a result recruits viewers to consume the suffering of others as an aesthetic pleasure, yet still remain sure of their own righteousness.

The Wire also recruits viewers to inhabit masculinity. The masculinist stamp on *The Wire* is unmistakable. During the show's first two years, when its style book was being established, only three episodes were directed by women and only one woman worked as a writer for the show.[9] Although a few white women characters (attorney Rhonda Pearlman and police officer Beatrice Russell) are allowed moments of partial agency, subjectivity, and individuality in the show, action on *The Wire* is usually the preserve of men. Almost without exception, the job of Black women is to support men, remind them of their obligations, and clean up after them, literally and figuratively.[10] Two Black women do exercise agency effectively and heroically: police officer Kima Greggs and criminal Snoop Pearson. Greggs is a lesbian character. Pearson's sexuality is unmarked but her mannerisms, speech, and dress perform masculinity. The appealing qualities of these nonnormative characters help distinguish *The Wire* from other television programs, but Greggs and Pearson exhibit agency largely in the ways that male characters do: by fighting, killing, and fitting in with the heteromormative groups of men whose agency moves the action along.

Both the professional football games played in the St. Louis domed stadium and the dramatic stories that appear in *The Wire* revolve around violence, aggression, competition, and masculine solidarity. These frames are not unique to our era; they have permeated the culture of the West (and other cultures) from antiquity to the present. Yet in the wake of deindustrialization, globalization, repudiation of the egalitarian and democratic movements of the middle of the twentieth century, and an era of perpetual war, these deployments of violence, aggression, competition, and masculine solidarity take on new significance. They express the structures of feeling emanating from unjust social relations as they have been structured in dominance. As Raymond Williams argues, in our culture pervasive alienation generates violent competition and impersonal appetites. Repeated dislocations and dispossessions become understood as proof of the arbitrariness of life and the inevitability of isolation and powerlessness.[11] False social subjects crave false cultural objects. The culture they consume stokes desires for "conscious insults" and "deliberately perverse exposures."[12] Dominant powers, Williams alleges, use humiliation as a mechanism of social control. They turn degradation into diversions that collectively make up what he terms "the pastime of callused nerves." Television shows and sporting events encourage people to think "if we are as filthy as this ('and we are') there is no point in anything else. . . ."[13] Thus, if our society believes today that there is no point in enforcing civil rights laws, no point in making a reality out of the dreams of Dr. King, no point in addressing climate change and its attendant environmental crises, no point in stopping the stagnation of real wages for most Americans, no point in challenging educational inequality, no point in opposing mass incarceration and the organized abandonment of aggrieved communities, no point in rejecting the recreational hate that stands at the center of our political life, it is, at least in part, because the spectacles staged by the state and capital direct our energies away from these ends and toward the compensatory pleasures of cruelty and sadism.

Under these conditions, warfare becomes the biggest spectacle of all, so much so that rather than being regretted as a necessity, war is embraced, celebrated, and deployed as the central metaphor of everything, including forms of commerce, recreation, and work that do not resemble actual wars at all. The violence, aggression, competition, and masculine solidarity displayed on *The Wire*, in professional football games, and in many other venues in commercial culture are logical parts of the pastimes of a people at war. Our national leaders tell us that the wars now raging in Afghanistan and Iraq will last throughout our lifetimes. These conflicts come on the heels of repeated military actions from World War II through the Korean War, the Vietnam War, and the lesser military actions in El Salvador, Nicaragua, Panama, and Kosovo. Decisions about armed conflict shape the state and society in important ways, but they also promote particular kinds of expressive culture.

Walter Benjamin spoke prophetically about the relationship between spectatorship, citizenship, and war in his famous 1939 essay "The Work of Art in the Age of Mechanical Reproduction."[14] Wondering how it came to be that masses of people seemed now "to experience the destruction of humans as 'an aesthetic pleasure of the first order,'" Benjamin argued that "warfare mobilizes the masses to experience a wide range of emotions, to consume the state's public performances of sadism, cynicism, sentimentality and sensationalism."[15] To prevent people from inhabiting the identity of witnesses to exploitation, inequality, and injustice, the state in a nation at war invites them to become consumers of cruelty. Spectacles in sports arenas and on television provide consumers with cultural reparations for society's inability to solve actual social problems. They give people things to watch but not meaningful work to do. They privilege the passive pleasures of the spectator over the active responsibilities of the citizen. Moreover, people who have become consumers of cruelty, people whose callused nerves lead them to embrace pastimes that are structured in dominance, are poorly positioned to imagine or enact new social relations. When the places where they live, work, and play are also structured in dominance, people can become enemies of their own best interests.

The white spatial imaginary does not simply disadvantage nonwhites by excluding them from the fruits and benefits of mainstream society. It also disadvantages whites by preventing them from seeing how we are actually governed in this society and how new oppositional ideas, actions, and associations might be developed. Whites recruited to police the boundaries of white spaces, to pursue comparative advantage for themselves at the expense of communities of color, to consume spectacles that provide only symbolic psychic solutions to serious social problems deny themselves the possibility of living in a decent, dignified, and democratic society. The white spatial imaginary is only one part of what sociologist Joe Feagin calls the "white racial frame," an entity that he defines as "an overarching worldview, one that encompasses important racial ideas, terms, images, emotions, and interpretations."[16] Feagin observes that slavery and legal segregation dominated social relations for three hundred and fifty years in the United States between 1619 (when African slaves were first purchased by English settlers) and 1969 (when the Fair Housing Act went into effect). Those years account for 85 percent of our national history. For that reason, Feagin notes, they exert continuing epistemological and ontological influence on the present. As I argued in the introduction and Chapter 1, links between race and place created in the past continue to shape social relations in the present. Pointing to the pervasiveness of residential racial segregation, Feagin notes, "For the most part, these racially segregated areas and geographical dividing lines are not recent creations, but have been shaped by white decisionmakers' actions over centuries."[17] Some of these actions, such as redlining and steering, are now against the law but rarely prosecuted. Others, such as racial zoning and restrictive covenants, are no longer used directly, but their legacy continues to shape perfectly legal policies about planning, zoning, and investment that powerfully skew opportunities and life chances along unequal racial lines. The practices of the past impede progress in the present, acting as a kind of self-reinforcing perpetual motion machine. No single actor needs to make an intentional decision to discriminate for space to be racialized and race to be spatialized. As the Polish intellectual Stanislaus Lec observed in another context, in an avalanche, every snowflake pleads not guilty.

The cynicism about social change expressed by *The Wire* is completely understandable. The prevailing power relations of this society offer ample reasons to be cynical. The corruption, cruelty, and callousness depicted on *The Wire* are not exaggerated; they are all too real. Yet the show's cynicism is also a shortcut, an evasion, a self-pitying preference for the path of least resistance. The program lacks the moral imagination and intellectual complexity that Dr. King urged us to develop. It does not recognize that out of necessity and hard historical experience, Blacks often see things differently from whites. The Black spatial imaginary has long been a crucible of creativity, an alternative archive of new democratic imaginaries, epistemologies, and ontologies. As James Baldwin argued decades ago, "The doctrine of white supremacy, which still controls most white people, is itself a stupendous delusion: but to be born black in America is an immediate, a mortal challenge."[18]

In the chapters that follow, I explore the origins and evolution of a Black spatial imaginary that finds value in devalued spaces, that elevates people over profits, that offers alternatives to hostile privatism, defensive localism, and competitive consumer citizenship. These ideas entail more than removing negative racist obstacles in the way of Black assimilation and upward mobility. Within the Black spatial imaginary, centuries of slavery and segregation have undercut the moral authority and political legitimacy of the dominant society. The Black freedom struggle has always been about more than simple legal equality. The goal has not been to disappear as Blacks and become honorary whites, but rather to change the entire society by bringing into it the situated knowledge of the Black spatial imaginary. In their 1967 book *Black Power*, Kwame Ture (Stokely Carmichael) and Charles Hamilton saw that new ideas were emerging out of Black spaces. In sharecroppers' cabins and on big city streets, Black people raised challenges to "the very nature of the society itself; its long-standing values, beliefs and institutions."[19] Central to those challenges was a rejection of the core ideas of what I am calling the white spatial imaginary, not just its exclusion of Black people. As Ture and Hamilton explain,

> The values of the middle class permit perpetuation of the ravages of the black community. The values of that class are based on material aggrandizement, not the expansion of humanity. The values of that class ultimately support cloistered little closed societies tucked away neatly in tree-lined suburbia. The values of that class do *not* lead to the creation of an open society. That class *mouths* its preference for a free, competitive society, while at the same time forcefully and even viciously denying to black people as a group the opportunity to compete. . . . This class wants "good government" for *themselves*; it wants good schools *for its children. . . . This class is the backbone of institutional racism in this country.*[20]

Ture and Hamilton were sensitive to this critique because Ture had learned it in spaces created by Black people inside the Mississippi freedom movement in the early 1960s. At the peak of the movement, the curriculum in freedom schools run by the Student Nonviolent Coordinating Committee asked students questions that looked beyond equality. Teachers asked their adult students: (1) What does the majority culture have that we want? (2) What does the majority culture have that we do not want? (3) What do we have that we want to keep?[21]

The works of expressive culture discussed in the chapters that follow ask and answer these very questions. My intent is not to present discursive space as an escape from the inequalities of physical place. On the contrary, I seek to demonstrate the importance of subaltern spaces as incubators of new democratic practices and institutions. Nor do I wish to romanticize the ghetto, diminish opposition to its injustices, or evade the terrible costs it imposes on its inhabitants. But I believe there we have much to learn from people who have learned to transform spaces of deprivation into places of possibility.

The moral imagination that emerges from Black feminist activism and artistry offers an especially important alternative to the white spatial imaginary. The chapters that follow demonstrate how Black women's agency appeared in the cultural organizations created by Horace Tapscott, the paintings of John Biggers, and the social sculpture of Rick Lowe, but achieved full theorization in the visual art of Betye Saar and writings by Paule Marshall and Lorraine Hansberry. Black feminism contains the moral complexity that *The Wire* lacks. It offers alternatives to the ideal of the citizen as a spectator promoted by the stadium project in St. Louis. The art activism delineated in Chapters 7 and 8 was crafted by women engaged in the Black freedom movement but who were wary of the ways that its normative sex and gender roles replicated and normalized the kinds of hierarchy on which the white spatial imaginary depends. The works of expressive culture produced by this activism offer more than entertainment, escape, and uplift. Crafted in the context of mass action and democratic upheaval, they are material archives of oppositional ideas and actions but also instruction manuals for mobilization and organization in the future. From bitter experiences with the ways in which women's experiences, ideas, and agency have been ignored in the public sphere and suppressed in domestic settings, Saar, Marshall, and Hansberry came to see that struggling for social justice requires commitment to intimate interpersonal justice, to incorporating the changes we need to make in society at large into the most immediate spheres of our emotional and romantic lives. Betye Saar's art reveals how the gendered division of household labor and demeaning representations of Black women in popular culture function as impediments to democratic social change, but also how we might creatively redeploy those very practices and representations and turn them into instruments of liberation. Paule Marshall's fiction grapples with the ways in which structural racism in society at large produces agonizing contradictions inside individuals, families, households, neighborhoods, and communities. While critiquing what Miranda Joseph would later term "the romance of community," Marshall also challenges the bourgeois ideal of individual escape, arguing that the problems of our shared social life can be solved only by working on them together. Lorraine Hansberry's plays and essays explore how collective oppression fuels radical divisiveness inside aggrieved communities. People who have been hurt may well want to hurt others. Only rarely can they strike back against their oppressors, but they have ample opportunities to attack each other. Crowded together in cramped quarters, competing with each other for scarce resources, and seeing the mark of their own humiliating subordination in the people whose identities they share, their hatred of oppression can easily become channeled into self-hatred. People forced to live close together by oppression are often at each other's throats. Especially in *A Raisin in the Sun*, Hansberry demonstrates how radical solidarity can cure the ills of radical divisiveness. It is not that members of aggrieved groups are likely to like each other more than members of other groups like each other, but rather that their linked fate requires them to recognize "something left to love" in each other as a means of preserving it in themselves. Saar, Marshall, and Hansberry do not allow us the luxury of dividing the world into heroes and villains, but instead call us to do the difficult intellectual, social, and moral work of recognizing how contradictions writ large in society are writ small in our everyday lives, how the things that can kill us can also cure us, if we learn how to use them in the right way.

Drawing on the ideas of James C. Scott, Robin Kelley calls our attention to why culture counts in history. Racism, heterosexism, and class oppression leave members of aggrieved groups with few opportunities to advance their interests directly inside the political system. Cultural practices enable them to expand the sphere of politics, to take actions that interrupt the workings of power, undermine their legitimacy, and prefigure the politics of the future. Kelley calls these everyday forms of resistance "infrapolitics." Scott refers to them as weapons of the weak. Yet as we shall see, people who are weak in the calculus of unequal power can make themselves quite strong in other ways.

SECTION III

Visible Archives

5

Horace Tapscott and the World Stage in Los Angeles

We did what we had to do, with the things
we had to do it with.
—KAMAU DAAOOD

The World Stage Performance Gallery at 4434 Degnan Boulevard in
the Leimert Park neighborhood of Los Angeles has never received the
kind of state subsidies available to the domed stadium in St. Louis.
The gallery's cultural productions have never received the kinds of critical
acclaim and financial remuneration given to the creators of *The Wire*. Yet the
World Stage is an important place, a site of struggle created by and for Black
people, a venue where democratic ideas and ideals get made and remade
every day. The poetry, prose, dancing, and music performed on the World
Stage are more than moments of entertainment; they are repositories of collective memory, sites of moral instruction, sources of radical solidarity, and
mechanisms for calling new communities into being through performance.
The World Stage is a visible archive of ideas and experiences from the past,
but also a meaningful site for the production of new activist identities appropriate for the urgent conditions we confront in the present.

Founded in 1989 by spoken-word poet and performance artist Kamau
Daaood, musician, composer, bandleader, and cultural visionary Horace
Tapscott, and Billy Higgins (probably the most recorded jazz drummer in history), the World Stage is haunted by the history of racialized space in Los
Angeles. It is the successor to places for producing culture that no longer
exist, places demolished by freeway construction and urban redevelopment
schemes, places subjected to contagious destruction (see Chapter 4) by systematic disinvestment and municipal abandonment, places defunded by cuts
in public spending on the arts and education demanded by the "balanced

budget conservatism" emanating from the white spatial imaginary. Patrons and performers at the World Stage remember things that most of white Los Angeles has long forgotten: the vibrant performance spaces and dynamic street life along Central Avenue in the 1940s, the quality of music instruction in public schools during the1940s and 1950s, the networks of apprenticeship in the Black community that produced world-class artists, writers, and musicians. Yet the existence of the World Stage also emanates from a history of violent confrontation and conflict, from struggles against restrictive covenants and police brutality, from the self-help and self-defense philosophies of Black nationalist organizations, and from the brutal causes and bitter consequences of the 1965 and 1992 civil insurrections.

The performers and patrons at the World Stage know that having access to such a place cannot be taken for granted. They remember how the government's counterinsurgency programs against the Black community in the1960s and 1970s focused on destroying Black-controlled spaces. In one instance, a former army intelligence officer named Ed Riggs who called himself Darthard Perry infiltrated the Watts Writers Workshop and other activist art collectives. He spied on the groups and reported to his superiors the details of their discussions and activities. Perry sabotaged equipment and disrupted performances. In 1973 he set fire to building that housed the Writers Workshop's rehearsal space and theater, burning it to the ground.[1]

Horace Tapscott's oral history and memoir offers important insight into the guiding racial and spatial logic of the World Stage. Tapscott begins his life story with an unusual turn of phrase. Describing his birth in "segregated Houston, Texas" in a hospital named Jefferson Davis, he asserts that from the moment he entered the world, Tapscott was "locked here on this earth."[2] Located in the midst of references to segregation and to a hospital named in honor of the president of the slave-owning Confederacy, Tapscott's term connotes containment and confinement. It links the life of this supremely successful Black intellectual, artist, and activist to the chains that shackled his slave ancestors as well as to the stone walls and iron bars that locked in more than one million Black inmates in the prisons of the contemporary United States in 2001, the year when Tapscott's book was published posthumously two years after his death. *Songs of the Unsung* presents story after story of spatial segregation, carceral confinement, and cultural containment, both in the Houston ghetto where Tapscott spent the first nine years of his life and in the Los Angeles ghetto to which his family moved in 1943. Tapscott delineates with excruciating specificity the effects of housing segregation, employment discrimination, and racially motivated incidents of police harassment and brutality. He demonstrates convincingly the degree to which the marginalization and devaluation of Black cultural creations (and their creators) stems from the spatialization of race and the racialization of space. Yet Tapscott tells another story as well. To be "locked" also denotes locating and following a moving target. His memoir reveals that Taspcott was "locked on this earth" in that sense as well, methodically "moving" (literally and figuratively) to achieve his goals despite the shackles and bonds designed to keep him and his community contained and constrained.

One particular move proved to be especially important. While performing in nightclubs with the Lionel Hampton Orchestra in 1961, Tapscott enjoyed the artistry and skills of the musicians and composers with whom he was associated. It seemed as if everyone played perfectly every night. He appreciated Hampton's encouragement of the musicians, his invitations to them to write the kinds of challenging arrangements and compositions they enjoyed playing. Tapscott found himself with a steady and secure job for the first time in his life. He received more money for playing music in the Hampton band than he had ever anticipated, more than enough to support his growing family back in Los Angeles. Yet he was miserable.

Tapscott felt that the music he was playing in Hampton's band had no substantive meaning for nightclub audiences, that they did not really pay any attention to it, did not understand it, and did not appreciate it. Music created originally by Black artists in Black communities for Black audiences seemed to lose much of its identity, purpose, and force in the spaces of expensive nightclubs geared to a mostly white clientele. Despite the obvious commercial value of Black music, Tapscott observed that its true creators derived little recognition or reward for their efforts. He resented the anonymity and poverty that he knew to be the lot of musicians who he respected, people like his Jefferson High School classmate Richard Berry, who wrote the original version of the song "Louie Louie," and jazz trombonist Melba Liston, who had attended Jefferson and Los Angeles Polytechnic high schools and had played a key role teaching Tapscott how to read music.[3] At the peak of his profession, at a time when he had finally secured the fruits and benefits of many years of hard work to become a skilled player, Tapscott told himself, "This is it brother, I've had it."[4] He handed Hampton his resignation and returned to the segregated Los Angeles neighborhoods that had nurtured and sustained his artistry during his formative years.[5]

Initially without any support at all from cultural institutions, municipal agencies, or philanthropic organizations, Tapscott started the Pan Afrikan People's Arkestra and, later, the Underground Musicians Association. He declared that his goal was to "preserve, teach, show, and perform the music of Black Americans and Pan-African music, to preserve it by playing it and writing it and taking it to the community."[6] By coming back home to Los Angeles, Tapscott chose to burrow in, to change the scale of racialized space.

He abandoned the national and international scale of the music industry in favor of the possibilities that might exist in small spaces at the local level in Black Los Angeles. Tapscott created ensembles to perform and teach different forms of music, dance, theater, and poetry. He launched these efforts in a series of seemingly unlikely places for art: in the living room of singer Linda Hill's small house on Seventy-Fifth Street between Central and Hooper, on the bandstand stage of the city-owned South Park at Fifty-First Street and Avalon, inside artist Percy Smith's big house at Fifty-Sixth Street and Figueroa, at the Watts Happening Coffee House on 103rd Street near Central, in three rented rooms in an office building near the Crenshaw–Baldwin Hills Shopping Center, inside a small office in a house near Western Avenue, and in the unfurnished spaces of an abandoned print shop on Vermont near Eighty-Fourth Street that was donated to the group by its Jamaican American owner.[7] Music composed and rehearsed in these venues was not necessarily aimed at performances in nightclubs or recording studios, but designed instead to be played in middle school auditoriums, churches, hospitals, public parks, and prisons. Tapscott secured assistance from Marla Gibbs, who used part of the money that she earned playing the family maid Florence on the television program *The Jeffersons* to purchase a building that Tapscott could then use for practice spaces and community arts projects. Regular viewers of *The Jeffersons* knew that Florence was feisty, but probably few suspected that she secretly funded a Black nationalist community space.[8]

Tapscott deployed spatial metaphors to name the projects that he started in these small spaces, emphasizing the new kinds of cognitive mapping he hoped to achieve. Calling his band the *Pan Afrikan* People's Arkestra referenced the global diaspora of African people created by the slave trade, but also Tapscott's desire to play, preserve, and celebrate the music of African people all around the world. In that way, the local spaces of the ghetto expanded beyond the juridical and geographic boundaries of Los Angeles and the United States. Houses, streets, and neighborhoods far from Los Angeles's main thoroughfares and its celebrated corridors of power became imagined as nodes in a larger network, as privileged parts of an Afro-diasporic global relay system transmitting experiences, ideas, and aspirations back and forth. In classic Black nationalist fashion, this identification transformed African Americans from members of a national minority into part of the global majority of nonwhite people.[9] Later, when Tapscott's group's activities expanded to include collaboration with poets, actors, and dancers, instruction programs for children, and support for radical community groups, they changed their name to the Underground Musicians Association, and still later, Union of God's Musicians and Artists Ascension (UGMAA). By declaring themselves to be "underground," Tapscott's group referenced the Underground Railway:

the network of slaves, free Blacks, and abolitionists who worked together to enable slaves to flee to freedom before the Civil War. The name also evoked memories of those enslaved Africans in Georgia and Alabama in the 1850s who sought freedom by a different route, by going underground literally, hiding in holes dug in the earth by day, and then coming out at night to forage for food. Some slave children were born in these underground dwellings and never saw daylight until emancipation.[10] The word "underground" also connotes countercultural space and covert resistance against superior power. The name *Union of God's Musicians and Artists Ascension* evoked allusions to important institutional spaces in Black communities that owned their own buildings, institutions like trade unions, fraternal orders, and sanctified churches.[11]

The term "arkestra" associated the orchestra with the mission of Noah's ark, which Tapscott described as an enclosed space that went somewhere to help save part of the world. His pun also borrowed from the "Arkestra" of jazz musician Sun Ra, another cultural worker who attempted to change the scale of racialized space by presenting himself (often convincingly) as a traveler through time from his home on the planet Saturn.[12] Tapscott derived the spelling of the name for his group from Sun Ra, but explained "while he [Sun Ra] was thinking in terms of space, of an ark traveling through space, I was thinking in terms of a cultural safe house for the music."[13]

In fashioning the spatial metaphor of a cultural safe house, Tapscott drew upon a rich personal and collective history. In his early years in Houston, his mother made a public cultural site out of the tiny shotgun house the Tapscott family occupied at 2719 Dowling in Houston's segregated Third Ward (a street and neighborhood discussed more fully in Chapter 6).[14] Mary Tapscott placed the family piano right across the front door of the house, requesting guests to play a tune on the instrument before they entered the dwelling.[15] The family moved from Houston to Los Angeles in 1943, when Horace's father, Robert Tapscott, secured wartime employment in the San Pedro shipyards. Mary Tapscott and her son traveled west by train. Upon reaching their destination, Tapscott's mother hailed a taxicab and instructed the driver to take them immediately to Harry Southard's barbershop on the corner of Central Avenue and Fifty-Second Street. She had selected Southard, a barber but also a trombonist, to be young Horace's music teacher. Tapscott later mused, "We hadn't got to the house yet, I don't know where I live. And before we get there, I'm introduced to my music teacher."[16]

As a teenager in Los Angeles in the late 1940s, Tapscott helped create his first cultural "safe house." At that time, the local symphony orchestras and recording studios excluded Black musicians from employment, claiming that none of them had the musical skills required for such demanding assignments. Black and white musicians held memberships in separate segregated local unions. The local for whites monopolized almost all of the best-paying jobs. To challenge these practices, a group of Black and white musicians worked together to found the Community Symphony Orchestra, also known as the Humanist Orchestra. The CSO rehearsed together as a group and played some concerts, but its main purpose was to attack segregation by creating a new kind of space, a place where players of different races could work together and share ideas, information, and skills in order to desegregate the unions, symphony orchestras, and recording studios.[17] Another effort to circumvent the music industry and gatekeepers from the arts establishment came from Buddy Collette and Bill Green, who organized weekly jam sessions at the Crystal Tea Room at Avalon and 50th Street to help jazz musicians develop their skills. Future Arkestra members Walter Benton, Ernest Crawford, and Sweetpea Robinson attended these sessions regularly.[18]

Tapscott's desire for a cultural "safe house" also grew logically out of the complicated politics of place that African Americans confronted on the streets of Los Angeles. Racial zoning, restrictive covenants, mortgage redlining, steering by real estate brokers, and direct discrimination by sellers and landlords confined African Americans to segregated neighborhoods and an artificially constricted housing market. This system relied on violence for its perpetuation.[19] Hate crimes by individuals, mob attacks on the houses and bodies of people attempting to cross the color line, and police brutality worked in concert to make public space dangerous for African Americans. In Los Angeles, the twin legacies of restrictive covenants and racialized policing continued to shape the moral geography of the city for African Americans in the 1960s.[20] Tapscott later remembered the 1960s and 1970s as a time when "the police would come through a neighborhood and just tear it up," noting, "You'd have to get off the street. You couldn't just be walking. Because the white policeman would call you 'nigger' and shoot you."[21]

Yet streets shaped by segregation could also function as sites for congregation.[22] Sites for self-activity such as cultural safe houses could serve as places for preserving, honing, and refining the resources of the street free from white surveillance and control. Tapscott valued the vibrant and dynamic street life along busy Central Avenue in the 1940s, considering it a key source of inspiration for his art.[23] He developed rhythms based on the ways that different people walked. He heard musical notes in people's voices and street sounds. He drew inspiration from the ferocious theatricality and exuberant festivity of urban crowds.[24] Whiling away minutes and hours sitting on the stoop in front of the two-story house on Central Avenue that served as the headquarters for the segregated Black local of the Musicians Union, Tapscott constantly encountered members of an older generation eager to share their experiences and opinions. "How many mentors you'd have in a day was impossible to count," he noted in retrospect. "They'd be telling us about being musicians, about life, about dealing with segregation and racism."[25] When his mother and sister offered him money from their savings so that he could matriculate at the prestigious Julliard School of Music in New York, Tapscott refused their offers (and Julliard's letter of acceptance) because he felt that he was already "attending" the best school for him: "SWU—Sidewalk University, because these cats would be on your case all the time."[26]

The Pan Afrikan People's Arkestra collected music from the streets, orchestrated it according to their own ideas, rehearsed it in safe spaces, and then brought it back out to the streets again to diverse performance venues. After their first few months of jam sessions, writing, and rehearsals at Linda Hill's house, the Arkestra decided to bring the music outside, to the otherwise unused bandstand at nearby South Park. Although the musicians' union and municipal cultural institutions in Los Angeles frequently sponsored concerts in parks, they had never invited Black groups to play, and never staged performances in Black neighborhoods. The Pan Afrikan People's Arkestra invited themselves to fill this void, playing for free at South Park on weekends. At first, the members of the Arkestra outnumbered the audience, but the quality of their playing soon attracted crowds. The park supervisor found an old piano in storage, had it tuned up, and brought it out to the bandstand. Actors and poets just seemed to appear and participate in the performances, presenting skits and spoken-word art about life in the community—especially about police harassment and brutality. Without any advertising or publicity in newspapers, on radio, or on television, members of the community found out about the Arkestra and adopted it as their own. In response, however, Los Angeles Police Department officers cracked down. They charged Tapscott and his musicians with the crime of using park facilities without a permit. Performers and audience members routinely discovered parking tickets on their cars after the concerts. Many were subjected to traffic stops and questioning by officers about alleged outstanding parking tickets and bench warrants.[27]

Unable to secure its space in the park, the Arkestra tried to reach the community by other means. They performed in housing projects, prisons, recreation halls, schools, and on street corners.[28] They "backed up" prizefighting champion and Vietnam War draft resister Muhammad Ali when he spoke to a crowd at the intersection of Fifty-Sixth Street and Broadway.[29] During one street corner performance, Tapscott noticed a flatbed truck parked nearby. He found the owner, asked permission to borrow the vehicle, and soon had the entire Arkestra playing on the back. They drove through different neighborhoods, stopping periodically to allow for impromptu dancing in the street by surprised but delighted pedestrians who waved their arms in approval.[30]

Tapscott cultivated an intimate relationship between his musicians and their audiences. Sometimes he would introduce songs the band was to play without giving them titles, saying merely, "This is one more you wrote through us."[31] Rather than seeking approval from critics, nightclub owners, or record company executives, Tapscott sought to integrate his orchestra into the active life and mixed-use spaces of the community. "Man, I don't get comfortable playing until I hear a baby cry," he once confided to Kafi Roberts.[32] Tapscott drew particular gratification from an incident that took place one day when the band was unable to conduct its daily rehearsal at Linda Hill's house. An inebriated street person evidently noticed the silence that replaced the usual sounds coming from the dwelling. He ambled up to Tapscott and asked, "Hey, man where's our band?" This was a band he had heard, but never seen. Yet he described it as "our" band. Tapscott felt a peculiar validation in this description. It gratified him tremendously that rehearsals of innovative music very different from what was played on the radio, composed by and played for the musicians themselves, did not strike people within hearing distance as a community nuisance, but rather as a community resource. It mattered to Tapscott that the man said "our band" rather than "your band."[33]

Performing under unusual circumstances in unusual spaces gave the members of the Arkestra an expanded notion of art. It enabled them to see powerful links between Black culture and the Black community. It encouraged them to fashion new forms of artistic and social practice.[34] Dadsi Sanyika later recalled, "The idea was that African people or black people don't know who they are and they can't travel to the Pan-African world. So we were going to gather the fragments together, so that when they came into the center, they could experience themselves in different phases of the culture, gospel stuff, rhythm and blues, jazz, the poetry, African Stuff, Caribbean things. It was a whole idea of gathering the culture, gathering the culture together."[35]

Like many other artists, intellectuals, and activists of the mid-twentieth century, the Arkestra's hopes for a more democratic and egalitarian society motivated them to imagine a more egalitarian and democratic understanding of the arts: not so much "community-based art making" as "art-based community making." They experimented with forms of expressive culture that enacted the kinds of social relations they envisioned.[36] Yet they also responded to concrete imperatives emanating from the realities of racialized space. The vibrant jazz scene that dominated Central Avenue in Los Angeles during the 1940s disappeared in the 1950s, a victim of police repression, urban renewal, suburbanization, and repressive licensing laws deployed to close down public spaces where Blacks and whites might mingle. Like the Association for the Advancement of Creative Musicians collective in Chicago chronicled by George Lewis in his magnificent book *A Power Stronger Than Itself*, Tapscott and other Black musicians in Los Angeles confronted a sharp decline in live music venues where they could play in the 1950s and 1960s.[37] The Arkestra enabled these musicians to turn disadvantage to their advantage. They enjoyed getting away from the standard playlists and loud conversations they encountered in nightclubs. They relished stretching out beyond the limits of short songs and short sets designed to encourage patrons to buy more drinks. Rather than playing music merely for their own amusement or performing it in commercial venues they did not control, they began to envision a new kind of cultural politics, especially in respect to changing relations among musicians and between the musicians and their audiences. Tapscott encouraged his flock to think of their work as "contributive rather than competitive," to make decisions collectively, to respect decisions reached by the entire group, to embrace unconventional musical lineups (at one time his ensemble had five bass players and four drummers), and to write music that spoke to the aspirations and experiences of the community.[38]

Tapscott also tried to encourage interpersonal behavior congruent with the group's musical philosophy. "We watched each other's back and took care of each other as a group," he remembers, emphasizing, "Everywhere we went, the whole group would be with me." They committed perhaps the ultimate spatial transgression in Los Angeles—riding together in cars in groups of four or five rather than following the one car/one driver pattern so common in the city. "That became intimidating to the point where we were called a gang or a 'perversion against the country,'" he recalls.[39] Although they almost always received no pay for their performances and did not charge admission to the audience, the Arkestra rehearsed for their appearances and performed at the level they would if they were playing for pay. "There was no such thing as practice," Kamau Daaood recalls; every time they played, they tried to play well.[40] Some events at the Watts Happening Coffee House asked patrons to pay an admission "fee," by bringing canned goods to the performance. "People would come in with a can of beans," Tapscott recalls. "And somebody else would be happy because they'd have something to eat that day. And we'd take it to them personally after the concert. The community started functioning."[41]

The Pan Afrikan People's Arkestra became the Underground Musicians Association, using another spatial metaphor to describe themselves.[42] Tapscott explains that "because the music we played wasn't accepted on top of the ground, we just separated ourselves." That separation entailed more than music, however. It extended to departing from older ways of knowing and developing new approaches to education, theater, and politics.[43] Linda Hill offered important leadership as the group transformed itself. She recruited members to assist her in devising a unique pedagogy to teach children how to read, write, and spell. Hill had first met Tapscott while she was working as a nurse at General Hospital helping administer treatment to the musician for his painful kidney stones. She had never studied music, but had always wanted to learn. Tapscott soon recognized her as a person of extraordinary talent. He taught her to play the piano, to write music, and to bring her pedagogical and social vision to the broader community. Hill developed a theory of teaching based on the idea that learning could take place in many different ways. She constructed a curriculum and pedagogy especially for students diagnosed by the school system as slow learners, encouraging them to develop skills in music and art that could then be applied later to learning reading, writing, and spelling.[44] The UGMAA regularly enlisted children as participants in musical events, rather than as mere listeners. Bass player Eddie Mathias decided to start what he called the Flute Society. He obtained several boxes of wooden flutes, and passed them out to school children so they could play along with the band, especially on the Linda Hill composition "Children."[45]

Playwright and director Cecil Rhodes explored new frontiers in theater in collaboration with the UGMAA, instructing actors to improvise lines and facial expressions in response to particular chord progressions played by the musicians.[46] A distinct spatial imaginary shaped new relations between artists and audiences. Tapscott believed that the UGMAA could reach the younger generation and have credibility with them only if it shared the spaces in which they lived. He remembered that when he was growing up, he respected the authority figures in his neighborhood, especially the teachers whose homes he could visit because they lived nearby and to whom he could pose questions when he encountered them in the grocery store. Looking back later on the influence that his own efforts with the Arkestra and UGMAA had on young people, Tapscott emphasizes, "We didn't just give them a big speech and then leave." [47] Tapscott's strategy revolved around shrinking the scale of space. Just as he had come off the road with the Lionel Hampton band to set up shop in Los Angeles, he urged other musicians to devote their efforts to community projects rather than to tours and recordings. As Daniel Widener notes astutely, "Forays outward were conceived as threatening aesthetic stagnation, penury, and racist hostility."[48] Tapscott invited successful African Americans who no longer lived in the ghetto to come back to the community. Children attending UGMAA workshops learned acting from the great film star and Shakespearean actor William Marshall, music from Rahsaan Roland Kirk, and poetry from Jayne Cortez. Marla Gibbs helped set up the UGMAA Foundation and the Sisters of Music, a women's group that helped produce events.[49] Bass player (and supremely successful studio session player) Red Callender frequently donated his services to the group.[50] When

Sun Ra and his Arkestra came to Los Angeles in 1971, they performed at the J. P. Widney Junior High School, where the UGMAA played on the last Sunday of every month.[51] For eight years the group gave regular performances at the Immanuel United Church of Christ.[52]

It meant a great deal to Tapscott that successful artists known all over the nation and the world demonstrated that they were willing to spend time in and with the community. He thought it would build the confidence of young people and help the artists as well. "If you're really thinking of trying to help the community," he reasoned, "you can't just jump into it. You have to really figure it out and it's not easy."[53] He felt confirmed in his beliefs when he witnessed the ways the young people in the community treated him and his musicians. He recalled that he could park his car in crime-ravaged neighborhoods, leave his keys in the ignition with the windows rolled down, and store his equipment on the back seat. Nobody stole anything from the car, he claims, because "the youngsters out there knew whose car it was, that it belonged to one of the band."[54] Musician Tommy Trujillo recalls that he always felt safe leaving his guitar and amplifier in his car, because people in the neighborhood knew who he was and what he did in the community.[55]

Living and working in small spaces within the Black community compelled Tapscott and the other members of the UGMAA to devise new artistic practices and principles, but the pervasive presence of active movements for social change gave those activities distinct political significance. In the wake of the 1965 Watts Riot and the rise of the local Civil Rights and Black Power movements, closeness to the community meant dealing directly with political issues. UGMAA members played at events supporting Black political prisoners Angela Davis and Geronimo Ji-ga Pratt, as well as at rallies featuring Bobby Seale and H. Rap Brown.[56] In typically nonsectarian fashion, the UGMAA supported any group they deemed committed to the community, including both the Black Panther Party and their bitter rivals, Maulana Karenga's US organization.[57] Percussionist E. W. Wainwright recalls, "We involved ourselves with anything that would speak to justice or talk about injustice. We did things in the park, we did concerts, we did free stuff, we did stuff for the homeless, [we took] up a collection for the homeless, and [did] fundraisers."[58]

As early as 1965, the UGMAA ran a preschool breakfast program for children in Watts, a program that later came under the purview of the Black Panther Party. Los Angeles Black Panther leader John Huggins (murdered in 1969) had participated in the UGMAA choir and enjoyed a warm relationship with Tapscott. Black Panther Party member Elaine Brown wrote and recorded an album of militant revolutionary songs, *Seize the Time*, for which Tapscott played piano, wrote the arrangements, and conducted the band.

Tapscott also arranged the music and organized a band for Brown's follow-up album, *Elaine Brown*, which contained a tribute to Jonathan Jackson (the teenaged brother of prison activist George Jackson) who died in a shoot-out with police after taking a judge hostage in an attempt to free his sibling.[59] Tapscott's composition "The Giant Is Awakened" paid tribute to the Black Power movement so effectively that community members stood up when it was played—a treatment previously accorded by Blacks to James Weldon and J. Rosamond Johnson's 1900 composition "Lift Every Voice and Sing," long considered the Black national anthem.[60]

Tapscott described the goals of the UGMAA in expressly spatial and racial terms: to depict "the lives of black people in their communities all over this country."[61] The organization's artistic and political work thrived in the racialized spaces of the Los Angeles ghetto, attracting a devoted following through its affective, intellectual, moral, and political appeal. Those very successes, however, also brought government surveillance and repression. The Federal Bureau of Investigation and the Department of Justice placed the group on their list of Black nationalist "hate groups."[62] Tapscott remembers being followed for about a year by agents driving a particular automobile every time he drove away from his house. Often when he came back home, he found two men wearing dark sunglasses and Hawaiian shirts on his doorstep waiting to question him. He took evasive action, staying away from home for long periods of time, refusing to sign his name on any document, and writing studio arrangements for other musicians under pseudonyms so that the government could not easily bring pressure against them in retaliation for Tapscott's participation in UGMAA.[63] Yet repression was not so easily avoided. In September 1972, Tapscott arranged for the Arkestra to record an album tentatively titled *Flight 17* in anticipation of a national tour sponsored by local Black arts collectives across the country. During the recording session, musicians noticed two strangers in the studio. They guessed the men might be from the musicians union or the mob. The observers never identified themselves, but when Tapscott came to the studio the next day to edit and mix the music, he saw that the part of the studio where they had been working had been set on fire, destroying everything the band had recorded. Tapscott and the other musicians suspected that the fire had been started by the two men they saw in the studio who they believed had been sent by the government to harass them.[64]

It came as no surprise to Tapscott that Black people could not really control the spaces of the Black community, that the activities of the Pan Afrikan People's Arkestra would provoke attempts at regulation and repression by those in power. For all Tapscott's talk about creating a cultural safe house, preparing Black people for their inevitably unsafe struggles over space constituted the core aim of his activity. As he ruminated shortly before his death in

1999, "We wanted our grandchildren to grow up realizing that they were not just here, that they had something to do with this country. People who were trapped in this society, mind wise, would always come to the Ark to relax, to listen, to be able to function outside, to get some more strength, so they could leave and go back into the war zone."[65]

The accumulated legacies of slavery and segregation that shaped the circumstances of Horace Tapscott's birth in Jefferson Davis Hospital in segregated Houston, Texas, manifested themselves throughout his life in the form of spatial constraints. They placed racialized limits on where he could live, work, and play, on where he could safely shop, speak, and travel. Tapscott responded with activism aimed at changing the scale of racialized space in his life by burrowing into small spaces in the Black community to carve away sites of solidarity and struggle. Retreating to those small spaces, however, did not mean disconnection from a wider world. The name "Pan Afrikan People's Arkestra" registered a desire to hear from and be in dialogue with the global African diaspora, to construct identities that looked beyond national citizenship in the United States of America. The Los Angeles ghetto included people who could provide that perspective—immigrants from Mexico and Central America, the Caribbean, and Africa, foreign students, artists, activists, and intellectuals from all over the world drawn to the "global" city of Los Angeles for personal or professional reasons. "Our concern was our particular area and black people," Tapscott recalls, "but we sympathized with peoples' struggles around the world."[66]

Immigrants, exiles, and expatriates visited the group, giving talks about the political issues that had driven them out of their native lands. One of them was Fela Kuti, soon to be one of Nigeria's most important musicians, activists, and intellectuals, who spent the 1969–1970 year in Los Angeles. Kuti performed in a nightclub owned by Black actor Bernie Hamilton by night, learning about Black nationalism by day from the spoken-word art of the Last Poets, the writings of Angela Davis and Stokely Carmichael (Kwame Ture), and conversations with Black Panther Party member Sandra Smith and her circle of friends that included actors Melvin Van Peebles and Jim Brown as well as singer Esther Phillips.[67] Because of the presence in Los Angeles of Blacks from outside the United States, newspapers and magazines from all over the world were scattered around Tapscott's organizations' meeting and rehearsal spaces. This global perspective encouraged the group's members to recognize racism as a global as well as a national project, to see that around the world the power of racism had intimate connections with forms of empire and exploitation that did not only concern Blacks. This critical cosmopolitanism helped build a sense of purpose and purchase on a wider world. "We were always up on what was going on in the world that had to do with any person, black or not, who was subjected to being a work hog," Tapscott remembered proudly.[68] Tapscott and his group traveled a great distance together, simply by staying home. By concentrating initially on race in one small space, they found their way eventually to seeing racism as part of a larger set of interrelated problems. By embracing work inside a small bounded locality, they ultimately came to see themselves as part of a wider world. Yet their optic on that wider world came from and remained loyal to the spaces they knew in Black Los Angeles.

Tapscott's politicized art was in many ways a response to the 1965 Watts Rebellion, an event that compelled him and other artists to produce new kinds of cultural ideas and practices. One event can often make a huge difference in the life of an individual, a community, or a society. Philosopher Alain Badiou contends that some events are so powerful that they force a decisive break with the past, requiring people to develop new ways of knowing, thinking, and being. These events make established meanings obsolete. They overthrow the authority of knowledge as it is currently constituted. They enable people "to exceed their own being" and perceive a new future that becomes possible only from the perspective of the galvanizing event. Badiou argues that particularly important advances occur from events that reveal "how injustices are not marginal malfunctioning but pertain to the very structure of the system."[69] The Watts Rebellion of 1965 was one of those turning points from which there was no turning back. A seemingly routine traffic stop of a Black motorist by white California Highway Patrol officers on August 11 rapidly escalated into a massive insurrection. Rioters broke into stores and looted their inventories. They set buildings on fire. They pelted police officers, firefighters, and National Guard soldiers with bricks, bottles, and stones. In slightly more than five days, rioters damaged or demolished nearly six hundred buildings and an estimated two hundred million dollars worth of property. The state responded with massive and deadly force. As historian Gerald Horne establishes in his fine book *The Fire This Time*, what began as a popular uprising against the police soon turned into a police riot against the populace.[70] Fourteen thousand soldiers and fifteen hundred police officers poured into the riot area, ostensibly to protect property and restore order. They arrested four thousand people, wounded nine hundred, and killed thirty-four. More Americans died in Los Angeles during that week than died in the war in Vietnam during the same period of time. The death toll from the riot exceeded the combined number of people killed in all of the riots that had convulsed cities across the nation during the preceding year.

The fury and rage of the rebellion grew out of long-standing unaddressed tensions between law enforcement officials and Black citizens, but also from the collective, continuing, and cumulative consequences of systemic racial discrimination in housing, employment, and education. Yet while the community lashed out, it did not do so blindly. A Black-owned bank was left untouched on a block where every other building was destroyed. A furniture store owned by whites was looted and burned to the ground, but the storefront next door housing an Urban League employment project remain untouched by the rioters. Inside stores known for charging deceptively high interest rates for installment purchases, looters first demolished the establishments' credit records sections before helping themselves to the clothing, furniture, and appliances on display. The riot demolished many commercial buildings, but almost no private homes, libraries, or churches.

Contemporary observers noted that despite its destructive fury and tragic consequences, the insurrection also produced a collective sense of pride and power. A psychologist conducting interviews with riot participants found that they did not think of themselves as criminals, but as "freedom fighters liberating themselves with blood and fire." They told him that the rebellion proved that they had overcome the fears of the previous generation, which they portrayed as helpless and intimidated by white authority figures.[71] A Black journalist discerned "a certain sense of triumph" in the Black community after the riots, what she described as "a strange, hushed, secretive elation in the faces of the 'bloods.'"[72] Spoken-word artist Richard Dedeaux of the famous Watts Prophets performance group celebrated the insurrection in a piece that proclaimed that while it takes millions and trillions of watts to light up most big cities, it took only one "Watts" to light up Los Angeles.[73]

For many African American artists, the 1965 uprising compelled them to become the kinds of "subjects" Badiou describes, people changed by an event and its moral imperatives to "exceed their own being" and develop a new consciousness. Noah Purifoy maintained that he did not really become a true artist until the violence in Watts. The rebellion challenged him to think about what art might be able to accomplish for an aggrieved yet clearly insurgent community. Purifoy scavenged and salvaged materials from the riot area "while the debris was still smoldering."[74] By September, he had collected three tons of fire-molded metals, charred wood, and broken shards of glass that he molded into works of sculpture. Purifoy's Sir Watts and other pieces that he created from objects littering the streets after the conflagration conjured the material remnants of the riot's destruction into works of art that remained faithful to the event while calling for a different future. The violence of the Watts Rebellion forged the very materials that Purifoy used to construct Sir Watts. Long after the rebellion had ended, the smells of burnt wood and metal could be discerned in his assemblage. "Assemblage provided a map for where the people of America could go if they had the courage of their dreams," he explained.[75]

David Hammons offered his own rendition of America in the midst of the riots in his 1970 work *Injustice Case*. "Buildings were burning," he recalls, explaining that the rebellion led him to juxtapose depictions of Black people against the American flag. He rubbed margarine and powder on his body and crawled on paper to make images of gagged, hanging, and mutilated Black men bordered by evocations of the flag. As the grease and powder evaporate and fade, these Black bodies disappear from Hammons' art just as Black bodies disappear in U.S. society because of premature death, mass incarceration, and marginalization.[76]

The violence of the Watts rebellion was destructive and tragic, but it also exposed the routine violence of the ghetto's very existence: the violence of brutal police occupation, overcrowding, hunger pangs, and the internalized aggression promoted by the social death that segregation imposed on its victims. In Los Angeles, restrictive covenants, mortgage redlining, direct discrimination, and mob violence confined African Americans to overcrowded neighborhoods in a tiny part of the huge metropolitan area. Aggressive police practices protected these physical boundaries, routinely exposing Black citizens to traffic stops, groundless arrests, and brutality whenever they ventured into white areas. Deliberate and overt school segregation skewed educational opportunities along racial lines while employment discrimination reserved high-paying jobs for whites. City, county, and state officials followed segregated residential patterns in drawing electoral district lines, minimizing the political power of Blacks while guaranteeing overrepresentation to whites.

The same power imbalances that prevented Blacks from achieving political representation also impeded cultural and artistic representation. Film and recording studios, the segregated white musicians' union, conservatories, museums, educators, and journalists all routinely excluded Blacks from meaningful participation in the city's cultural industries and its other image-making and meaning-making apparatuses. Local newspapers almost never published pictures of African Americans; they rarely even reported on the acts of Black individuals unless they were criminals wanted for offenses against whites. In the 1930s, a group of radical Los Angeles artists created portable mural panels in support of the Scottsboro Boys, a group of Black men falsely accused and wrongly imprisoned for the alleged rape of two white women in Alabama. The artists planned to exhibit their paintings in Barnsdall Art Park in East Hollywood. Los Angeles Police Department officers intervened, however, seizing the panels the night before the exhibit was to open, and returning them several days later filled with bullet holes.[77] Sculptor Beulah Woodard broke the color barrier when she secured the first exhibition by a Black artist in the county museum of art in 1935, but newspaper reviewers dismissed her display of African-themed masks and sculpted heads as a collection of bizarre artifacts that did not deserve to be called art.[78] Woodard helped establish the Los Angeles Negro Art Association, which was invited to mount an exhibition at the Stendahl Gallery. When they arrived at the scene, however, the Black artists discovered that their exhibit would be on the gallery's back patio, not its main exhibition space.[79]

The visual art that emerged out of the Watts Rebellion could not erase this history, but it could confront it and transform it. Betye Saar, John Outterbridge, Noah Purifoy, Judson Powell, Charles Dickson, Charles White, Curtis Tann, and others produced works of art capable of registering the enormity of the event, not just as the destruction of a part of the past, but also as the first step in creating a new future. With creativity and sophistication, they aimed to produce an art that acknowledged the hurts of history but was not defeated by them. Their art helped prepare Black people to become what Toni Cade Bambara describes as being unavailable for servitude. This emergence of this art was an event in itself. It drew upon what Jacques Ranciere calls "the properties of spaces and the possibilities of time" to create physical objects that expressed new sense perceptions and encouraged new forms of political consciousness.[80]

In 1992, another insurrection broke out in response to the acquittal of the police officers who had been caught on videotape brutalizing motorist Rodney King. During the 1980s, the combined pressures of deindustrialization, capital flight, computer-generated automation, outsourcing, economic restructuring, the repudiation of the civil rights revolution, and massive incarceration devastated Black Los Angeles. The 1992 rebellion added to that damage. Rioting damaged and destroyed some twelve hundred buildings worth more than a billion dollars. Seventeen thousand people were arrested, two thousand were injured, and fifty-two were killed.[81] Yet these devastating events also motivated Tapscott, Daaood, Higgins, and other Black artists and activists to create the World Stage as a place of their own, as a visible archive of all they had learned from what they had experienced. Just as the 1965 rebellion produced a new flow of creative Black expressive culture, the events of 1992 brought forth people in Leimert Park eager to testify about what they knew. "All of a sudden things started happening here," singer Dwight Tribble recalls. "It seemed like it happened overnight."[82] Artists set up studios in neighborhood homes and apartments, and entrepreneurs opened new dance studios, record shops, clothing stores, nightclubs, and galleries. Ben Caldwell started the KAOS Network to teach filmmaking and Project Blowed to promote hip-hop artistry among young people. The World Stage became an important place for arts and education, which it remains to this day.[83] Through its everyday functions as an arts center, through the educational work that it does on its Web site (http://www.theworldstage.org), through the recorded music and videos made on site over the years, and through second-ary accounts of its origins and evolution in books by Horace Tapscott, Steven L. Isoardi, Daniel Widener, and Joao Costa Vargas, the World Stage is a place that does important work in the world as a repository of collective memory, a site of moral instruction, and a visible archive of past struggles and their still unmet demands for justice.[84]

6

John Biggers and
Project Row Houses in Houston

Either the oppressed continuously struggle in forms
of their own choosing or they are defeated by life.
Only they can know what they can and must do.
—GEORGE P. RAWICK

Just as the history of struggles over racialized space in Los Angeles led to
the creation of the World Stage as a visible archive of collective memory
and a prominent mechanism for collective struggle, Project Row Houses
in Houston came into existence in the context of a long history. Perhaps the
best place to start that history is on Dowling Street in Houston's Third Ward
on a summer evening in 1970. On July 26 of that year, Carl Hampton spoke
to a crowd of about one hundred people. Although only twenty-one years
old, Hampton had emerged as an important political force in the city's Black
community. After a sojourn in Oakland, California, where he witnessed the
Black Panther Party's efforts to "serve the people" through free breakfast programs for children and through patrols that monitored and challenged police
misconduct, Hampton started the People's Party II in Houston. He directed
the group's efforts to feed and clothe poor people in the Third Ward from
the party's headquarters in the 2800 block of Dowling (one block from the
site of Horace Tapscott's boyhood home, discussed in Chapter 5). The material deprivation of Black people loomed large in shaping Hampton's politics.
"If black people did not live in substandard housing, poor conditions, or suffer all the other unequal indignities," he declared, "there would be no People's Party II."[1]

The impromptu rally on July 26 offered Hampton an opportunity to tell
the community about the arrests of two organizers and to ask for help in raising bail. These rallies had become frequent occurrences on Dowling Street
ever since an incident ten days previous when Hampton encountered two

uniformed police officers attempting to prevent a young man from selling the Black Panther Party newspaper on the street outside the People's Party II headquarters. When Hampton attempted to converse with the officers, they noticed the unconcealed .45 caliber automatic pistol outside his shirt in a holster strapped across his shoulder. Although it was completely legal to carry a weapon in public in Texas at that time, the officer challenged Hampton about his gun. When the Black militant replied that he had a constitutional right to bear arms, the officer reached for his own gun. Aware of the wave of police shootings of Black militants and ordinary Black citizens in recent years, Hampton drew his weapon from his holster in self-defense. Two members of the People's Party II emerged from the headquarters carrying weapons. The police officers sent in a call by radio for other officers to assist them at the scene. Hampton and the other party members retreated to the headquarters, barricading themselves inside. Police reinforcements rushed to the scene. Fearing assassination, Hampton refused to surrender. Fearing a mass insurrection, the police declined to open fire.

For the next ten days, the police and the People's Party II found themselves locked in an uneasy standoff. On one occasion, as many as thirty police cars with sirens blaring rushed down Dowling Street to party headquarters, but a crowd estimated at more than two thousand people surrounded the building and forced the officers to retreat.[2] A warrant had been issued for Hampton's arrest, but the police had not yet found a way to take him into custody. For his part, Hampton made no attempt to flee, but instead placed his safety in the hands of the community that he hoped would protect him.

As Hampton spoke to the crowd on July 26, sharpshooters affiliated with the Houston Police Department's Central Intelligence Division perched behind the parapet on the top of St. John's Baptist Church across the street. They carried high-powered rifles with telescopic night vision scopes. An informant able to verify Hampton's identity accompanied them. As Hampton spoke to the crowd, the police opened fire, shooting Hampton several times in the chest and stomach with hollow-point dumdum bullets. A woman in the crowd hustled the People's Party II leader into her automobile and took him to a hospital, where he died early the next morning. Police bullets struck three other people on the street. Officers arrested some sixty people at the scene. Police spokespersons claimed that the officers on top of the church had been fired upon from the crowd below and were merely defending themselves. Representatives of the Peoples Party II and other Black organizations described the killing of Carl Hampton as an assassination.[3]

Carl Hampton died on Dowling Street, a ghetto thoroughfare named after an Irish immigrant who had become a Confederate general and a Texas hero in the war to destroy the Union and preserve slavery. The Peoples Party

II located its headquarters on a block that seemed to them to represent all the ills of the racialized space of the ghetto: dilapidated housing, streets that needed paving, inadequate bus service, inefficient storm drains, garbage that sat uncollected, and police harassment of ordinary citizens while drug dealers, pimps, gamblers, and gunrunners conducted their business unimpeded. These conditions in the ghetto were not created by ghetto residents themselves, but rather stemmed from decades of discriminatory land-use practices ranging from restrictive covenants and mortgage redlining to steering and blockbusting by real estate brokers, from a city government that collected taxes from Black people but routinely shortchanged them on city services to a police department that behaved more like an occupying army protecting white property than as a force for protecting the safety and security of neighborhood residents.

During the 1930s, relatively equal numbers of Blacks and whites lived in the Third Ward. Between 1945 and 1965, however, the neighborhood became almost entirely Black. The expressly racist preferences given to whites by the Home Owners Loan Corporation and the Federal Housing Administration and the ban on state enforcement of restrictive covenants declared by the Supreme Court's decision in *Shelley v. Kraemer* enabled Jewish American and other white residents of the ward to move west and southwest into new exclusively white suburbs.[4] By 1950, nearly 70 percent of Blacks in Houston lived in the Third, Fourth, and Fifth Wards.[5] Racialized space so marked the identities of these places that even when charter reform dissolved the ward system as the unit of political representation, Houston's Black neighborhoods retained their ward names in a way that was never true of formerly white wards. The designation of Third, Fourth, or Fifth Ward marked a certain kind of Blackness: the Third Ward of Dowling Street and Texas Southern University, the Fourth Ward of Gray Avenue and Allen Parkway Village, and the Fifth Ward of Lyons Avenue and Louisiana Creole social clubs and churches.[6] All the Black wards suffered from municipal neglect. Residents of Andrews Street in the Fourth Ward, for example, decided to buy their own bricks and lay them by hand in the dirt road that divided their houses because the city would not pave the street on its own.[7]

The city exacerbated an already artificially constricted housing market for the city's Black population by demolishing the eastern third of the Fourth Ward during the 1950s in order to clear land for the construction of the Gulf Freeway.[8] Building the I-10 Freeway inflicted similar devastation on the Lyons Avenue business district in the Fifth Ward. Booker T. Caldwell ran a custom tailoring business in the Fifth Ward near Don Robey's Bronze Peacock nightclub on Lyons Avenue, but found himself forced to move to the Third Ward near the El Dorado ballroom on Dowling Street when the Lyons

Avenue neighborhood became bisected by the freeway. Some residents of the Third Ward in 1970 were doubly displaced, having moved there in the first place only after having been driven out of the Fifth Ward because of the construction of the I-10 Freeway, after having been displaced previously from the Fourth Ward because of the construction of the Gulf Freeway.[9]

In the year that Carl Hampton was killed, more than 90 percent of Houston's Black residents lived in Black majority neighborhoods.[10] Although the city prided itself on the absence of zoning control over land use, in fact, private deed restrictions covered most of the white residential areas, locking out nuisances and hazards that then were located in minority neighborhoods. City officials had a moment of panic about these zoning practices in the late 1960s when the federal government tried to create fair housing opportunities through the subsidized 236 housing program. Houston officials recognized that the lack of local zoning regulations might enable subsidized housing available to Blacks to be placed in white neighborhoods. To prevent this outcome, the city council passed a resolution that created an unprecedented system of land-use review that required "neighborhood analysis committees" to approve any subsidized housing projects. Municipal officials in Houston, who had long celebrated the lack of zoning as the key to the city's prosperity, finally found a zoning practice they liked, because it was one that enabled them to subvert the promises of fair housing proclaimed as a vital national interest in the 1968 federal Fair Housing Act. As Richard Babcock noted in the journal *Planning*, "Houston managed to practice exclusionary zoning even without a zoning ordinance."[11]

Discriminatory land-use policies made Dowling Street very different on the day that Carl Hampton was killed than it had been in the past. Memorialized in the song "I Was on Dowling Street" by the great blues guitarist and singer Lightnin' Hopkins with lyrics that described the thoroughfare sardonically as "a nice place to go to get an education," Dowling Street was once a bustling thoroughfare in a vibrant community.[12] Patrons flocked to the upscale El Dorado ballroom on the corner of Elgin and Dowling to dance to the music of jazz and blues musicians. The ballroom featured a downstairs restaurant and close proximity to the corner liquor store where customers could purchase bottles they brought into the club in brown paper bags because the establishment did not have its own liquor license. Street-level businesses in the El Dorado building and nearby included a drugstore, an appliance store, a shoe-shine parlor, a photography studio, a clothing store, and a custom tailor.[13] Lightnin' Hopkins sometimes played at the El Dorado, but he also turned all of Dowling Street into his own personal entertainment venue. Hopkins routinely boarded the buses that cruised up and down Dowling Street, playing for the passengers and collecting tips from them. Several of the bus drivers liked his music so much that they let him ride for free. One driver even made unscheduled stops at liquor stores so Hopkins could spend his tip money on whiskey that helped him keep playing. According to Hopkins, passengers frequently got up and danced in the center aisle of the bus when he played. Sometimes they would ride past their stops because they did not want to get off the bus and leave the party.[14]

Houston Blacks turned segregation into festive congregation on Dowling Street and other ghetto thoroughfares, but they suffered terribly from the ways in which freeway construction and other civic projects constantly compelled them to move, disrupting social, political, and personal networks, lowering property values, and undermining successful business establishments. Overcrowding proved to be an especially nettling consequence of the artificially constricted housing market. As early as the 1930s, Houston's Fourth Ward housed one of the highest population densities in the nation, nearly six times the national average. In a city with very few apartment houses and many single-family dwellings, one of the key mechanisms enabling this population density was the shotgun house. Blacks in Houston first built shotgun houses after the civil war in the Fourth Ward area known as Freedman's Town in celebration of the end of slavery. Black people who had been designated *as* property before emancipation owned very little property after it. The shotgun house was both a sign of material deprivation and an ingenious strategy to combat it. Often measuring no more than six hundred square feet, the typical shotgun home was one room wide and two or three rooms deep, with no hallways and the front and back doors aligned. Faced with the high costs of land and materials, emancipated African Americans built these narrow dwellings on small plots of land using a traditional form of African-influenced architecture common to the slave south and the Caribbean.[15] People in Houston often say that these buildings were called shotgun houses because their size and shape made it possible to fire a shotgun through the front door and see the shot exit through the back door without leaving a mark on the inside. Yet the name may actually stem from the word *shogun*, which in West Africa means "God's house."

Shotgun houses make efficient use of small spaces and sparse materials. They work well in Houston's hot and humid climate because with both doors open a breeze can blow through the entire house. They also compensate, however, for the limited space available for Black settlement by promoting and enabling population density. Local residents sometimes joked about the proximity of these homes to one another, as when the editor of the *Houston Informer* newspaper wrote that residents of shotgun houses could sit in their homes and actually hear their next door neighbors changing their minds.[16] Yet density also promoted mutual recognition and conversation. Porches close to sidewalks served as ideal gathering spots for conversation. The uniform design of the houses emphasized the unity of their inhabitants as people who not only lived in their own individual dwellings, but also shared a neighborhood and a community.

Although shaped by the harsh realities of discrimination and exclusion, shotgun houses promoted egalitarian solidarity and inclusion. Horace Tapscott remembers the Third Ward of his 1930s childhood as a place where neighbors helped guide and mentor each other's children, where many different kinds of family configurations could connect with community networks of instruction, discipline, affection, and apprenticeship.[17] Part of Tapscott's efforts as an adult (discussed in Chapter 5) to create a band in which musicians could be "contributive rather than competitive" stemmed from the sense of solidarity he learned in Houston neighborhoods dotted with shotgun houses. He recalls that people who lived in these houses had specific ways of doing things. When he started school in Houston with his neighborhood friends, Tapscott observes, "We had to learn things in groups. They gave us the feeling of always working together with someone, that you could do things much better with someone else, and that you could trust the person you were working with."[18]

The brilliant work of Robert Farris Thompson enables us to see how the shotgun houses themselves played a role in promoting that sense of solidarity. Thompson's studies reveal that shotgun houses functioned not merely as dwellings or investments, but also as sites of cultural creation and moral instruction. A block of row houses might appear to the casual observer as identical, undifferentiated, and uniform—like the brownstone row houses in Paule Marshall's novel about Brooklyn, *Brown Girl, Brownstones* (discussed in Chapter 7). Yet the solidarities of sameness engendered by the row house also allow for dynamics of difference, for individual improvisation, ornamentation, and expression. Thompson notes that residents of shotgun houses place jugs, jars, baskets, and pots by their doors, adorn trees and porches with bottles, and fasten mirrors and shiny metal objects to outside walls. Yard artists surround plants with tires and wheels, and dot their lawns with spinning pinwheels and figurative icons. Thompson argues that, like the shotgun house itself, these decorative arts reflect the enduring presence of the African and slave past in present-day Black life. Ornamental objects exist to do work in the world. Wheels, tires, hubcaps, and pinwheels convey the importance of motion, especially for people seemingly trapped in a ghetto. Mirrors and shiny metal objects throw back envy onto the beholder, while also conveying the "flash of the spirit," relaying communications from ancestors and symbolizing enduring connections with them. Containers at the boundary of a house or yard capture and contain evil before it can enter. Figurative sculptures, fans, and medicinal herbs protect and guard the house. In this cosmology, every problem has a solution and imbuing objects with seemingly unexpected properties increases the chances of making "right things" come to pass.[19]

John Biggers became fascinated with these shotgun houses while teaching art at Texas Southern University in Houston's Third Ward between 1949 and 1983. Biggers had been raised in a shotgun house in Gastonia, North Carolina, where he learned about racialized space at an early age. His family "medicated" their home in an African way, tying a nail to a string inside a mayonnaise jar filled with water and placing it under the doorstep. The string and the nail represented a serpent prepared to strike at anyone attempting to harm the house or its inhabitants.[20] Despite its small size, the house served as a social center for friends and relatives. Similar to Paule Marshall's remembrances of the "poets in the kitchen" (discussed in Chapter 7), later in life Biggers remembered fondly the nights when he and his brother Joe would lie on blankets and fall asleep in the front room by the fireplace as his mother and other women made quilts together. Yet Gastonia also taught him bitter lessons about race and space. Biggers's mother took in washing from white families and assigned her sons the task of delivering to her clients the clothes that she cleaned, starched, and pressed. John and Joe quickly discovered that as soon as they set foot in the white parts of town, they would be attacked by white boys armed with rocks and sticks. They learned to fend off their attackers with one arm while protecting the crisp clean laundry with the other.[21]

Teaching at Texas Southern presented Biggers with an introduction to the moral geography of race and place in Houston. The school itself came into existence through an elaborate and bizarre effort to preserve segregation. A Black man named Heman Sweatt had applied for admission to the law school at the University of Texas. The school rejected his application because of a state law prohibiting integrated schools. Sweatt sued the university, arguing that it had violated the rights promised to him by the "separate but equal" language of *Plessy v. Ferguson* by denying him access to the educational opportunities it provided routinely for whites. Rather than abandon segregation, the legislature authorized the establishment of an entire new university and law school only for Blacks. The state of Texas claimed that Sweatt could attend this school (even if he were its only student) and therefore receive an equal, if separate, education. The U.S. Supreme Court saw through the racist ruse, however, ruling in 1950 that the facilities, faculty, and social contacts available at the University of Texas Law School surpassed those that Sweatt or others would receive at a school cobbled into existence merely to preserve UT as an all-white space. In addition to a segregated law school, the college established on the site of an existing community college became a state-funded general education institution for Blacks, albeit one that never received the kinds of support that the state regularly made available to its white campuses.[22]

Working as a Black artist in a city whose cultural institutions were generally open only to whites, Biggers found himself in constant contact with the Black community. He staged one of the first public exhibits of his art work at the Hester House community center in the Fifth Ward. Commissions to create murals compelled him to think carefully about the role that works of art could play in constituting Black public space and telling the hidden histories of Black people. Reverend Fred Lee asked Biggers to paint a portrait of the minister's late wife, Dora Lee, at the YWCA building. Biggers persuaded Lee to allow him to create instead a mural celebrating the past and present accomplishments of all Black women. The emphasis in this early work on Black history, on the roles played by women in the community, and on the importance of spaces created and controlled by Black people informed many of Biggers's subsequent creations.[23]

From their location in the Third Ward, Biggers and the rest of the TSU campus community faced the challenges of racialized space every day. Students from the campus conducted eight months of sit-in demonstrations in 1960 that eventually succeeded in desegregating the lunch counters in the city's major downtown department stores.[24] In the years preceding the killing of Carl Hampton on Dowling Street, student militancy increased steadily. When an eight-year-old Black girl drowned in a landfill in the Sunnyside neighborhood southeast of downtown on May 16, 1967, TSU students participated in demonstrations protesting the city's policy of concentrating landfills and waste incinerators in Black neighborhoods.[25] These same protestors and their fellow students confronted another issue of racialized space right on campus that very evening. For several years, white male students from the nearby University of Houston amused themselves by driving their cars at high speeds down Wheeler Street and shouting racist epithets and insults at TSU students, especially women. Activists at TSU petitioned the city to close the street to through traffic, but their request was denied. On the evening of May 16, 1967, a caravan of cars proceeded down Wheeler from the UH. White drivers and passengers shouted their usual insults at Black women. This time, some TSU students responded by throwing rocks and bottles at the cars. No white students were injured, but the police department considered the actions by the TSU students to be a threat to public order. Chief of Police Herman Short sent more than thirty police vehicles to the campus. He deployed officers wearing helmets and armed with riot guns and tear gas projectiles. The police contingent included canine squads. Officer R. D. Blaylock was wounded in the thigh by a bullet that he claimed had come from a student dormitory.[26] In response, five hundred police officers fired more than three thousand rounds of carbine and shotgun fire into the men's dormitory, Lanier Hall. Officers rampaged through the building, using axes and the bolts of their shotguns to destroy students' personal property and nearly all of the 144 rooms in the building.[27] Half-dressed and undressed students were dragged from their rooms by officers and forced to lie prone on cold, wet streets with guns pointed at them. Male officers searched female students rudely and assaulted male students with clubs and rifle butts. When a bullet from a police rifle ricocheted and killed police officer Louis Kuba, five TSU students were charged with murder.[28] The charges against the students were eventually dropped, but no police officers were disciplined for their brutal and destructive attack on the campus.

Biggers's location at Texas Southern in the Third Ward exposed him to the criminal injustices of racialized space, but it also enabled him to see and appreciate how Black people creatively used the spaces to which they were consigned by discrimination and segregation. Asked to paint a mural in tribute to local NAACP activist Christa Adair in 1980, Biggers toured the Third Ward neighborhoods where she had grown up and felt himself drawn powerfully to its shotgun houses and to the community life that they sustained.[29] He felt that the women who lived in these houses possessed remarkable powers and had accomplished important things. Biggers thought of these Third Ward women as "organized women, women who, when they voted took the whole block with them."[30] The repetition of geometric forms on a block of shotgun houses made the sum greater than its parts, constituting a social aesthetic system grounded in Black visual memory.[31] The abstract interconnected patterns that linked together shotgun houses on Third Ward or Sunnyside streets evoked for Biggers the sharing of responsibility necessary for Black survival. Individual people and objects are drawn with consummate care in his art, but the full impact of his paintings and murals replies on repetitions and rhymes that make distinct objects and people cohere into a unified totality.

In a series of drawings, murals, and paintings that included the extraordinary piece *Shotguns* in 1987, Biggers places shotgun houses at the center of a linked and integrated sign system composed of material objects deployed by Africans in America to do important work in the world. In his art, washboards become ladders, houses are held like lanterns to light the way, rain soaked sidewalks become mirrors, shotgun houses appear dressed in shawls and overalls, porches and pediments fit together like textile patterns, railroad tracks signify time, motion, connections, and ruptures.[32] *Shotguns* plays with space to represent and reinforce Afro-diasporic beliefs and practices. Railroad tracks traverse a quilt placed in front of a row of five women holding miniature shotgun houses standing on their front porches. Over their heads, an alternating pattern of peaked roofs makes it appear as if these houses are standing on each other's shoulders.[33] Birds in upward flight signify spirits ascending to the heavens. As Robert Farris Thompson interprets it, the painting "illustrates numinous qualities in complex interaction; it carries us into a process, where black Creole vision takes the poetic measure of three worlds—Europe, Africa, and America—and combines them. It does this in order to make a medicine, an *nkisi*, as artistic images and charms for healing and protection are called in *Kongo*."[34]

The porch decorations, yard art, and medicated shotgun houses of the Houston ghetto inspired John Biggers to create visual art that passed on their message to a wider world, traveling to places like elite museums that the inhabitants of these houses rarely entered. Yet Biggers's art also came full circle as the inspiration for the creation of a new generation of shotgun houses. In 1992, Houston artist Rick Lowe participated in a tour of the Third Ward. His guides described the rows of shotgun houses as unsafe habitats, obsolete dwellings, and impediments to development. At first Lowe did not disagree with that assessment, even though the row of rust-colored roofs on the dwellings shining in the Houston sun struck him as exceptionally beautiful. But then Lowe thought about John Biggers's paintings. He remembered that they proceeded from very different assumptions about the shotgun house. After contacting Biggers and engaging in extensive conversations with him, Lowe came to believe that the Black spatial imaginary animating Biggers's paintings pointed the way toward new and exciting work by artists and architects. Biggers believed that successful communities possessed good architecture, lively artistic and cultural activities, democratic educational opportunities, and a strong social safety net. Moved by those ideas, Lowe set out to create "a living John Biggers painting" through Project Row Houses.

Lowe and his collaborators secured small grants that enabled them to renovate twenty-two houses near Holman and Live Oak Streets, about two blocks from Dowling Street. Following Biggers's formula for artistic activity, education, and a social safety net, the project invited artists to create installations in ten of the buildings and to turn five of them into arts education centers for neighborhood children, reserving the rest for transitional housing for single mothers. One artist distributed disposable cameras to neighborhood residents and displayed their photos in jars in a Third Ward Archive that invited viewers to write messages on the backs of the photos. Another artist created an installation aimed at airing issues of sexual abuse. Project Row Houses proceeded from the premise that art could change social relations, that expressive culture could not just cry out for change but instantiate change by creating new democratic practices and institutions.[35]

Project Row Houses provoked neighborhood participation and outside interest. Vacant lots near the houses became impromptu public parks as neighbors and artists worked together to set up benches and tables near trees where people congregated. These developments attracted the attention of speculators who viewed the activity through different eyes. Intrigued by the proximity of the Third Ward to the University of Houston and the Texas Medical Center, they viewed the emerging community as an ideal site for gentrification. They hoped to buy property cheaply, drive out the neighborhood's working-class Black inhabitants, and build and sell new housing to urban professionals. To stave off gentrification, Project Row Houses formed a nonprofit housing and community development corporation to hold down land and housing prices, move bungalows and shotgun houses from other parts of town to the Third Ward, and promote community control over neighborhood development. Consistent with the collective and community-oriented vision of the Black spatial imaginary, they realized that their success in refurbishing and rehabilitating one group of houses on one block would be undermined if they lost control of the neighborhood around it to speculators and gentrifiers. The only way to protect their success on one block was to spread the project to a larger thirty-five–block area, to build duplex rental units in addition to refurbishing shotgun houses and bungalows.

The project eventually came to control forty-seven buildings, five of them commercial spaces. In keeping with John Biggers's philosophy about the importance of creative artistic activity to a neighborhood, one of those commercial buildings was the El Dorado Ballroom located two blocks from the Row Houses on the corner of Elgin and Dowling. The El Dorado's owners donated the vacant building to the project. Artists and volunteers refurbished and reopened the ballroom with a performance on May 17, 2003, evoking nostalgic memories of its central place in Third Ward life from the 1930s through the 1970s. "The El Dorado Ballroom made us feel like we were kings and queens," blues vocalist Carolyn Blanchard recalled, adding, "We always held our heads a little higher after leaving the El Dorado."[36]

The Project Row Houses initiative contrasts sharply with the racial and spatial imaginary that has traditionally shaped development in Houston. In 1980, when the city contained nearly as many potholes (1.5 million) as people (2 million), Mayor Jim McConn announced he did not worry about how this reflected on his administration's provision of public services. Houstonians may need to have the front end of their automobiles aligned frequently because of the potholes, the mayor conceded, but lower taxes left them with enough money to pay for the repairs in his estimation. It did not appear to occur to him that this philosophy of privatism endangered public safety, wasted resources, and contributed to shredding the social safety net for the

city's most vulnerable residents.[37] Critics long complained that Houston's
aversion to planning contributed to expensive and environmentally destructive urban sprawl. One alleged that privileging development of far-flung suburbs over fill-in development in the inner city left Houston spread out "like a
spilled bucket of water." The contrast between subdivisions protected by deed
restrictions and largely unzoned and unregulated commercial strips made the
city's public spaces look to one acerbic critic like "a cluttered dime store, a
garage sale gone wrong, a leaking sewer pipe."[38] In a metropolis plagued by
the absence of planned development, a notable dearth of public parks, and
grievous racial inequality, Project Row Houses attracted considerable attention and support. Its artists built upon, but also augmented and extended, the
seemingly eccentric architecture and ornamentation traditionally associated
with the shotgun house. In the process, they created a public place guided by
a Black spatial imaginary, promoting an understanding of urban life that challenged the defensive localism and hostile privatism that prevailed historically
in the rest of the city. These artists also contested the separation between art
and life, rejecting the notion that the proper places for art are museums and
private collections. As project artist Bert Long explains in Andrew Garrison's
fine film *Third Ward TX*, "Art is life. You don't go *to* it, you're *in* it."[39]

Rick Lowe and his associates in Project Row Houses recognized that
Houston's free-market philosophy never served the needs of inner-city Blacks.
Elevating the exchange values of property over the use values of neighborhoods destroyed communities and shattered social bonds. The civic boast
that Houston was "open for business" meant complete disregard for the health
and well-being of the city's neighborhoods. Yet in fact, the city never actually practiced the free-market principles that it preached. Over the years
whites in Houston had not operated as market actors, but rather as collaborators in a racial cartel designed to monopolize wealth and amenities for
themselves while dumping the costs and burdens of development on communities of color. It was not the free market that bisected the Fifth Ward
with the I-10 Freeway or that demolished huge sections of the Fourth Ward
for the Gulf Freeway. Coordinated white political power rather than free-
market activity led white elected officials to place all five of the city-owned
landfills in Black neighborhoods and four of its five large garbage incinerators in Black neighborhoods and the fifth in a Mexican American area.[40] For
decades, whites in Houston carved out unearned advantages for themselves
by conspiring to create an artificially constrained housing market for Blacks
through antimarket actions including restrictive covenants, mortgage redlining, real estate steering, blockbusting, and direct refusal to sell or rent homes
to Blacks. The very civic boosters who celebrate the city's unregulated and
unzoned development live in private subdivisions rigorously regulated by pri-

vate deed restrictions. Owners and investors fight to maintain low tax rates on their own wealth, leaving insufficient funds available for vital city services. Yet they have no reluctance to pay fees to homeowners' associations so that they can hire private police and maintain streets and landscaping near their own property, providing for themselves services that their antitax fervor denies to others. Houstonians have kept their own taxes low, but starting in the 1970s they did so only by relying on federal funds to finance the construction of the elaborate infrastructure of roads, water and sewer conduits, and electric power grids that make dispersed (and segregated) urban settlement possible. A patchwork of special tax districts hoards resources for those who need them least, raising the costs of necessary services for those who need them most. This system is supported and sustained by acts of housing discrimination that violate laws that have been on the books for more than forty years. Testing carried out by fair-housing advocates in Houston in 2001 revealed that Latinos seeking housing encountered discrimination 65 percent of the time, while Blacks seeking shelter experienced discrimination 80 percent of the time.[41]

The success of this white racial cartel in Houston created the problems that face the Third Ward. Its residents are not simply disadvantaged, but rather taken advantage of by a complex system of racial exclusion and subordination. Art might seem like a feeble form of self-defense against this system, but in a quintessentially Afro-diasporic way, the artists of Project Row Houses have fashioned ways of turning disadvantage into advantage, of transforming humiliation into honor, of making a way out of no way. Even before the first house was refurbished, Project Row Houses was already a success. Abandoned and boarded-up shotgun houses previously provided protective cover for drug dealers and drug users, for prostitutes and their customers. Once artists started scraping, cleaning, painting, and restoring houses, they brought new attention to the area. Like Tyree Guyton's artwork on abandoned houses in Detroit in 1998 (discussed in Chapter 2), artistic activity filled the streets and sidewalks with traffic that made drug users and "johns" nervous, while bringing unwanted surveillance to dealers, pimps, and prostitutes. Of course, this would never have happened if pure free-market principles had been allowed to prevail, since the trade in drugs and sex was clearly the most profitable market activity in the neighborhood.

Resistance to market logic fueled another vital part of the work of Project Row Houses. The project's work sought to benefit the people of the Third Ward by creating art exhibitions, instructional programs for neighborhood children, impromptu parks, and transitional housing for single mothers trying to complete their college educations. When these programs proved successful, they increased property values and made the area more attractive to developers. Market logic would dictate selling the land and housing to these developers so they could create new dwellings near downtown for wealthy suburban young professionals and retired "empty nesters." Individuals might profit from these new market opportunities, but the exchanges would destroy the community. Residents working with Project Row Houses responded with a campaign encouraging community members to stay. In a frontal assault on the white spatial imaginary, they came up with a slogan that they placed on signs posted on their property: "Third Ward Is Our Home, Not for Sale." What had started out as an exercise in community-based art making had evolved into a project in art-based community making.

The activities of Project Row Houses also challenged prevailing notions of art. Rick Lowe's initial desire to make a living John Biggers painting evolved into an expanded understanding of art, which Lowe (following the German artist Joseph Beuys) described as social sculpture. Lowe had been trained initially as a landscape painter, but felt that his work in that genre "just wasn't getting it" because the stakes were too low.[42] The very practices on which the social status of art seemed to depend—its autonomy from social life, the credentialing powers of curators and critics, the money paid by collectors—now seemed to trivialize rather than ennoble artistic creation compared to a project that actually changed social conditions and social relations. Experienced artists discovered new principles from the process of working with vernacular art. Designer and planner Walter Hood worked as a visiting artist with the project. Long a distinguished and generative proponent of new approaches to social space, Hood found that working on the shotgun house reminded him of how working people recognized untapped capacities in houses that were not capacious. He remembered how as a child he witnessed his own family arrange space inside small dwellings to enable more people to live in them comfortably. Houses designed for traditional nuclear families could be suitable for extended family use with the proper imagination and ingenuity.[43]

New artistic principles also emerged from new kinds of art work. Even before Project Row Houses began, Third Ward resident Cleveland "Flower Man" Turner had already turned his home on the corner of Sampson and Francis Streets into a spectacular exhibition featuring wreaths of brightly colored flowers, sculptures made from objects rescued from the city dump, and an extraordinary spatial imagination that made his small house seem to blend seamlessly with the array of decorations Turner placed on and around it. John Biggers had described folk artists medicating their houses to keep them safe from harm. For Flower Man, working on the house had direct medicinal and curative powers. He had previously spent seventeen years living homeless on skid row. One night he had a vision of a house that was so beautifully decorated he felt he had to create it. Laboring on the building helped cure him of substance abuse and made him a neighborhood celebrity. Pointing to a house in the film *Third Ward TX*, one artist proclaims, "This stopped being nothing, and got converted into something,"[44] an observation that applies to both the artists and their creations.

Perhaps the most important part of the intervention staged by Project Row Houses is its role in strengthening the social safety net. When Rick Lowe initiated conversations with neighborhood residents about his plans to create a work of art that illustrated issues important to the Third Ward community, one youth advised him that the community already knew what the issues were. They did not need artists to teach them about conditions they confronted every day. What they needed were solutions to those problems. If artists are creative people, the youth contended, then they should solve problems, not just represent them. "That was the defining moment that pushed me out of the studio," Lowe explains. Instead of creating cut-out sculptures and billboard-size paintings about social issues, he pursued the idea that life could be a work of art, that "art can be the way people live."[45]

This challenge to create a new kind of art resonated with Lowe because it spoke to his own already well-formed inclinations about art and social life, but also because they touched on John Biggers's insistence that communities needed a strong social safety net. One of the biggest problems facing the community concerned the shortage of affordable housing and support services for single mothers. In response, the project created the Young Mothers Residential Program to provide transitional housing for single mothers attempting to complete a college education. The proximity of the houses to one another enables the YMRP to share resources including a parenting class, counseling, and the help of a "mentor mom." This program picks up on Biggers's insistence on both the strength of Black women as a community resource and on his understanding of Third Ward women as people who are organized and who do things in groups. This part of the program also advanced an innovative understanding of art. Assata Richards discovered not only that she lived in proximity to art and artists, but that in a way she had become an artist as well. She remembers wondering what kind of art Lowe created. "Then I realized we were his art," she relates, adding, "We came into these houses, and they did something to us. This became a place of transformation. That's what art does. It transforms you. And Rick also treated us like artists. He would ask, 'What's your vision for yourself?' You understood that you were supposed to be making something new, and that something was yourself."[46] The YMRP also defied the market logic of competitive individualism through its emphasis on mutuality and solidarity. The film *Third Ward TX* depicts one of these women attending her graduation ceremony at Texas Southern University. When asked if she is sad that graduation means that she now has to leave her house, the woman replies that she is happy that she can pass it on to another single mother who needs it just as she did.[47]

Project Row Houses breaks with tradition in many ways. It challenges the land-use philosophy that privileges profits over people. It views art as a vital part of the life of a community, finds value in devalued spaces, and offers alternatives to possessive individualism and competitive consumer citizenship. Yet the project also builds upon tradition, tapping into a long local history of vernacular art making and collective community building. Cleveland "Flower Man" Turner had already turned his home into a showplace long before art activists descended on the Third Ward. He drew inspiration from the art that Cortor Black had created as a yard artist in the Sunnyside area of Houston during the 1970s. Black placed pinwheels, fans, and revolving and whirring metal blades in his yard, covered the inside walls of his house with tinfoil, and transformed an old Pontiac automobile into a "light chariot" by attaching red glass lights that resembled bullets to its sides and placing clusters of chrome on its roof.[48] The provocative theatricality and persistent transgression of size and scale created by Black, Turner, and other Third Ward artists both echoed and answered prevailing aesthetic practices in commercial vernacular art and architecture outside the ghetto in Houston as well. Without zoning codes or regulations on the size and shape of signs, local highways and streets in Houston have long been places where eccentric art thrived. A giant 12-foot by 24-foot porcelain man's dress shoe lined with red neon illuminated the facade of the Houston Shoe Hospital at the corner of Kirby and Bissonet. An 8-foot-wide and 15-foot-long grand piano with 88 individual keys and white neon trim advertising the Holcombe Lindquist piano company towered over the Southwest Freeway. A 30-foot-high and 18-foot-wide orange wooden root beer barrel invited patrons to the Lucky Burger Orange Barrel at Richmond near Shepherd. Holder's Pest Control on the Southwest Freeway featured a 27-foot-long and 9-foot-wide porcelain black cockroach trimmed in white neon. At Christie's Seafood Restaurant on South Main, a sharpshooting neon shrimp wearing a Stetson hat and bandanna decorated the building, while a fiberglass crab with light bulb eyes guarded the entrance.[49]

The imagination that enabled the artists connected with Project Row Houses to *see* abandoned and dilapidated shotgun houses and perceive them as potential spaces for art exhibition, instruction, and apprenticeship, as transition housing for single mothers, and as sites of intergenerational association and mentoring also drew on local traditions. During the 1940s and 1950s, the El Dorado Ballroom served many different purposes. Its dance floor and restaurant functioned as a node in a neighborhood network of business establishments that drew people to Dowling Street, not only to shop, but also to socialize on the street, to gossip about each other and converse about social issues, to display creative mastery of new clothing styles, and to find romantic partners. Shady's Playhouse, nearby on the corner of Simmons and Sampson, catered to another clientele in equally diverse ways. A rough blues joint devoid of the flash and glamour of the El Dorado, Shady's featured small cabins behind the main building where musicians and their associates could crash for the night, help themselves to food simmering on stoves, participate in impromptu jam sessions, and receive instruction from more experienced players.[50]

Project Row Houses' novel approach to space also promotes alternative conceptions of time. In its environs, local collective memory challenges dominant understandings of history. In a city where elected officials, civic boosters, journalists, and academic historians celebrate municipal growth and progress, the Third Ward remembers what the official story forgets. In February 2008, Project Row Houses hosted a showing of *Who Killed the Fourth Ward?*—a brilliant and prophetic film made originally in Houston in the 1970s and revised in the 1980s. Directed by James Blue and Bryan Huberman, the film details the struggle by Black residents of the Allen Parkway Village housing project to save their dwellings from demolition and prevent gentrification of their Freedman's Town neighborhood. Although unjustly neglected by critics and all but ignored by people with the power to make decisions about urban space in Houston, *Who Killed the Fourth Ward?* reveals a tragic past that can become the Third Ward's future if endeavors like Project Row Houses are not successful.

A different part of that past that haunts the present motivated a new initiative among Project Row Houses supporters starting in 2008. On the thirty-eighth anniversary of the police killing of Carl Hampton, Third Ward residents assembled on Dowling Street. On a summer day when the temperature climbed to nearly 100 degrees, they surveyed the vacant lot where the People's Party II headquarters used to stand, traveled to the Golden Gate Cemetery where Hampton's body is buried, and assembled in Project Row Houses Park for a commemorative ceremony. Sensei Benton remembered Hampton as a man "who gave his life so that all could have a place to stay and clothes on their backs and good food to eat." Delineating the importance of excavating the buried history of past struggles, Benton concluded, "We don't need a monument or a symbol but some serious work in the community."[51] Some of that serious work involves Project Row Houses. In 2009 the initiative hosted and supported a community coalition commemorating Hampton's death and celebrating his life.[52]

Early in 2010 the organization posted a notice on the World Wide Web expressing its support of the Carl B. Hampton Fortieth Anniversary Memorial scheduled for Saturday, July 24, 2010. In preparation, participants and supporters began collecting archival material and film footage that might serve as the basis for an exhibit to accompany the event. On the fortieth anniversary of the shooting of Carl Hampton, Project Row Houses joined with the Carl Hampton Memorial Committee to stage an art exhibition in the ground floor spaces of the El Dorado Ballroom of historical and contemporary works of art about the Black freedom struggle. An anniversary commemoration in Emancipation Park at 3018 Dowling Street on July 24, 2010, featured speeches by distinguished academics and activists.[53]

Forty years after the death of Carl Hampton, the work he did on Dowling Street remains to be completed. Yet the neighborhood in which he lived continues to produce places and people that generate new ideas and new imaginaries. Like the World Stage in Leimert Park in Los Angeles, Project Row Houses does significant work as a site for the generation and display of art, but it also functions as a visible archive of past struggles, as a repository of collective memory, a site of moral instruction, and a vital crucible for preserving and extending the ideas of the Black spatial imaginary.

SECTION IV

Invisible Archives

7

Betye Saar's Los Angeles and Paule Marshall's Brooklyn

The terms of oppression are not only dictated by history,
culture, and the sexual and social division of labor. They
are also profoundly shaped at the site of oppression, and
by the way in which oppressors and oppressed continuously
have to renegotiate, reconstruct, and reestablish their
relative positions in respect to benefits and power.
—ARTHUR BRITTAN AND MARY MAYNARD

The self-activity of Black women plays a central role in art produced by
Horace Tapscott, John Biggers, and Rick Lowe. Tapscott describes the
home in which he was raised as "a house full of women" that included
his grandmother, two great-aunts, his mother, and a Miss Chaney who rented
a room. He credits his mother with shaping his interest in music because
of her example as an independent person who led her own performing jazz
quartet before he was born and as the mentor who introduced him to the
piano, bought him his first trombone, and took him to his first music teacher.
Tapscott's composition *Ancestral Echoes* contains a line based on the special
whistling sound his mother made to signal him to stop playing outside and
come into the house.[1] Another composition, *Drunken Mary/Mary on Sunday*,
presents an affectionate tribute to a woman from his neighborhood. Women
including composer/activist Linda Hill, flutist and vocalist Adele Sebastian,
and the guitarist who called herself Avotcja played important roles in Tapscott's many endeavors. The Arkestra promoted collaborations that opened up
new opportunities for women musicians that enabled some of them to feel
deeply invested in Tapscott's projects. As Adele Sebastian proclaimed about
the Ark, "We are a family and the music is not just something you do. It's a
way of life and you live it, and you breathe it, and you are it, and you don't sell
out. You hold fast, and you stay strong and play it. And you say what you have
to say. And you put it in the archives and you write it down, and you don't let

anybody take it. And you don't abuse it or destroy it. And you leave it for the children. And that's what it's about. And that's us: dedication."[2]

Comparison of Tapscott's group to a family contains both positive and negative implications. The amount of time they spent with each other and the shared sense of purpose they enjoyed replicated the dynamics of a close and smoothly functioning family. Yet traditional gender roles still held sway. Tapscott refused to play the piano as a child because he feared that the other boys in the neighborhood thought of it as a girl's instrument and would beat him up for playing it. He did not switch to piano until later in life when he injured his lips so badly in a car crash that he could no longer play the trombone.[3] Nearly all the male musicians in Tapscott's group had the leisure time to play music because their female partners worked traditional jobs, supporting the men with their earnings. Bass player Al Hines later recalled, "We hung out together all the time. Horace wouldn't get no job and I wouldn't get no job. Our old ladies were running us crazy because we wouldn't do nothing but play."[4] The man known to his musicians as "Papa" could devote his life to music because his wife Cecilia supported her husband and their five children by working as an administrator at the Los Angeles County Hospital.[5] Guitarist Avotcja had many good musical experiences playing with the group, but she objected to how her independence and self-assertion put her at odds with Tapscott's preferred traits in women. "As much as I loved Horace," she recalls, "I wasn't the follow the leader kind of sister. And those were the kind of sisters they wanted."[6]

The art of John Biggers and Rick Lowe also displays special attention to the dignity and agency of Black women. Biggers's painted tributes to the "organized" Black women who lived in shotgun houses and his murals about Black women in history evidence an advanced consciousness about gender. Lowe's decision to reserve houses for single mothers attempting to get college degrees and his establishment of the special mentoring program for them recognize the important tasks that many Black women find themselves forced to fulfill because of the intersectional oppressions of race and gender. Yet works of art that speak *for* the interests of Black women are not the same as works of art that emanate *from* the experiences of Black women. Establishing archives and institutions has been even more difficult for Black women than for Black men. Women interested in starting their own collectives did not have access to the male camaraderie and sexual division of labor that made Tapscott's Arkestra possible. Black women artists did not receive the kinds of commissions that John Biggers secured in the 1960s and 1970s, and Black women arts activists have not received the level of foundation funding that makes Project Row Houses viable. Perhaps even more important, the tradition of radical resistance embodied in the Watts Rebellions and the People's Party

II in Houston speaks to an insurgent consciousness and persona that despite important exceptions has been more available to men than to women. Despite the fact that aggrieved groups need solidarity that crosses gender lines, and despite the perverse ways that white supremacy, since the days of slavery, has denied Black women the same kind of split between public and private spheres that shaped distinct gender roles for middle-class whites, Black women have only rarely created visible archives like the World Stage or Project Row Houses. Yet for that very reason, the invisible archives available in expressive culture have been tremendously important to Black women, as the visual art of Betye Saar and the fiction writing of Paule Marshall demonstrate.

People act in the arenas open to them with the tools they have at their disposal. Betye Saar's art works and Paule Marshall's novels establish the discursive spaces of expressive culture as invisible archives, as homes from which women cannot be evicted, as neighborhoods that cannot be gentrified. Saar and Marshall turn to the spaces of their youth and the lessons they learned in them about self-activity and artistry to create works of expressive culture that guide Black women's efforts to find their places in the world. They burrow in to the spaces of the household to find the ways in which the instruments of oppression might be turned into tools for liberation. They find important knowledge inside the home, ways of knowing and ways of working that understand racism and sexism without succumbing to them, discursive frames that critique sexism, caste divisions, and class prejudice while still finding something left to love in people living the only lives that are open to them.[7]

Betye Saar spoke powerfully to gendered as well as racial inequalities in the works of art that she fashioned starting in the same years that Tapscott's Ark did its work. Her creations in the wake of the Watts Riot of 1965 echoed Tapscott's efforts to reduce the scale of space, to find value and meaning in Black people's everyday lives in their communities. Yet Saar also recognized, in ways that Tapscott largely did not, that struggles against racism could be undermined by uncritical absorption of sexist hierarchies, that Black women's experiences gave them especially important things to say about race and space. Like Tapscott, Saar responded by changing the scale of space, by burrowing in, constructing works of art from material items, images, and ideas grounded in everyday life, emphasizing connections between the physical places of the city and the discursive and political spaces that shaped Black consciousness and culture. As Daniel Widener observes, Saar's deployment of vernacular images and artifacts echoes Tapscott's efforts to emphasize "the popular community-based focus of the jazz collective by using language accessible to everyday black folks."[8]

Saar's assemblages and installations have earned deserved and widespread praise for their extraordinary aesthetic innovations and achievements. Yet the ultimate import of her creations cannot be confined within the boundaries of the categories that our society ascribes to art. A former social worker, Saar has long understood the "social" work she wants her artwork to do. She embodies and extends a long and honorable tradition of Afro-diasporic conjuring, relying on ways of knowing and being that conceive of the artist as being what Theophus Smith describes as "a quasi-medical practitioner who transforms reality by means of prescribed operations involving a repertory of efficacious materials."[9] Saar works on ordinary objects of everyday life and labor in order to imbue them with transformative potential. She presents medicine cabinets as mechanisms for curing society's ills. She displays ironing boards and steam irons to press for social change. Domestic laborers brandishing brooms in her pieces remind audiences that sweeping changes still need to be made. She offers viewers an art saturated with the particularities of place and time, creating spectacles made up of objects and images that confront the hurts of history and challenge viewers to face up to the demands of ethical witnessing.[10]

At first glance, some of the images, artifacts, and objects deployed in Saar's art seem to be unlikely instruments for liberation. Corpulent mammies, smiling Sambos, and ingratiating Uncle Toms populate her assemblages and installations. Images and slogans appear on materials that evoke memories of racist stereotyping and subordination including watermelons, washboards, and banjos. Saar zeroes in on these dangerous places and spaces, reviving the racist ridicule of the minstrel show stage while referencing directly and indirectly the hurtful racial and sexual exploitation that Black women have endured as domestic laborers. The sadism of the slave owner and the blood lust of the lynch mob permeate the history of spectatorship that she references and repositions. Yet Saar delves into these poisonous images and experiences for much the same reason that the physicians of antiquity turned to poison as an antidote to illness. Things that kill can also cure if they are deployed in the right ways. Just as the individual body can build up immunity to diseases by being injected with small doses of toxins, the body politic might be inoculated against racism through representations that deprive the racist insult of its deadly sting. For aggrieved racialized peoples, freedom from the fetters of negative ascription frequently entails inhabiting temporarily the identities that others have constructed about them in order to subvert, invert, and contest the devalued nature of their collective identity. They must speak back to power within the terms and logic created by power in the first place. As film theorist Laura Mulvey explains, "It cannot be easy to move from oppression and its mythologies to resistance in history; a detour through a no-man's land or threshold area of counter-myth and symbolisation is necessary."[11]

Saar's "detour" through the threshold areas of countermyth and symbolization leads her to materials that have memories inscribed inside them. In *Sambo's Banjo* (1971–1972), a musician's case does not contain the stringed instrument of African origin saluted in the assemblage's title, but rather a smiling Sambo doll hung by a thread. A "secret" panel above the doll expresses a hidden truth by displaying two items: a Black skeleton hanging from a noose around its neck and a photograph of white spectators at a lynching of a Black man. Sambo's forced smile and the playful promise of joy-filled banjo music hide the harsh realities out of which African American music historically emerged. Similarly, a carefree nappy-headed "darkie" dancing in striped pants and a long coat with tails decorates the front of a working metronome in *I've Got Rhythm* (1972). A crucifix beneath the figure on the front of the metronome and fragments of newspaper clippings on its sides that describe lynchings posit a relationship between minstrelsy and murder. Unlatching the front of the metronome reveals more open secrets: a Black skeleton attached to the arm of the metronome "dances" in front of a photograph of a white mob and an American flag. The metronome that enables musicians to keep to the beat in this case references another kind of beating. The clicking of the metronome in this context sounds more like a ticking time bomb than an invitation to dance. Saar's piece inverts the identity of popular music, showing that its bright promises hide brutal practices. Yet she also recognizes that entertainment helped Black people survive in a country built upon their subordination and suppression. Entertainment provided employment, enabled movement, and offered opportunities to display disciplined virtuosity.[12] Saar's art reveals how visual images that defame and demean can also be used to affirm the dignity of Black people. For Saar, freedom entails the practical work of survival and negotiation with power. *I've Got Rhythm* invites viewers to manipulate material objects by opening closed doors and finding hidden compartments. *The Liberation of Aunt Jemima* (1972) focuses on the tasks performed by domestic workers. "For years I have collected vintage washboards," she relates, "and to me, they symbolize hard labor. By recycling them I am honoring the memory of that labor and the working woman upon whose shoulders we now stand."[13]

In *Gone Are the Days* (1970), built around a found photograph that Saar obtained in a secondhand store, two beautiful Black children from the era of Jim Crow segregation become the focal point for a presentation of the persistent struggle by past generations of African Americans for self-respect and dignity in the midst of an avalanche of racist representations and realities. "What happened to these people?" Saar asks. Another photograph serves a dramatic role in *Blackbird* (2000). A posed group photo of the third grade class taught by Saar's great-aunt in Missouri in 1911 sits in a wood frame above figurines of Blacks eating watermelons, a Black crow, and other degrading contemporaneous images of Blackness. The dignity of the third grade students contrasts sharply with the racially tinged images beneath them. Saar describes these photos as "a mystery with clues to a lost reality," a reality not so much lost but stolen. Nostalgia for a lost past is a powerful trope in much Western art, but the relationship between past and present in Saar's creations is especially charged because white supremacist domination of the mechanisms of artistic representation and the writing of history make her respectful of memory, but suspicious about uncritical nostalgia.

For Saar, the retrieval of lost realities requires her to mine alternative archives and imaginaries already present in her own biography. Born in Los Angeles in 1926, Saar learned about art from a broad range of teachers situated in the geographic spaces of her childhood. The Watts Towers, created near her home by Italian immigrant Sabato Rodia, offered an eccentric but unforgettable example of assemblage and installation. She took craft classes for children administered by the local parks and recreation department. Museum exhibits exposed her to art from Egypt, sub-Saharan Africa, and Oceania.[14] Saar's work resonates with influences from many different cultures and subcultures including Latino altars, assemblage, feminist iconography, and pop art.[15] She did her undergraduate work at the University of California at Los Angeles, completed graduate studies at California State University at Long Beach, and studied printmaking and film at the University of Southern California, California State University at Northridge, and the Pasadena School of Fine Arts.[16] Much of her entry-level work as an artist exposed her to quotidian and vernacular forms. She executed interior design commissions, created posters, and produced studio cards based on artist sketches to be sold in small boutiques. Saar worked with Curtis Tann making jewelry and other fine crafts from enamel. Saar also worked as a costume designer for a small local theater group, remembering their performance of Lorraine Hansberry's *A Raisin in the Sun* (discussed in Chapter 8) as one of her first projects.[17] These forms of art heightened Saar's appreciation of the expressive qualities of everyday life, of the possibilities of mixed media, of the communicative powers of items found in the home, and of the seductive allure and unexpected contradictions of commercial culture. They also placed her in direct dialogue with an integrated and socially conscious community of artists living in and near Pasadena and Altadena who provided models for a full-time career in art.[18] These artists worked in many different media and at many different levels, but they also shared a belief system about art as a social force, as something to produce new social relations not just as the making of elaborate ornaments to be enjoyed for their own sake.[19]

In *The Liberation of Aunt Jemima* (1972) and the long series of mixed-media assemblages that follow it, Saar counterpoises the violence of white supremacy with the retaliatory violence of civil insurrections. The piece is based on a pair of found objects: a 1930s plastic "mammy" memo and pencil holder that Saar purchased at a rummage sale, and a small image of a smiling mammy holding a squirming and screaming white child. "Aunt Jemima" holds a broom in her right hand as an emblem of her life of domestic labor, but she also has a rifle by her left side. A clenched fist symbolizing the Black Power movement blocks out the lower half of the mammy with child. "My intent was to transform a negative, demeaning figure into a positive empowered woman . . . ," she explains, "a warrior ready to combat servitude and racism."[20]

Saar's seemingly paradoxical pairing of Aunt Jemima with a weapon of urban insurrection emanated directly from her response to the Watts Rebellion and the broader Black freedom movement. The insurrection in Watts in 1965 served as a kind of final verdict on the legacy of racialized space in Los Angeles. It entailed a mass collective refusal of the unlivable destiny authored by the white spatial imaginary. She describes the images she made in response as "a way to express anger; to start my own revolution with my materials and symbols," as a way to respond to a time of "black revolution and the death of Martin Luther King."[21]

Historian George P. Rawick made a connection similar to Saar's image of Aunt Jemima holding a rifle in his book *From Sundown to Sunup*, which was written as part of Rawick's attempts to come to grips with what he called the "process of truth" unleashed by the insurgencies in Watts, Detroit, Newark, and hundreds of other cities during the 1960s. Rawick argued that the humiliating subordination of slavery depended upon fear and intimidation. Always consigned to social death or frequently forced to face actual physical death, the slave knuckles under and accepts servitude as an unalterable reality. Yet this very submission produces anger and rage. "Unless the slave had had a tendency to be Sambo," Rawick writes, "he can never become Nat Turner. One who has never feared becoming Sambo, never *need* rebel to maintain his humanity."[22]

Like Rawick, Saar recognized that Aunt Jemima and the gun-toting rebel are not opposite personalities, but rather can be opposing strategies and possibilities inside the same person. Aunt Jemima, Uncle Tom, and other "sambo" figures experience the degradation of humiliating subordination, but they survive. Nat Turner and other insurrectionary rebels enjoy the dignity of self-active struggle, but they lose their lives because of their open rebellions. In the wake of the assassinations of Dr. King and Malcolm X, of the martyrdom of many freedom fighters and the loss of lives in the Watts Rebellion, Saar saw that militant and assertive people can became maimed or eliminated. Her art asked for another view of the mammy and the Uncle Tom.[23] Only one who has endured the indignities of being Aunt Jemima truly understands the imperatives of revolutionary violence. Only a person aware of the dreadful and mortal consequences of revolutionary insurrection would stoop to become Aunt Jemima. In these works of art, Saar engages in conjuring, creating images that promote revolution as a form of healing, that find hope in the midst of despair, that locate something left to love even in what seem to be the most craven, cowardly, and cowed members of the community.

For Betye Saar, the meaning and the matter of art are closely intertwined. As Richard Candida Smith notes, Saar's art identifies a resemblance between discarded objects and the "misunderstood and dismissed cultural heritage that black women forged over the centuries."[24] Her work takes inert materials, finds human memories inside them, and transforms reality by revealing the mutually constitutive relationships that link accommodation and resistance. Just as Fannie Lou Hamer's labor as a plantation timekeeper during the 1960s made her perfectly attuned to knowing what "time" it was in more ways than one, Betye Saar's situated knowledge as a Black woman enables her to create art that deploys the tools of domestic labor to urge the nation to iron out its problems, cure its ills, and clean up its act. Saar's strategic reconfiguring of objects found in domestic spaces to make comments about broad systems of power reduces the scale of space; it burrows into domestic settings but finds the whole world compressed and compacted in them. Paule Marshall deploys a different spatial strategy in her books and short stories. Equally concerned as Saar with the domestic sphere and women's negotiations with it, Marshall's characters nonetheless alter the scope of space by branching out, by moving back and forth across and within borders and boundaries of all kinds. Wary of the parochial closures and oppressive confinements of household and neighborhood life in the ghetto, Marshall's characters seek connections to a wider world. Yet they reject the deracination and disidentification with other Blacks that a disembodied universalism would require. Marshall's characters find their places in the midst of displacement. They make an art out of homelessness by carrying out into the wider world lessons they have learned in different kinds of homes along the way.

Marshall's first novel, *Brown Girl, Brownstones* was published just before her thirtieth birthday in 1959. It presents a thinly veiled *roman à clef*, a deft artistic rendering of Marshall's experiences growing up as the Brooklyn-born daughter of immigrants from Barbados. Although clearly a work of fiction, Marshall's narrative contains many similarities to the author's life. It depicts an immigrant girl's childhood in Brooklyn and her academic success at a local public college. It describes a father's desertion of his wife and children to join a religious cult. It delineates complicated and continuing negotiations with the protagonist's Caribbean identity.[25] Marshall struggled in life with many of the gendered hierarchies she critiques acerbically in the novel. The passivity promoted by patriarchal religions comes in for special scorn in the novel, perhaps because of Marshall's personal memories of her own father deserting the family to become a follower of Father Divine, a desertion that she remembered later as compounding her mother's bitterness as she grappled with cancer before succumbing to an early death.[26] Moreover, Marshall completed the writing of this first novel successfully only after securing enough time to write by defying her husband's objections and hiring a babysitter to take care of their children.

Marshall portrays the Brooklyn ghetto in global terms in *Brown Girl, Brownstones*. Her characters' memories, minds, and bodies move back and forth between the city spaces where they have settled in Brooklyn and their ancestral homeland in the Caribbean. The powerful allure of place in *Brown Girl, Brownstones* is haunted by multiple histories of displacement. Poverty, hard labor, and landlessness drive Barbadians to Brooklyn. There they encounter southern-born U.S. Blacks who have migrated to the North fleeing southern segregation, sharecropping, and vigilante violence. A distinct racial and spatial economy confronts both these groups in Brooklyn. They move into previously all-white neighborhoods that are rapidly becoming all Black. They ride buses and subway trains to white neighborhoods where they clean other people's homes. They venture out into a city whose sidewalks, streets, and stores have unmarked racial prohibitions and dangers that they must learn quickly and negotiate successfully. All these movements make Marshall's immigrant characters long for safety, security, and even stasis. They want to own their own homes and dwell in stable neighborhoods. Yet they discover that real estate steering, blockbusting, and urban renewal create continuous new displacements that keep them constantly moving. The containments they experience as a result of racialized space compel constant movement, but that very movement only augments their desire for stability and rest.

Marshall depicts a community that wishes for homelands and homes because they have never really had either one. Colonialism and class oppression in Barbados and residential discrimination and urban renewal in New York deny them the stability and security of being "at home" in either locale. In the metropolis, they start their U.S. sojourn in East Brooklyn, move to Fulton Street, and hope to continue on to Crown Heights. On the periphery, the African American south and the Afro-Caribbean West Indies are places slaves were brought to and workers passed through. They might signify "home," but they are also transient sites shaped by Euro-American conquest, colonization, and slavery. Marshall's characters seek mastery over spaces, yet find their hopes perpetually frustrated. Marshall fashions her particular spatial imaginary by referencing her distant ancestors' experiences with colonialism and slavery as well as her parents' struggles to inhabit, own, and move freely through city space. Her particular optic on place emerges out of the immigrant status of her parents, her own experiences as a Black woman, and her historically and socially situated political critiques and commitments as a participant in mid-twentieth-century freedom movements including the Harlem Writers Guild and the Association of Artists for Freedom.[27] In writing *Brown Girl, Brownstones*, Marshall drew as well on her experiences working for *Our World*, a general-interest magazine aimed at Black readers. The commercial viability of that journal depended upon finding topics of broad interest capable of appealing to all sectors of the diverse multinational Black community that was its target market. It required empathy and generosity toward groups with many divisions and disagreements among them. It helped Marshall cultivate the openness to different ways of being Black that permeates *Brown Girl, Brownstones*.

Literary artistry itself for Marshall was a product of a particular place. In her essay "The Making of a Writer: From the Poets in the Kitchen" and in her short story "Reena," Marshall evokes fondly her childhood fascination with the group of Black women who sat around her mother's table in the basement kitchen of the family's brownstone house in Brooklyn. Women like these, she claims, were the first "poets" she encountered. None of these women actually wrote poetry or even thought of themselves as poets, but Marshall honors them with that designation to emphasize how their richly passionate and playful speech influenced her later life and art. Paule remembered sitting with her sister in a corner of the kitchen pretending to do their homework, but actually listening attentively to their mother and her friends as they conversed over cocoa and tea at a large dining table. Eavesdropping enabled the young girls to enjoy, admire, and absorb the older women's verbal artistry and creative imagination.[28] Noting Czesław Miłosz's claim that "language is the only homeland," Marshall emphasizes how these kitchen conversations enabled a small circle of immigrant women to speak in ways that made them feel at home far away from home, hundreds of miles from their country of birth. They reveled in conversation, deploying verbal art creatively to keep parts of their Barbadian pasts alive in the Brooklyn present.[29] Yet it was not just their verbal skills that impressed Marshall. Many of these women participated in Marcus Garvey's pan-African Universal Negro Improvement Association (UNIA). As Ula Taylor explains in her splendid biography of Amy Jacques Garvey, participation in the UNIA held particular importance for women. The organization promoted a cosmopolitan "community feminism," that encouraged women to be serious critical thinkers. It authorized activism in the world to advance the race.[30] The women in the kitchen fashioned

identities out of imagined and real connections between places. They cultivated diasporic intimacy and pan-African identification with other Black people around the world, but felt solidarity with other oppressed communities as
well. From these women, Marshall learned a sophisticated sense of world-
transcending citizenship. "They saw themselves," she recalls, "not only as
Black Americans or Afro-Caribbeans living in this hemisphere, but they saw
themselves as part of that larger world. And this has become of course, one
of the themes of my work."[31] Burrowing into the small spaces of kitchens in
Brooklyn enabled them to branch out to a wider world. Marshall explains that
displaced immigrants gain a powerfully productive optic on power, that living in two places expands the range of ideas, identities, and imaginaries available to them. Being an immigrant, she argues, provides the opportunity "to
live not between but within two worlds."[32] This way of living offers a unique
optics on identity and power that evokes more general epistemological principles. It affirms that "a thing is at the same time its opposite, and . . . the contradictions make up the whole."[33]

In *Brown Girl, Brownstones,* as in much of her subsequent work, Marshall focuses on the Caribbean and its role in the spatial imaginaries and
moral philosophies of migrants to the United States. The Garvey Movement
and other forms of Black nationalism referenced in Marshall's writings under-
score a desire to make a home out of homelessness, exile, and diaspora. Yet
Black nationalist organizations pursue this goal in complex and theoretically
sophisticated ways. As James C. Hall notes, "To desire to reconstruct what it
was like to *be a people* is not necessarily a crude nationalism; it is instead an
attempt to figure out the relationship, as Marshall herself puts it, between our
past and the 'overturning of the present order.'"[34]

Marshall cautions, however, that these desires can become counterproductive. They run the risk of substituting one form of confinement and
containment for another. Women can easily be trapped inside both the patriarchal domains of the nuclear family and the patriotic spaces of nationalism. Solidarities of sameness receive eloquent approbation from Marshall;
they are logical responses to shared suffering. Yet solidarity can become tyr-
anny. Groups can come together through coercion as well as consensus. Desires for unity can lead to insistence on uniformity. Solidarity inside a family,
community, race, or nation can soothe pain and offer succor, but it can also
suffocate and suppress mutual recognition and respect by denying important
differences.

The challenges of owning a home, leaving home, and feeling at home in
the world form the foundational conflicts in *Brown Girl, Brownstones.* Marshall begins her story with an illustrative anecdote that prefigures how these
issues will shape the contours of the entire book. The novel begins with its

adolescent protagonist leaving the "safe, sunlit place" on the upper landing of the top floor of her house. She walks down the stairs to face the challenges that await in "the dark hall and beyond." This phrase refers literally to the inside of the house, but figuratively it speaks to the wider world beyond it.[35] The young Selina Boyce is on a journey that will compel her to leave the safety—but also the suffocating surveillance of her home—to journey out into an unstable ever-changing world and try to make her way.

The novel's protagonist learns about the wider world beyond her family through experiences in the urban spaces that surround her childhood home. Marshall presents rich and evocative descriptions of these places, attaching particular promises and perils to each one. She compares "the concatenation of traffic and voices" and the "gaudy empty displays" in Manhattan shop windows to the "shrill-green" grass in Fulton Park and the "smoke-blurred windows" of a beauty shop in the Brooklyn ghetto.[36] The raucousness of Brooklyn's Fulton Street with its "cars, voices, neon signs, and trolleys" contrasts sharply with the "gentility" on Chauncey Street with its old buildings adorned with Ionic columns, bay windows, and black-iron grille fences.[37] These vivid descriptions of urban spaces pay tribute to the sights and sounds of the social world of Marshall's childhood, a world that no longer exists in reality as she writes (because of urban renewal), but persists as an invisible space of memory and moral instruction.

The brownstones appear in the novel even before the brown girl, a temporal sequence with considerable significance. Marshall's narrative voice directs our attention to a row of red-brown-stone three-story houses on a Brooklyn street standing side by side in the summer sun. It is as if these edifices are characters with personal qualities rather than inanimate buildings. At first, the uniform design and color of dwellings attached to one another makes the entire block seem like one connected house. Closer inspection, however, reveals unique architectural features in each of them. We learn that these houses are both alike and different. Differences exist even though they appear the same. Later, we discover the same about the Black people who live inside these brown buildings.[38]

Yet row houses on a Brooklyn street possess a value that their inhabitants lack. People come and go, live and die, but property appreciates in value and produces wealth across generations. In a telling passage, Marshall's narrator explains that "the West Indians, especially the Barbadians who had never owned anything perhaps but a few poor acres in a poor land, loved the houses with the same fierce idolatry as they had the land on their obscure islands."[39] This fierce idolatry emanates, in part, from the deprivations of the colonial past. Not owning land consigned impoverished West Indians to harsh, unremitting, and unrewarding labor on lands owned by others. They sought to change their place in the social order by moving into new spaces in Brooklyn. Yet in the metropolis they pursue diverse spatial strategies. Some immigrants want to own homes in Brooklyn because they believe that acquiring and then selling property in New York will enable them to return to Barbados in triumph, to purchase the homes "back home" that they could not previously afford. Others associate "back home" with hardship. They have no desire to return. They hope instead to use ownership of brownstones in Brooklyn as a base for putting their children in positions where they can succeed in the United States, where they can acquire the full fruits and benefits of citizenship and social membership.

Yet people who pay a terrible price for not owning property can become willing to do terrible things to obtain it. Marshall's description of the immigrants' desire for property as a kind of idolatry is more than a passing remark. Idolatry is not just worshipping graven images; it entails valuing things more than people, elevating property rights over human rights. For people whose ancestors were treated by law as if they were property, this is an especially grievous failing. Marshall explains in one of her essays that *Brown Girl, Brownstones* revolved around her efforts to "articulate feelings . . . about the acquisitive nature of the society and . . . its devastating impact on human relationships."[40] In one memorable scene, the teenage protagonist stands in her parlor adorned in gifts given to her by her materialistic father. Instead of making her happy, her new clothes make her feel "that she did not quite belong to herself. She was owned by the yellow taffeta gown her father had bought her, her feet imprisoned in the new shoes, her fingers estranged in gloves and her wrists bound by the gold bangles she wore on such occasions."[41]

In Marshall's view, immigrants' efforts to assimilate into U.S. society run the risk of "almost blind absorption in the material." A critique of avarice and materialism pervades *Brown Girl, Brownstones*.[42] The protagonist's father squanders his inheritance buying flashy clothes that make him feel important. Her mother makes her family and boarders in her home miserable in order to maintain the property values of their dwelling. Yet true to Marshall's epistemological appreciation of contradictions, there is always something left to love, even in people who cause us enormous pain. Both the father's frivolity and the mother's materialism evidence laudable determination to act in the world rather than merely being acted upon. Immigrant homes are material objects and possessions, but they are also places to be occupied, enjoyed, and controlled. The community's fierce idolatry expresses a distorted reverence for property, but as Barbara Christian observes, it also embodies a collective will to overcome obstacles and resist subordination.[43]

The fierce idolatry of houses displayed by the Barbadians in Brooklyn cannot be attributed solely to their immigrant status. The residents of these brownstones in Brooklyn carry the double burden of being "twice Black." They are both noncitizen immigrants and black people.[44] Employment discrimination relegates them to low-wage jobs that make it extremely difficult to *earn* their way from rags to riches. Acquiring property might make it possible to *own* their way up the social ladder, if not to obtain riches, at least to attain respectability.[45] The Blacks born in Barbados and those born in the United States are often at odds with another. United by their common color and the racist treatment it brings, their different histories divide them in many different ways. Yet they share similar, if not identical, experiences of displacement that make them equally sensitive to the politics, economics, and moral geographies of space. The Barbadians articulate their estrangement by referring to the United States as "this man country."[46] African Americans also feel that the nation belongs to "the man," and not to them. Although differently marginalized, both groups are united by a linked fate that shapes these perceptions of race, space, and place. Negative racial ascription entails prohibitions about place. As a character in one of Marshall's short stories observes, color can be more significant than immigrant status in this estrangement. "I can never lose the sense of being a displaced person here in America because of my color," she says.[47]

Selina Boyce, the brown girl in the novel's title, comes from a family deeply connected to the broader Barbadian immigrant community in Brooklyn. Shared skin color, ancestry, and history provide important sources of solidarity in their once white, but now increasingly black, Brooklyn neighborhood. Because of white flight enabled by blockbusting, real estate steering, mortgage redlining, and subsidies for the suburbs, the West Indians move en masse into the previously segregated spaces that have opened up to them. Their entry into a Brooklyn neighborhood comes "like a dark sea nudging its way onto a white beach and staining the sand."[48] Yet the Boyce family itself, no less than the neighborhood in which they live, is deeply divided—by gender and generation, by class and caste, by immigration status and citizenship. The people that Selina encounters daily inhabit identities that embody the sharp oppositions that structure the social world. In their lives, morality clashes with materialism, sensuality with self-control, sociability with selfishness. These conflicts *between characters* manifest themselves repeatedly in the novel in the form of battles *between places*, between Barbados and Brooklyn, between Fulton Street and Fifth Avenue, between the houses that the Barbadian immigrant women live in but leave every morning and the houses in Flatbush and Sheepshead Bay where they scrub floors hoping to earn enough money to become homeowners themselves.

In this novel, different places encode different histories. Miss Thompson's beauty shop on Fulton Street serves as a symbolic repository of African

American collective memory, as an alternative academy where Selina learns the importance of empathy, compassion, and solidarity.[49] Inside that shop, the traditions of radical egalitarianism and abolition democracy forged by newly freed slaves after the Civil War live on. In contrast, the converted factory that functions as the meeting place for the Association of Barbadian Homeowners and Businessmen signals the start of deindustrialization in Brooklyn. At the same time, it preserves the island past as a site converted for use for celebrations, rituals, and feasts that enable this diverse community to pool resources for self-help and mutual aid. An expensive apartment in an exclusive building on Manhattan's east side is the kind of place that Selina's mother and her friends have made their livelihoods cleaning. Its connection to this history is made clear when Selina ventures into one of these homes with a college friend and encounters there a torrent of patronizing, dismissive, and racist comments by her classmate's mother. The incident reveals that there can be no simple movement from Brooklyn to Manhattan, from segregation to assimilation. The Black neighborhood in Brooklyn is not only different from the upper east side, but the upper east side's luxury and privilege depend upon contempt for and exploitation of the Black people in Brooklyn. The alienations and indignities of low-wage labor endured by the immigrant workers bear a metonymic relationship to the places where the work occurs. Rural cane fields, urban factories, office buildings, luxury apartments, and a tiny, cramped beauty parlor in Brooklyn draw their moral prohibitions and possibilities in direct relation to the work that is done in them. These places resonate with social hierarchies that produce particular kinds of people.

Although Selina lives comfortably in a modest brownstone with her mother, father, sister, and boarders, the concept of home remains something of a mystery to her. When her parents speak of "home," they mean Barbados, a place Selina has never seen. Deighton Boyce, her middle-class father, remembers Barbados with nostalgia, as a natural paradise and playground. Silla Boyce, her working-class mother, recalls the island as place of punitive poverty and racist subordination. Both parents seek to make money in the United States, but for different reasons. Her father longs to build a stately house in Barbados, while the mother hopes for homeownership in New York.[50] Yet both imagine that owning a home will create a safe haven, a hope that Marshall's narrator eventually recognizes as misplaced. The differences in personality and character that distinguish the mother and the father come from their different histories with places, from diametrically opposed memories, experiences, and aspirations in Barbados and Brooklyn. The cane fields where Silla labored taught lessons very different from those that Deighton learned in his middle-class neighborhood. Marshall's narrator observes, "It seemed to Selina that her father carried those gay days [of his youth] in his

irresponsible smile, while the mother's formidable aspect was the culmina-
tion of all that she had suffered."[51]

Parental homelands are often problematic for immigrant children. They
are sources of both obligation and guilt. Like the other Barbadian girls in
the novel, Selina's tangible connection to Barbados comes from the two silver bangles she has worn on her wrist since birth. This jewelry comes from
"home" and signifies attachment to it. But whether the bangles are bracelets
or handcuffs is never quite clear. The meaning of home in Brooklyn is no
less a mystery to Selina than the meaning of home in Barbados. Her mother
and the other immigrant women clean other people's homes in order to earn
money to have homes of their own. Some, like the Boyce family's boarder
Suggie, work as live-in maids who rarely get to enjoy the fruits of their labor.
Even if they eventually purchase homes of their own, they must leave their
own dwellings, families, and friends for the entire workweek.[52] The house
that Selina's family rents and hopes to buy seems to her like "a museum of all
the lives that had ever lived there." She feels haunted by the presence of the
white family that inhabited the dwelling before her family moved into it. The
white family is gone but their "ponderous furniture and potted ferns" remain
in the entrance hall, and their elderly and infirm white servant still occupies
an upstairs room.[53]

In addition to the ghostly presence of the previous occupants, Selina's
home is also a business, containing boarders as well as family members. Her
mother runs the household with an eye toward making enough money to purchase a home of her own. The poetics of home in our society might make us
expect Silla's hopes to be suffused with maternal generosity and care, but
we quickly learn otherwise. In order to pursue the dream of the companion-
ate family home, Selina's mother has to privilege pecuniary concerns over
personal relationships. Exposing the class structure that the mythology of
the middle-class family obscures, Marshall reveals that Silla Boyce views the
humans in her household as a means to monetary ends. She hectors her tenants for the rent money. She evicts Suggie, a lonely, hardworking tenant who
has befriended Selina. The woman's male visitors seem to Silla to give the
building "an unsavory reputation and thus [lowering] its property value."[54]
Silla turns to forgery so that she can sell a small parcel of land that Deighton
has inherited in Barbados in order to purchase property for the family in New
York. She monitors her roomers' conduct closely in order to protect the value
of her building, hiding in the halls to catch them running down the stairs or
playing the radio too loud. Even Silla herself appears appalled at the things
she feels she has to do for money. At a wedding celebration, she exclaims
guiltily to a group of friends, "Houses! That's all the talk. Houses! When
you does have to do some of everything short of murder to get them some-

times."[55] Marshall offers us overwhelming evidence that being without assets that appreciate in value and that can be passed down to subsequent generations causes Black people tremendous pain, but she also shows that wanting too much to acquire assets can distort personalities and produce costs of different kinds.

Yet while Silla's seeming avarice shows what happens when Black people value material gain too much, Deighton's irresponsibility demonstrates the dangers of taking asset accumulation too lightly. When his charming entreaties induce Silla to return the money due him from his inheritance, Deighton selfishly squanders the windfall on fine clothes and expensive presents designed to prop up his grandiose and narcissistic self-image at the expense of the family. Locked in bitter battle with one another, each parent opts for a spatial solution to the problem. After being injured in an industrial accident, Deighton leaves the family home and moves into a temple run by the charismatic patriarchal religious leader, Father Peace. Silla notifies the immigration and naturalization service that Deighton is an undocumented immigrant, engineering his deportation back to Barbados. On the trip home, he dies from either an accidental fall or a deliberate suicidal leap. Unable to rely on her normative biological family for a home in which she can believe, Selina pursues personal associations and affiliations with non–family members to fill the void. Like her family members, these diverse characters manifest personal characteristics and traits infused with the histories of different physical and social spaces.

Miss Thompson runs the local beauty parlor by day and cleans offices by night. She helps raise the children of the woman who owns her rooming house, and she provides Selina with important counsel and advice. Many of the Barbadians look down on Miss Thompson because she is a native-born black, an immigrant from the South, a person whose business smells from the fried fish sandwiches she eats at her workplace, and whose leg emits an unpleasant odor because of an untreated sore. Both her suffering and her solidarity with other Blacks (African Americans *and* immigrants) come from the part of the country she is from—the Jim Crow south. Miss Thompson received the wound on her leg resisting rape by a white man, and she carries that experience with her in a wound that refuses to heal. She feels angry and exasperated by both white supremacy and the irresponsibility of her neighbors who drink too much, spend their money on frivolous entertainment, and neglect their children. Yet she channels that anger into empathy, compassion, and connection, helping to parent children who are not her own, including Selina. She advises the young girl to understand and appreciate her parents and her community despite all their faults, to know them well enough to discern which of their values she wishes to keep and which ones she wishes to discard.[56] The beauty shop that she runs is part of the capitalist system, albeit a minor and only marginally successful part. Yet like her emancipated slave ancestors who created new democratic practices and institutions in the plantation-dominated southern states after the Civil War, Miss Thompson transforms a place of alienated labor into a space for moral instruction, intergenerational friendship among women, and intraracial recognition.

Barbadian immigrant Claremont Sealy draws on the physical and discursive spaces of the past in Barbados to teach lessons similar to the ones that Miss Thompson derives from slavery and the Jim Crow south. He urges the Businessmen and Homeowners Association to strike the adjective "Barbadian" from its title and replace it with "Negro." He advocates solidarity with the larger African American community so they can fight together for mutual benefit, especially against the planned urban renewal project that threatens their neighborhood.[57] The Barbadians in the novel emphatically reject his suggestion, but Sealy exemplifies the spatial and racial stance that Marshall endorses. She describes her writing as "a bridge that joins the two great wings of the black diaspora in this part of the world" by portraying West Indian immigrants as people with "the opportunity to live not between but within two worlds." Drawing on a political slogan popular in Jamaica and other Caribbean islands, Marshall emphasizes that Afro-Caribbeans and Afro-Americans share a linked fate, explaining, "All o' we is one as far as I'm concerned. And I, myself, am both."[58]

Yet it is not only the Caribbean and the U.S. South that become reconciled in Marshall's vision. Her protagonist grapples with the contradictions between the culture of uplift and the culture of the blues. The proper demeanor and repressed behavior of the upwardly mobile striving Barbadians contrasts radically with the ferocious theatricality and Dionysian hedonism of the Black working class. The culture of uplift attempts to bring order to a disorderly reality, to perform normative Victorian values so persuasively that racist presumptions about Blacks as lazy, licentious, gluttonous, impulsive, and rapacious will be disproved. The culture of the blues embraces pleasure as a way of defying social death, affirming life, and refusing an unlivable destiny.[59] Participants in the culture of the blues often view adherents to the culture of uplift as self-hating, brainwashed, and deluded in thinking that it is Black behavior—rather than white privilege—that causes racism. For their part, proponents of the culture of uplift frequently feel undermined by the culture of the blues and consequently try to police popular behavior. Class and caste play insidious roles in these disputes because the culture of uplift is more accessible and more rewarding to those with wealth, education, and lighter skin color, while the culture of the blues survives and thrives among the dark-skinned Black working class.

Suggie, who boards in the Boyce family home, uses the culture of the blues to escape the dreary work she has to do as a domestic worker. Miss Thompson loves 125th Street in Harlem because it is where Black people dress well, eat fancy food served by white waiters, and ride around in Cadillacs. "Honey, I seen it just once and got all choked up inside," she tells Selina, adding, "I was so proud to see my peoples living so swell."[60] Yet the things that make Miss Thompson proud make the members of the Barbardian Association ashamed. They view the taverns where Black people congregate as similar to the rum shops back home in Barbados, which Silla describes as places that "keep we pacify and in ignorance."[61] Marshall's preferred resolution of this conflict in *Brown Girl, Brownstones* comes through Selina's recognition of identifying with both cultures rather than choosing one or the other. Near the end of the novel, Marshall writes that Selina "was one with Miss Thompson, she knew as she pulled herself up the subway steps to Fulton Street and saw the closed beauty shop. One with the whores, the flashy men, and the blues rising sacredly above the plain of neon lights and ruined houses, she knew, as she stumbled past the White Drake Bar."[62] This is the resolution we might expect, one where the moral power of Miss Thompson and the traditions of the Abolition Democracy she represents teach a young woman to overcome her family's pretensions and prejudices. But Marshall does not stop there. Selina immediately sees the building that housed the Barbadian Association headquarters sharing the same spaces inhabited by the culture of the blues. Marshall writes, "And she was one with them: the mother and the Bajan women, who had lived each day what she had come to know. How had the mother endured, she who had not chosen death by water. She remembered the mother striding home through Fulton Park each late afternoon, bearing the throw-offs under her arm as she must have borne the day's humiliations inside."[63]

The Barbadians and African Americans in the novel have come to the physical spaces of Brooklyn from places they did not own or control. Their common skin color relegates them to the same neighborhoods and exposes them to the same forms of discrimination. Their need to pool resources in the face of this consistent negative ascription from the outside produces powerful desires for solidarities of sameness. Yet the very invocation of sameness immediately brings into their sights all the ways in which they are different, not just across group lines but within them. Afro-Caribbeans and Afro-Americans have different histories, memories, and cognitive mappings. Even within the groups, the number of things that divide them equal the number of things that unite them. There is no one way to be Barbadian, no one way to be Black. Moreover, as important as race is, there is no guarantee that rallying around a common racial identity will end their oppression. In an important moment in the novel, Silla Boyce concedes that the oppressive power they confront in their lives at present works through the categories of race. Yet she argues that it is power itself that is the problem. "Take this world," she says. "It wun always be white. No, mahn. It gon be somebody else turn soon—maybe even people looking near like us. But plenty gon have to suffer to bring it about. And when they get up top they might not be so nice either, 'cause power is a thing that don make you nice."[64]

Selina Boyce experiments with the identities available to her in diverse spaces, by sporadically leaving her community and then returning to it. At home, on the streets, in the youth group of the Barbadian Association, at the Greenwich Village apartment of her artist lover, in her bourgeois friend Beryl's home, at the rehearsals and performances of her college dance troupe, each space produces a different character zone for her to inhabit, but all fall short. The novel ends, however, with two specific spatial transformations that express Marshall's preferred solutions.

Just when her mother is about to complete the purchase of a brownstone in a better neighborhood, Selina decides to return to Barbados. A Jewish white female friend from her college dance group uses her family connections (and her white privilege) to secure a job for Selina dancing as an entertainer on a cruise ship. She can now run away to sea and leave Brooklyn behind. Yet even nomadic spaces have their histories. Selina's plans to return to Barbados as a dancer on a tourist ship position her as a black artist performing a self-tropicalizing spectacle for mostly white tourist audiences. She knows from her father's experiences as a boy that tourism brings into stark relief the decidedly unequal relationships between the hemispheric north and south. Deighton Boyce's fond memories of his Barbadian boyhood included diving in the ocean for coins thrown by tourists who derived amusement from watching the local youths risk their lives for sums of money that passengers could easily afford to throw away. The cruise ship that provides Selina with her opportunity to visit the Caribbean sets sail from a country suffused with images of tropical tourism.

Her friend suggests that once she is in the Caribbean, she can jump ship. This decision might seem to represent choosing the father's Barbados over the mother's Brooklyn. "Jumping ship" to start her new life echoes how Deighton came to New York in the first place as an undocumented immigrant, but also his fatal leap when he returned to Barbados. Selina sees herself, however, as also following in the footsteps of her mother who left home at the age of eighteen to start a new life on her own. Her journey to Barbados expresses independence from both her mother and her father in a way that does not preclude returning to Brooklyn. Nor does it succumb to any romantic foundational identification with the island.

Selina mourns the loss of all that she leaves behind in the racialized space of Brooklyn—"those faces, those voices, those lives touching hers."[65] Yet because Black people do not control the spaces in which they live, Brooklyn does not remain static. Miss Thompson returns to the South to take a rest from her work in the beauty shop. No one knows when, or if, she will be back. The houses that the Barbadians have worked so hard to own get knocked down as part of the city's urban renewal program, undermining all their hard work and draining them of the assets they had managed to acquire.[66] "All those houses we sweat to buy and now, at last making little money from," laments Cecil Osborne, "gon soon be gone."[67]

At the conclusion of the novel, Selina walks through the neighborhood and surveys its ruins, the "vast waste" of an area where blocks of brownstones had been blown up to make way for a public housing project. As she walks through the rubble, Selina imagines that she hears "footsteps ringing hollow in the concrete halls."[68] Selina walks away, feeling like the "sole survivor amid the wreckage." She wishes to leave something behind. She takes one of the two silver bangles worn on her wrist since childhood to remind her of "home," and tosses it behind her, high over her shoulder. It strikes a stone, and makes "a frail sound in that utter silence."[69] She leaves one bangle in the ruins, but carries its twin on her wrist as she ventures out into her future. Instead of making a once-and-for-all decision between Brooklyn and Barbados, between ethnic affirmation and universal affiliation, between acquisitiveness and artistry, between the irresponsible joy of the father and the determined resolve of the mother, between the endless obligations imposed by the Barbadian Association and commitment-free dalliance with her lover, Selina Boyce chooses "both/and" rather than "either/or." This moral and political stance has no home, but it encourages us to create homes on the run in fugitive spaces that offer only temporary possibilities.

In a short story that also seems based on Marshall's life written nearly a quarter century after the publication of *Brown Girl, Brownstones*, Marshall delineates the devastating ruptures that urban renewal projects caused, disrupting the continuity and emotional ecosystem of the Black community in which she was raised. Her narrator laments that "the places no longer matter that much since most of them have vanished."[70] Her memory of them, however, still matters a great deal, because struggles over places continued to shape battles for rights, resources, and recognition. The patterns of the past perpetually impede progress in the present. Places that have vanished like Paule Marshall's Brooklyn neighborhood could have generated assets that appreciated in value across generations for millions of Black families. Instead, Black children like the fictional Selina Boyce and the historical Paule Marshall confronted the realities and restrictions of racialized space. Near the end of *Brown Girl, Brownstones*, Selina thinks about the people she knew growing up and how the radical divisiveness of life in a segregated city pitted them against each other. Marshall's narrator notes "those faces, those voices, those lives touching hers had ruined her, yet, she sensed—letting her gown trail on the sidewalk—they had bequeathed her a small strength."[71] That bequest seems small compared to the assets that white children receive from their ancestors. It is small consolation for housing discrimination and urban renewal, for the decapitalization of Black communities that simultaneously subsidized asset accumulation for whites. As an inheritance, it pales in comparison to the unfair gains and unjust enrichments that white families pass down across generations. Yet the small strength that Marshall identifies may not be so small after all. It is a spatial imaginary that recognizes the full harm done to individuals and society by racialized space and idealized fantasies about the properly gendered prosperous private home. It is an imaginary that seeks to be at home everywhere in the world, but to resist the closures and containments of being home bound. In its efforts to change the scope of space, it refuses Manichean binary oppositions and instead embraces complexity and contradiction. Perhaps most important, it recognizes both the enduring hold that the past has on the present while insisting on the imperative of action to shape a new future. The places of the past may disappear, but the moral lessons learned inside them can be carried on to new temporal and spatial locations. A brownstone house in a Brooklyn neighborhood, whose inhabitants devoted enormous energy to burrowing in and building up, turned out for Marshall to be the perfect place to learn about branching out. Its lessons also entail the importance of recognizing "the something left to love" inside other people, a recognition that forms the core challenge in Lorraine Hansberry's play *A Raisin in the Sun*, which forms the focal point for the next chapter.

8

Something Left to Love

Lorraine Hansberry's Chicago

An awareness of social space . . . always entails an
encounter with history—or better, a choice of histories.
—KRISTIN ROSS

During the time Paule Marshall explored the contradictions of Caribbean and North American identities in *Brown Girl, Brownstones*, images of the West Indies took on special prominence in the United States with the sudden and unexpected popularity of calypso music. At the very moment when Marshall imagined that a dialogue with Caribbean culture could help her learn to embrace a kind of global citizenship that transcended the parochial prejudices of North American racism, executives in the music business were busy turning part of Caribbean culture into a lucrative commodity. Audiences who derived economic benefits every day from imperialism's exploitation of the West Indies' labor, markets, and raw materials sought amusement and escape in songs that seemed to present the region as a tropical paradise suffused with colorful customs and quaint cultural expressions. North American musicians and singers "covered" calypso songs, simplifying them musically and lyrically, repressing their rich history of social criticism. This appropriation and exploitation of calypso by North American artists and entrepreneurs transformed Caribbean self-activity and self-expression into a spectacle that reinforced white supremacy. It changed the scope of space, but in a manner completely contrary to the principles articulated by Paule Marshall by expanding the white spatial imaginary to include the rest of the world.

Yet oddly enough, the commercial success of calypso music played an indirect role in bringing into being a tremendously significant challenge to the logic of racialized space. The profits generated by one calypso recording enabled Lorraine Hansberry to work full-time time writing the play *A Raisin in the Sun*, a poignant and powerful protest against segregation. The relationship between *A Raisin in the Sun* and the popularity of calypso music evidences the kind of unexpected and ungainly contradiction in real life that Paule Marshall wrote about so effectively in her fiction. In the late 1940s and early 1950s, African American rhythm and blues songs began to secure significant sales even though they were released on small independent labels not under the control of the major corporations in the music industry. Threatened by the social and sexual messages in some of these songs, but also concerned about losing market share to small entrepreneurs, the major companies responded by promoting calypso music from the West Indies. Rhythm and blues music had risen to popularity in no small measure because of racialized space; it emerged from the new African American communities created during and after World War II in the wake of the mechanization of southern agriculture and subsequent mass migration of Blacks to northern cities. The major record labels attempted to counter the popularity of these products that they *did not control* emerging from the racialized spaces of African American ghettos by promoting products from another racialized space that they imagined they *could* control: the Caribbean.[1]

Just as employers encouraged migration to the North American mainland by Puerto Rican and Jamaican labor after World War II to undermine the solidarity and bargaining power of African American workers, executives in the music industry turned to Caribbean music as a means of undercutting the earnings and social influence of these African American artists.[2] Yet consonant with dominant industry practices, the fruits and rewards of commercial calypso went to North American interpreters and promoters, not to the music's original Caribbean creators. The extraordinarily talented Harry Belafonte recorded a long-playing album titled *Calypso* that made the best-seller charts in 1956, retaining its popularity for eighty-four weeks, thirty-one of them as the best-selling album in the land.[3] Belafonte's song "Jamaica Farewell" entered the best-selling single charts on October 20, 1956, where it would remain for the next twenty-six weeks. Although the Harlem-born Belafonte had long established an admirable personal résumé as a resolute, irrepressible, and militant fighter for Black freedom and human rights (a distinction he enjoys to this day), the commercial success open to him came from the unearned privilege he derived from his identity as a North American, albeit the son of an immigrant father from Jamaica. In contrast, West Indian calypsonians Lord Kitchener and Mighty Sparrow represented places with long histories of politically radical, topical, or sexually themed songs. Their associations with these places and their noncitizen status in the United States made it impossible for them to secure the kinds of corporate support required for U.S. chart success that was available to Belafonte.[4]

One week before Belafonte's "Jamaica Farewell" hit the charts, a white group, Vince Martin and the Tarriers, placed a song titled "Cindy, Oh Cindy" in the top forty.[5] Written by Robert Nemiroff and Burt D'Lugoff, the song's genealogy illustrates the inequalities between spaces that characterize relations between North America and the Caribbean.[6] Its lyrics express a sailor's longing for a letter from his lover back home whose charms exceed those of the women he meets on his travels. Nemiroff and D'Lugoff, two white male New York songwriters, credited themselves as composers on the recording, receiving substantial royalties from its commercial success. Yet the song actually was a folk song well known in the West Indies and the Georgia Sea Islands originally titled "Pay Me, My Money Down." In the original version, the song expressed a class-conscious insistence by a dockworker that he get paid for his labor. With obvious commercial acumen in the politically and culturally repressive atmosphere of the 1950s, Nemiroff and D'Lugoff transformed this workers' song into a love song, changing "pay me, my money down" to "Cindy, don't let me down."[7] Nemiroff and D'Lugoff may not have realized that they based "Cindy, Oh Cindy" on "Pay Me, My Money Down." When music publisher Philip Rose asked the Tarriers (Erik Darling, Bob Carey, and Alan Arkin) to back up Vince Martin's recording of the song, however, they noticed immediately its resemblance to the West Indian song because they remembered its appearance on an early 1950s album by the Weavers. The Tarriers reinserted the Jamaican rhythm underlying "Pay Me, My Money Down" into the recording of "Cindy, Oh Cindy" to produce an arrangement with enormous popular appeal. The money they made from recording "Cindy, Oh Cindy" helped launch the Tarriers on extremely successful career paths. Erik Darling later joined the Weavers before launching a successful recording career as a studio musician, solo artist, and founding member of the Rooftop Singers. Alan Arkin left folk music to devote himself to a full-time acting career, a career that took off quickly once he won a Tony award for starring in Carl Reiner's semiautobiographical play *Enter Laughing*.[8] Many people profited from the popularity of "Cindy, Oh Cindy," but the original creators and interpreters of the song did not.

The reward structure of the music industry obliterated the identities of the original composers and lyricists of "Pay Me, My Money Down." Transforming the song into "Cindy, Oh Cindy" occluded the life circumstances of low-wage labor in the colonized country from which the song initially emerged. Yet the royalties secured from "Cindy, Oh Cindy" took an unpredictable turn when one of its white songwriters, Robert Nemiroff, used the money he made from the song to support the efforts of his Black wife, Lor-

raine Hansberry, as she wrote the play *A Raisin in the Sun*. Once the play
had been written, the song's publisher, Philip Rose, used part of his royalties
from it to help finance bringing *A Raisin in the Sun* to the stage. The first dramatic play produced on Broadway written by an African American, *A Raisin
in the Sun* went on to do more important work in the world. More than any
other single work of expressive culture, it called (and still calls) public attention to the indignities and oppressions of racialized space in the United States
at mid-century. Revived on Broadway and as a made-for-television movie in
2004 (released on DVD in 2008), *A Raisin in the Sun* remains a powerful
part of the invisible archive of Black memory, struggle, and spatial imagining. Financed in part by a song that succeeded in the market by pandering to
the seeming naturalness of racial and spatial inequality, *A Raisin in the Sun*
serves as a powerful weapon in the struggle to challenge the fatal coupling of
race and place.

In the play, Hansberry changes the stakes of space by depicting sympa-
thetically a Black family's plans to move into a forbidden place. Blessed with a
sudden inheritance, the Younger family wishes to leave their cramped inner-
city apartment and purchase a new home in the suburbs. Yet their new white
neighbors try to keep them out. Hansberry's protagonists do not have an overwhelming desire to live next door to white people. Rather, they recognize that
homeownership offers them the possibility of securing once and for all the
full fruits and benefits of their labor by acquiring an asset capable of appre-
ciating in value and being passed down to future generations. The Younger
family knows they will surely face harassment and ostracism in their new
dwelling, but they are determined to deny whites the right to exclude them.
The Younger family does not deepen and enrich ghetto spaces in the manner of Horace Tapscott, Betye Saar, John Biggers, and Rick Lowe. Nor do
they move back and forth across spaces like Selina Boyce in Paule Marshall's
Brown Girl, Brownstones. Instead, the Younger family challenges the stakes
of space by attempting to move into a place that is likely to be unpleasant in
order to defy prohibitions against their free movement and the consequences
of those prohibitions for their dignity as humans.

Nemiroff and Hansberry met each other for the first time on a New
York City picket line during a protest against racial discrimination. Hansberry had come to the city to work as an editorial assistant for Paul Robeson's
monthly newspaper *Freedom*, where her associates included Harold Cruse
and Julian Mayfield. She was a twenty-year-old dropout from the University of Wisconsin. Dissatisfied with the comparatively cloistered atmosphere
on the Madison campus, Hansberry threw herself into the vibrant life of
the streets in New York. In a letter to a friend in 1951, she talked about
how much she learned from the city itself, from the lively public sphere that

Black people created for themselves in public places. Just as Ella Baker had done in the 1930s when she came to New York from her native North Carolina, Hansberry attended meetings, ushered at rallies, made street corner speeches, went for long walks, and talked "to my people about everything on the streets."[9] Nemiroff and Hansberry married in 1953. He wrote songs and plays, while she worked in radical journalism until Nemiroff's success with "Cindy, Oh Cindy" enabled her to carve away time to write her first play.

Like Paule Marshall's first book, Hansberry's first play evidenced strong connections with the spatial possibilities and prohibitions of her childhood. Born in Chicago in 1930, Hansberry grew up in a successful entrepreneurial African American family. Her father played a key role in founding that city's first Black-owned bank. He started a real estate corporation that controlled properties that housed some four thousand families. Yet for all his wealth and business acumen, Carl Hansberry's Blackness prevented him from purchasing the home he wished to buy for himself and his family at 6140 South Rhodes Avenue in Chicago. Deed restrictions on the property barred its sale to African Americans. In May 1937, a white associate purchased the house for Hansberry and transferred its title to him. When the family (including seven-year-old Lorraine) attempted to move in, violent mobs of whites from the neighborhood repeatedly laid siege to the dwelling. On one occasion a brick crashed through the living room window with such force that it remained lodged in the opposite wall. The terror of that incident stayed with Hansberry for the rest of her life. She later recalled, "I was on the porch one day with my sister, when a mob gathered. We went inside, and while we were in our living room, a brick came crashing through the window with such force that it embedded itself in the opposite wall. I was the one the brick almost hit."[10] Her mother refused to remove the projectile from the wall, leaving it there as a permanent reminder of the family's "welcome" to the neighborhood.

The Hansberry family fought a six-year battle to stay in their home. When the Illinois Supreme Court ordered them evicted, Carl Hansberry moved to Washington, D.C., to shepherd the case through proceedings before the United States Supreme Court. His wife, Nantille, stayed with the children in the house for eight months in order to establish themselves as legal residents. Although the Supreme Court reversed the Illinois decision, the episode drained Carl Hansberry of most of his wealth. His experience with the case embittered him so deeply that he moved to Mexico in protest. When he died of a cerebral hemorrhage in that country in 1945, fifteen-year-old Lorraine Hansberry concluded that "American racism helped kill him."[11]

The horrors that the Hansberry family confronted could not be construed as personal. Systemic and impersonal forces created and maintained the boundaries that relegated members of different races to different places, exposing them to decidedly different and unequal opportunities and life chances. George Lewis's oral history interviews with the performers who established the Association for the Advancement of Creative Musicians has uncovered a pattern of double violence in the lives of Black people in Chicago. Several of Lewis's interview subjects said their families came to Chicago in the first place because whites in the south used mob violence to drive them off the land, then seized their property through various forms of legal subterfuge like adverse possession. Once the families arrived in Chicago, discrimination and zoning relegated them to overcrowded areas where landlords could charge high rents for dilapidated dwellings because segregation artificially constricted the housing choices available to Blacks.[12] When they tried to move into better areas, white mob violence confronted them once again.

Historians Arnold Hirsch and Thomas Sugrue have detailed the centrality of mob violence in preserving the privileges of segregated space for white homeowners in northern cities during the 1940s and 1950s. Hirsch notes that, in Chicago alone, white mobs launched forty-six separate attacks on Black residences between May 1944 and July 1946. Starting in January 1945, at least one attack took place every month. Twenty-nine of the incidents entailed arson. Three of assaults took the lives of Black people.[13] White mobs attacked Black families attempting to move into houses in the Fernwood area in 1947, in Englewood in 1949, in Cicero in 1951, and in Trumbull Park in 1953 and 1954. Police officers generally condoned these assaults. The Chicago Housing Authority used this violence as justification for its policy (later ruled illegal in federal court) of locating public housing projects only in segregated Black neighborhoods.[14] Author Frank Loudon Brown's novel *Trumbull Park*, published in the same year as *A Raisin in the Sun*'s first performance, captures the terror and chaos of one of these episodes brilliantly. The novel is based on what actually happened to Brown, his pregnant wife, and their two daughters, who were among the first Black families to move into the previously all-white Trumbull Park public housing project in 1954. Whites living in the project and their allies from the neighborhood threw sulfur candles, bricks, and stones through the windows of apartments occupied by Blacks. They set off loud explosive devices at three- to five-minute intervals for hours at a time.[15] Whites massed in hostile groups on the streets, circulated hate-filled pamphlets, and yelled racial insults at Blacks in neighborhood parks, stores, and even churches. City authorities, elected officials, community members, and religious leaders were cowed by the violence, although one church bulletin timidly reminded parishioners that "hissing, hooting, and assaulting anyone for going to Mass is very un-Christian."[16] Police officers stood by watching the violence, but they made no arrests. Blacks simply attempting to go to work downtown had to be transported out of the neighborhood in police wagons for their own safety.[17] Oddly enough, Brown's life paralleled Hansberry's in many ways. Both were born in Chicago, both combined activism with intellectual work (in his case doctoral studies at the University of Chicago), and both succumbed to fatal diseases before their thirty-fifth birthdays.[18]

Even without the kinds of spectacular assaults that Lorraine Hansberry and Frank London Brown experienced and chronicled, normal slum conditions entailed a kind of violence by themselves. Residential segregation created artificially high demands for an artificially scarce supply of housing. It enabled slumlords to subdivide houses and apartments, to pocket profits from their buildings without having to do maintenance on them. Lack of maintenance, overcrowding, and stress on building infrastructures created the preconditions for the thousands of fires that consumed South Side apartments between 1947and 1953. Two hundred people, sixty of them children, perished in these blazes. The *Chicago Defender* described the blazes as "another Chicago Fire on the installment plan."[19]

James Baldwin attributed the success of Hansberry's *A Raisin in the Sun* to the recognition of systematic oppression that it provoked for African American viewers, especially in respect to their relationship to racialized space. "Black people," he claimed, "supplied the play with an interpretive element, which could not be present in the minds of white people; a kind of claustrophobic terror, created not only by their knowledge of the house but by their knowledge of the streets."[20] Amiri Baraka credited the appeal of the play to the ways in which it "typifies American society in a way that reflects more accurately the real lives of the Black U.S. majority than any work that ever received commercial exposure before it, and few if any since."[21] Writing in 1995, Baraka noted that "*Raisin* lives in large measure because black people have kept it alive."[22] They do so, Baraka argues, because the play speaks to the central problem they face every day as Black people in America, a problem he describes as "the powerlessness of black people to control their own fate or that of their families in capitalist America where race is place, white is right, and money makes and defines the man."[23]

A Raisin in the Sun exposes the ways in which Black people have to struggle for the kinds of assets, inheritances, and opportunities that whites take for granted. Moreover, the stubborn persistence of white supremacist practices insures its relevance to succeeding generations. In 1975 the cast of a musical based on the play found itself called upon to support a Black family in Queens, New York, whose home had been firebombed because they had the temerity to move into a previously white neighborhood. The actors discovered a report from 1972 by a city commission describing eleven cases in the preceding eighteen months in New York where minority-owned homes had been set on fire or vandalized. For good measure, a church had also been bombed and a school bus had been attacked.[24]

In a 1964 letter to the *New York Times* that the newspaper's editors thought was not fit to print, Hansberry recalled her family's fight against restrictive covenants as she answered critics complaining about civil rights activists in that year who threatened a "stall-in" to block traffic headed for the opening of the New York World's Fair. The critics claimed that the activists manifested an impatience that would harm their own cause.[25] Hansberry strongly defended the activists' plans to obstruct public space as part a needed remedy for the obstacles against free movement that African Americans had experienced for centuries. She recalled how her father's passionate embrace of the "American way" led him to spend his fortune, time, and talents battling against white supremacy in a way that the critics of the stall-in might find legitimate. She explained, however, that these properly legal tactics required her as a young girl to face howling mobs, to risk her life, to be spat upon, cursed, and pummeled every day on her way to and from school. As her mother sat up all night guarding her children with a loaded German Luger handgun in her lap, Hansberry's father won his case in federal court but lost the home anyway. The Black ghetto in Chicago and other cities became even more segregated in the years that followed. Citing the costs in "emotional turmoil, time and money which led to my father's early death as a permanently embittered exile in a foreign country," Hansberry concluded her letter by endorsing the refusal of the young demonstrators at the World's Fair to play by the same rules. She lauded their willingness to "lie down in the streets, tie up traffic, do whatever we can—take to the hills with guns if necessary—and fight back."[26]

The racialized spaces of the segregated South Side Chicago neighborhoods of her youth loomed large in Lorraine Hansberry's writing and consciousness. She advised travelers to the city to ride the elevated trains because they afforded choice views of her neighborhood's back porches where "the tempo of my people" could be observed. "Our Southside is a place apart," she proclaimed; "each piece of our living is a protest."[27] Hansberry remembered the elementary school she attended as a place programmed for failure. Its students were Black, but the people who made decisions about the education it offered were white. She observed that Ross Elementary School existed more to withhold education rather than to provide it, "just as the ghetto itself exists not to give people homes but to cheat them out of as much decent housing as possible."[28] Yet Hansberry also received early lessons from her family about how the schemes of racialized space might be rearranged and contested. She recalled riding in the family car one time as her father drove through the hills of Kentucky on a family vacation. She listened while her mother explained how Lorraine's slave grandfather ran away from his owner and hid in these hills, and how her grandmother stashed away food for him in secret places in the woods.[29]

Hansberry drew on the hate crimes perpetrated against her family during her childhood in telling *Raisin in the Sun*'s story. As the play opens, Lena Younger, her daughter Beneatha, her son Walter Lee, his wife Ruth, and their son Travis eagerly await delivery of a check from a life insurance company owed to them because of the death of Lena's late husband, "Big Walter." Walter Lee wants to use the check to purchase an interest in a liquor store so that he can leave his job as a chauffeur and relieve his wife of her work as a domestic. Beneatha plans to go to medical school and envisions the check as payment for tuition. Lena, however, adamantly hopes to spend the money on a home for the family. She selects the all-white Clybourne Park neighborhood because the houses there are in her price range, not because of any abstract commitment to integration.

The brilliant, complex, and multilayered plot of *A Raisin in the Sun* touches on an impressive array of issues, from fissures between genders and generations to the cumulative consequences of colonialism and slavery, from class tensions within the Black community to the power of racial categories to divide white and Black workers of the same class, from the seductive appeals of popular culture to the logic behind strategies of uplift among aggrieved groups. Yet the dramatic tensions at the center of the drama stem specifically from the racialization of space and the spatialization of race. For Hansberry, changing either the scale or the scope of racialized space will not suffice. Instead, she argues for changing what is at stake in struggles over space.

The recreational spaces of the ghetto described so lovingly by Paule Marshall in *Brown Girl, Brownstones* seem like traps to Hansberry. Speaking reverently about the music played by a small combo at the Green Hat bar, Walter Lee explains, "You can just sit there and drink and listen to them three men play and you realize that don't nothing matter worth a damn, but just being there."[30] Like Silla Boyce in *Brown Girl, Brownstones*, Hansberry views the demotic culture of the ghetto as an opiate, one that soothes real pain, but only by promoting resigned detachment from social problems. Yet Hansberry refused either to disidentify with the Black working class or to embrace fully the culture of uplift in which she was raised. She sometimes explained her adult commitments as the inevitable product of one unforgettable childhood experience. She recalled that her wealthy parents sent her to her first day of kindergarten wearing a fur coat. In the midst of the Great Depression, a five-year-old Black girl in an expensive fur coat must have been a rare sight. Offended by this ostentatious display of privilege, some of her classmates roughed her up and stained her coat with ink. Although she did not under-

stand what was happening at the time, she later remembered the incident as
a formative life lesson. She explained that the incident left her with a life-
long antagonism to flaunting symbols of affluence, and insisted pointedly that
after her first day of school, she deliberately chose her friends from the ranks
of her assailants.[31]

The Younger family came from those ranks. Walter Lee works as a chauffeur and takes a wealthy white man from place to place. He drives around
in circles, going nowhere on his own. Walter Lee wants to own a business,
to have a place to be where nothing matters "but just being there." Yet his
dreams lock him into the limits of racialized spaces of the ghetto. The most
utopian dream he can conjure up is to own a liquor store. Hansberry portrays this choice as already constrained by the racialization of space. For Walter Lee, no less than for the customers he hopes to attract, liquor will help
him endure intolerable conditions, but do nothing to change them. His sister Beneatha occupies the other extreme. She embraces the anticolonial and
Pan-African dreams of a Nigerian boyfriend who gives her a Yoruba name
that means "she for whom bread is not enough." Beneatha rejects the history
that she feels has led Black people tragically from the plantation to the ghetto.
She wants a new identity, aspiring to be a Black nationalist and a physician,
someone capable of curing both society's and her own people's ills. Unlike her
brother, she sees far beyond the ghetto and its values. Yet for that very reason,
she also distances herself too much from the very people she purports to represent, disidentifying with and heaping scorn on her mother's alleged back-
wardness—her seeming accommodations to white supremacy, her ignorance
of Africa, and the faith in God that strikes her daughter as mere superstition.
Beneatha also looks down on her brother's desire for pleasures and places of
his own. Walter Lee seeks to change the scale of space; he wants to burrow
into the ghetto, imagining that the liquor store will be a safe haven, a source
of power and profits. Beneatha wants to branch out, to change the scope of
space, to see the Chicago ghetto as only a tiny and powerless part of a majestic Afro-disaporic world now coming into its own in Africa and all around
the globe. Yet neither Walter nor Beneatha can resolve the Younger family's
problems with racialized space through these strategies. Hansberry's play pro-
poses changing the stakes of space as the preferred solution.

Through the character of Lena, Hansberry champions burrowing in,
building up, and branching out all at once. Lena wants a new home for her
family, not for its cash value, but because it represents a chance for a better life for her grandson. She also makes it clear that she sees purchasing a
home as the best way of giving her late husband something he never received
in life, fair compensation for all his hard labors. Yet Lena also understands
the dreams that guide Walter Lee and Beneatha. She sees their legitimacy.

After using part of the money for a down payment on the house, Lena gives
the rest to Walter Lee, instructing him to deposit some of it in an account for
Beneatha's medical school tuition and to use the rest to purchase a share of
the liquor store. Although disappointed that her children are neither satisfied
nor proud of what she and her husband have done for them, Lena recognizes
that they need money in order to become actors in the world, rather than simply people who are acted upon. She knows they need money to look the world
in the eye. Yet Walter gets swindled out of the money foolishly by a confidence man. The family gets an opportunity to recoup their loss when a representative of the all-white Clybourne Park homeowners' association offers
to buy back the house at a profit to the Youngers in order to keep the neighborhood all white. The Younger family now needs the money. They know full
well the hostility that awaits them if they move into Clybourne Park. At one
point Walter Lee argues that they should accept the offer. The most valuable
thing the family owns, he decides, is the fear the possibility of their presence
provokes among their new neighbors. He contends that they should put on a
show for the man and get the money, no matter how debased it makes them
feel. At the end of the play, however, the family decides to keep the house.
Their decision is not based on hopes for financial security; they would have
gained more wealth by accepting the money offered them not to move. Nor
do they imagine that their new suburban home will be blissfully peaceful,
given what they now know about the people who will live near them. They do
not even have a particularly strong moral or political commitment to integration. Instead, they decide that they cannot allow anyone to determine where
they can or cannot live, where they belong, or what they can do with their
money. The right to inhabit and own space is more valuable to them than the
space itself. They see that they have been called to do work in the world that
makes a difference.

Hansberry recognizes Walter Lee's frustrations as real and sees his anger
and ambition as fully justified. Yet she argues that he would be better off
challenging the system than merely hoping to find a safe space inside it.
Hansberry locates Walter Lee and the rest of the Younger family on the "frontiers of challenge" against white supremacy. Although she thinks of these
frontiers as limited because they do not in themselves question the basic
premises of the social order, these frontiers are nonetheless important to
Hansberry because they offer potential places for the creation of new kinds of
consciousness, for Blacks to become a new people.[32] When one critic wrote
that the family's decision to move to the suburbs gave the play a happy ending, Hansberry responded, "If he thinks that's a happy ending, I invite him
to come live in one of the communities where the Youngers are going!"[33] The
point for her was not to envision how one family might have a more enjoy-

able life, but rather how their decision—as well as the play she wrote depicting it—might advance the cause of Black freedom. Hansberry believed that works of expressive culture contained energy necessary for social change.[34] She opposed the ghetto not because it was Black, but because it constrained opportunities and life chances. She was not looking for reconciliation with resistant whites. As she wrote shortly after *A Raisin in the Sun* had its New York premiere, "Negroes, for instance, simply do not live as long as white people in America. I think we must begin to remember facts like that and chatter less about the sensibilities of our bigots. We have been pathetically overgenerous with their malignant whimsy for three centuries."[35]

Hansberry's play staged a symbolic rebuke of the white spatial imaginary. Yet even offstage she found herself forced to battle for space, for a place where her play could reach the public. After raising sufficient funds from 147 different investors, the producers of *A Raisin in the Sun* could not find a single theater owner on Broadway willing to rent space to a play based on the experiences of African Americans. The producers had to take the production out on the road and first demonstrate that it could succeed at the box office in New Haven and Philadelphia before opening in New York.[36] When the commercially and critically successful play became a film in 1961, the film studio's director and producer deleted dialogue to soften its critique. They cut out lines Hansberry added to the work describing a Black family that had been bombed out of their home in a white neighborhood. In writing the screenplay, Hansberry added scenes that depicted Walter Lee feeling rebuffed by a white liquor store proprietor whom he asks for business advice. She augmented her portrayal of Lena by showing her work as a domestic and her frustration in paying high prices for inferior goods in a neighborhood store. Neither scene appeared in the final version of the film.[37]

The self-activity valorized in *A Raisin in the Sun* expresses what Hansberry elsewhere termed "the religion of doing what is necessary in the world."[38] Combining the sense of "doing for self" encapsulated in the creations by Tapscott, Saar, Biggers, and Lowe with Marshall's advanced understanding of situational affiliations and allegiances, Hansberry's play envisions and enacts a politics of space that puts ultimate faith not in property or places, but in people. The play prefigured the degree to which struggles over racialized spaces would take center stage in the civil rights movement of the 1960s, from the marches for fair housing in the Chicago suburbs of Gage Park and Marquette Park led by Dr. Martin Luther King, Jr., in 1966 to the electoral battle over California's fair-housing law in 1964, from the passage of the federal Fair Housing Act of 1968 to the issuance of the Supreme Court's monumental housing desegregation decision that same year in the *Jones v. Mayer* case.

Although it is always difficult to gauge with precision the exact relationship between works of expressive culture and movements for social change, *A Raisin in the Sun* played an important if indirect role in placing the vexed connections between race and place before the public. It also played a direct role in making possible one of the most significant moments in the civil rights struggles of the 1960s. Hansberry used the notoriety and resources she derived from the success of the play to participate fully and enthusiastically in the Black freedom movement. New Orleans civil rights activist Jerome Smith contacted Hansberry and asked for help for the Congress of Racal Equality's "Freedom Summer" voter registration drive in Mississippi. The playwright organized, chaired, and spoke at a public meeting at Croton-on-Hudson, New York, to raise funds for the project. CORE used the money generated from that particular meeting to buy the station wagon that Michael Schwerner, Andrew Goodman, and James Chaney were driving at the time of their abduction and murder near Philadelphia, Mississippi. This brutal act of repression carried out by Ku Klux Klan members (including local law enforcement officials) demonstrated to the world in dramatic and unambiguous fashion the corruptions of white supremacist power in the United States, and helped build popular support for passing and enforcing substantive civil rights laws for nearly the first time in a century.[39]

In 1966, seven years after the debut of *A Raisin in the Sun* on Broadway, five years after its film premiere, and two years after Lorraine Hansberry succumbed to cancer at the age of thirty-four, Martin Luther King, Jr., set up a temporary headquarters in her beloved city of Chicago. King and the Southern Christian Leadership Conference hoped to show that the nonviolent tactics that they had used successfully to challenge southern segregation and disenfranchisement could be effective in addressing the problems facing northern Blacks, such as poverty, residential segregation, educational inequality, and police brutality. King quickly learned the degree to which white control over space in Chicago kept Blacks in their place. After weeks of unsuccessful mobilizations and demonstrations in the inner city, the coalition that King led decided to bring the struggle to the suburbs by staging open-housing marches in all-white neighborhoods in Gage Park and Chicago Lawn.

Open-housing advocates assembled clear evidence of discrimination by individuals and real estate agencies that clearly violated local fair-housing statutes: one hundred and twenty-one instances in Gage Park alone.[40] Forty-seven whites and sixty-one Blacks attempted to secure housing from thirteen real estate agencies in the Belmont-Cragin neighborhood. The white housing seekers were shown available dwellings in the neighborhood, but Blacks were directed toward properties in the ghetto. Only one of the thirteen real estate companies made its regular listings available to Blacks.[41] An integrated group of fair-housing advocates marched into Gage Park on the weekend of July 29. They were met by white mobs. Men, women, and children waved signs decorated with swastikas and racist epithets. Signs proclaimed, "Nigger Go Home," "White Power," and "I'd Love to Be an Alabama Trooper, that is what I'd truly like to be, because if I were an Alabama trooper, I could shoot niggers, one, two three."[42]

White residents of Gage Park shouted obscenities at the marchers and pelted them with rocks and bottles. One of the demonstrators, a ten-year-old girl, got hit with a rock. A nun and first grade teacher at Sacred Heart School, Sister Mary Angelica, fell to the pavement after being struck in the head by a stone. As marchers picked up the unconscious nun and hurried her into a nearby police car, their assailants screamed in triumph, "We've got another one." Young men yelled, "Burn them like Jews" and "White power." One held a noose and chanted "KKK" while others burned a cross in the street. Protest leader Al Raby was struck with projectiles on four separate occasions. Cars belonging to the demonstrators were vandalized. Twelve of them were burned, another twelve were overturned, and two were pushed into a nearby lagoon.[43] Many more demonstrators would have been injured save for the brave efforts of young Black street-gang members who acted as parade marshals. They batted down hundreds of bottles and bricks with their bare hands, but did not fight back against their assailants out of respect for Dr. King's commitment to nonviolence.[44]

Two weeks later, Dr. King and gospel singer Mahalia Jackson led a march by six hundred demonstrators demanding open housing in Gage Park. Twelve hundred police officers stood between the marchers and a mob estimated to be anywhere from four thousand to eight thousand people. Counterdemonstrators pelted the marchers with firecrackers, bricks, bottles, and even one knife. A rock hit Dr. King in the head as members of the crowd chanted, "Niggers go home." "We want King," "Get the Witch Doctor," and "Kill him, kill, him." They surged against police lines and pushed and shoved the outmanned detail of officers at the scene. King and his staff had witnessed violence frequently in the South, but nothing like what they encountered in Chicago. The mobs in Gage Park were not composed solely of street toughs. Entire families poured out of houses to confront the marchers. The size of the crowd and the hysteria and hatred they voiced surpassed anything the SCLC veterans had seen before. "I have never seen such hostility and hatred anywhere in my life," King remarked, "even in Selma."[45] On August 14, men wearing business suits and women wearing Sunday dresses (some of them returning home from church services) confronted open-housing marchers with signs featuring swastikas and threats against Blacks. One marcher was hit with a brick and two automobiles belonging to demonstrators were vandalized. After a rally by the American Nazi Party, police officers were attacked by a mob of whites.[46]

In the South, outbursts of mob violence had redounded to the benefit of nonviolent civil rights protestors. The conscience of the nation had been touched by scenes of white mothers spitting at Black schoolchildren trying to desegregate schools in New Orleans, of young white men attacking and beating Black students asking for service in previously segregated lunch counters in Nashville and many other cities, of firefighters aiming high-pressure hoses at nonviolent marchers in the streets of Birmingham. Yet when similar violence occurred in the North perpetrated by working-class suburban dwellers seeking to keep their neighborhoods white, the conscience of America was not touched. Instead, representatives of the city of Chicago, the state of Illinois, and the federal government generally blamed the peaceful nonviolent marchers for the conflict. Pundits, politicians, and journalists opined that Dr. King had gone too far, that the movement wanted change too fast, that whites had the right to defend the advantages that accrued to them from residential discrimination. Stunned by the violence, abandoned by their white liberal northern allies, and humiliated by defeat, Dr. King and his staff negotiated a face-saving exit from Chicago. They signed an agreement pledging an end to all street demonstrations but especially a planned march to the white suburb of Cicero in return for promises that the city would enforce its fair-housing ordinances (already on the books) and stop locating public housing projects exclusively in Black neighborhoods. The agreement included no timetable, no deadlines, no benchmarks, and no means of accountability. Dr. King moved on to other campaigns in other cities, while Blacks in Chicago faced the bitter possibility that the campaign might have left them in an even worse condition than before. Not only had they failed to secure better conditions, but they had provoked white supremacist vigilante violence that now stood triumphant, validated by its success in driving Dr. King from the city.

Like the Younger family in A Raisin in the Sun, Blacks in Chicago in 1966 decided that they could not allow white exclusion to go unchallenged. In the play, Walter Lee proclaims his family's right to inhabit the house in Clybourne Park as something they have already earned. He presents his son Travis to the representative of the white homeowners' association as the sixth generation of their family in this country. Walter Lee explains they have decided to move into the house because "my father—my father—he earned it for us brick by brick." The unpaid and underpaid labor of Blacks like Big Walter made the accumulation of white wealth possible. Walter Lee changes his mind about inhabiting suburban space because the fight over the house positions him differently in time. If only the present counted, it would make sense to take the money offered by the homeowners' association. But to do so, would be to disidentify with history, with the work Big Walter did and the remuneration he never received for it. Knuckling under to the association would also send the wrong message to Travis about his future, depriving him of the kind of courageous intergenerational example that Big Walter and Lena had set for Walter Lee and Beneatha. Like the fictional Younger family, the real-life Black families participating in the Chicago movement in the summer of 1966 decided to cross the line, to go to the suburbs out of respect for the past and with a sense of obligation to the future. For the movement activists, that meant conducting the march in Cicero, despite the agreement not to do so between the SCLC and city leaders. Cicero held symbolic meaning for the moral geography of race in Chicago. Although as many as fifteen thousand Blacks worked in that city every day, none lived there. Cicero had a reputation among Blacks as a place that you did not venture into alone or stay too long. Just a few months earlier in May 1966, four white teenagers in Cicero attacked Jerome Huey, a Black teenage honors student who had traveled to the suburb to apply for a job. His attackers knocked Huey's eyes out of skull, killing him in the process.[47] Yet the fear that Cicero provoked and the level of hatred that it represented posed an important challenge to the freedom movement. Despite the evident dangers, in fact because of them, marching in Cicero had great appeal for the movement's rank and file. Like the Younger family in Lorraine Hansberry's play, they viewed backing down as giving up, as betraying both their ancestors and their descendants. As protester Linda Bryant-Hall later recalled, "I looked forward to the time that I could march down those streets in defiance of all of the people there."[48]

Without the participation or approval of Dr. King or Jesse Jackson, the rank and file of the Chicago freedom movement made a decision very similar to the one made by the Younger family in *A Raisin in the Sun*: to go where they were not wanted, to affirm their conviction that no one had the right to keep them out. They announced that they would march on Cicero. Activist Nancy Jefferson declared, "I am a citizen of this city. I am Black American. I have a right to move where I want to move if I have the money to move. What's wrong with that?"[49] Chester Robinson of the West Side Association described the decision to take the struggle to Cicero as an important turning point. He announced that movement no longer sought to touch the conscience of whites. They had seen what that had produced in Gage Park and Marquette Park. Instead, they marched this time to demonstrate that they could not be intimidated, that they were not guided by fear. They would not come to whites hat in hand begging for justice, Robinson emphasized, but instead intended to walk anywhere, anytime, as humans entitled to human and humane treatment. The demonstrators also announced that this march would not be a "Dr. King march." Anything thrown at them, they warned, would be thrown back. On the Labor Day weekend, a small group of two hundred and fifty blacks and whites marched together for open housing on the streets of Cicero. Three thousand police officers assigned to protect them could barely restrain the howling mob that taunted and attacked the marchers. As the march proceeded, whites from Cicero shouted obscenities at the marchers, threw things at them, and threatened them. The protestors stopped to pray at the spot where Jerome Huey had been murdered. Huey's mother cried as a theology student led the group in a prayer for her deceased son's memory. As they prayed, the white mob swirled around them, shouting insults and waving swastikas.[50]

The marchers in Cicero confronted exactly what the Younger family might have faced in Clybourne Park. But they marched anyway. They did so to pursue the worthy and fully justified goal of open housing, but they also acted out of a sophisticated understanding of the dignity that comes from fighting back. Hansberry dramatizes that argument brilliantly in an important moment in A Raisin in the Sun. Beneatha's progressive politics and activist militancy cause her to confuse self-righteousness with righteousness. Furious at her brother for foolishly squandering part of the family inheritance in pursuit of a license to operate a liquor store and embarrassed by his willingness to knuckle under to the Clybourne Park Improvement Association and take the money they offer to keep the Younger family out of the neighborhood, Beneatha speaks bitterly about him. In her eyes, Walter has internalized the corruptions of white society. He is willing to bribe state officials, to sell liquor to other Blacks despite the harm it does to them and their community, to debase himself by taking money from whites for not moving into their neighborhood. Lena Younger cautions her daughter against rejecting her brother, explaining that now more than ever he needs her love. Beneatha replies scornfully that he has fallen so low that there is nothing left in him to love. Drawing on the hard lessons she has learned from a lifetime of racist subordination, Lena stiffens her back and rebukes her daughter. She explains that Walter has become the way he is because of the things that have happened to him. With a fire in her eyes, Lena insists to Beneatha that there is always something left to love. Lena does not like the things Walter has done. She is critical of them herself. She is not saying he should not be accountable for his actions and corrected when they are wrong. She recognizes, however, that writing him off would be giving up. It would mean accepting the social death to which white supremacy has consigned him. Beneatha thinks she is being militant, but Lena sees that she is simply being dogmatic, and selfishly so. The temporary pleasures of feeling superior to her brother prevent her from seeing how her fate is linked with his. The plot of A Raisin in the Sun turns on this scene. By recognizing something left to love in Walter,

Lena creates the possibility for her son to return to the fold, to save himself and serve his family.

Like Paule Marshall's novel, Lorraine Hansberry's play served as an invisible archive of struggles against racialized space. Although reflecting individual aesthetic choices and personal preoccupations, these creations also offer evidence of the central role played by space in the cognitive mapping and structural economy of race in the mid-twentieth century. The innovative, imaginative, and even eccentric character of their work stems from their unusual ambition to blend aesthetic and political goals into a unified totality. No one spatial strategy sufficed to solve the diverse and plural problems that white supremacy posed for Black communities. Yet changing the scale, scope, and stakes of space served different purposes at different times. All three strategies worked together as a reticulated web that accomplished more collectively than any one tactic might have achieved individually.

In order for history to take place, it takes places. Among aggrieved groups, history also takes places away, leaving people displaced and dispossessed. In the United States, racial subordination has often manifested its full force and fury through physical segregation and spatial subordination. Works of expressive culture emerged in twentieth-century Black communities as both symptoms and critiques of that nexus between race and space. Their enduring appeal and relevance offer powerful evidence of the shameful duration, depth, and dimension of the racialization of space and the spatialization of race. In Section V, I will explain how intransigent attachments to human diversity in Black culture manifest themselves in contemporary struggles for democracy by the Black working class in New Orleans and by proponents of fair housing all across the nation.

SECTION V

Race and Place Today

9

New Orleans Today

We Know This Place

Unless we can control the space we occupy,
we will not be able to really love one another.
—Kalamu ya Salaam

Hurricane Katrina hit New Orleans at the end of August in 2005. Water broke through and overflowed defective levees built and maintained by the Army Corps of Engineers. Leaders of local and state government bodies undermined by decades of defunding the public sector delayed declaring a state of emergency to escape responsibility for helping people get away. Working-class and poor Blacks suffering from the cumulative consequences of the repudiation of the civil rights movement and the egalitarian social programs of the 1960s lacked the private vehicles needed to escape the city. Federal officials failed to provide food, water, and sanitation to thousands of people herded into the city's domed stadium and neglected to rescue those trapped in their neighborhoods. Armed police officers stood on bridges leading out of the city to prevent Blacks fleeing the flooding from escaping to predominately white municipalities. After the hurricane, city, state, and federal officials colluded with private investors to disperse nearly half of the city's population to far-flung destinations in an effort to fulfill the promise made by George Bush's Secretary of Housing and Urban Development Alphonso Jackson that "New Orleans is not going to be as black as it was for a long time, if ever again."[1]

The organized abandonment of the New Orleans Black working class conformed completely to the logic of the white spatial imaginary. Assertions of the community's right to return, right to rebuild, and right to determine democratically its own future came largely out of the Black spatial imaginary, from social movement groups, community organizations, and arts activists. Spoken-word artist Sunni Patterson spoke for these people powerfully in her poem "We Know This Place." Patterson's piece placed the problems facing Black people in New Orleans in the aftermath of Hurricane Katrina in the context of a long history of struggles over race and space. "We know this place," the first line of her poem proclaims, referencing not only the physical place of New Orleans but also the place in history created by the continuous displacement and dispossession of Black people. This is a place of social death, Patterson explains, "for we have glanced more times than we'd like to share into eyes that stare with nothing there behind them but an unfilled wish and an unconscious yearning for life though death rests comfortably beside us." Patterson connects the agonized cries of people slowly dying of hunger and thirst at the Superdome to the moans and wails emanating from slave quarters and slum neighborhoods for centuries. Plans to rebuild the city at the expense of local residents for the profit of investors are another "feast for the beast at their table of shame with napkins 'round necks that catch the blood that drains from the flesh they chew, it's hell to gain." In words that echo Malcolm X, Patterson writes, "And we know this place. It's ever-changing yet forever the same: Money and power and greed, the game."[2]

Yet the place that Patterson knows is also a special place, a site where a Black spatial imaginary has long honed and refined the arts of burrowing in, building up, and branching out. It is a place where the global Blackness honored in Paule Marshall's writing has long had proximate and tangible meanings. People all over the world revere New Orleans as a significant center of the African diaspora. The Crescent City's music, dance, food, architecture, speech, religion, and performance styles all display African influences and retentions. Hand-drawn illustrations by Henry Benjamin Latrobe of performances by Black musicians in Congo Square in the nineteenth century depicted instruments that closely resembled those made and played traditionally in Africa. These images displayed traces of African practices such as carving figures on stringed wooden instruments and making drums by stretching the skins over hollowed-out pieces of wood.[3] Dena Epstein explains that vivid displays of African culture persisted openly in New Orleans before the Civil War to a greater degree than in any other North American city.[4] Sidney Bechet claimed that when slaves dreamed, "things would come to them out of Africa."[5] In his *American Patchwork* program on public television in 1991, Alan Lomax showed a film he made in the late 1970s that highlighted parallels between New Orleans parades and African festival celebrations. Lomax focused especially on a street dancer named Spiderman whose penchant for dancing on rooftops and under cars embodies the African aesthetic of contrasting heights with depths.[6] Today, the parade umbrellas and percussive polyrhythms of second liners display the enduring and irrepressible

African presence in the local culture. As Gwendolyn Midlo Hall reminds us, "New Orleans remains, in spirit, the most African city in the United States."[7]

Yet life in New Orleans is riddled with contradictions. African retentions are everywhere in the city, but they interact in complex and sometimes contradictory ways with currents of culture, history, and politics that originate in other places. Louisiana's Native Americans encountered Spanish and French colonizers in the sixteenth and seventeenth centuries. The Louisiana colony was established initially by settlers from Canada, but built by the labor of slaves, many of whom originated in Senegal. Filipinos came to Louisiana as early as 1763 and started to settle in New Orleans in the nineteenth century.[8] French settlers in Louisiana captured some Native Americans and exported them for sale as slaves on Caribbean islands controlled by France. Benito Juarez, later president of Mexico, made his home in exile in New Orleans in the 1850s, working as a cigar maker in the French Quarter as he mobilized opposition to the dictatorial regime in his home country. General Antonio Maceo also used New Orleans as a base for Cuban exiles mobilizing for independence from Spain in 1884 and 1885.

New Orleans has thus long been "always African," but never "only African." Its history helps us see how diasporic models of exile and return home to a mother land tell us less about the way Afro-diasporic identities are lived in the world than do frameworks based on practices that entail world-traversing and world-transcending citizenship. The complex culture of New Orleans offers us an opportunity to rethink how the history of the Africa diaspora has taken place. We owe a great debt to past scholars for establishing the persistence of African beliefs, practices, and processes in North America. African retentions helped Black people to counter the dominant culture's racist erasures of the African past and its presumptions that Africans in America lacked any enduring or meaningful connections to their native lands. Yet in the United States, as Rachel Buff observes, African retention has always been paired with New World invention.[9]

Cut off from ancestral homelands in Africa and denied full franchise and social membership in the United States, many Blacks forged ideals of world-traversing and world-transcending citizenship through cultural production. Some retained hopes of return to Africa, not just by participating in Black nationalist "back to Africa" movements, but also by instantiating memories of Africa in everyday practices of household decoration, healing, craft work, and religious rituals.[10] As Charles Joyner notes, even when slaves were compelled to work exclusively with American or European tools, they nonetheless employed them in African ways.[11] These practices could not function the same way they did in Africa, however, because of the grim realities of slavery and white supremacy in the United States. Instead, these African retentions provided the basis for New World inventions, evidencing not so much a literal desire to return to Africa as much as demonstrating a commitment to living and working in African ways in the new world. They help produce a diasporic imagination that affirms that wherever Africans are, Africa is. Yet African retentions also promote connections to the wider world that makes its presence felt in the global crossroads that is New Orleans.

New Orleans serves as both the southernmost port of the Mississippi River Valley and metaphorically as the northernmost port of the Caribbean Sea. Every day for centuries, ships and sailors from Cuba, Haiti, Mexico, and Trinidad have entered and departed the local port. Migrants from Haiti, Martinique, and other Francophone Caribbean islands have brought a distinct inflection to local African American identity. Historic preservation in the French Quarter makes New Orleans seem like one of the most European cities in North America. Yet in the rest of the metropolitan area outside the central city, the local petrochemical industry played a crucial role in shaping the predictable North American pattern of the automobile-centered city with suburbs that prevails in the rest of the country.[12] Largely because of refugees and exiles from Vietnam, between seven thousand and twelve thousand Asian immigrants now inhabit the New Orleans metropolitan area. Migration from Central America propelled by opportunities for low-wage construction jobs in the wake of the destruction surrounding Hurricane Katrina has raised the Latino population of the city to more than fifteen thousand. New Orleans is not only a city but a crossroads as well, a place where collisions occur, but where creative new paths also emerge.

New Orleans has served historically as the headquarters of the white supremacist Mississippi Delta "plantation bloc,"[13] as well as what David C. Estes (drawing on Zora Neale Hurston) terms the "urban mother of all African American culture, a sacred place where myth becomes a potent force in history."[14] As the financial and political center of plantation power, the city has been a place where profits made from the exploitation and repression of nonwhite labor have been secured, invested, and expanded. New Orleans and its surrounding hinterlands have been laboratories for the development of cruel and regressive policies about incarceration and taxation, low-wage labor and welfare, and environmental destruction and educational inequality. These policies have been implemented subsequently in the rest of the nation and the world because of the political power of the plantation bloc in the United States. Yet the stark imbalances of power in New Orleans have also provoked the creation of a relentless and continuing series of egalitarian and antiracist artistic, social, and political mobilizations that continue to this day in the wake of the plundering of the city by neoliberal interests and institutions in the wake of the destruction that accompanied Hurricane Katrina in 2005.

African Americans throughout the United States have developed a diasporic imagination that embraces exile as a permanent rather than temporary condition, as a source of strength rather than as a source of deprivation. Living in exile without the practical possibility of returning home generated an imagination that envisioned and enacted coalitions to other communities that transcended national borders. For example, both Canada and Mexico served as possible destinations for individual runaway slaves. In the 1850s, Martin Delany and Mary Ann Shadd Cary pursued "colonization" projects in Canada that entailed building cross-border networks valuable to the abolitionist cause.[15] Frederick Douglass sought support for the antislavery movement from white workers in Ireland, Scotland, and England.[16] Four thousand fugitive slaves made their way to Mexico to live in settlements protected by the Mexican government, like the one established by the Seminole Indian chief Wild Cat.[17]

Blacks in the United States cultivated real and imagined affinities with other diasporic Africans, but they also identified with other aggrieved communities from all races, with people struggling at home and around the world for rights, resources, and recognition. Anna Julia Cooper famously proclaimed that "every interest that has lacked an interpreter and a defender" becomes the concern of Black women.[18] Black communities in the United States have long viewed their fate as linked to anticolonial and antiimperialist struggles throughout the world, not only in Africa, but in the Caribbean, Latin America, and Asia as well.[19] The global interests and affiliations of North American Blacks have a long history that encompasses stories in the Black press about Corporal David Fagen, who defected from the U.S. Army to join Emilio Aguinaldo's rebels in the Philippines in 1899, efforts by W. E. B. Du Bois to promote what he termed the common cause of the darker races, the grassroots popularity of the Black internationalism of the Universal Negro Improvement Association, and the anticolonialism manifested in popular support in U.S. Black communities for Ethiopians resisting Italian aggression, antifascists in Spain, and struggles against British colonialism by the Indian National Congress, as well as Malcolm X's insistence on taking the concerns of Blacks to the United Nations so that representatives of nations in Asia, Latin America, and Africa could help adjudicate Black demands.[20]

The history of diasporic identification, intimacy, and creativity in New Orleans is especially relevant at the present moment, at a time when transnational processes, practices, and institutions seem to have eclipsed the autonomy of the nation-state. In a brilliant rumination on the need to craft new understandings of citizenship and social membership at this historical moment, Etienne Balibar calls for political projects that attend to *both* the legitimate democratic aspirations of particular aggrieved groups *and* to the necessity of creating broader spheres of interdependence. In that context, the history of New Orleans can serve as a valuable archive of generative ways of knowing and ways of being.[21]

The history of New Orleans has made the city a place where multiple languages, national histories, and traditions collide, conflict, and coalesce. These interactions do not diminish the importance of the African diaspora to the city's culture. Indeed, it is precisely the adaptability, syncretism, gregariousness, and generosity at the core of West African culture that accounts for much of the ability of generations of New Orleaneans to make creative use of conflict, to forge balance and unity out of opposites, to fashion life-affirming and pleasure-affirming artistic expressions as a central form of revolt against what Franklin Rosemont describes as "the shameful limits of an unlivable destiny."[22] Complicated lineages of suffering, struggle, sacrifice, tragedy, and triumph intersect in New Orleans, but it has been the work by diasporic Africans of creating a world-traversing and world-transcending citizenship that explains the unique role of the world in New Orleans and New Orleans in the world. As musician Dr. John (Mac Rebennack) explains, "In New Orleans, everything—food, music, religion, even the way people talk and act—has deep, deep roots; and, like the tangled veins of cypress roots that meander this way and that in the swamp, everything in New Orleans [is] interrelated, wrapped around itself in ways that aren't always obvious."[23]

The poetics of place play a central role in these practices and processes, not just in the links between Africa and America, but also in the connections that link the city of New Orleans and the rest of the Mississippi Delta to the American South, the nation at large, and the world beyond the geographic and juridical borders of the nation-state in the Americas and around the world. The African rhythms and African sensibilities that pervade New Orleans music became tools for creating panethnic unity among diverse groups. Slaves brought to Louisiana during the colonial era tended to be Senegambians and Bakongo people, but as Michael Gomez demonstrates, the brutal racial oppression mandated by the slave system compelled diverse African peoples to coalesce into a unified if not uniform Afro-American culture.[24] Robert Farris Thompson identifies six core techniques and practices as central to African culture (specifically Yoruba): the dominance of percussive attack in sound and motion, deployment of multiple meters all at once, inner pulse control, suspended accents, call and response between musicians and between the musicians and their audiences, and the centrality of social allusions in songs and dances.[25] All these serve as easily identifiable core practices for New Orleans musicians. Yet it would be a mistake to separate the aesthetics of music making in New Orleans from the moral and political imperatives of community making. The emphasis in New Orleans music on networks of apprenticeship and instruction echoes J. H. Kwabena Nketia's description of the Akan idea of musical instruction as a process of "slow absorption through exposure to musical situations and active participation, rather than formal teaching."[26] As Thompson argues about the art of the African diaspora in general, the labor needed to produce works of art trains artists and audiences to learn to recognize significant communications. Expressive culture in this tradition entails gradual immersion into social groups. In the Afro-diasporic context, music, religion, and art make things happen in the world. They invoke ancestors, imagine future descendants, and summon the god of the oppressed to intervene in this world. Thompson explains that the Yoruba vision of the world revolves around the "metaphoric capture of the moral potentiality inherent in certain powers of the natural world—thunder, oceans, herbs, and stones—and a demonstration that creative persons have shaped certain images, pillars of lateritic clay, implements of iron, metal fans, brooms decorated with leather and cowrie-shell embroidery, so that they illumine the world with intuitions of the power to make right things come to pass."[27]

Generations of Black people in New Orleans have voiced allegiance to Africa openly, publicly, and politically. At the turn of the twentieth century, *Voice of Missions*, an emigrationist "back to Africa" magazine published in Georgia by African Methodist Episcopal Church Bishop Henry M. Turner, circulated widely within the New Orleans Black working-class community.[28] In the 1920s, Audley "Queen Mother" Moore mobilized a crowd of armed blacks to encircle the Longshoreman's Hall to defend successfully Marcus Garvey's right to speak in the city. Community activist Virginia Young Collins remembers her Garveyite father instructing his family that "Africa is wherever Africans are."[29] Collins drew upon Garvey's Pan-Africanism in her own work. She participated in a campaign waged by a group calling itself the Universal Association of Ethiopian Women asking the United Nations to strike down laws in Louisiana that denied welfare benefits to many Blacks. Later she became active in the Republic of New Africa, a group organized around the demand for a territorial homeland for Blacks in the South. These identifications with Africa blended with other frames for seeking freedom, including home-grown Abolition Democracy and the residual effects of the first successful slave revolt in history in Haiti.[30] Contemporary New Orleans musicians still look to Africa for inspiration, affiliation, and identification. Cyril Neville explains, "The drum comes to me as a symbol of what I, or we, used to be. I can't speak on the drums, but I try to convey my feelings . . . I think about Africa when I play. To me, right now, my Africa is the drums 'cause when I feel like going back to Africa I play my drums."[31]

An African presence is clearly evident in the religious life of New Orleans both inside and outside houses of worship. Spiritual, Holiness, and Pentecostal congregations stage emotional services replete with ecstatic praise, powerful music, spirit possession, and promises of healing. The activities carried out inside these churches influence life outside them, teaching people about the presence of the sacred in their lives. William Paden argues that these kinds of rituals entail "the deliberate structuring of action and time to give focus, expression, and sacredness to what would otherwise be diffuse, unexpressed or profane."[32] Thus the sacred appears in seemingly prosaic and ordinary items: in mirrors, bottles, and stones that decorate trees, yards, and the exteriors of houses, in tires and hubcaps that serve as planters and decorations, in cosmograms composed of flowers, herbs, shells, and fragments of ceramic dishware, at intersections that become treated as sacred crossroads. This spirit of deploying material objects and ritual practices to do work in the world helps explain what might otherwise seem like mere superstition. Blues singer and guitarist Deacon John relates that he cried so loud as a baby that it startled his parents. Wanting to channel that voice into singing rather than cries of rage, they carried their infant son outside and cut his fingernails under a fig tree in the belief that doing so would enable him to grow up to be a singer.[33] Many cultures around the world honor and extol self-activity and self-help, but in the African diaspora the emphasis on doing work in the world that makes a difference has been a primary means of survival. In the Afro-diasporic tradition, what matters is not so much the path you take, but rather the path you make.

The African presence in New Orleans is pronounced and unmistakable, but it is not discrete, autonomous, or unmediated. The experiences of the Neville Brothers illustrate how African retention in New Orleans blends with New World invention. Charles Neville recalls learning about relatives and ancestors who were Native American, French, Spanish, and Martinican as well as African.[34] When Art Neville's band the Meters played in Trinidad with calypso star the Mighty Sparrow, Neville recognized parts of the music he heard in the Caribbean as "the old sounds of my childhood."[35] Cyril Neville remembers moving to New York and feeling at home because the city surrounded him with Haitians, Jamaicans, and Puerto Ricans whose customs, speech, and demeanor reminded him of New Orleans. He began to think of himself as being from "the island of New Orleans," not because the city is actually an island but because of what he called its heritage of island life, island dreams, island songs, and island rhythms. Cyril Neville felt the Caribbean called to him because it shared with New Orleans "the slave trade with Africa, souls being shipped and abandoned, culture confused and commingled, the sense of oppression, the sense of relaxation, humid heat hanging over your head like a hammer, carnivals and rituals and a beat that goes from morning till night, drums that talk like singers and singers who sing like drums."[36] He developed a special affinity for Bob Markey's reggae music from

Jamaica, even playing the Rastafarian's "No Woman No Cry" over and over again as he successfully kicked his heroin habit. But Marley's music offered no easy path to liberation for Cyril. He learned from Marley's music that while the island spirit might be free, "the islands themselves were no freer for a black man than anyplace else."[37]

Some Black musicians from New Orleans learned and honed their art far from home. Nineteenth-century composer and conductor Edmond Dede joined the exodus of creoles of color and other free Blacks from New Orleans in response to increasing anti-Black antagonism, repressive legislation, competition from white immigrants, and significant economic and social changes before the Civil War. He migrated to Mexico in 1848, but illness compelled him to return to New Orleans in 1851. Dede booked passage to Europe in 1857, settling around 1860 in Bordeaux, France, where he secured employment as a theater conductor and composer of ballets, operettas, and overtures.[38] Pianist, singer, and bandleader Tommy Ridgley took a different route. He grew up singing in a church choir, but did not think about becoming a professional musician until he was shipped overseas to Okinawa as a member of the U.S. Navy. Homesick for New Orleans and with plenty of time on his hands, Ridgley taught himself to play piano at the base PX. When he returned to the Crescent City, he embarked on a music career, playing initially with Roy Brown and later fronting his own groups at the Dew Drop Inn and other local venues.[39]

The life of New Orleans piano player Champion Jack Dupree encapsulates in microcosm the global reach and scope of New Orleans's music. Dupree's father came from the Belgian Congo, his mother was a Cherokee Indian, and he grew up in the section of New Orleans known as the Irish Channel. After Dupree's parents died in a fire, he moved into the Colored Waifs Home, where he received instruction on the piano from an Italian priest. As a youth he apprenticed himself to the local Black musician known as "Drive 'Em Down" and served as "spy boy" for the Yellow Pocahontas tribe of Mardi Gras Indians. As an adult, Dupree lived the life of an itinerant musician. He settled in Chicago before serving in the Pacific in the U.S. Navy during World War II. Dupree spent two years in a Japanese prisoner of war camp. After his discharge from the service, he worked cooking kosher food for the faculty at New York's Yeshiva University. He moved to England in 1958, where he married a local woman. In his later years he made his home in Hanover, Germany, but spent summers at his horse ranch in Sweden. Champion Jack carried the music of New Orleans out into the world, but the music he played contained traces of the musical cultures of many continents.[40]

Discriminatory hiring practices and racist repression frequently provoked members of the Black working class in New Orleans to travel to California on the railroad lines and interstate highways that led out of the city. In 1908, Mississippi bass player Bill Johnson, who had assembled his band in New Orleans, brought the ensemble to San Francisco. Migrants from New Orleans obtained gigs in Los Angeles at Wayside Park, where they played music and cooked buckets of red beans and rice on the job.[41] The first published reference to jazz music anywhere in the world appeared in a San Francisco newspaper in 1913. The next year, Freddie Keppard joined Johnson's band in California. Kid Ory started a six-year stay in Los Angeles and Oakland in 1919.[42] Jelly Roll Morton invited musicians Buddy Petit, Wade Whaley, and Frank Dusen to leave Louisiana to join his band in Los Angeles in 1917 and 1918. When they arrived wearing box coats and tight pants that would have been stylish in New Orleans, Morton was appalled. He took them to a tailor immediately to purchase outfits more in keeping with the look accepted on the West Coast. In addition, Morton scolded them for bringing a bucket of red beans and rice to work and cooking it on the job. Shocked by Morton's transformation into a Californian, Petit, Whaley, and Dusen quickly returned to New Orleans in disgust.[43]

The first recorded session of New Orleans "Dixieland" jazz by Black musicians did not take place in New Orleans, but in studios in Santa Monica, California, in 1922.[44] Morton and many other New Orleans musicians remained or returned to the West Coast in succeeding decades. Despite occasional forays to other cities, Morton came back to Los Angeles and died there in 1941. Kid Ory followed a similar path, performing in Oakland and Los Angeles during the 1920s before spending five years in Chicago and then returning to California to run a chicken ranch with his brother during the 1930s. In the 1940s, Ory spearheaded a Dixieland revival on the strength of club engagements on Sunset Boulevard in Los Angeles accompanied by fellow New Orleanean Barney Bigard on clarinet. He appeared on Orson Welles's radio show, and made brief but memorable contributions to the Hollywood films *New Orleans* and *Crossfire*. In the 1950s, Ory appeared regularly at Disneyland in a band that included Caughey Roberts and Teddy Buckner.[45] New Orleans musicians who spent a significant amount of time in Los Angeles include Otis and Leon Rene, Lee and Lester Young, Roy Brown. Lee Allen, Henry Butler, Irma Thomas, Harold Battiste, and Aaron Neville.

While these musicians lived a part of New Orleans history in other cities around the world, James Booker exemplifies the ways in which the rest of the world influenced music in New Orleans. A child prodigy on the piano, Booker astounded audiences with his mastery of diverse musical styles taken from Chopin, Bach, Errol Garner, Liberace, and his New Orleans teacher Tuts Washington. Southern University in New Orleans Professor Jo Dora Middleton challenged Booker to play some difficult pieces by Bach. The young pianist looked over the sheet music quickly and asked his teacher, "Do you want me to play them from the front to the back or the back to the front?" Booker noted his proficiency at classical music in typically mischievous fashion in the title of his 1982 composition that described his playing as "classified." Booker grew up in a middle-class family in New Orleans and nearby Gulf Coast cities, but served a sentence "at the mercy of merciless men" in Angola Prison. He also mastered the codes of European classical music. When piano virtuoso Arthur Rubenstein came to New Orleans to perform in 1958, Booker's music teachers arranged for the star to hear their pupil play. Rubenstein marveled at the skill of the young pianist, volunteering that he could never match the speed with which Booker's fingers flew across the keyboard.[46]

Before it was destroyed by the floods that followed Hurricane Katrina, the home of Cyril Neville contained an altar that honored a cosmopolitan roster of heroes: Jamaican reggae singer Bob Marley, Native American warriors Crazy Horse and Sitting Bull, and U.S. Black nationalist leader Malcolm X (whose mother came from the island of Grenada and whose Baptist minister father participated in Marcus Garvey's Universal Negro Improvement Association). The altar itself is an interesting transcultural symbol, invoking Catholic, Caribbean, and African religious imagery. Drawing on Zora Neale Hurston's ethnographic observations about home altars in New Orleans, David C. Estes describes altars as "conjure sites that de-center power in order to sacralize New Orleans as the entryway for the African gods into the North American continent. Hoodoo altars are a means of contesting the exclusive association of power with white commercial, judicial, and religious edifices and re-situating it within the homes of African Americans."[47]

White piano player and singer Mac Rebennack has spent his musical life immersed in Black culture, but those experiences also led him to close affiliations with Latinos. Shortly after being expelled from Jesuit High School in 1954, Rebennack played in a band with Earl Stanley, son of a Yaqui Indian from Mexico who migrated to New Orleans to work as a chef in local restaurants. Years later, Rebennack joined forces musically with Richard "Didimus" Washington, a musician who had grown up in Ethiopia and Cuba before moving to New Orleans. Washington studied in Cuba with the great jazz and Santeria drummer Chano Pozo, and he brought a special Caribbean flair to the local music scene. Washington frequently played five conga drums at once, while nestling two bongo drums between his legs. Rebennack remembers Washington's music as a blend of Cuban jazz, Haitian finger-style drumming, and African rhythms.[48]

The pre-Lenten carnival celebrations that have made New Orleans famous throughout the world contain retentions of practices from medieval Europe as well as Cuba, Haiti, Trinidad, and Africa. Afro-Caribbean practices loom large in New Orleans music as well. Douglas Henry Daniels notes that Jelly Roll Morton attributed his earliest musical education to his Haitian godmother, Eulalia Echo (sometimes written as Eulalie Hecaud). Morton's musical tributes to other artists such as "King Porter Stomp" and "Mamie's Blues" (honoring trumpeter Porter King and blues singer and pianist Mamie Desdunes), along with his habanera rhythms and "stomps," resonate with the vocabulary and grammar of Afro-Caribbean musical forms. Daniels notes that tenor saxophonist Lester Young asserted that he drew on a variety of vodou practices and beliefs gleaned during his early years growing up in New Orleans. Daniels reports that Young believed that everyday events like the sight of a bird flying contained occluded signs and messages from spirits. Young gave his songs titles that reflected Afro-Caribbean dance styles emphasizing upward movement off the earth such as "Lester Leaps In," and "Jump Lester Jump."[49]

The diasporic Africa that emerges in New Orleans draws its determinant features from interactions with many cultures that are not African, or at least are African several times removed. The Canadians who played a central role in establishing European settlement in New Orleans established Indian as well as African slavery in Louisiana. Indians and Blacks intermarried in the colonial era, while some slaves ran away to freedom in Indian territory. Native Americans maintained a visible public presence in New Orleans until the 1920s when they tended to become absorbed into the local Black community.[50] The Indian imagery central to both Spiritual churches and Mardi Gras fraternal orders in Black New Orleans sometimes reflects inaccurate and mass-mediated images of Indians, and Native Americans in the region with Black ancestors have also frequently disidentified with the Black part of their heritage. Yet in both communities, interracial identities and identifications have served as incentives for interracial affinity and affiliation, for interracial marriage, and for joint recognition of conquest and slavery as the foundations of white power and privilege.

Benito Juarez was neither the first nor the last Mexican to find refuge, succor, and support in New Orleans. A triumphant appearance by the Mexican army's Eighth Cavalry Military Band at the 1884 World's Cotton Exposition popularized habanera and *danza* music in the city. Local publishers sold sheet music featuring songs with these styles, which they advertised "as played by the Mexican band.[51] Thomas Tio came from a New Orleans creole family that settled for a short time in the Eureka Colony near Tampico, Mexico. He studied in New Orleans with Italian opera conductor Luigi Gabici, who traveled with an opera troupe that appeared in Havana before settling in New Orleans. Thomas Tio's grandson Lorenzo became a distinguished clarinetist and teacher who trained Barney Bigard, Jimmie Noone, Omer Simeon, Paul Barnes, and Darnell Howard. Mexican American Baldemar Huerta sang

Louisiana two-chord blues classics like "Wasted Days and Wasted Nights" in Bourbon Street nightclubs in the 1960s before serving a stretch in Angola for drug possession. In the 1970s he secured success recording blues-inflected bilingual country songs under the stage name Freddy Fender. Haitian music influenced generations of New Orleans musicians from Louis Moreau Gottschalk's classical compositions in the nineteenth century through the Neville Brothers collaborations in the 1980s and 1990s with Les Freres Parent, a musical group exiled from Haiti because of their sharp criticism of the U.S.-backed ruling elite.

Like the Black community in Paule Marshall's Brooklyn, African American life and culture in New Orleans drew energy and imagination from its links to a wider world. Yet local spaces and spatial imaginaries produced distinct local inflections. In New Orleans, spectacular streamers of Spanish moss hang from the branches of oak trees. Summer breezes carry the fragrant and appetizing smells of simmering red beans and rice through the air. Characters with names like Two-Weed, No-Toed Joe, and Seven-Come-Eleven hang out on corners and in taverns. Street names in New Orleans proclaim Virtue, Desire, Piety, Community, Humanity, Mystery, Music, and Pleasure. Ned Sublette notes that there is an intersection in New Orleans where Jefferson Davis Parkway meets Martin Luther King Boulevard.[52] The city is a place where musicians have been known as Nookie Boy, Hold That Note Sam, and Half-a-Hand, where disc jockeys have called themselves Ernie the Whip, Poppa Stoppa, and Doctor Daddy-o.

Some of the residents of the Faubourg-Treme area can trace their family's history in the oldest continuous free Black neighborhood in North America back hundreds of years.[53] Family, church, and neighborhood networks loom large in the lives of Black people in New Orleans. When Fats Domino started to enjoy commercial success as a rhythm and blues singer and piano player in the 1950s, he did not move out of the Ninth Ward, where he grew up in a small house on Jourdan Street. Instead, Domino built a big dwelling on the corner of Marais Street and Caffin Avenue, close to the homes of many his relatives. Domino's split-level mansion with its terrazzo-floor entrance inlaid with dominos contrasted radically with the rest of the neighborhood, but he never considered moving to another part of town.[54] Similarly, the success enjoyed by the Neville Brothers in the 1980s led them to purchase an abandoned fire station on Valence Street and turn it into a center serving the youth of their uptown neighborhood. The late Mardi Gras Indian Chief of Chiefs, Allison "Tuddy" Montana, took pride in his Seventh Ward neighborhood, using his skills a construction worker to help neighbors fix up their dwellings and reminding them that the homes in which they lived had been built initially by skilled Black craftsmen.

Yet as Ninth Ward poet and journalist Kalamu ya Salaam reminds us, "Living poor and Black in the Big Easy is never as much fun as our music, food, smiles, and laughter make it seem."[55] The joyful artistry that has delighted people all over the world has emerged from spaces pervaded by oppression, cruelty, and brutality. The barbarism of the Louisiana state prison system has inspired song lyrics by Juvenile, Bottom Posse, Dr. John, and Robert Pete Williams, all of whom reference the slave-like conditions confronting inmates at the Angola Penitentiary in central Louisiana. Leadbelly, James Booker, Aaron Neville, Charles Neville, and Freddy Fender served sentences in Angola. In the city itself, illegal housing discrimination, racially targeted urban renewal policies, school segregation, police brutality, and state-supported subsidies for "white flight" to the suburbs have relegated many Black people in New Orleans to spaces of last resort packed with hazards and bereft of amenities.

The city of New Orleans has systematically destroyed the spaces most important to Black people. The decision by local authorities to rename Place Congo as Beauregard Square in honor of a Confederate general prefigured subsequent insults and incursions, including the destruction of the Treme Market in the 1930s.[56] In the uptown area, Dryades Street (now Oretha Castle Haley Boulevard) served as a center of commerce and culture for African Americans until white merchants moved their shops to the suburbs or went out of business entirely rather than concede to demands by civil rights activists in the 1960s to employ African Americans as workers in their stores. New Orleans poet Tom Dent hailed the downtown Rampart Street area of his youth as "the commercial center of the struggling Black nation within the city we had all emerged from."[57] The construction of Louis Armstrong Park, however, destroyed much of what was Congo Square and reconfigured the street front along Rampart. Urban renewal efforts destroyed sixteen blocks of historic buildings in the Treme neighborhood. Residential segregation made Claiborne Avenue an important thoroughfare in the Black community by the mid-twentieth century. Nearly two hundred businesses on the street attracted a lively clientele, while the one-hundred-foot-wide and sixty-one-hundred-foot-long grass median dividing the street provided space for picnics, games, and washing cars. Forty-year-old live oak tress lined the "neutral ground" median, while a paved path in the center made it ideal for walking. Construction of the downtown section of the I-10 Freeway in the 1960s, however, destroyed hundreds of oak trees, divided the neighborhood, marred its appearance, and eliminated twelve blocks of historic homes as well as miles of thriving neighborhoods.[58] The Freeway made it easier for suburban commuters to enter and leave the city, but it turned the previously crowded Claiborne Avenue into an eerie and empty buffer zone. Instead of vibrant streets filled with pedestrians who frequented nightclubs and restaurants, the street became a sparsely populated thoroughfare pockmarked by the occasional discount drug store or drive-through fast-food outlet. Yet to this day, Mardi Gras Indian tribes and local artists still claim the neutral ground under the freeway and the pylons of the overhead expressway as sites for creative expression.

Even before the disastrous aftermath of Hurricane Katrina, the Greater New Orleans Fair Housing Action Council received fifty to one hundred complaints per week about housing discrimination. Testing by fair-housing advocates revealed that Black apartment seekers in the city encounter discrimination 77 percent of the time. Attorneys won more than one million dollars in actual and punitive damages for victims of housing discrimination in the 1990s, but neither city nor state nor federal officials took any serious steps to open up opportunities for fair housing and homeownership to Blacks. On the contrary, the HOPE VI program before Katrina, and the planned bulldozing of nearly four thousand serviceable public housing units after it, have only led to an even more constricted housing market for New Orleans Blacks.[59]

The cumulative impact of urban renewal, disinvestment, and the evisceration of the social wage in New Orleans has left Black people with little control over the exchange value of the spaces they occupy. Yet they have worked tirelessly to occupy, inhabit, and transform the use value of those spaces, establishing sites for collective cultural expression and creative coalescence. New Orleans remains a place of unexpected spaces. Members of social clubs dance in the streets on the way home from funerals. Tribes of Mardi Gras Indians parade through neighborhoods on Mardi Gras Day and St. Joseph's Day, stopping for ceremonies at seemingly ordinary intersections that they treat as sacred sites. Some of the most memorable music made in New Orleans emerged out of unexpected urban spaces. Parade beats permeated the rhythm and blues drumming of onetime tap dancer Earl Palmer. Trumpeter Dave Bartholomew derived the rhythm for his composition "Whole Lotta Lovin'" (recorded by Fats Domino) from a parade beat that featured the bass drum of the streets rather than the snares and kettles usually foregrounded in the recording studio.[60] Toussaint McCall made his hit record "Nothing Takes the Place of You" on a cheap tape recorder in the den of his home. Johnny Adams, Joe Jones, and Eddie Bo recorded hit songs for Joe Ruffino's Ric Records label in a studio that master carpenter Bo built by himself with his own hands.[61]

Composer and guitarist Earl King wrote many of his songs in his "office," at the counter of the K&B Drugstore at the intersection of Louisiana and St. Charles Avenues. When the K&B closed, he moved his operations inside the Tastee Donut Shop on the corner of Louisiana Avenue and Prytania. King got ideas for songs as he watched people pass by, sitting in the donut shop every day for eight hours for years, consuming as many as twenty cups of coffee as he composed music and lyrics.[62] When he worked for entrepreneur Frank Paina, who ran the Dew Drop Inn and promoted music at clubs in nearby rural areas, King selected musicians by using the "shape-up" system that shipping companies used to hire stevedores on the docks. Musicians would congregate in front of the Dew Drop Inn at Lasalle and Washington, and King would pick out individuals and assign them to work crews to play different gigs.[63] Just as King drew his manner of hiring musicians from the riverfront docks, promoter Percy Stovall booked performances by New Orleans artists throughout the South by calculating when farm workers got paid. Stovall sent his artists to Mississippi when the cotton crop had been picked, to the Carolinas when tobacco was in the sheds, to Georgia when peanuts and peaches had been harvested, and to Florida after the oranges had been picked.[64] When these musicians returned to New Orleans, they participated in a local economy shaped by exports of oil and cotton, by imports and reshipments of coffee and bananas.

Saxophonist James Rivers drew on his relationship to city space by composing and practicing on the banks of Lake Pontchartrain. Rivers liked to play his music at night by the side of the lake because the beating of the waves and the water against the seawall helped him think. When performing on stage, he would try to visualize and hear the lake so he could remember his inspiration for the tunes he played.[65] Streams of traffic served similar purposes for singer Aaron Neville and producer-composer-performer Allen Toussaint. They rode around town in a car carrying a portable tape recorder in case they came across inspirations for songs. Stopped behind a big semitrailer one day, they noticed the truck's engine had a steady beat, so they recorded it and used it as the basis for a song when they arrived at the studio.[66] Black artists used the segregated spaces of New Orleans to turn segregation into congregation, but white supremacist control over public spaces also made musical performances precarious undertakings. In the era of Jim Crow segregation, Black entertainers playing in white clubs could not use dressing rooms or stay backstage. They had to spend their time between sets in storerooms and closets. At one show, Lee Allen came out into the club from the storeroom to play some selections on the jukebox. Defending their space from this intrusion, white patrons and club employees attacked Allen and beat him up.[67]

New Orleans is a place where things can change quickly, where human will and desire can make things happen suddenly. Dorothy LaBostrie quit her job as a cook for a white woman one day in 1955, declaring she wanted to write a hit record. The next day LaBostrie wandered into Cosimo Matassa's recording studio and wrote "Tutti Frutti" in fifteen minutes during a lull in a Little Richard recording session.[68] She lived off the royalties from that song for decades. It took only one day in the Malaco Recording Studios in Jackson, Mississippi, for New Orleans pianist and producer Wardell Quezergue to turn Loyola University cafeteria baker Jean Knight and New Orleans postal worker King Floyd into stars. On his first day on the job at Malaco, Quezergue produced "Mister Big Stuff" for Knight and "Groove Me" for Floyd.[69]

One day was also all it took for Edgar Blanchard's Gondoliers to break the color barrier and become the first Black band hired in the Perez Lounge on Airline Highway. Pete Fountain's all-white Basin Street Six had previously played a regular gig at that establishment. Fountain's group consisted of three whisky heads and three pot heads. One night the pot heads got into a fistfight with the whiskey heads, so the owner fired them all and decided he could get better behavior from a Black band, giving Blanchard and the Gondoliers their big break.[70] Not all the sudden changes that take place in New Orleans have been happy ones, however. The racialized spaces of New Orleans stem from long and mean-spirited traditions of residential segregation, unequal education, environmental racism, and perpetual police and vigilante violence. While driving to a performance in Monroe, Louisiana, in 1963 with guitarist Irving Bannister, singer Sugar Boy Crawford encountered a state trooper who directed their car to the side of the road. Crawford's claim that the driver of the vehicle had done nothing wrong led to an altercation. The officer whipped the singer with his pistol so badly that Sugar Boy had to be hospitalized for nearly a year. When he secured his release from the hospital, Crawford found that the beating damaged him so badly that he could no longer keep up with the band when he sang up-tempo numbers. His injuries forced him to retire from singing as a professional.[71] Similarly, the Neville Brothers remember the time that New Orleans police officers picked up their uncle George Landry (Chief Jolly) for questioning about an alleged sexual assault. When the policemen could not get Landry to confess to a crime he had not committed, they had him straddle a desk drawer naked and slammed the drawer shut on his testicles. The authorities eventually found the culprit who actually committed the crime. They released Landry, but did not apologize to him for his treatment.[72]

This brutal and systematic oppression is responsible in part for the ferocious theatricality that permeates life in New Orleans on and off stage. In New Orleans nightclubs, audiences listening to music clap hands on the after beat rather than on the beat. Musicians cook food backstage during their performances. Shows do not really start until well after midnight. Local entertainers speak fondly of the legendary Iron Jaw Harris. His act consisted of dancing barefoot on beer bottle caps to make them stick to his feet and sound like taps. He held a table in his mouth with his teeth while he danced and ate thumb tacks, razor blades, and bits of broken glass "washed down" by swallowing fire.[73] Evidently, Harris wanted very much to be in show business. His flamboyant act, however, may have also had Afro-diasporic origins. In his study of the Maroon people in Jamaica, Kenneth Bilby notes that they draw on their Kromanti heritage in celebrating those who "can eat glass bottles, dance on fire, deflect bullets and knives, and miraculously close up gaping wounds."[74]

The ferocious theatricality and aggressive festivity that permeate expressive culture in Black New Orleans might seem foolish and frivolous to outsiders. To insiders, however, the flamboyance stems from the long fetch of history, from centuries of struggle to assert and affirm that Black lives matter. As Karla Holloway explains in her analysis of the spectacles enacted by New Orleans Black funeral processions, "Their visual excess expressed a story that African Americans otherwise had difficulty illustrating—that these were lives of importance and substance, or that these were individuals, no matter their failings or the degree to which their lives were quietly lived, who were loved."[75]

"In New Orleans," says Aaron Neville, "you learn to combine everything."[76] Musicians blended their music with many other kinds of performance. One featured act in New Orleans nightclubs during the 1950s was the "Three Hair Combo," made up of musicians known as Professor Longhair, Professor Shorthair, and Professor No Hair. They wore their hair three ways: parted, unparted, and departed.[77] Trumpeter Melvin Lastie repeatedly imitated the sounds of chickens on his horn; a stripper at the Club Tiajuana went him one better. She called herself "the chicken lady" and laid an egg at the conclusion of her act.[78] Guitar Slim used to appear on stage wearing lime green pants and red coats with his shoes dyed to match his pants and his hair dyed to match his coat.[79] One bartender at the Club Forest mixed and served drinks efficiently even though each of his fingers ended at the first joint. Customers called him "Nubs" in deference to his truncated fingers. Nubs explained his disability calmly, "I owed some people some money." Dr. John recalls a night in the 1950s when a fight broke out at Spec's Moulin Rouge Lounge in Gretna. The club's security guard panicked and fired wildly into the crowd, wounding several patrons. When police officers arrived and tried to get people to leave, one customer would not give up his seat at the bar and leave the establishment. He had two bullets lodged in him, but he wanted to finish his drink.[80] During a 1962 performance of the song "A Certain Girl" at the Municipal Auditorium, Ernie K-Doe kept a clothes rack with nine suits on it backstage. Every time he came to the instrumental part of the tune, K-Doe would run behind the curtain and with the help of a valet change into another suit, run back out on stage, and sing the next chorus.[81] When Soul Machine performed its scintillating cover version of "Light

My Fire" by the Doors at the Desert Sand Club at Esplanade and Claiborne in the early 1970s, enthusiastic fans lit matches and waved them over their heads. The club's owner eventually asked the band members to remove the song from their playlist because he was afraid the fans would set the entire building on fire.[82]

Some performers won allegiance from New Orleans audiences simply by making the most of what they had. An accident took two fingers from Frank Mitchell's right hand. Known sarcastically as "Lefty" and "Half-a-Hand," Mitchell won praise and admiration for the unique styles he developed as a pianist because his injury prevented him from playing in the usual fashion. South Carolina native Clayton "Peg Leg" Bates thrilled New Orleans audiences as a tap dancer with an artificial leg. After he proved he could make as much noise with one leg and one peg as other tap dancers made with two legs, Bates would unstrap his peg and continue dancing on one leg, not only keeping up the complex tapping rhythm of the earlier part of his act, but jumping in the air and turning head over heels flips that ended with perfect landings on his one leg.[83] Poverty compelled Professor Longhair to learn to play music on a piano that he found abandoned in an alley. His mother had taught him how to play scales and chords, but the piano he used had inoperable and missing keys that made conventional playing impossible. Necessity forced Longhair to develop unusual and novel fingerings that helped him eventually to become a unique and much-sought-after artist. Longhair could not duplicate the reach and dexterity that he admired so much in Tuts Washington's piano playing, so he learned to ball his left hand into a fist and roll it over the keys to approximate Washington's sound.[84]

In New Orleans things may not be what they seem; seeing is not always believing. Before television made it easier for fans to know what the musicians they admired looked like, impersonators routinely played gigs under star's names. On any given night in the 1960s, audiences thinking they were watching Shirley and Lee were actually being entertained by a duo called Sugar and Sweet. Ricky Ricardo passed himself off as Frankie Ford, while James Booker and assorted friends performed as if they were Huey Smith and the Clowns.[85] Drummer Walter Lastie believed that he was the only sighted musician in an all-blind band performing at the Club Tiajuana until one night when a fight broke out. In the midst of the melee, one of the "blind" band members shouted to another, "Watch it, Popee, here comes a Regal beer bottle at you."[86] Even skin color, that most obvious visual cue, can be highly deceptive in New Orleans. Complex patterns of migration and intermarriage can make it difficult to deduce the race of a local resident from his or her face. The city's population has roots in Europe, Africa, Asia, the Mediterranean, and the Caribbean. Historian Kim Lacy Rogers found her research on the 1950s civil rights movement complicated by the fact that it was impossible to discern the race of any given civic leader from newspaper photographs alone.[87] Black activist Virginia Collins fought ferociously on behalf of her people in civil rights and Black nationalist organizations, yet never broke ties completely with light-skinned relatives who had decided to pass for white in order to obtain jobs that would otherwise be closed to them.[88] New Orleans Black activist Matt Suarez remembers how his light skin enabled him to sneak into "whites only" bars in the French Quarter routinely during the days of legal segregation. An often-repeated story in the Suarez family related how Matt's uncle passed for white so successfully that he did not even tell his wife he was Black until after the wedding, only to find out then that his new bride was a Black woman who had been passing for white as well.[89]

Trumpet player and singer Louis Prima grew up in the Treme neighborhood near Congo Square in a family that migrated from Sicily to Argentina before settling in New Orleans. Prima had dark skin, copied the hoarse tone and scat singing of Louis Armstrong in his vocals, and dressed like a street hustler. He peppered his song lyrics with Italian and Yiddish words and phrases as well as African American slang. Prima took trumpet lessons from Black musicians Lee Collins and Henry "Kid" Renna. In the 1930s the manager of a New York night club fired Prima because he believed him to be Black.

In subsequent years, Prima's orchestra performed at the Apollo Theater in Harlem and other primarily Black venues where audiences sometimes perceived him to be Black as well. Prima married his band's lead singer, Keely Smith, an olive-skinned woman with short-cropped black hair whose family tree blended Cherokee and Irish ancestry. Prima and Smith carried out romantic and sexual banter on stage, leading some managers of nightclubs catering to whites to ban the act because they suspected that Prima was Black. At some hotels, managers refused to rent a room to Prima and Smith because they believed strongly that they were an interracial couple. Yet hotel personnel were not always so sure which race should be attributed to whom. Different managers at different times identified both Prima and Smith as the Black member of the couple, even though neither one was Black.[90]

Another kind of passing appeared in the career of Irving Ale, a man who sang and hosted shows in New Orleans disguised as a woman named Patsy Valdalia at the famed Dew Drop Inn. Among her many achievements, Valdalia hosted the club's annual Halloween Gay Ball.[91] A generation of New Orleans entertainers—both male and female—patterned their stage shows after Valdalia's performances. "He gave me tips on how to wear makeup, what clothes to wear, how to move on stage and how to get off and on the bandstand," Irma Thomas recalls.[92] Thomas learned the choreography and the song "Hip Shakin' Mama" from Valdalia, sensuously provoking desire among the men in her audiences with an act that was her impersonation of a female impersonator. Female fans often lusted after handsome Larry Darnell, but few of them knew that Darnell preferred sex with men.[93] Oscar James Gibson performed as Bobby Marchan at the Dew Drop Inn on weekends, but took stage in drag as female impersonator "Roberta" on weekdays in the Powder Box Revue at the Dew Drop and later at the Club Tiajuana, wearing cocktail dresses that he sewed by hand himself.[94]

Strategic masquerades and impostures of different kinds by cross-gender and cross-race performers in New Orleans have helped encode aggressive festivity and creative contradictions inside the local culture. These gestures are easily misunderstood by members of privileged and powerful groups whose recreations and rituals often perform a temporary escape from respectability by pretending to embrace identities they despise. A long history of contemptuous mimicry by mummers and minstrels has been used to bolster the privileged status ascribed to whiteness, masculinity, and wealth. The titillations of transgression and the appeals of contact with putatively uninhibited others function as compensation and reparation for the toll that propriety takes on propertied people. They serve as a safety valve, as a way to let off steam and indulge in forbidden passions temporarily before returning to a normative identity. No doubt many of the consumers of New Orleans Black expressive culture derive precisely these satisfactions from the performances they view. For the oppressed, however, masquerade and imposture are what James Scott calls weapons of the weak. (See the Bridge following Chapter 4.) In New Orleans, they are necessary tools for self-defense and survival in the one-sided war that white supremacy wages against African people in America. Just as African American artists and musicians turn ordinary objects, movements, and sounds from everyday life into powerful forms of expressive culture, the Black community in New Orleans defends itself by using all the means at its disposal in the arenas that are open to it. In their art, Black people in the city break down the binary oppositions that divide the sensual from the spiritual, the political from the performative, and the intellectual from the aesthetic.

Pianist and singer Dr. John (Mac Rebennack) explains, "In New Orleans, in religion, as in food or race or music, you can't separate nothing from nothing."[95] A white musician who has spent his life immersed in Black culture, Rebennack and Harold Battiste created the character Dr. John based on the pseudonym adopted by Jean Montanet, a nineteenth-century New Orleans vodou practitioner reputed to have been born in Senegal.[96] Rebennack originally intended the character to be performed by Ronnie Barron, but when those plans fell through, he assumed the role himself.[97] Local legends sometimes present the original Dr. John as the tutor to Marie Laveau, the city's most famous servant of the spirits (although as Brenda Marie Osbey often observes, Laveau is a person more interesting to whites than to Blacks). Popularized in stories written by the enthusiastic if often uncomprehending white writer Robert Tallant, Laveau acquired fame and prestige as a vodou practitioner whose clients included both Blacks and whites. Reputed to be of Native American and African ancestry, Laveau married a light-skinned Haitian man and lived with a white man after her husband's death.[98] Mac Rebennack's performances on stage as Doctor John "The Gris-Gris Man," most likely reinforce exotic and condescending white supremacist notions about the mysterious and mystical beliefs, practices, and superstitions of a purportedly "primitive" people for many of his fans. Yet the term "gris-gris" probably comes from *gerregerys*, a Mande word that connotes a destructive charm.[99] From the perspective of diasporic imagination, the use of charms and other practices to serve the spirits is connected to the concept of ashe: the practical work done in the world that makes a difference. As evidenced in Dr. John's statement, religion is like food, music, or race, that is, a social construction in which everything is related to everything else, a way of working in the world and on the world so that the work you do speaks for you.

Like musical performances and Pan-African politics, religion in New Orleans has functioned as a crucible for world-traversing and world-transcending citizenship. Vodou from Haiti and syncretism from Africa fuse with Euro-American religious practices and beliefs. The Black population of New Orleans contains large numbers of both Catholics and Protestants whose worship practices include sanctified, spiritualist, holiness, and vodou ceremonies. The racial configurations of religion in New Orleans reveal the contradictions of church and state in the Spanish, French, and British empires, the psychopathology of religion and race in the antebellum, postbellum, Jim Crow, and post–civil rights eras in the United States, and the traditions of conquest, conversion, resistance, and inversion in Africa, the Caribbean, and Latin America.

African American religion serves as a repository of many different forms of diasporic connection to Africa. In North America, Black Christianity historically also promoted a world-traversing and world-transcending consciousness that included Africa but was not confined to it. Some spiritual churches in New Orleans with Black congregations venerate nineteenth-century Sauk Indian war Chief Black Hawk as an adopted spiritual ancestor in the struggle for freedom. The tradition of honoring Black Hawk in New Orleans Spiritual Churches dates back to the 1920s evangelism of Leafy Anderson, who claimed to be of mixed Black and Mohawk descent. Intermarriage between Indians and Blacks as well as respect for Native American spirituality helped popularize these churches, but they also drew adherents because of the utility for Blacks of masquerading as Indians. Like the Mardi Gras Indian tribes who mask as heroic warriors defending their turf against conquering invaders, the spiritualist churches have often provided a mask of legitimacy for vodun. As Zora Neale Hurston explained in 1931, "Hoodooism is in disrepute, and certain of its practices forbidden by law. A spiritualistic name protects the congregation, and is a useful device of protective coloration."[100]

Black people comprise the major ethnic group in the New Orleans Catholic Church, numbering more than 80,000 parishioners. There are more than one hundred historically Black colleges and universities in the United States and more than two hundred and fifty Catholic institutions of higher learning, but the only expressly Black Catholic college is Xavier University in New Orleans. Reviewing Zora Neale Hurston's descriptions of vodun altars ornamented with candles, incense, holy water, and blessed oil, David C. Estes concludes that New Orleans has been a "neo-African Vatican in which elements of Roman Catholic belief and ritual have been incorporated into a vibrant, traditional black religion. It is a holy metropolis, sacralized through folk rituals and various forms of traditional speech by which religious leaders regularly and confidently invoke the power of the spirit world into the lives of ordinary people."[101]

Important on its own as a collective ritual and personal refreshment of the soul, African American religion has blended with other forms of social, cultural, and intellectual work to connect Black people in New Orleans with a wider world. For Africans in America, biblical figuration emerged out of the exigencies of exile. The Middle Passage severed Black Americans from many sources of meaningful connection to their African ancestors, but they filled that void by adopting imaginary ancestors from the stories in their master's sacred book. They honored these fictive ancestors in the names they gave their children, in the sacred songs they composed, and in the folk tales they told. They focused on flawed figures who sought, summoned, and served the god of the oppressed, on heroes like Moses and David who won freedom for themselves and their people in this world, and on people who spoke truth to despotic power like the prophets Joshua and Isaiah. They sang spirituals about the prophet Ezekiel "connecting dry bones" because it mattered to them that the Old Testament prophet breathed new life into a shattered and scattered people. Diasporic imagination and biblical figuration rendered histories of bloodlines less important than shared or similar histories of bloodshed, while venerating a savior who came into the world "to make one blood of all nations."[102]

The devastation of much of New Orleans before, during, and after Hurricane Katrina in 2005 has once again focused attention on the debilitating poverty produced by institutionalized racism in the Mississippi Delta. The hurricane was a natural disaster, to be sure, but its disproportionate impact on the Black working class stemmed from decidedly unnatural, deliberate, and socially constructed causes. For decades and even centuries, the unchecked power of the plantation bloc in the Mississippi Delta has led to policies deliberately designed to make white property more valuable than black humanity, to craft increases in institutional rents for the rich out of the suffering of the black working class.[103] The organized abandonment of poor and working-class black people in the region preceded the hurricane and contributed significantly to its devastating impact.

In the wake of the devastation that accompanied Hurricane Katrina in 2005, the federal, state, and municipal governments, and local elected officials (including Blacks) from both major parties, conspired with private developers and investors to make sure that displaced residents of housing projects and poor neighborhoods could not return to the city or participate meaningfully in planning its future. The power of the plantation bloc in the Mississippi Delta has played a central role in shaping the racial order of U.S. society. The region's patterns of racial power are not a local aberration, but rather the crucible from which national and international policies have emerged. Clyde Woods explains that the price of white privilege and plantation bloc power in the Mississippi Delta is paid by Black working-class people in the form of racialized impoverishment, enclosure, displacement, neoplantation politics, the arbitrariness of daily life and prospects for survival, denial of human rights, cultural imposition, the manufacture of demonized images of black "savagery," different kinds of regionally distinct traps (urban renewal, spatial isolation, environmental racism), the desecration of sacred places, and the suppression of spatial use values.[104] The South is not a periphery of the U.S. racial order; it is its center. Any serious effort to create racial democracy, to break the bonds of dependency, and to produce social justice must be rooted in the ethnoracial and ethnospatial imaginaries of the southern Black working class.

Hurricane Katrina evidenced the failures of neoliberalism in many ways, from levee failures to the erosion of wetlands, from the impact of global warming on hurricanes to the unwillingness and/or inability of federal agencies to save lives or deliver food and medical equipment to evacuees, from the destruction of public housing to the manufacture of homelessness. Clyde Woods reminds us, "Katrina revealed the present and future costs of a fragmented, de-linked, privatized, and devolved state; no one is in charge."[105] Contemporary responses to Hurricane Katrina propose only the creation of new corporate subsidies and new dependency-creating institutions, ignoring the possibilities of rebuilding New Orleans from the bottom up, and refusing to hear the voices of the region's black working class as it confronts the collective, cumulative, and continuing realities of racialized space and subsidies to the institutional rents of the plantation and neoplantation elites. Attempts to break the bonds of dependency at the grassroots manifest themselves in community organizations and their struggles for the right of displaced residents to return to New Orleans, to rebuild their communities, and to build constituencies for democratic renewal in New Orleans.

Instead of neoliberal privatization schemes, we need to pay special attention to community knowledge, not only to activist organizations, but also the epistemologies emanating from the work of poets, actors, musicians, visual artists, and fraternal organizations and sororities. The activities of Students at the Center (SAC) are especially important because they involve young people in community-based art making and art-based community making in New Orleans. Artists and activists associated with SAC, including Kalamu ya Salaam, work with students to stage public performances that revolve around dialogue and debate about ways of improving local schools and neighborhoods. The key mechanism deployed by SAC is the story circle, an activity that uses listening to stories and telling stories as a means of developing capacities for citizenship and leadership in ordinary people. Students involved with SAC turn the reviled and often abandoned spaces of the city into rich sites for collective expression and action. As Ninth Ward poet, activist, and teacher Kalamu ya Salaam explains, "Our program is based on what can work within the conditions in which we find ourselves. . . . That's part of the jazz aesthetic—when it's your turn to take a solo, you can't say, 'Well, wait, that's not the song I wanted to play,' [No], it's *your* turn."[106]

The stakes of art and activism in New Orleans and in the wider world beyond it are very high. As Clyde Woods argues, "The translation of working class African American aesthetic and ethical movements into the reorganization of regional life in the Delta is, by definition, a transformation that will reconstruct the United States and the world."[107] The neoliberal reconstruction of New Orleans is part and parcel of what Naomi Klein calls predatory disaster capitalism. Privatization schemes in development long before the hurricane struck—but implemented fully by the Republican Bush administration, enabled by the craven capitulations of a Congress controlled by Democrats, and ultimately embraced by the Obama administration—produce unearned bounties for private consultants, developers, and security forces while closing public hospitals and schools, and refusing to pay salaries of public employees. These policies are simply a form looting in a time of disaster, but because the looting is being done by white-collar criminals, it draws none of the attention that journalists and elected officials allocated to fears of poor Black people taking water and food in order to survive when the hurricane hit. Neoliberal reconstruction of New Orleans enacts a massive redistribution of wealth from the poor to the rich; it creates new opportunities for asset accumulation by uprooting poor and working people from their homes, neighborhoods, church congregations, and family and community networks. Neoliberal reconstruction of New Orleans also entails cultural genocide. It elevates market space and market time over historical and social spaces and times. The gentrified tourist-directed simulacrum to be built where housing projects once stood will no doubt serve as sites for purchasing souvenirs that evoke the histories of jazz, blues, and vodou. But the people who created jazz, blues, and vodou will not be present. They will not be able to profit from the merchandising of their cultural history.

Yet the battle is not over. The struggle over space continues in New Orleans. The Greater New Orleans Fair Housing Action Council continues to investigate and contest illegal acts of housing discrimination. Public housing residents and their allies in the New Orleans Survivor Council continue to fight to prevent the destruction of habitable buildings, a destruction that will only exacerbate the shortage of affordable housing for people who are Black and working class. City schoolteacher Cherice Harrison-Nelson supervises a curriculum that includes a Mardi Gras Indian Hall of Fame honoring the local tradition. The Ashe Cultural Center on Oretha Castle Haley Boulevard (formerly Dryades Street) serves as a meeting place for community groups, a site for creating and exhibiting works of expressive culture, and the locus of an annual commemoration of ancestors lost in the Middle Passage. The New Orleans Women's Health Center functions as a focal point for political mobilizations based upon the situated knowledge of working-class women of color.

People all over the world have been inspired, entertained, and sustained by the cultural creativity of the Black working class in New Orleans. They have savored the pleasures of the city's music, food, dance, and dress. They have discovered serious and sacred purposes beneath the facade of the forbidden, the frowned upon, and the foolish. But there is a politics behind the masks that needs to be discerned, appreciated, and acted upon as well. Neither seeking an unproblematic return to Africa nor uncritical entrance into a white-supremacist and plutocratic nation, the Black working class in New Orleans has suppressed desires for a temporal homeland and instead sought a world-traversing and world-transcending citizenship, connecting its own freedom dreams to the struggles of oppressed people around the globe. Now at the moment of its greatest need, this community needs to know that we support it, to hear our voices on behalf of its right to return, its right to rebuild, and its right to reclaim democratic participation in shaping its own future. The neoliberal plans for reconstructing New Orleans require the destruction of the very Black neighborhoods and Black culture that give the city

its distinctive identity. In their place, developers will create gentrified neighborhoods and sanitized tourist sites that will evoke the city's history in the
process of erasing it. Instead of promoting art that does work in the world
by registering injuries, healing wounds, and calling communities into being
through performance, the post-Katrina neoliberal culture of New Orleans
will advance a spatial imaginary devoted solely to spectatorship and shopping.
This elevation of market time and market space over the rich Afro-diasporic
temporalities and spatialities of New Orleans portends a disaster even greater
than the flooding that followed Hurricane Katrina, not just for New Orleans,
but for the entire nation and the entire world.

10

A Place Where Everybody Is Somebody

This whole phantasmagoria has been built on the most
miserable of human fictions; that in addition to manifest
differences between men there is a deep, awful and
ineradicable cleft which condemns most men to eternal
degradation. It is a cheap inheritance of the world's infancy,
unworthy of grown folk: My rise does not involve your fall.
No superior has interest in inferiority. Humanity is one
and its vast variety is its glory and not its condemnation.
—W. E. B. Du Bois

When Reverend James Cleveland founded the Gospel Music
Workshop of America (GMWA) in 1967, he gave his new organization an unusual motto. This is a place, Cleveland declared,
"where everybody is somebody."[1] As Christians, participants in the GMWA's
conventions and competitions no doubt perceived this message in religious
terms: everybody is somebody because we are all children of God, because
Jesus died for everyone. But the motto also resonated with the core imperatives of the Black spatial imaginary with its long history of making spaces
where new social relations might take place. It reflected lessons learned from
turning segregation into congregation, competition into cooperation, negative ascription into positive affirmation, and parochial attachments to property and place into cosmopolitan allegiances to a world-traversing and world-
transcending citizenship.

Cleveland's ideas about the gospel music association as a place where
new identities might emerge grew logically out of his experiences in Black
churches. Born in 1932 in Lorraine Hansberry's Chicago (see Chapter 8),
he sang as a boy soprano in the choir at the Pilgrim Baptist Church, where
Thomas A. Dorsey served as minister of music and where Roberta Martin
was the featured pianist. One of Cleveland's first jobs entailed delivering

newspapers to his neighbors, one of whom was Mahalia Jackson. Because his parents were too poor to afford a piano, Cleveland taught himself to play by pretending to play notes on a keyboard that he drew with a pencil on a windowsill filled with cracks and crevices.[2] Like the narrator of Harriet Jacobs' *Incidents in the Life of a Slave Girl* and many others in Black history, Cleveland turned a small space of confinement into a big arena of creativity. He got a lot of work done in a small space. Reverend Cleveland went on to become an important presence in the gospel field by incorporating many blues and popular music devices into his arrangements and singing. He moved to Horace Tapscott's and Betye Saar's Los Angeles in 1963 (see Chapters 5 and 7). Cleveland served as pastor at the New Greater Harvest Baptist Church until he got fired because the congregation felt he devoted too much during his services to music and too little time to preaching. As a result, Cleveland founded the Cornerstone Institutional Baptist Church in 1970. He served as pastor there until his death in 1991.[3]

Cleveland viewed the Gospel Music Workshop Association as a new democratic institution. He hoped it would function as an alternative academy to train musicians to develop their skills more fully. Gospel music, he noted, had no colleges or schools devoted to passing on its traditions. Talented musicians were often untrained. They lacked access to places where they could learn sight-reading, harmony, composition, and performance techniques. Cleveland asked professional musicians to donate a portion of their time each year to conventions and competitions, to put their knowledge, achievements, and fame to work in service to other people in an atmosphere where everybody could be treated as if they were somebody.[4]

The very practices and processes of gospel music had something to do with the vision informing Cleveland's creation of the GMWA. Not every gospel singer has the vocal range or voice control needed to be a soloist. But the architecture of gospel music turns this disadvantage into an advantage. Singers with limited range as individuals can sound great when blended together with others in a group. Voices vibrating inside bodies enact the fellowship and solidarity that the lyrics of gospel songs envision. In gospel music it is not necessarily the kind of voice that you have, but rather what you do with that voice that matters. Effort and empathy can count for a lot in this realm. A recording like "I'm All Right Now" by the Soul Stirrers is extraordinary despite the limited vocal range of soloist Julius Cheeks. Part of the song's power comes from Cheeks's battle with the limitations of his own voice, his changes in pitch and his deployment of growls and shouts to create and resolve aesthetic tension. Cheeks communicates how hard he is working to make the song come out well. Regular listeners of gospel learn to recognize and reward this kind of effort. The mode of listening that this kind of performance cultivates can be an important part of the gospel music experience. Jazz great Louis Armstrong knew this kind of listening well from his childhood experiences in a sanctified church. Late in Armstrong's life, a reporter asked him if he resented playing with musicians of lesser ability. The trumpet virtuoso responded with a story about a member of the congregation of the church he attended as a child. Proud of their regular preacher, most of the church members disdained the sermon delivered one Sunday by a substitute pastor. One woman in the church, however, seemed as moved by the inadequate oratory of the newcomer as she had been by the eloquence of the regular clergyman. When challenged on her enthusiasm, the woman explained that despite the speaker's shortcomings, when she looked over his shoulder, she saw Jesus there just the same. Armstrong explained that he applied the same principle to playing with less-skilled musicians. As long as they worked hard and played as well as they could, Armstrong explained, he could look over their shoulders and see Joe Oliver and Bunk Johnson and play his music for them. Armstrong's biographer Thomas Brothers explains the meaning of this anecdote in an analysis that applies as convincingly to gospel music as it does to jazz. "It is possible to listen as Armstrong listened," Brothers notes, "to grant conviction and passion a place in the first line of valuation, with technical sophistication pushed slightly to the rear. One can value *willingness* and learn to hear it, even to think about it as carrying a glimpse of spiritual or artistic purity—at a certain point it does not seem to matter how this is phrased."[5]

Even beyond the aesthetic contours of the music, gospel performances can be seen logically as places where everybody is somebody. A successful gospel performance benefits tremendously from great singing, but it also requires participation from people who do not sing at all, from those who compose music, play instruments, write lyrics, design and sew costumes, move equipment, set up microphones, operate sound boards, manage spotlights, direct lighting systems, transport equipment and personnel, sell tickets, and do publicity. How the audience listens and responds can be as important to the event as the music that is played. The sum total of activities that go into creating a gospel concert or caravan is greater than its parts, and in the mix everybody is somebody.

James Cleveland came to his vision of a place where everybody is somebody directly through his activities as a Christian minister and musician, by way of encounters with these ideas and ideals in the concrete physical spaces and places of Black churches. In the century that followed Emancipation and its subsequent betrayal by Jim Crow segregation, the church was one of the few physical places Blacks could inhabit and control. Many churches, especially those created by working-class Blacks, preserved the radical solidarity and primal hope that permeated slave religious practices and beliefs. In sanctified and holiness churches, congregants made joyful noises, uttered ecstatic praise, and moved their bodies freely. Music, movement, and prayer sometimes led to talking in tongues and other forms of spirit possession. Like African shamans, preachers and worshippers in these places expressed spiritual dilemmas, social tensions, and emotional problems through movements of the body.[6] Perhaps most important, religious services in holiness churches especially affirmed belief in the healing properties of worship and expressive culture, a principle firmly grounded in the religious traditions of west Africa.[7] The slave ancestors of twentieth-century Black church members preserved these African practices in secret Wednesday night prayer meetings. They kept them alive in a variety of conjuring and healing practices that helped shape the contours of Black religion long after slavery ended.[8]

Many of the cultural, social, and spatial practices needed for survival during slavery continued to be important after emancipation. Exploited as workers, disenfranchised as citizens, and persecuted because of their color and their culture, many African Americans flocked to small storefront churches that helped them to endure white supremacy without knuckling under to it. Working-class Black Christians called on the God of the oppressed to come into their lives. They felt that they knew Him personally, and they perceived His presence at every service. This connection neutralized some of the power realities of their society. The strict rules for living they learned in the church and the demands on their time that church membership entailed evoked a sense of living in America as if they were in exile, as if white supremacy was only a temporary burden to be endured, as if their real home was in heaven rather than on earth. More than escapism, these beliefs brought into being new kinds of individuals and new kinds of communities. As Ephraim Radner explains, "For Christians, exile has been not only a condition forced upon a small group of people, but a state into which everyone was called by God for their human maturation—a place of formation, where attitudes and motivations were molded into a community without earthly roots."[9] Imagining oneself in exile temporarily neutralized the power hierarchies of U.S. society, rendering them relative, provisional, and contingent rather than universal. White supremacy ruled in the times and places of man, but it had no place in the time of God.

The term "exile," however, does not quite capture the experiences created inside working-class Black churches. Exiles get to leave the land of their oppression. Black Americans, on the other hand were compelled to remain inside it. As Henry Highland Garnett phrased it in the years before the Civil War, African Americans were even worse off than the Hebrews in the Bible. For the Jews in ancient Egypt, an exodus was possible. For American Blacks, Garnet exclaimed, "The Pharaohs are on both sides of the blood-red waters."[10]

Black people had to stay and fight, to transform rather than simply escape the society that oppressed them. Exile thus functioned as a useful metaphor to help distance oneself from the iniquities of a segregated society, but by necessity it also served as the basis for oppositional and activist social consciousness inside it, for what Lorraine Hansberry called the religion of doing what is necessary in the world (see Chapter 8). Black churches grounded in this culture created distinct alternatives to the practices and premises of materialism, hierarchy, and white supremacy that dominated the rest of U.S. society. Speaking in tongues could convey democratic principles. It proved that the Holy Spirit could strike anyone in the congregation, even the least educated, thereby undermining the authority of the specialized knowledge and ecclesiastical language of the clergy.

The churches also cultivated covert resistance to racism. During the times and inside the places where the repressive forces of white supremacy made direct expression of antiracist views impossible, the culture of exile in Black churches provided protective cover. Gospel music composer William Herbert Brewster explains, "Before the freedom fights started, before the Martin Luther King days, I had to lead a lot of protest meetings. In order to get my message over, there were things that were almost dangerous to say, but you could sing it."[11] Working-class Black churches also challenged the surface appearances of prevailing power relations and social hierarchies to posit a deeper reality of piety accessible through spirit possession, dances, songs, dreams, and healing. They expressed what theologian Harvey Cox calls "primal hope"—a refusal to believe that the appearances and social relations of this world are all that exist and an insistence on living as if ultimately they do not matter.[12] They cultivated the state of mind that Toni Cade Bambara called being indifferent to power. Primal hope encouraged the creation of new identities and institutions. The white male propertied power that pervaded a broad range of American institutions even provoked at least some African Americans to question hierarchies based on gender as well as hierarchies based on race.

Many observers have noted the prominence of Black women in sanctified religion, especially their key role in the Azusa Street Revival of 1906–1909. Students of social movements have argued that the organizational skills learned and refined in church activities enabled Black women to play prominent roles in the civil rights movement.[13] The Black church developed a different gender economy than the white church. A 1986 study found that a clear majority of ordained women clergy in the United States led sanctified, holiness, or Pentecostal churches, many of them Black churches. This research revealed that these denominations ordained many more women than the mainstream Protestant churches.[14] Reverend Cleveland's success drew productively on that history, on the perception of church music and church choirs as a woman's sphere, on the work done by women to sustain churches and gospel singing. These ties were exemplified in the arrangements that Reverend Cleveland created for Albertina Walker, Aretha Franklin, and many other women singers. In his own music, moreover, Cleveland provided a clear alternative to the privileged forms of masculinity favored by the Black preachers of his era. As the important research of Johari Jabir demonstrates, Cleveland built his arrangements and stage shows around performance styles of gospel music replete with the displays of intense emotion, vulnerability, and passion generally favored and advanced by (often closeted) gay men in the gospel community. This openness to a continuum of gender and sexual identities fits perfectly with Cleveland's early musical syntheses of gospel music and the blues as well as his later fusions of gospel and pop. Even on religious matters, Cleveland described himself as a synthesis: part Baptist and part sanctified.[15]

Reverend Cleveland's desire for a place where everybody is somebody drew on the ideas, ideals, practices, and politics forged in Black churches and other alternative academies over the years. Like Horace Tapscott, Betye Saar, and John Biggers, he changed the scale of space by finding and nurturing extraordinary resources inside the confined spaces of the ghetto. Like Rick Lowe and Paule Marshall, he recognized the exceptional resourcefulness of Black women. Like Marshall and Lorraine Hansberry, he found conventional gender and sex roles to be too narrow. Like Tapscott's Arkestra and Rick Lowe's Project Row Houses, the GMWA functioned as an alternative institution, making important things happen in seemingly unexpected spaces. Like the celebrations of Afro-Caribbean hybridity in the fiction of Paule Marshall and the practices of Afro-disaporic musicians in New Orleans, Cleveland's persona and projects used the situated places and experiences of Black life to create alliances and affiliations across borders to envision and enact a world-transcending citizenship.

It should not come as a surprise that the racial and spatial subordination of African Americans has led to the emergence of particular kinds of people. Indeed, the age of repudiation's conservative and liberal mobilizations against the gains made by the egalitarian and democratic Black freedom movement of the mid-twentieth century have insisted on this point, although in a bizarre and distorted formulation. They argue that our nation's history since the passage of civil rights laws proves that Black people are different and deficient, that the problems they face are of their own making, that having been "given" equal rights they have shown themselves to be unfit for freedom. This judgment depends upon fervent denial of the realities of racialized space. It evades the ways in which discriminatory land use and lending policies impede asset accumulation by Blacks. It confuses the impact of racism with the nature of race. It ignores the impact of educational inequality and environmental and transit racism on the lives of children of color. Politicians, pundits, and the creators of popular culture often present us with elaborate delineations of incidents of allegedly nonnormative behavior by Blacks devoid of the contexts in which they occur. Because of the absence of context, we are led to conclude that people who *have* problems *are* problems, that places where people are poor exist because of the people who live in them. What we do not see is that relations between races are relations between places, that the racial problems we confront have spatial causes.

Of course, people do pay a price for centuries of oppression and suppression. Poverty and racism are not designed to make people nice. Individuals who have been hurt often want to hurt others. In its terminal stages, genocide can look like suicide. As the character Silla Boyce contends in Paule Marshall's *Brown Girl, Brownstones*, "It's a terrible thing to know that you gon be poor all yuh life, no matter how hard you work. You does stop trying after a time. People does se you so and call you lazy. But it ain' laziness. It just that you does give up. You does kind of die inside."[16] Yet it makes no sense for a society to decry these outcomes while perpetuating the very practices that produce them in the first place. As Dr. King maintained, "It is a strange and twisted logic to use the tragic results of segregation as an argument for its continuation."[17]

What I have tried to demonstrate in *How Racism Takes Place* is that Black people *are* often different, but not because of pigment and phenotype. We know nothing about anyone by knowing the color of his or her skin. The existence of the Black spatial imaginary does not tell us anything about what any or all Blacks think, believe, or perceive. But because the spaces we have been forced to inhabit produce distinctive optics on power, because people of different races inhabit different places, the Black spatial imaginary contains important evidence about how we are actually governed in this society.

I focus here not so much on what has been done to Black people by others, or on how they have suffered as a result, or even on what they have done for themselves in response. Instead, in this book, I concentrate on what it is possible to learn from the ethnoracial and ethnospatial imaginary that has been forged out of struggles with racialized space. The ideas and artistry of Tapscott, Saar, Marshall, Hansberry, Biggers, and Lowe emerge from and speak to collective struggles about place and power. The works of expressive culture examined earlier in this book can be read as part of the diagnosis and the cure for the pathologies of white supremacy. The capacity to envision places where everybody can be somebody can be of tremendous value to everyone in this society, especially to white people. But the possessive investment in whiteness and the white spatial imaginary work to blind us to the healing and liberating properties of the Black spatial imaginary, to obscure and distort its deep commitments to more dignified, democratic, and decent social relations. Just as segregation and subordination have worked over the years to produce particular kinds of Black people, the unfair gains and unjust rewards of whiteness have produced particular kinds of whites. This has nothing to do with biology, nor is it a form of social determinism. All groups of people have honorable histories of social justice on which they and we can draw. There are whites who are not white supremacists and white supremacists who are not white. Yet the same racialized places that have compelled African Americans to develop knowing optics on power prevent most whites from understanding fundamental features of the society in which they live. Gated communities offer an illusion of autonomy in an interdependent world. Hostile privatism and defensive localism produce the very problems they purport to prevent. The relentless segregation of our society cuts off whites from valuable sources of information. It leads them to misinterpret cries for social justice as appeals to guilt, obscuring the need for all of us to take collective responsibility for shared social conditions and problems. The white spatial imaginary promotes a self-renewing culture of denial and disavowal. It produces a debilitating refusal to recognize the role of race as a social force. It provokes resistance to democratic reforms. As legal scholar Catharine McKinnon observes, "Change is not slow; it is resistance to change that makes it take a long time."[18]

Yet even time can become distorted because of differential relationships with space. The white spatial imaginary is innately ahistorical. It accepts the prevailing imbalances of wealth and power between racialized spaces as a baseline reality that should not be disturbed, as an accurate register of the achievement and worth of the people who live in those spaces. If whites live in wealthy suburbs and Blacks live in impoverished ghettos, the white spatial imaginary says, it is because whites have worked hard and succeeded while Blacks have exerted too little effort and failed. The long history of rewards for racism and subsidies for segregation disappears from this equation. The wealth that whites inherit from previous generations is rarely mentioned. We do not acknowledge the cumulative vulnerabilities that Black individuals and communities face from centuries of impediments to asset accumulation, decapitalization, and discrimination. In contrast, the Black spatial imaginary encourages us to see that how "things are" is, at least in part, a consequence of how they came to be. The white spatial imaginary, however, encourages people to think the world begins when they walk into the room. It leads people born on third base to believe they hit a triple.[19]

The manner in which different spatial imaginaries produce different temporalities took center stage in the *Missouri v. Jenkins* case decided by the

Supreme Court in 1995. For twenty-three years after the Supreme Court's *Brown v. Board* decision, city and state officials in Kansas City, Missouri, refused to desegregate local schools. Black parents sued the school board and the state, winning a judgment in federal court in 1977. Although the city and state lost their case in court, they continued to fight against integration. Kansas City school officials did not even come up with a *plan* for desegregation until the courts mandated one eight years later in 1985, some thirty-one years after *Brown v. Board*. The actual plan was not implemented until another three-year delay came to an end in 1988. Then the plan was implemented for seven years. In 1995, however, the Supreme Court ruled that desegregation in Kansas City had gone on too long, that while initially justified, it was now an intolerable burden for whites. The Court decided in *Missouri v. Jenkins* that after seven years of desegregation, racial inequality in education in the Kansas City area no longer had anything to do with the policies in place before *Brown v. Board*, policies that persisted for thirty-four years after it. School segregation owed nothing to the past any more, the Court ruled, but now stemmed instead from contemporary "voluntary" and "natural" decisions about where people wanted to live. Although more than a century of segregation preceded their ruling, the Court majority decided that residential choices in Kansas City in 1995 had nothing to do with the legacy of segregation, even though these purportedly innocent and independent decisions concentrated white people in affluent suburbs with well-funded schools while relegating blacks to poverty-stricken inner-city neighborhoods where schools were literally falling apart.[20] Moreover, as soon as Blacks became a majority of the school population in Kansas City, the majority white electorate refused to pass a single tax levy or bond issue to fund the schools.[21] As Justice Ruth Bader Ginsburg pointed out in her dissenting opinion in *Missouri v. Jenkins*, the Court majority had decided that remedial desegregation programs had in a mere seven years effectively countered the entire legacy of discrimination that started in Kansas City with the proclamation of the Code Noir by King Louis XV of France in 1724, a legacy that included slavery, state laws prohibiting public education for blacks, mandatory Jim Crow segregation, and thirty-four years of direct resistance to the *Brown* decision.[22]

The Supreme Court's belief that two hundred and seventy-one years of white supremacy had been wiped out by seven years of modest school desegregation programs was of course a hollow fabrication designed to privilege the interests of white property over the interests of Black humanity. The Rehnquist Court in 1995 was determined to bend the law to suit the interests of whites. The mechanism for doing so, however, the denial of history's hold on the present, is part of the broader damage done by the white spatial imaginary. We see this denial in evidence often in discussions of affirmative action, fair housing, and school desegregation. It is both intellectually dishonest and socially destructive. It is as if people living alongside a river downstream from the source of pollution argue that the river should not be cleaned up because they did not personally pollute it. Or as if a person who smoked cigarettes as a youth and stopped cannot contract cancer later in life because the person no longer smokes. If the toxins are in the body, the smoker still had a problem. If the history of racism creates cumulative vulnerabilities in the present, it will not help the body politic to pretend they are not there.

The Black spatial imaginary presents a more sophisticated understanding of time, a more accurate delineation of the relationships linking past and present. Jesus Hernandez's research on the geography of mortgage foreclosures in Sacramento, California, shows how past practices of redlining dating back at least to the 1930s that would now be illegal made certain neighborhoods in that city particularly susceptible to capital extraction and the meltdown of the deregulated subprime market during the first decade of the new millennium.[23] The patterns of the past impede progress in the present.

Just as the white spatial imaginary distorts white understanding of time, it also occludes basic facts about money. David Freund's research (see Chapter 1) shows how whites after World War II gained privileged access to government-supported mortgages that enabled them to move into white suburbs with infrastructures paid for by federal funds. Yet they came to view themselves not as recipients of government largesse, but as winners in free and fair market competition. These whites and their descendants (and heirs) do not acknowledge that housing markets have never been free, nor do they see how an artificially constrained housing market imposes a racial tax on Black people. This blindness in a central part of their lives prevents them from recognizing the true contours of the entire U.S. class system and their place in it. For example, having declared themselves winners in the market, they cannot acknowledge how the growing concentration of wealth at the top undermines their own well-being. The total share of the national income going to wages and salaries is presently at its lowest level since 1929 while the percentage of national income garnered by corporate profits is higher than it has been at any time since 1950.[24] Suburban whites often imagine themselves to be overtaxed, imagining that Blacks and other people of color collect generous welfare benefits for not working. Suburban wage earners are in fact overtaxed, but not because of welfare. They suffer from the very tax "cuts" for which they routinely vote, cuts in taxes on income, capital gains, and inheritance that benefit the rich but deprive governments of needed income that then must be raised from the taxes that hit hardest on the middle class and the poor—sales taxes, fees for services, and payroll taxes. During the 1960s, payroll taxes were 6 percent, but after the Reagan tax cuts of the 1980s (in reality, tax shifts) they grew to their present level of 15 percent.[25] Sixty percent of consumption in the United States is done by the wealthiest 20 percent of households, while only 10 percent comes from the poorest 40 percent.[26] The bottom 50 percent of the population controls less than 3 percent of the nation's wealth. The bottom 85 percent accounts for only 16 percent. But the wealthiest 1 percent of households own more than a third of the country's total wealth.

The detachment from reality required by the white spatial imaginary appears most powerfully in widespread efforts to attribute the 2007 meltdown of the financial system to programs designed to help Blacks become homeowners rather than to the deregulation and securitization of the home mortgage lending industry. Politicians, editorial writers, and right-wing pundits always eager to "stand up" to Blacks but timid in the face of corporate malfeasance blamed the Community Reinvestment Act and other modest efforts to promote homeownership among the groups most harmed by illegal discrimination. They reiterated their interpretation even when observers across the political spectrum, including liberal sociologist Douglas Massey and conservative historian Niall Ferguson, correctly identified how deregulation and securitization created profitable opportunities for lenders to make bad loans, including those that exploited the cumulative financial vulnerabilities of Black home seekers by engaging in deliberately racist predatory lending practices.[27] A 2008 "State of the Dream" report by the United for a Fair Economy organization revealed that a majority of subprime borrowers would have qualified for conventional prime-rate loans and that only 11 percent of subprime loans in 2008 went to first-time home buyers.[28] Federal Reserve Bank economists Elizabeth Laderman and Carolina Reid found that CRA lenders made only a small percentage of loans to low- and moderate-income borrowers, that loans that originated under CRA were significantly less likely to lead to foreclosure than other loans, and that only 12 percent of CRA loans were high-priced, compared to 52.4 percent of loans by independent mortgage companies marketing in low-income communities. Conservative economist and federal Reserve Board governor Randall Korzner noted that the evidence "makes it hard to imagine how this law [CRA] could have contributed in any meaningful way to the current subprime crisis."[29]

The most sophisticated and accurate analysis of the subprime crisis reveals the degree to which links between race and place have damaged the entire economy. Economist Gary Dymski explains that the systematic exclusion of minority home seekers from the mortgage market by redlining and discrimination before 1990 created structural weaknesses that served as the enabling precondition of the economic meltdown. The cumulative vulnerabilities of these borrowers made them susceptible to predatory lending practices. But it was the strategic transformation of banking in the 1980s, the position of the

United States in the world financial system, and the securitization and finan-
cialization enabled by the 1999 banking "reform" act that made home lending
not just extortionary but also speculative. Dymski's study shows that the loss of
wealth suffered by people of color because of mortgage foreclosures was an essential part of a broader expropriation of working-class wealth by financial capital, an expropriation hidden to most whites because of its racial dimensions.[30]

The white spatial imaginary thus obscures an increasingly unequal, unjust, and (in the wake of the economic crisis) untenable economy. Many of
the people whose material well-being has been damaged most by these economic changes still believe that unleashing private greed can produce public gain. Steeped in the ideology of ownership, they imagine that business
is a benign and moral presence in our society. They do not dream of allying
with Blacks because the racialization of space, the possessive investment in
whiteness, and the white racial frame prevent them from seeing the circumstances that Blacks face or what they might gain from adopting the Black spatial imaginary. They have been so busy policing perceived threats from poor
people with dark skins that they do not seem to have noticed how they are
being exploited by their fellow whites who are wealthy. They have become so
accustomed to blaming Blacks for social problems that even when confronted
with overwhelming evidence of white criminality in the form of the predatory
and fraudulent lending practices that precipitated the economic crisis, they
absolve their fellow whites of all accountability and responsibility by blaming
the crisis (inaccurately) on federal programs designed to fight discrimination
in the home loan industry. This aspect of the white spatial imaginary has a
long history. It has also served the interests of elites very effectively. As Toni
Morrison observes,

> There is still much ill-gotten gain to reap from rationalizing power
> grabs and clutches with inferences of inferiority and the ranking of
> differences. There is still much national solace in continuing dreams
> of democratic egalitarianism available by hiding class conflict, rage
> and impotence in figurations of race. And there is quite a lot of juice
> to be extracted from plumy reminiscences of "individualism" and
> "freedom" if the tree upon which such fruit hangs is a black popula-
> tion forced to serve as freedom's polar opposite; individualism is fore-
> grounded (and believed in) when its background its stereotypified,
> enforced dependency.[31]

Joe Feagin notes how little whites actually know about Blacks. He points
to surveys that show that half of whites believe that Blacks have the same levels of education and quality of jobs as whites and that 60 percent of whites

believe that the average Black person has the same access to health care as the average white person. Only one in five whites is able to estimate accurately the amount of racial discrimination that Blacks confront.[32] Other studies confirm Feagin's findings. More than 80 percent of whites tell pollsters that housing discrimination is no longer a serious problem. A similar percentage believes that Black applicants have the same chance of being hired as whites. Only slightly more than a third of whites believe that continuing racial discrimination explains the socioeconomic standing of Blacks relative to whites. More than half of whites attribute the lack of racial progress to the absence of motivation among Blacks. Sixty-five percent of whites contend that racial inequalities would disappear if only Blacks would "try harder." Half of whites believe that government has no obligation to correct racial inequality, and 77 percent of whites insist that Blacks deserve "no special favors in society."[33] Yet the facts are far different from what whites imagine them to be. As of December 2009, unemployment among Blacks reached 16.2 percent, compared to 9 percent among whites. Blacks earn 62 cents for every dollar of income earned by whites. Blacks are nearly three times more likely to live in poverty than whites. For every dollar of net worth owned by whites, Blacks have 10 cents. Whites are 34 times more likely than Blacks to have a median net wealth over $3.5 million. The median value of white families' net financial assets is $39,500, while the assets of families of color have a median value of $5,500.[34] Whites have much to learn from the Black spatial imaginary. It would teach them about why race matters, but also make available to them a less Pollyannaish view of market practices and a more serious commitment to moral behavior and social relations. Horace Tapscott walked away from the most lucrative employment of his career in order to re-create the collaborative social spaces of his Houston childhood in Los Angeles. Betye Saar's installations and John Biggers's paintings imbue the everyday tools of working women with enormous dignity. Paule Marshall wrote *Brown Girl, Brownstones* to protest "a blind absorption into the material." The family that Lorraine Hansberry depicts in *A Raisin in the Sun* passes up material gain to follow the religion of doing what is necessary in the world. Parade musicians and marchers in New Orleans create art that cannot be contained inside commercial venues. James Cleveland's GMWA called on successful musicians to volunteer their services to help people who had no other way of getting help. From slavery to sharecropping, from the forced labor camps administered by large corporations in the South in the postbellum era to the systematic discrimination practiced by real estate agents and bankers in the North throughout the twentieth century, business has long been a central force in the establishment and maintenance of white supremacy. In a true capitalist society, the only color that would matter would be the color of money. Neoclassical economists continuously assert that civil rights laws are not needed because market principles should make discrimination impossible. Yet the way markets actually work is to reward cartels of all kinds, including racial cartels. As Pulitzer Prize–winning author and *Wall Street Journal* Atlanta bureau chief Douglas A. Blackmon notes, individual businesses have been the main perpetrators of employment discrimination, and wealthy bankers were among the chief financial backers of organized opposition to the 1964 Civil Rights Act. "Indeed," Blackmon adds, "the commercial sectors of U.S. society have never been asked to fully account for their roles as the primary enforcers of Jim Crow segregation, and not at all for engineering the resurrection of forced labor after the Civil War."[35]

The white spatial imaginary encourages whites to believe that hiding social problems is the same as solving them. It deploys zoning and other land-use regulations as a proxy for segregation rather than as part of a rational program for distributing rewards, risks, and responsibilities fairly. Just as it separates people into discrete privately held domains, the white spatial imaginary promotes the disaggregation of social problems into their constituent parts. For example, schemes to reform schools almost always focus exclusively on the classroom, the curriculum, and pedagogy. These are important areas to address, but many of the most severe school problems start outside the school in environmentally caused learning and developmental disabilities, inadequate nutrition and health care, parents who find themselves compelled to work too many hours to be involved in their children's schooling, transit racism, and violence. Shortages of fair and affordable housing can relegate Black children to overcrowded dwellings with no study spaces, expose them disproportionately to lead poisoning and asthma, and cut them off from networks of information about educational enrichment opportunities. Compared to white children, Black youths attend schools with fewer credentialed teachers, guidance counselors, supplies, books, and advanced courses. If they do not manage to outperform more privileged whites on high-stakes tests despite these obstacles, their schools run the risk of losing funding. Housing shortages and residential segregation also compel Black students to move more frequently than whites. Frequent moves disrupt the continuity of classroom learning for the students who move as well as for the ones who do not. These moves contribute directly to low achievement and high dropout rates. A study of over four thousand students in Oregon and California revealed that students who move frequently during their elementary school years also have a 20 percent higher chance of being involved in violent incidents.[36] Changing peadagogies and curricula will do little to remedy these ills.

As the white spatial imaginary distorts our understanding of time and money, it also does harm to our moral reasoning. Rather than accountability and responsibility, practices of refusal, resistance, and renegotiation dominate white responses to Black demands for justice.[37] When Malcolm X declared that "the names change but the game stays the same," he identified a core dynamic of the possessive investment in whiteness. When slavery ended in the nineteenth century, sharecropping, Jim Crow segregation, forced labor, and mass incarceration emerged to take its place. At the same time, federal judges inverted the meaning of the Fourteenth Amendment, turning anti-subjugation laws designed to protect Black humanity into anti-racial-recognition principles that protected white property and privileges. In the twentieth century, the Supreme Court's proclamation in favor the principle of desegregating public schools has been foiled in practice by massive resistance from whites in both the North and the South. The 1964 Civil Rights Act and the 1965 Voting Rights Act succeeded in desegregating public accommodations and voting, but white opposition to fair employment practices, affirmative action, school desegregation, and fair housing leaves opportunities and life chances unfairly skewed along racial lines.

The meanness and mendacity of white resistance to desegregation deserves special mention. For example, lengthy litigation by fair-housing advocates finally convinced a federal judge in 1969 that the Chicago Housing Authority had violated the law by locating public housing exclusively in Black neighborhoods. The judge instructed the city to build seven hundred new public housing units, and he ordered them to locate three-quarters of them outside the ghetto. Housing Authority officials at first resisted this order. When compelled by a court order to comply with it, moreover, they announced that the decision was moot because they had decided to cease construction of all new public housing.[38] Similarly, in the 1970s, an organization composed of Black residents of Sumter County, Alabama, received federal funds to promote land and home ownership under the aegis of a program set up to aid minorities in accumulating assets. When Ronald Reagan became president, officials in his administration tried to overturn that decision. Blacks could not take advantage of this program to help minorities, they charged, because in Sumter County Blacks were a numerical majority. When African Americans went to court to have the funds restored, the Reagan administration simply defunded the program and then terminated it.[39]

When Martin Luther King was murdered, Congress passed the Fair Housing Act of 1968. As a condition of allowing the bill to pass, Republican Senate Minority Leader Everett Dirksen insisted on removing all provisions that might guarantee effective enforcement.[40] Justice William O. Douglas noted in the 1972 *Trafficante* case that the resulting Fair Housing Act required ordinary citizens to act as "private attorneys general," investigating complaints without subpoena powers and prosecuting malefactors without the threat of penalties sufficient to deter illegal acts.[41] The law that emerged was one that Senator Edward Kennedy later described as "a toothless tiger," a statute that proclaimed fundamental rights but precluded meaningful remedies.[42] Yet over the years, fair-housing advocates have turned disadvantage into advantage. They have taken a law deliberately designed to be weak and made it strong. The reliance on civilian enforcement rather than action by the attorney general or the Department of Housing and Urban Development has compelled grassroots groups around the nation to form fair-housing councils. These groups engage in education and litigation. They support new legislation and promote political mobilization. They have filed structural lawsuits securing prospective relief to prevent ongoing discriminatory actions as well as individual lawsuits winning retroactive damages for past discrimination.[43]

As the white spatial imaginary develops new forms of exclusion, fair-housing advocates and their allies devise appropriate responses. Malcolm X's comparison of racism to a Cadillac because they make a new model every year and his observation that "the names change but the game's the same" still shed light on the U.S. racial order. For example, as balanced-budget conservatism increasingly pits subunits of government against each other, municipalities and counties have tried to ease their financial burdens at the expense of communities of color. The device of underbounding entails managing annexations and service provision to provide covert subsidies for whites through systematic exploitation of nonwhites. Government agencies draw district lines in such a way as to deny sewer and water connections and garbage collection to neighborhoods inhabited by Blacks and Latinos. These underserved neighborhoods become dumping grounds for refuse and junk. Their inhabitants are forced to use outhouses and septic tanks because they are denied sewer service. They pay more for water connections. In some cases, they cannot call on police officers stationed inside city limits but must rely instead on county sheriffs who serve large territories of unincorporated areas. Fair-housing advocates have developed new strategies to oppose these practices. A structural lawsuit in Ohio led to a federal court ruling that compelled officials from the city of Zanesville, Muskingham County, and Washington Township to pay nearly eleven million dollars to the residents of a predominantly Black community (Coal Run) for denying it water connections for more than half a century. Similar lawsuits are currently in progress in Moore County, North Carolina, and in Modesto, California.[44]

An especially important victory emerged from a lawsuit filed by the Anti-Discrimination Center alleging that officials in Westchester County, New York, evaded their responsibilities to affirmatively further fair housing despite receiving federal funds contingent on those efforts. County officials initially ridiculed the charges as "garbage," but Federal Judge Denise Cote ruled that the county misrepresented itself to federal officials by affirming action on fair housing issues while making little or no actual efforts to combat housing segregation. In a settlement that could serve as a model in many other communities where officials have evaded their fair housing responsibilities, Westchester County agreed to spend more than $50 million to build or acquire homes and apartments and to place 630 of them in municipalities where Blacks comprise less than 3 percent of the population and Latinos make up less than 7 percent.[45]

The fight for fair housing is a lot like gospel singing. It brings together people with very different levels of expertise and vastly different experiences, opinions, and intentions. Progress in the field of fair housing comes from hard work by people in widely dispersed venues. It relies on litigation, legislation, education, and mobilization by people in fair-housing centers and legal clinics, law offices and court rooms, city councils and state legislatures, administrative agencies and research libraries. The fight for fair housing is a place where what people do together is greater than anything they can do as individuals. It is a place where people sing the songs of the unsung, a place where everybody is somebody. It is a place where you don't have to be a big dog to do big deeds. It is not a struggle that storms from triumph to triumph, where people win "once and for all" victories. It is a place, however, in the words of the great organizer Ella Baker, where "we who believe in freedom cannot rest until it comes."[46]

We need to destroy the fatal coupling of race and place. A first step in disconnecting the nation's racial regimes from their spatial grounding would be to support the struggle for fair housing, to turn the promises of the 1968 and 1988 fair-housing acts into concrete practices. Changing fair-housing laws by giving judges the power to issue "cease and desist" orders and impose higher penalties would make it harder for discriminators to break the law. Insisting that cities fulfill their legal responsibilities to fund fair-housing activities when they receive federal grants would empower citizen enforcement at the local level. Systematic fair-housing testing and enforcement programs could be financed by the federal government through elimination of the home mortgage deduction for second homes, an end to the federal tax deduction for local property taxes, and increases in inheritance and capital gains taxes. Closer scrutiny of tax-increment financing arrangements and tax abatements for developers could stop diversion of general tax dollars to private interests that are unaccountable to the public. An amendment to the U.S. constitution reversing the 1973 Rodriguez decision and the 1974 Milliken decision by guaranteeing all students in public schools an equal education and allowing busing across jurisdictional lines would remove one the key incentives for white flight from integrated schools and for the educational inequality that results from property-tax-based school-funding systems.

The Black spatial imaginary can function as a key resource in struggles for social justice, for fair housing and fair hiring, school desegregation and affirmative action, equal opportunity and democracy. Where the white spatial imaginary disaggregates and divides, the Black spatial imaginary produces unexpected connections and coalitions. Horace Tapscott's Arkestra and Rick Lowe's Project Row Houses transformed ordinary houses, commercial buildings, and parks into schools, conservatories, libraries, art galleries, and performance spaces. Tapscott fought hunger by asking audience members to bring cans of food to concerts as the price of admission. After these performances he led his musicians in distributing the food to hungry people. Lowe and his collaborators make works of art that help single mothers finish their educations by giving them places in which to live. Their project aids recovering substance abusers by helping them find meaningful work that gives them new reasons to live. Tapscott, Betye Saar, John Biggers, Paule Marshall, Lorraine Hansberry, and Afro-diasporic musicians and marchers in New Orleans provide us with ways of viewing the immediate problems facing Black communities not as parochial or particular issues, but as nodes in a global network of struggles for dignity and justice. The social imagination envisioned and sometimes enacted by these artists pervades the work done by social movements in the fields of fair housing and fair hiring, school desegregation, environmental justice, transit equity, and sustainable growth.

The dynamic, syncretic, and dialogic properties of the Black spatial imaginary have much to offer. They possess creative possibilities for remapping time and space, for renegotiating the links between past and present as well as between the local and the global. They can clear up confusion about the relations between people and property, independence and interdependence, materialism and morality, race and place. Yet advancing the creative potential of the Black spatial imaginary is not simply or solely the task of Black people. Changing the spatial imaginary of society is an enormous and daunting task. It cannot be engineered by experts or called into being by charismatic leaders. It requires endless agonistic struggle by ordinary people. As Martin Luther King understood, ""No great victories are won in a war for the transformation of a whole people without total participation. Less than this will not create a new society: it will only evoke more sophisticated token amelioration."[47] Most people assume that our society lacks the will to change, that the kind of total participation that Dr. King envisioned can never happen here. Some readers no doubt think this vision has nothing to do with them. But I hope others will recognize what the Black spatial imaginary shows us. It reveals the tremendous power of work done in the world by serious people who believe that there is important work to do and decide that it is up to us to do it.

Decoupling race from place requires us to make an enormous and miraculous transformation of our society. Yet the mere survival of Black people in America has been a miracle. The enduring humanity of Black people in the face of relentless dehumanization has been a miracle. The unwavering devotion to democracy by Black people has been a miracle. The fact that the very people who have been farthest from realizing democracy's fruits and benefits have valued it the most has been a miracle. Making miracles is not impossible. Miraculous change can not *take place*, however, until we change the racialized meanings *of place*. No one will do this work for us. No knight on horseback will come to our rescue. No election will do for us what we need to do for ourselves. Within the electoral system, as Julian Bond observes, the Republicans have been shameless in perpetuating and exploiting racial divisions. The Democrats have been spineless in opposing them. We have choices in elections, but they are choices between voting for the shameless or the spineless. We cannot wish away these realities. These are problems that require some backbone, not a wishbone. They require imagination, education, agitation, organization, legislation, litigation, and mobilization. Yet everything we need to solve our problems is already here. The tradition of the Black spatial imaginary teaches us that every problem has a solution, that the terms and tools of oppression can be turned into instruments of emancipation, that strong people don't need strong leaders.

One of the songs regularly sung by participants in Reverend James Cleveland's Gospel Music Workshop Association expresses the kind of thinking that we so badly need. In that space "where everybody is somebody," soloists and choirs sing, "May the Work I've Done Speak for Me." Many of the people who sing those words know a lot about work. They labor every day as low-wage workers, cleaning hotel rooms they could never afford to rent and cooking food they could never afford to buy, working hard, dirty, dangerous jobs for meager pay. They do their jobs and do them well. But when they sing, "May the Work I've Done," they probably are thinking about another kind of work, the kind described by Toni Cade Bambara as "the work of walking upright and seeing clearly, breathing easily and thinking clearly, being better than we've been programmed to believe we can be, helping a neighbor experience the best of himself or herself."[48] This is the lesson of the Black spatial imaginary, whether it is sung, painted, danced, written, or spoken. In this world, the work you do speaks for you.

Notes

INTRODUCTION

Epigraph: Martin Luther King, Jr., *Where Do We Go from Here: Chaos or Community?* (Boston: Beacon, 2010), 10.

1. George Lipsitz, *The Possessive Investment in Whiteness: How White People Profit from Identity Politics* (Philadelphia: Temple University Press, 2006).

2. Thomas R. Shapiro, *The Hidden Cost of Being African American* (New York: Oxford, 2004), 190.

3. Kenneth Jackson, *Crabgrass Frontier* (New York: Oxford, 1975), 216.

4. Daria Roithmayr, "Racial Cartels" (University of Southern California Law and Economics Working Papers Series, Working Paper 66, 2007).

5. Melvin L. Oliver and Thomas M. Shapiro, *Black Wealth/White Wealth: A New Perspective on Racial Equality* (New York: Routledge, 2006). Shapiro, *Hidden Cost.*

6. Oliver and Shapiro, *Black Wealth/White Wealth.*

7. Shapiro, *Hidden Cost.*

8. Richard Rothstein, "How the U.S. Tax Code Worsens the Education Gap," *New York Times*, April 25, 2001, p. A-17.

9. Thomas M. Shapiro, Tatjana Meschede, and Laura Sullivan, "The Racial Wealth Gap Increases Fourfold" (Research and Policy Brief, Institute on Assets and Social Policy, Heller School for Social Policy and Management, Brandeis University, 2010), 1–3. Accessed on June 5, 2010, from IASP.Brandeis.edu/pdfs/racial-wealth-gap-brief.pdf.

10. James H. Carr and Nandinee K. Kutty, "Attaining a Just Society," James H. Carr and Nandinee K. Kutty, *Segregation: The Rising Costs for America* (New York: Routledge, 2008), 333.

11. Laura Pulido, "Rethinking Environmental Racism: White Privilege and Urban Development in Southern California," *Annals of the Association of American Geographers* 90, no. 1 (2000): 13.

12. Quoted in Dolores Acevedo-Garcia and Theresa L. Osypuk, "Impacts of Housing and Neighborhoods on Health: Pathways, Racial/Ethnic Disparities, and Policy Directions," in Carr and Kutty, *Segregation*, 197.

13. Scott Burris, Ichiro Kawachi, and Austin Sarat, "Integrating Law and Social Epidemiology," *Journal of Law, Medicine, and Ethics* 30 (2002): 510–521.

14. Quoted in Burris, Kawachi, and Sarat, "Integrating Law," 513.

15. Dennis R. Judd and Todd Swanstrom, *City Politics: Private Power and Public Policy* (New York: Harper and Collins, 1994), 222.

16. Acevedo-Garcia and Osypuk, "Impacts of Housing," 215.

17. John P. Caskey, *Fringe Banking: Check-Cashing Outlets, Pawnshops, and the Poor* (New York: Russell Sage Foundation, 1994), 1, 144.

18. James H. Carr and Nandinee K. Kutty, "The New Imperative for Equality," in Carr and Kutty, *Segregation*, 21.

19. Gregory D. Squires and Charis E. Kubrin, *Privileged Places: Race, Residence, and the Structure of Opportunity* (Boulder, CO: Lynne Rienner, 2006), 14.

20. Carr and Kutty, "New Imperative for Equality," 20.

21. Caskey, *Fringe Banking*, 86–87.

22. Gertrude Ezorsky, *Racism and Justice: The Case for Affirmative Action* (Ithaca, NY: Cornell University Press, 1991), 25. Richard Child Hill and Cynthia Negry, "Deindustrialization and Racial Minorities in the Great Lakes Region, USA," in D. Stanley Eitzen and Maxine Baca Zinn, eds., *The Reshaping of America: Social Consequences of the Changing Economy* (Englewood Cliffs, NJ: Prentice Hall, 1989), 168–178. Caskey, *Fringe Banking*, 96.

23. Carr and Kutty, "New Imperative for Equality," 22.

24. Kathleen C. Engel and Patricia A. McCoy, "From Credit Denial to Predatory Lending: The Challenge of Sustaining Minority Homeownership," in Carr and Kutty, *Segregation*, 92.

25. Paul D. Davies, "Beg, Borrow, Besieged," *Philadelphia Daily News*, February 5, 2001.

26. Engel and McCoy, "From Credit Denial," 92.

27. Carr and Kutty, "New Imperative for Equality," 22.

28. Angel O. Torres, Robert D. Bullard, and Chad G. Johnson, "Closed Doors: Persistent Barriers to Fair Housing," in Robert D. Bullard, Glenn S. Johnson, and Angel O. Torres, eds., *Sprawl City: Race, Politics, and Planning in Atlanta* (Washington, DC: Island Press, 2000). Dolores Acevedo-Garcia, Theresa L. Osypuk, and Nancy McArdle, "Racial/Ethnic Integration and Child Health Disparities," in Chester Hartman and Gregory D. Squires, *The Integration Debate: Competing Futures for American Cities* (New York: Routledge, 2010).

29. Squires and Kubrin, *Privileged Places*, 12.

30. Colin Gordon, *Mapping Decline: St. Louis and the Fate of the American City* (Philadelphia: University of Pennsylvania Press, 2008), 111.

31. Gregory D. Squires, "Insurance Redlining: Still Fact, Not Fiction," National Housing Institute, January/February 1995, http:///www.nhi.org/online/issues/79/isured.html, 1.

32. Joe Feagin, *Racist America: Roots, Current Realities, and Future Reparations* (New York: Routledge, 2000), 156.

33. *Inner City Press*, "Insurance Redlining," http://www.innercitypress.org/insure. html, accessed October 29, 2010.

34. Gordon, *Mapping Decline*, 111.

35. Torres, Bullard, and Johnson, "Closed Doors," 103–105.

36. Engel and McCoy, "From Credit Denial," 92.

37. Feagin, *Racist America*, 157.

38. Torres, Bullard, and Johnson, "Closed Doors," 101.

39. Jesus Hernandez, "Connecting Segregation to Contemporary Housing Credit Practices and Foreclosures: A Case Study of Sacramento" (written testimony submitted to the National Commission on Fair Housing and Equal Opportunity, Los Angeles Hearing. July 9, 2008).

40. Torres, Bullard, and Johnson, "Closed Doors," 101.

41. Feagin, *Racist America*, 159.

42. Feagin, *Racist America*, 158.

43. Squires, "Insurance Redlining," 3.

44. George Lipsitz, *American Studies in a Moment of Danger* (Minneapolis: University of Minnesota Press, 2001), 117–138, 169–184, 213–233. George Lipsitz, *Footsteps in the Dark: The Hidden Histories of Popular Music* (Minneapolis: University of Minnesota Press, 2007), 26–78, 133–153, 211–237. George Lipsitz, "Walleye Warriors and White Identities: Native Americans' Treaty Rights, Composite Identities, and Social Movements," *Ethnic and Racial Studies* 31, no. 1 (January 2008), 101–122.

45. Charles J. McLain, *In Search of Equality: The Chinese Struggle against Discrimination in Nineteenth-Century America* (Berkeley: University of California Press, 1994), 223–233.

46. Mindy Thompson Fullilove, *Root Shock: How Tearing Up City Neighborhoods Hurts America, and What We Can Do about It* (New York: Ballantine Books, 2004), 40.

47. Judd and Swanstrom, *City Politics*, 146.

48. Russell Thornton, *American Indian Holocaust and Survival: A Population History since 1492* (Norman: University of Oklahoma Press, 1987), 225–239. Duane Champagne, *Social Change and Cultural Continuity among Native Nations* (Lanham, MD: Alta Mira Press, 2007), 174–179. Robert D. Bullard, ed., *Unequal Protection: Environmental Justice and Communities of Color* (San Francisco: Sierra Club, 1994).

49. Excellent work on these questions has been done by Arlene Davila, Laura Pulido, Raul Homero Villa, Mary Pat Brady, Al Camarillo, Roberto Alvarez, Chiou-Ling Yeh, Kathleen Yep, Duane Champagne, Al Gedicks, and Joane Nagel.

50. King, *Where Do We Go*, 71.

51. The concept of a "racial order" comes from Claire Jean Kim, *Bitter Fruit* (New Haven, CT: Yale University Press, 2000), 14–15.

52. Kimberle Williams Crenshaw, "Race, Reform, and Retrenchment: Transformation and Legitimation in Anti-Discrimination Law," in Kimberle Crenshaw, Neil Gotanda, Gary Peller, and Kendall Thomas, eds., *Critical Race Theory: The Writings That Formed the Movement* (New York: New Press, 1996), 103–125.

53. King, *Where Do We Go*, 95.

54. Ibid., 181.

55. Ibid., 3.

56. Ibid., 12.

57. Ibid., 86.

58. Ibid., 10.

59. Ibid., 141.

60. Ibid., 142.

61. Ibid., 212–213.

62. Ibid., 213–214.

63. Ibid., 214.

64. Ibid., 146.

65. Ibid., 137.

66. Ibid., 21.

67. Charles W. Mills, *The Racial Contract* (Ithaca and London: Cornell University Press, 1997), 131.

68. Raymond Williams, *The Politics of Modernism* (London: Verso, 1999), 134.

69. Ibid.

70. King, *Where Do We Go*, 4.

CHAPTER 1

Epigraph: Frances E. W. Harper, *Iola Leroy* (New York: Oxford University Press, 1988), 265–266.

1. *Fundamentals of Real Estate Practice*, quoted in Colin Gordon, *Mapping Decline: St. Louis and the Fate of the American City* (Philadelphia: University of Pennsylvania Press, 2008), 83.

2. John R. Logan and Harvey L. Molotch, *The Political Economy of Place* (Berkeley: University of California Press, 1987), 128.

3. Thomas Sugrue, *The Origins of The Urban Crisis: Race and Inequality in Postwar Detroit* (Princeton, NJ: Princeton University Press, 2005). Arnold Hirsch, *Making the Second Ghetto: Race and Housing in Chicago, 1940–1960* (Cambridge, UK: Cambridge University Press, 1983). Gordon, *Mapping Decline*. Clarence Lang, *Grassroots at the Gateway: Class Politics and Black Freedom Struggle in St. Louis, 1936–75* (Ann Arbor: University of Michigan Press, 2009). Josh Sides, *L.A. City Limits: African American Los Angeles from the Great Depression to the Present* (Berkeley: University of California Press, 2006).

4. Lang, *Grassroots at the Gateway*, 83–84.

5. Hirsch, *Making the Second Ghetto*, 243.

6. Johnny Otis, "Johnny Otis Says 'Let's Talk,'" *Los Angeles Sentinel*, March 24, 1960, p. 4A.

7. Eugene Meehan, *The Quality of Federal Policymaking: Programmed Failure in Public Housing* (Columbia: University of Missouri Press, 1979).

8. David M. P. Freund, *Colored Property: State Policy and White Racial Politics in Suburban America* (Chicago: University of Chicago Press, 2007), 359. The suburb also subsidized heterosexuality by funneling loans and tax breaks to encourage the construction and sale of housing units designed for properly gendered nuclear family units.

9. Charles W. Mills, *The Racial Contract* (Ithaca and London: Cornell University Press, 1997), 42.

10. Melani McAlister, *Epic Encounters* (Berkeley: University of California Press, 2001), 4.

11. David W. Noble, *Death of a Nation: American Culture and the End of Exceptionalism* (Minneapolis: University of Minnesota Press), 2002.

12. Evan McKenzie, *Privatopia: Homeowner Associations and the Rise of Residential Private Government* (New Haven, CT: Yale University Press, 1994), 10.

13. Ibid., 22.

14. Ibid., 22–23.

15. Ibid., 7, 12, 177.

16. George L. Jackson, *Blood in My Eye* (Baltimore: Black Classic Press, 1990), 182.

17. McKenzie, *Privatopia*, 186.

18. Ibid., 187.

19. The estimate of four million violations of the Fair Housing Act comes from the National Fair Housing Alliance. See "Fair Housing Enforcement at HUD Is Failing," http://www.nationalfairhousing.org?NationalCommission/FutureofFairHousingEnforcementHUD/tabid.3387/Default.Aspx.

20. Angel O. Torres, Robert D. Bullard, and Chad G. Johnson, "Closed Doors: Persistent Barriers to Fair Housing," in Robert D. Bullard, Glenn S. Johnson, and Angel O. Torres, eds., *Sprawl City: Race, Politics, and Planning in Atlanta* (Washington, DC: Island Press, 2000), 89.

21. Ibid., 90–91.

22. Clarence Lo, *Small Property versus Big Government: Social Origins of the Property Tax Revolt* (Berkeley: University of California Press, 1990), 58.

23. Philip J. Ethington, "Segregated Diversity: Race-Ethnicity, Space, and Political Fragmentation in Los Angeles County, 1940–1994" (final report to the John Randolph Haynes Foundation, July 17, 2000), 25, 27, http://www.usc.edu/dept/LAS/history/historylab/Haynes_FRIndex.html.

24. Daniel HoSang, *Racial Propositions: Ballot Initiatives and the Making of Postwar California* (Berkeley: University of California Press, 2010).

25. Freund, *Colored Property*, 337. Richard Dyer, "White," *Screen*, Fall 1998, 44.

26. Dolores Acevedo-Garcia and Theresa L. Osypuk, "Impacts of Housing and Neighborhoods on Health: Pathways, Racial/Ethnic Disparities and Policy Directions," in James H. Carr and Nandinee K. Kutty, *Segregation: The Rising Costs for America* (New York: Routledge, 2008), 197.

27. George Lipsitz, *The Possessive Investment in Whiteness: How White People Profit from Identity Politics* (Philadelphia: Temple University Press, 2006).

28. Douglas S. Massey, *Categorically Unequal: The American Stratification System* (New York: Russell Sage, 2007), 73, 74.

29. Eva Bertram, Morris Blachman, Kenneth Sharpe, and Peter Andreas, *Drug War Politics: The Price of Denial* (Berkeley: University of California Press, 1996), 38–42. Alexander C. Lichtenstein and Michael A. Kroll, "The Fortress Economy: The Economic Role of the U.S. Prison System," in Elihu Rosenblatt, ed., *Criminal Injustice: Confronting the Prison Crisis* (Boston: South End, 1996), 21, 25–26. Michelle Alexander, *The New Jim Crow: Mass Incarceration in the Age of Colorblindness* (New York: New Press, 2010), 7.

30. Scott Burris, Ichiro Kawachi, and Austin Sarat, "Integrating Law and Social Epidemiology," *Journal of Law, Medicine and Ethics* 30 (2002): 515.

31. Toni Morrison, *Playing in the Dark: Whiteness and the Literary Imagination* (New York: Random House, 1992), 38. On fear of the social aggregate as essential to

the modern bourgeois subject, see Nancy Armstrong, *How Novels Think: The Limits of Individualism from 1719–1900* (New York: Columbia University Press (2005), 25.

32. Massey, *Categorically Unequal*, 111.

33. Gregory D. Squires and Charis E. Kubrin, *Privileged Places: Race, Residence, and the Structure of Opportunity* (Boulder, CO: Lynne Rienner, 2006), 6.

34. Craig Haney, *Death by Design: Capital Punishment as a Social and Psychological System* (New York: Oxford University Press, 2005), 193–200.

35. No author, "Study Shows Racial Gaps in School Suspensions," *Louisiana Weekly*, September 20–September 26, 2010, 10.

36. Ibid., 194–200.

37. Naomi Murukawa, "The Origins of the Carceral Crisis: Racial Order as 'Law and Order' in Postwar American Politics," in Joseph Lowndes, Julie Novkov and Dorian Warren, eds., *Race and American Political Development* (New York: Routledge, 2008), 236. Thanks to Nikhil Pal Singh for making me aware of this piece.

38. Alexander, *New Jim Crow*, 97.

39. Ibid.

40. Ibid., 96–98.

41. Bill Quigley, "Examples of Systemic Racism in the U.S. Criminal Justice System," *Louisiana Weekly*, August 2–August 8, 2010, 7.

42. Ibid.

43. Ibid., 121.

44. Marc Mauer, "Two-Tiered Justice: Race, Class, and Crime Policy," in Chester Hartman and Gregory D. Squires, *The Integration Debate: Competing Futures for American Cities* (New York: Routledge, 2010), 170, 177, 179.

45. Massey, *Categorically Unequal*, 102.

46. Alexander, *New Jim Crow*, 92.

47. Mauer, "Two-Tiered Justice," 170, 177, 179.

48. Jackson, *Blood in My Eye*, 183–184.

49. Ruth Wilson Gilmore, *Golden Gulag: Prisons, Surplus, Crisis, and Opposition in Globalizing California* (Berkeley: University of California Press, 2007), 247.

50. Michael Omi and Howard Winant, *Racial Formation in the United States: From the 1960s to the 1990s* (New York: Routledge, 1994).

51. Edmund P. Morgan, "The Labor Problem at Jamestown," *American Historical Review* 76, no. 3 (June 1971): 595–611.

52. Gary Nash, *Red White, and Black: The Peoples of Early North America* (Upper Saddle River, NJ: Prentice Hall, 1999), 110–114.

53. Daria Roithmayr, "Racial Cartels" (University of Southern California Law and Economics Working Papers Series, Working Paper 66, 2007).

54. Herbert Blumer, "Race Prejudice as a Sense of Group Position," *Pacific Sociological Review* 1, no. 1 (Spring 1958): 6.

55. W. E. B. Du Bois, *Black Reconstruction in America, 1860–1880* (New York: Free Press, 1998), 30.

56. Peter Irons, *Jim Crow's Children: The Broken Promise of the Brown Decision* (New York: Penguin Books, 2004), 221.

57. Clayborne Carson, "Two Cheers for *Brown v. Board of Education*," *Journal of American History* 91, no. 1 (June 2004), 27. Ettinger, "The Quest to Desegregate Los Angeles Schools," *Los Angeles Lawyer* (March) 2003, 62.

58. Irons, *Jim Crow's Children*, 242–243.

59. Quoted in Stephen Breyer, "Dissenting, 551 U.S.,"_Supreme Court of the United States, Nos. 05-908 and 05-915, *Parents Involved in Community Schools v. Seattle School District No. 1 et al.* (2007), 48.

60. Irons, *Jim Crow's Children*, 238.

61. John Roberts, "Opinion of Roberts, C.J. 551 U.S.," Supreme Court of the United States, Nos. 05-908 and 05-915, *Parents Involved in Community Schools v. Seattle School District No. 1 et al.* (2007), 37.

62. Nathan Newman and J. J. Gass, "A New Birth of Freedom: The Forgotten History of the 13th, 14th, and 15th Amendments," *Judicial Independence Series*, Brennan Center for Justice at NYU School of Law, 2004, www.brennancenter.org (accessed February 20, 2010).

63. Ibid., 21.

64. Karyn McKinney, *Being White: Stories of Race and Racism* (New York: Routledge, 2004).

65. Martin Luther King, Jr., "The Drum Major Instinct," in James M. Washington, *A Testament of Hope: The Essential Writings and Speeches of Martin Luther King Jr.* (New York: Harper Collins, 1991), 264.

66. Irons, *Jim Crow's Children*, 237.

67. Shanna Smith and Cathy Cloud, "Welcome to the Neighborhood? The Persistence of Discrimination and Segregation," in Hartman and Squires, *Integration Debate*, 11–12.

68. Gabriel N. Mendes, "A Deeper Science: Richard Wright, Dr. Fredric Wertham, and the Fight for Mental Healthcare in Harlem, NY, 1940–1960" (PhD diss., Brown University, 2010), 185–186. Copy in author's possession.

CHAPTER 2

Epigraph: Ruth Wilson Gilmore, "Fatal Couplings of Power and Difference: Notes on Racism and Geography," *The Professional Geographer* 54, no. 1 (February 2002): 16.

1. Marsha Dean Phelts, *An American Beach for African Americans* (Gainesville: University Press of Florida, 1997). Alison Rose Jefferson, "African American Leisure Space in Santa Monica: The Beach Sometimes Known as the 'Inkwell,' 1900–1960," *Southern California Quarterly*, Summer 2009, 155–189.

2. Laurel Fredrickson, "Unintended Relations," *Winthrop University Visual and Performing Arts*, http://www2.wintrop.edu/vpa/Galleries/inint_relat.htm, accessed June 26, 2010.

3. See Stephen Steinberg, *The Ethnic Myth: Race, Ethnicity, and Class in America* (Boston: Beacon, 1982), 5–43. Joane Nagel, *American Indian Ethnic Renewal* (New York: Oxford University Press, 1997), 213–231. Nayan Shah, *Contagious Divides: Epidemics and Race in San Francisco's Chinatown* (Berkeley: University of California Press, 2001), 17–76. Sucheng Chan, *Asian Americans: An Interpretive History* (Boston: Twayne, 1991), 3–24. Mary Pat Brady, *Extinct Lands: Temporal Geographies: Chicana Literature and the Urgency of Space* (Durham, NC: Duke University Press, 2002). Carlos Velez-Ibanez, *Border Visions: Mexican Cultures of the Southwest United States* (Tucson: University of Arizona Press, 1996), 91–136. Rachel Buff, *Immigration and the Political Economy of Home: West Indian Brooklyn and American Indian Minneapo-

lis, 1945–1992 (Berkeley: University of California Press, 2001). Charles McClain, *In Search of Equality: The Chinese Struggle against Discrimination in Nineteenth Century America* (Berkeley: University of California Press, 1994), 223–233. Raymond Lou, "Chinese American Vendors of Los Angeles: A Case of Resistance, Political Organization and Participation," *Integrated Education* 19, no. 3–6 (Summer 1982): 88–91.

4. Robert Farris Thompson, *The Flash of the Spirit: African and Afro-American Art and Philosophy* (New York: Vintage, 1984).

5. Vincent Harding, *There Is a River* (San Diego: Harcourt and Brace, 1981), 40.

6. Deborah Gray White, "Let My People Go, 1804–1860," in Robin D. G. Kelley and Earl Lewis, *To Make Our World Anew A History of African Americans* (New York: Oxford University Press, 2000), 194.

7. George P. Rawick, *From Sundown to Sunup* (Westport, CT: Greenwood, 1972), 110.

8. Ibid., 107.

9. Theophus Smith, *Conjuring Culture: Biblical Formations of Black America* (New York: Oxford, 1994). W. E. B. Du Bois, *Black Reconstruction in America, 1860–1880* (New York: Simon and Schuster, 1995), 124.

10. White, "Let My People Go," 194.

11. On outside entrepreneurs, see Claire Jean Kim, *Bitter Fruit: The Politics of Black-Korean Conflict in New York City* (New Haven, CT: Yale University Press, 2000), 37–41. On the "economic detour" see Melvin L. Oliver and Thomas M. Shapiro, *Black Wealth/White Wealth: A New Perspective on Racial Inequality* (New York: Routledge, 1997), 45–50. See also Robert W. A. Fairlie and Alicia M. Robb, *Race and Entrepreneurial Success: Black-Asian and White-Owned Businesses in the United States* (Cambridge, MA: MIT Press, 2008) and Deirdre A. Royster, *Race and the Invisible Hand: How White Networks Exclude Black Men from Blue-Collar Jobs* (Berkeley: University of California Press, 2003).

12. John R. Logan and Harvey L. Molotch, *The Political Economy of Place* (Berkeley: University of California Press, 1987), 132.

13. Ibid., 138.

14. Dennis R. Judd, "Role of Government Policies in Promoting Residential Segregation in the St. Louis Metropolitan Area," *The Journal of Negro Education* 66, no. 3 (Summer 1997): 221–222.

15. James H. Carr and Nandinee K. Kutty, "The New Imperative for Equality," in James H. Carr and Nandinee K. Kutty, *Segregation: The Rising Costs for America* (New York: Routledge, 2008), 14.

16. Xavier de Sousa Briggs, "More Pluribus, Less Unum? The Changing Geography of Race and Opportunity," in Xavier de Sousa Briggs, *The Geography of Opportunity: Race and Housing Choice in Metropolitan America* (Washington, DC: Brookings Institution Press, 2005), 29.

17. Ibid., 26.

18. Martin Luther King, Jr., "Letter from Birmingham City Jail," in James M. Washington, ed., *A Testament of Hope: The Essential Writings and Speeches of Martin Luther King, Jr.* (New York: Harper Collins, 1991), 290.

19. Barbara Ransby, *Ella Baker and the Black Freedom Movement: A Radical Democratic Vision* (Chapel Hill: University of North Carolina Press, 2003), esp. 224–227.

20. Gregory D. Squires and Charis E. Kubrin, *Privileged Places: Race, Residence, and the Structure of Opportunity* (Boulder, CO: Lynne Rienner, 2006), 9.

21. Chenoa Flippen, "Unequal Returns to Housing Investments: A Study of Real Housing Appreciation among Black, White, and Hispanic Households," *Social Forces* 82, no. 4 (2004), 1523–1555.

22. Camille Zubrinsky Charles, *Won't You Be My Neighbor? Race, Class, and Residence in Los Angeles* (New York: Russell Sage Foundation, 2006), 43–44.

23. Melissa Harris-Lacewell, *Barbershops, Bibles, and BET: Everyday Talk and Black Political Thought* (Princeton, NJ: Princeton University Press, 2004). Vorris Nunley, *Keepin' It Hushed: The Barbershop and the African American Hush Harbor Rhetoric* (Detroit: Wayne State University Press, 2010). Ingrid Banks, *Hair Matters: Beauty, Power, and Black Women's Consciousness* (New York: NYU Press, 2000). Adia Harvey Wingfield, *Doing Business with Beauty: Black Women, Hair Salons, and the Racial Enclave Economy* (Lanham, MD; Rowman and Littlefield, 2009).

24. Clarence Lang, *Grassroots at the Gateway: Class Politics and Black Freedom Struggle in St. Louis, 1936–75* (Ann Arbor: University of Michigan Press, 2009), 72, 162. George Lipsitz, *A Life in the Struggle: Ivory Perry and the Culture of Opposition* (Philadelphia: Temple University Press, 1995), 177.

25. Suzanne Smith, *To Serve The Living: Funeral Directors and the African American Way of Death* (Cambridge: Harvard University Press, 2010), 65, 92, 95.

26. Theda Skocpol, Ariane Liazos, and Marshall Ganz, *What a Mighty Power We Can Be: African American Fraternal Groups and the Struggle for Racial Equality* (Princeton: Princeton University Press, 2006), 13.

27. Skocpol, A Liazos, and Ganz, *What a Mighty Power We Can Be*, 15.

28. Skocpol, Liazos, and Ganz, *What a Mighty Power We Can Be*, 178.

29. Ingrid Monson, *Freedom Sounds: Civil Rights Call Out to Jazz and Africa* (New York: Oxford, 2007), 165.

30. Cecile E. Harrison and Alice K. Laine, "Operation Breadbasket in Houston, 1966–78," in Howard Beeth and Cary Wintz, eds., *Black Dixie: Afro-Texas History and Culture in Houston* (College Station: Texas A&M Press, 1992), 226.

31. Clyde Woods, *Development Arrested: Race, Power, and the Blues in the Mississippi Delta* (New York: Verso, 1998).

32. Thomas Brothers, *Louis Armstrong's New Orleans* (New York: W. W. Norton, 2006), 17.

33. Ibid., 135.

34. Mindy Thompson Fullilove, *Root Shock: How Tearing Up City Neighborhoods Hurts America, and What We Can Do About It* (New York: Ballantine, 2004), 20.

35. Brothers, *Louis Armstrong's New Orleans*, 21.

36. Ibid., 88, 222.

37. Ibid., 20.

38. Herman Gray, *Cultural Moves* (Berkeley: University of California Press, 2005), 49.

39. Robert Farris Thompson, "Bighearted Power: Kongo Presence in the Landscape and Art of Black America," in Grey Gundaker, ed., *Keep Your Head to the Sky: Interpreting African American Home Ground* (Charlottesville: University Press of Virginia, 1998), 43–44.

40. Ibid., 44.

41. Margalit Fox, "Jim Gary, Sculptor Inspired by Junk, Dies at 66," *New York Times*, January 19, 2006, A18.

42. Lionel Hampton, *Hamp: An Autobiography* (New York: Amistad, 1999), 3.

43. Steven L. Isoardi, *The Dark Tree: Jazz and the Community Arts in Los Angeles* (Berkeley: University of California Press, 2006), 16.

44. Suzanne E. Smith, *Dancing in the Street: Motown and the Cultural Politics of Detroit* (Cambridge: MA: Harvard University Press, 1999), 41.

45. Ibid., 41–44.

46. Martin Luther King, Jr., "A Testament of Hope," in Washington, *Testament of Hope*, 325.

47. Robert D. Bullard, Glenn S. Johnson, and Angel O. Torres, *Highway Robbery: Transportation Racism and New Routes to Equity* (Boston: South End Press, 2004). Robert D. Bullard, Glenn S. Johnson, and Angel O. Torres, eds., *Sprawl City: Race, Politics, and Planning in Atlanta* (Washington, DC: Island Press, 2000), 3–4.

48. Bullard, Johnson, and Torres, *Highway Robbery*.

49. Beverly Wright, "New Orleans Neighborhoods under Siege," in Robert D. Bullard and Glenn S. Johnson, eds., *Just Transportation: Dismantling Race and Class Barriers to Mobility* (Gabriola Island, BC: New Society Publishers, 1997), 140.

50. Margery Austin Turner, "Residential Segregation and Employment Inequality," in Carr and Kutty, *Segregation*, 166–167.

51. Briggs, "More Pluribus, Less Unum?" 35.

52. Edward Barnes, "Can't Get There from Here," *Time*, February 19, 1996. http://www.time.com/time/magazine/article/0,9171,984137,00html.

53. "The Color Line and the Bus Line," *Nightline*, ABC News, November 22, 1999.

54. Lang, *Grassroots at the Gateway*, 197.

55. Celeste-Marie Bernier, *African American Visual Arts from Slavery to the Present* (Chapel Hill: University of North Carolina Press, 2008), 198.

56. Ibid., 199.

57. Ibid.

CHAPTER 3

Epigraph: Joe R. Feagin, "The Continuing Significance of Race: Antiblack Discrimination in Public Places," *American Sociological Review* 56, no. 1 (February 1991), 101–116.

1. "St. Louis Public School District Facts, 1999–2000," St. Louis Public Schools, http://dtd1.slps.k12.m0.us/articles/schlfact.htm, 1–2. Peter Downs, "Tax Abatements Don't Work," *St. Louis Journalism Review*, February 1997, 5.

2. Amy Stuart Wells and Robert L. Crain, *Stepping over the Color Line: African American Students in White Suburban Schools* (New Haven, CT: Yale University Press, 1997), 337.

3. John Portz, Lana Stein, and Robin R. Jones, *City Schools and City Politics: Institutions and Leadership in Pittsburgh, Boston, and St. Louis* (Lawrence: University Press of Kansas, 1999), 118.

4. Rick Pierce, "St. Louis Schools Get Year Reprieve While Kansas City Loses Accreditation," *St. Louis Post-Dispatch*, October 22, 1999.

5. D. J. Wilson, "The End of Desegregation as We Know It," *Riverfront Times*, January 6, 1999, 12, 13.

6. Colin Gordon, *Mapping Decline: St. Louis and the Fate of the American City* (Philadelphia: University of Pennsylvania Press, 2008), 11.

7. Ibid., 9.

8. Ibid., 12.

9. Ibid., 92, 96.

10. Dennis R. Judd and Todd Swanstrom, *City Politics: Private Power and Public Policy* (New York: HarperCollins, 2004), 206.

11. Gordon, *Mapping Decline*, 111.

12. Ibid., 41.

13. Jill Quadagno, *The Color of Welfare: How Racism Undermined the War on Poverty* (New York: Oxford, 1996), 109–110.

14. Gordon, *Mapping Decline*, 206.

15. Clarence Lang, *Grassroots at the Gateway: Class Politics and Black Freedom Struggle in St. Louis, 1946–1975* (Ann Arbor: University of Michigan Press, 2009), 139–140.

16. Dennis R. Judd, "The Role of Governmental Policies in Promoting Residential Segregation in the St. Louis Metropolitan Area," *Journal of Negro Education* 66, no. 3 (1997), 216–217.

17. George Lipsitz, *The Possessive Investment in Whiteness: How White People Profit from Identity Politics* (Philadelphia: Temple University Press, 1998).

18. Arthur Denzau and Charles Leven made these estimates in 1985 in a report to the St. Louis Board of Education's community advisory committee.

19. Matthew Ulterino, "The Great American Give-Away: Are Cities Selling Themselves Short for the Sake of Redevelopment?" (Center for Urban Research and Policy, Columbia University School of International and Public Affairs, 1998), http://www.sipa.columbia.edu/CURP/Resources/metro/v01n0401.html.

20. Mike Meyers, "L.A. Rams Finally Win Big but Most of Us Stand to Lose," *Minneapolis Star-Tribune* online, January 20, 1995. Melinda Roth, "At the Trough," *Riverfront Times*, September 17, 1997, 16.

21. Ulterino, "Great American Give-Away," 3.

22. Wells and Crain, *Stepping over the Color Line*, 313.

23. Kern Alexander, "The Impact of Fiscal Inequality on At-Risk Schoolchildren in St. Louis (Testimony of Kern Alexander)," *Journal of Negro Education* 66, no. 3 (1997), 304.

24. Judd, "Role of Governmental Policies," 226.

25. Wells and Crain, *Stepping over the Color Line*, 312.

26. Judd, "Role of Government Policies," 217.

27. Charles C. Euchner, *Playing the Field: Why Sports Teams Move and Cities Fight to Keep Them* (Baltimore: Johns Hopkins University Press, 1993), 67.

28. D. J. Wilson, "The Deal of the Century," *Riverfront Times*, February 23, 2000.

29. "Trans World Dome by the Numbers," www.transworlddome.ord/fact01.html. D. J. Wilson, "Ballpark Frankness," *Riverfront Times*, March 10, 1999.

30. Toby Eckert, *Indianapolis Business Journal* 18, no. 5 (April 21–27, 1997.

31. Reynolds Farley and W. H. Frey, "Changes in Segregation of Whites from Blacks during the 1980s: Small Steps Toward a More Integrated Society," *American Sociological Review* 59 (1994): 23–45.

32. Wells and Crain, *Stepping over the Color Line*, 24.

33. Portz, Stein, and Jones, *City Schools and City Politics*, 119.

34. Anthony J. Scalzo, "What the Companies Knew and When They Knew It," *St. Louis Post-Dispatch*, April 23, 2000. Alliance to End Childhood Lead Poisoning, http://www.aeclp.org/5/companies.html.

35. Robert D. Bullard, "Anatomy of Environmental Racism and the Environmental Justice Movement," in Robert D. Bullard, ed., *Confronting Environmental Racism: Voices from the Grass Roots* (Boston: South End, 1993), 21.

36. Senator Sam Ervin's quote appears in Euchner, *Playing the Field*, 65.

37. Joanna Cagan and Neil de Mause, *Field of Schemes: How the Great Stadium Swindle Turns Public Money into Private Profit* (Monroe, ME: Common Courage, 1998), 63.

38. Gerald W. Scully, *The Market Structure of Sports* (Chicago: University of Chicago Press, 1995), 116.

39. Euchner, *Playing the Field*, 34.

40. Roger G. Noll and Andrew Zimbalist, "Sports, Jobs, Taxes: Are New Stadiums Worth the Cost?" *Brookings Review* 15, no. 3 (Summer 1997), 1, http://www.brook.edu/pub/review/summer/97/noll.html.

41. Ibid., 45.

42. Euchner, *Playing the Field*, 46.

43. Cagan and deMause, *Field of Schemes*, 61.

44. George Cothran, "Hook, Line, and Sinker," *San Francisco Weekly*, May 1, 1996, 11.

45. Ulterino, "Great American Give-Away," 3.

46. Judd, "Role of Governmental Policies," 234.

47. Peter Asselin, "Supporting the Home Team . . . in More Ways Than One: An Analysis of the Public Financing of Philadelphia's New Sports Stadia," *Rutgers Journal of Law and Urban Policy* 3, no. 3 (2006), 411.

48. August A. Busch III, quoted in Peter Hernon and Terry Ganey, *Under the Influence: The Unauthorized Story of the Anheuser-Busch Dynasty* (New York: Simon and Schuster, 1992) 390.

49. Michael N. Danielson, *Home Team: Professional Sports and the American Metropolis* (Princeton, NJ: Princeton University Press, 1997), 256. George Lipsitz, "Sports Stadia and Urban Development: A Tale of Three Cities," *Journal of Sport and Social Issues* 8 (Summer/Fall 1984): 6.

50. Ray Hartmann, "Stadium Sale: The Name of the Game Is Deceit," *St. Louis Riverfront Times*, March 10, 1999, 2.

51. Fred Lindecke, "Here We Go Again: Will Taxpayers Have to Pay for Another New Stadium for Rich Owners?" *St. Louis Journalism Review* 40, no. 317 (January/February 2010), 10.

52. Asselin, "Supporting the Home Team," 389.

53. Ibid., 390.

54. John Logan and Harvey Molotch, *Urban Fortunes* (Berkeley: University of California Press, 1987).

55. John Mollenkopf, *The Contested City* (Princeton, NJ: Princeton University Press, 1993). Kenneth Jackson, *The Crabgrass Frontier: The Suburbanization of the United States* (New York: Oxford University Press, 1985).

56. Logan and Molotch, *Urban Fortunes*, 173. "By 1977, with Carter in the White House, urban aid benefits were now directed toward the suburbs and growing sunbelt cities; Dallas's receipts alone had grown tenfold in four years."

57. Euchner, *Playing the Field*, 64. Logan and Molotch, *Urban Fortunes*, 177.

58. Walden Bello, *Dark Victory: The United States, Structural Adjustment and Global Poverty* (London: Pluto Press, 1994), 91.

59. Sidney Plotkin and William E. Scheurman, *Private Interest, Public Spending: Balanced Budget Conservatism and the Fiscal Crisis* (Boston: South End Press, 1994), 22–24.

60. Ibid., 21.

61. Logan and Molotch, *Urban Fortunes*, 206–207. Euchner, *Playing the Field*, 63.

62. Euchner, *Playing the Field*, 280.

63. Euchner, *Playing the Field*, 83.

64. Cagan and deMause, *Field of Schemes*, 61.

65. Lindecke, "Here We Go Again," 11.

66. Randy Abelda and Chris Tilly, "Unnecessary Evil: Why Inequality Is Bad for Business," *Dollars and Sense*, no. 198 (March-April 1995): 20.

CHAPTER 4

Epigraph: James Baldwin, quoted in Robert Weems, *Desegregating the Dollar: African American Consumerism in the Twentieth Century* (New York: NYU Press, 1998), 67.

1. *The Wire*, Seasons 1–5. Home Box Office DVD 4000016795, 2008.

2. Jimmie Reeves and Rich Campbell, *Cracked Coverage: Television News, the Anti-Cocaine Crusade, and the Reagan Legacy* (Durham, NC: Duke University Press, 1994). Herman Gray, *Watching Race: Television and the Struggle for Blackness* (Minneapolis: University of Minnesota Press, 2004).

3. David Simon, "Season One Overview," in Rafael Alvarez, *The Wire: Truth Be Told* (New York: Grove Press, 2009), 47.

4. Ibid.

5. Jason Bartel, "Rewired for Change: Sonja Sohn's Road to Redemption," *Baltimore*, September 1, 2009, http://www.bthesite.com/archives/2009/09/rewired-for-change-sonja . . . (accessed February 15, 2010).

6. Oliver Burkeman, "When Pretend Is Real," *Guardian*, May 24, 2008, http://www.guardian.co.uk/media/2008/may24the.wire.season.five/ . . . (accessed February 15, 2010).

7. Karen Olson, "Old West Baltimore: Segregation, African American Culture, and the Struggle for Equality," in Elizabeth Fee, Linda Shoppes, Linda Zeidman, ed., *The Baltimore Book: New Views of Local History* (Philadelphia: Temple University Press, 1991), 61.

8. Samuel Kelton Roberts, *Infectious Fear: Politics, Disease, and the Health Effects of Segregation* (Chapel Hill: University of North Carolina Press, 2009, 219, 201–221.

9. Harold McDougall, *Black Baltimore: A New Theory of Community* (Philadelphia: Temple University Press, 1993), 47.

10. Ibid., 211.

11. W. Edward Orser, *Blockbusting in Baltimore; The Edmonson Village Story* (Lexington: University Press of Kentucky, 1994), 63.

12. Ibid., 68.

13. Ibid., ix.

14. Ibid., 91, 110, 111. John Logan and Harvey Molotch, *Urban Fortunes* (Berkeley: University of California Press, 1987).

15. McDougall, *Black Baltimore*, 100, 104.

16. Peter Clandfield, "'We Ain't Got No Yard': Crime, Development, and Urban Environment," in Tiffany Potter and C. W. Marshall, eds., *The Wire: Urban Decay and American Television* (New York: Continuum, 2009), 40–41.

17. Rhonda Y. Williams, *The Politics of Public Housing: Black Women's Struggles against Urban Inequality* (New York: Oxford, 2004), 229–230.

18. Philip Tegeler, "Back to Court: The Federal Role in Metropolitan Housing Segregation," *Shelterforce Online*, Issue 40, March/April 2005, http://www.nhi.org/online/issues/140/court.html (Accessed February 17, 2010). For full details on *Thompson v. HUD* see NAACP Legal Defense and Educational Fund, Inc., Issues: Housing Discrimination, *Thompson v. HUD*, http:www.naacpldf.org/issues.aspx?subcontext+50 (accessed February 17, 2010).

19. Stefanie Deluca and James E. Rosenbaum, "Residential Mobility, Neighborhoods, and Poverty: Results from the Chicago Gatreaux Program and the Moving to Opportunity Experiment," in Chester Hartman and Gregory D. Squires, *The Integration Debate: Competing Futures for American Cities* (New York: Routledge, 2010), 195.

20. Kathleen C. Engel and Patricia A. McCoy, "From Credit Denial to Predatory Lending: The Challenge of Sustaining Minority Homeownership," in James H. Carr and Nandinee K. Kutty, *Segregation: The Rising Costs for America* (New York: Routledge, 2008), 100.

21. *Mayor and City Council of Baltimore v. Wells Fargo Bank, N.A. and Wells Fargo Financial Leasing, Inc.*, L 08CV 062 (in author's possession, http://relmanlaw.com (accessed February 17, 2009).

22. Ben Popken, "Affidavits on How Wells Fargo Gave 'Ghetto Loans' to 'Mud' People,'" http://consumerist.com/2009/06/affidavits-on-how-wells-fargo-gave-ghetto-loans-to-mud-people.html (accessed February 17, 2010). Michael Powell, "Bank Accused of Pushing Mortgage Deals on Blacks," *New York Times*, June 7, 2009. http://www.nytimes.com/2009/06/07us/07baltimore.html?_r=2&part . . . (accessed February 17, 2010).

23. Powell, "Bank Accused."

24. Relman and Dane, "Latest News," http:/www.relmanlaw.com/ (accessed February 18, 2010).

25. Adrian Sainz, "Attorneys: Predatory Lending a Civil Rights Issue," *Louisiana Weekly*, July 26–August 1, 2010, 12.

26. Williams, *Politics of Public Housing*.

27. Ibid.

28. David M. Alff, "Yesterday's Tomorrow Today: Baltimore and the Promise of Reform," in Potter and Marshall, *The Wire*, 30.

29. Ben Bagdikian, *The New Media Monopoly* (Boston: Beacon Press, 2004), 116–117.

30. Mindy Thompson Fullilove, *Root Shock: How Tearing Up City Neighborhoods Hurts America and What We Can Do about It* (New York: Ballantine Books, 2004), 89.

31. David Simon, "Introduction," in Potter and Marshall, *The Wire*, 3.

32. Williams, *Politics of Public Housing*.

33. Ibid., 240.

34. Dennis R. Judd and Todd Swanstrom, *City Politics: Private Power and Public Policy* (New York: HarperCollins, 1994), 174.

35. Gregory D. Squires and Charis E. Kubrin, *Privileged Places: Race, Residence, and the Structure of Opportunity* (Boulder, CO: Lynne Rienner, 2006), 5.

36. Douglas S. Massey, *Categorically Unequal: The American Stratification System* (New York: Russell Sage, 2007), 99.

37. Ibid., 95.

38. Ibid., 100, 101.

39. Williams, *Politics of Public Housing*, 228.

A BRIDGE FOR THIS BOOK

Epigraph: Marshall Berman, "Eternal City," *Village Voice*, Voice Literary Supplement, November 1989, 12.

1. Peter Stallybrass and Allon White, *The Politics and Poetics of Transgression* (Ithaca, NY: Cornell University Press, 1986), 5–6.

2. Cedric Robinson, *Forgeries of Memory and Meaning: Blacks and The Regimes of Race in American Theater and Film before World War II* (Chapel Hill: University of North Carolina Press, 2007), xii.

3. Johnny Otis, *Upside Your Head! Rhythm and Blues on Central Avenue* (Hanover, NH: Wesleyan/University Press of New England, 1993), 151.

4. Nancy Armstrong, *How Novels Think: The Limits of Individualism from 1790–1900* (New York: Columbia University Press, 2005), 25.

5. Ryan Brooks, "The Narrative Production of Real Police," in Tiffany Potter and C. W. Marshall, eds., *The Wire: Urban Decay and American Television* (New York: Continuum, 2009), 76.

6. Rafael Alvarez, *The Wire: Truth Be Told* (New York: Grove Press, 2009), 232.

7. Ibid., 233.

8. Ibid.

9. Laura Lippman, "The Women of *The Wire* (No, Seriously)," in Rafael Alvarez, *The Wire: Truth Be Told* (New York: Grove Press, 2009), 60.

10. Courtney D. Marshall, "Barksdale Women: Crime, Empire, and the Production of Gender," in Potter and Marshall, *The Wire*, 156. Marshall views the Black women of *The Wire* as retaining more agency than I do. I agree with her emphasis on the importance of resisting the demonization and trivialization of Black women's lives, but believe that *The Wire* is more a symptom of this problem than a critique of it.

11. Raymond Williams, *The Politics of Modernism* (London: Verso, 1999), 132–133.

12. Ibid., 100.

13. Ibid., 100.

14. Walter Benjamin, "The Work of Art in the Age of Mechanical Reproduction," in Walter Benjamin, *Illuminations: Essays and Reflections* (New York: Schocken Books, 1968).

15. Benjamin, *Illuminations*, 242.

16. Joe R. Feagin, *The White Racial Frame: Centuries of Racial Framing and Counter-Framing* (New York: Routledge, 2010), 3.

17. Joe R. Feagin, *The White Racial Frame: Centuries of Racial Framing and Counter-Framing* (New York: Routledge, 2010), 2.

18. James Baldwin, *No Name in the Street* (New York: Vintage, 1972), 128–129.

19. Kwame Ture and Charles Hamilton, *Black Power* (New York: Random House, 1992), 34.

20. Ibid., 40–41.

21. Charles Payne, *I've Got the Light of Freedom* (Berkeley: University of California Press. 1995), 303.

CHAPTER 5

Epigraph: Author's notes, lecture presentation by Kamau Daaood and Medusa, University of California, Santa Barbara, February 5, 2008.

1. Steven L. Isoardi, *The Dark Tree: Jazz and the Community Arts in Los Angeles* (Berkeley: University of California Press, 2006), 83. Daniel Widener, *Black Arts West: Culture and Struggle in Postwar Los Angeles* (Durham, NC: Duke University Press, 2010), 113.

2. Horace Tapscott, *Songs of the Unsung* (Durham, NC: Duke University Press, 2001), 1.

3. Clora Bryant, Buddy Collette, William Green, Steve Isoardi, Jack Kelson, Horace Tapscott, Gerald Wilson, and Marl Young, eds., *Central Avenue Sounds: Jazz in Los Angeles* (Berkeley: University of California Press, 1998), 257, 301. Tapscott, *Songs of the Unsung*, 79, 80.

4. Isoardi, *Dark Tree*, 1.

5. Ibid.

6. Tapscott, *Songs of the Unsung*, 80.

7. Ibid., 85, 91, 94, 105, 147.

8. Isoardi, *Dark Tree*, 146, 163, 184–185. Widener, *Black Arts West*, 131.

9. Robin D. G. Kelley, *Freedom Dreams: The Black Radical Imagination* (Boston: Beacon, 2002), 13–35. Sterling Stuckey, *Going through the Storm: The Influence of African American Art in History* (New York: Oxford, 1994), 83–102. Nikhil Pal Singh, *Black Is a Country: Race and the Unfinished Struggle for Democracy* (Cambridge, MA: Harvard University Press, 2004), 101–133.

10. Vincent Harding, *There Is a River* (San Diego: Harcourt and Brace, 1981), 164, drawing on information in the slave narratives collected by the WPA and published by George Rawick as part of *The American Slave* (Westport, CT: Greenwood, 1972, especially vol. 1, no. 13, p. 6 and vol. 4, no. 2, p. 191.

11. Johnny Otis, *Upside Your Head! Rhythm and Blues on Central Avenue* (Hanover, NH: Wesleyan/University Press of New England, 1993). Tapscott, *Songs of the Unsung*, 138.

12. John Szwed, *Space Is the Place: The Life and Times of Sun Ra* (New York: Da Capo Press, 1997), 93–96, 111–128, 151–181.

13. Tapscott, *Songs of the Unsung*, 83.

14. Dowling Street served as the inspiration for Houston blues musician Conrad Johnson's 1947 recording "Howling on Dowling" (Gold Star 622).

15. Tapscott, *Songs of the Unsung*, 13.

16. Ibid., 18.

17. Bryant et al., *Central Avenue Sounds*, 132, 176.

18. Widener, *Black Arts West*, 123.

19. Raymond A. Mohl, "Shifting Patterns of American Urban Policy since 1900," in Arnold R. Hirsch and Raymond A. Mohl, eds., *Urban Policy in Twentieth Century America* (New Brunswick, NJ: Rutgers University Press, 1993), 1–45; Arnold R. Hirsch, "With or without Jim Crow: Black Residential Segregation in the United States," in Hirsch and Mohl., *Urban Policy*, 65–99.

20. Raphael J. Sonnenshein, *Politics in Black and White: Race and Power in Los Angeles* (Princeton, NJ: Princeton University Press), 1993. Becky M. Nicolaides, *My Blue Heaven: Life and Politics in the Working-Class Suburbs of Los Angeles, 1920–1965* (Chicago: University of Chicago Press), 2002. Greg Hise, *Magnetic Los Angeles: Planning in the Twentieth Century Metropolis* (Baltimore: Johns Hopkins University Press), 1997. Catherine Jurca, *White Diaspora: The Suburb and the Twentieth-Century American Novel* (Princeton. NJ: Princeton University Press), 2001.

21. Tapscott, *Songs of the Unsung*, 109. For more on the LAPD see Edward J. Escobar, *Race, Police, and the Making of a Political Identity: Mexican Americans and the Los Angeles Police Department, 1900–1945* (Berkeley: University of California Press), 1999. Charles Ogletree, Jr., Mary Prosser, Abbe Smith, and William Talley, Jr., *Beyond the Rodney King Story: An Investigation of Police Conduct in Minority Communities* (Boston: Northeastern University Press, 1995), 44–45, 46, 56–57, 61, 64–65.

22. Earl Lewis, *In Their Own Interests: Race, Class and Power in Twentieth Century Norfolk, Virginia* (Berkeley: University of California Press, 1991), 90–91.

23. See also Otis, *Upside Your Head!*, 7–35.

24. Tapscott, *Songs of the Unsung*, 44, 179.

25. Ibid., 27.

26. Ibid., 29.

27. Ibid., 91–94.

28. Red Callender and Elaine Cohen, *Unfinished Dream: The Musical World of Red Callender* (London: Quarter Books, 1985), 141.Tapscott, *Songs of the Unsung*, 121, 141, 163.

29. Tapscott, *Songs of the Unsung*, 119.

30. Ibid., 95–96.

31. Isoardi, *Dark Tree*, xvii.

32. Ibid., 268.

33. Tapscott, *Songs of the Unsung*, 89.

34. James Baldwin explains that isolation of artists from audiences can make the work of white artists irrelevant, but that it is even more damaging to cultural creators who are Black. Baldwin explains that as Black Americans, Black artists already experience isolation from the majority of the population of the country in which they live. Their continued growth depends upon the support, guidance, and correction of the Black community. The pressures of American life and the mechanisms of artistic recognition and reward, however, "conspire" to remove the Black artist from that very community. See James Baldwin, "Sweet Lorraine," introduction to Lorraine Hansberry, *To*

Be Young, Gifted, and Black: Lorraine Hansberry in Her Own Words, adapted by Robert Nemiroff (New York: Vintage, 1995), xviii–xix.

35. Isoardi, *Dark Tree*, 136.

36. See George Lipsitz, "Not Just Another Social Movement: Poster Art and the Movimiento Chicano," in Chon A. Noriega, ed., *Just Another Poster? Chicano Graphic Arts in California* (Santa Barbara: University of California Art Museum, 2001), 71–89.

37. George Lewis, *A Power Stronger than Itself: The AACM and American Experimental Music* (Chicago: University of Chicago Press, 2008), 85–86.

38. Tapscott, *Songs of the Unsung*, 201, 97, 104, 200.

39. Ibid., 88.

40. Author's notes, lecture performance by Kamau Daaood and Medusa, University of California, Santa Barbara, February 5, 2008.

41. Tapscott, *Songs of the Unsung*, 107.

42. Ibid., 87.

43. Ibid., 88.

44. Ibid., 89.

45. Ibid., 95.

46. Ibid., 99.

47. Ibid., 109.

48. Widener, *Black Arts West*, 137.

49. Tapscott, *Songs of the Unsung*, 89, 143, 148, 175.

50. Callender and Cohen, *Unfinished Dream*, 109.

51. Szwed, *Space Is the Place*, 285. Tapscott, *Songs of the Unsung*, 145.

52. Isoardi, *Dark Tree*, 146.

53. Tapscott, *Songs of the Unsung*, 109.

54. Ibid., 108.

55. Isoardi, *Dark Tree*, 96.

56. Ibid., 62.

57. See Angela Davis, *Angela Davis: An Autobiography* (New York: Random House), 1974. Scot Brown, *Fighting for US: Maulana Karenga, the US Organization, and Cultural Nationalism* (New York: NYU Press), 2003. Ward Churchill and Jim Vander Wall, *Agents of Repression: The FBI's Secret Wars against the Black Panther Party and the American Indian Movement* (Boston: South End, 1988), 79, 85, 87–88, 409. M. Wesley Swearingen, *FBI Secrets: An Agent's Expose* (Boston: South End, 1995), 84–86. Tapscott, *Songs of the Unsung*, 122–123.

58. Isoardi, *Dark Tree*, 97.

59. Tapscott, *Songs of the Unsung*, 108, 112, 123.

60. Sondra Kathryn Wilson, ed., *The Selected Writings of James Weldon Johnson*, Vol. 1 (New York: Oxford, 1995), xv. Tapscott, *Songs of the Unsung*, 114.

61. Tapscott, *Songs of the Unsung*, 137.

62. Widener, *Black Arts West*, 150.

63. Daniel Widener, "Something Else: Creative Community and Black Liberation in Postwar Los Angeles," PhD dissertation, New York University, 2003, 83. Tapscott, *Songs of the Unsung*, 118.

64. Isoardi, *Dark Tree*, 157–158.

65. Tapscott, *Songs of the Unsung*, 139.

66. Ibid., 90.

67. Carlos Moore, *Fela: This Bitch of a Life* (London: Allison and Busby, 1982), 83, 85, 91, 92, 95. Tom Cheney, "Sorrow, Tears, and Blood: Q&A with Fela Anikulapo Kuti," *Los Angeles Reader* 8, no. 41 (August 1, 1986), 1.

68. Tapscott, *Songs of the Unsung*, 90.

69. David Luis Brown, *Waves of Decolonization* (Durham, NC: Duke University Press, 2008), 71.

70. Gerald Horne, *The Fire This Time: The Watts Uprising and the 1960s* (New York: Da Capo, 1997), 128.

71. Ibid., 38.

72. Ibid., 67.

73. Richard Dedeaux, "I Remember Watts," on Watts Prophets, *When the 90s Came*, Payday/FFRR 422 828, 880–882.

74. Samella Lewis, *African American Art and Artists* (Berkeley: University of California Press, 2003), 198.

75. Richard Candida Smith, "Reverencing the Mortal: Assemblage Art as Prophetic Protest in Post–World War II California," in University of Michigan Museum of Art, *Betye Saar: Extending the Frozen Moment* (Ann Arbor and Berkeley: University of Michigan Museum of Art and University of California Press, 2005), 44.

76. Celeste-Marie Bernier, *African American Visual Arts from Slavery to the Present* (Chapel Hill: University of North Carolina Press, 2008), 200–201.

77. Sarah Schrank, *Art and the City; Civic Imagination and Cultural Authority in Los Angeles* (Philadelphia: University of Pennsylvania Press, 2009), 51.

78. Ibid., 62.

79. Ibid.

80. Jacques Ranciere, *The Politics of Aesthetics: The Distribution of the Sensible* (New York: Continuum Books, 2005), 9, 13.

81. Gerald Horne, *The Fire This Time: The Watts Uprising and the1960s*, (New York: Da Capo, 1997), 355.

82. Isoardi, *Dark Tree*, 227.

83. Tapscott, *Songs of the Unsung*, 174–175. Isoardi, *Dark Tree*, 227–228.

84. Tapscott, *Songs of the Unsung*. Isoardi, *Dark Tree*. Widener, *Black Arts West*. Joao Costa Vargas, *Catching Hell in the City of Angels* (Minneapolis: University of Minnesota Press, 2006).

CHAPTER 6

Epigraph: George P. Rawick, *From Sundown to Sunup: The Making of the Black Community* (Westport, CT: Greenwood, 1972), 96.

1. Thomas Wright, "Who 'Fingered' Carl Hampton," *Sepia Magazine*, November 1979, 12, www.itsabouttimebpp.com/chapter.../murder_of_Carl_Hampton.pdf (accessed February 7, 2010).

2. Ibid., 10.

3. Gloria Rubac, "Activists Honor Panther Leader Carl Hampton," *Workers World*, July 26, 2008, www.workers.org/2008/UShampton_08071 (accessed February 7, 2010).

4. Roger Wood, *Down in Houston: Bayou City Blues* (Austin: University of Texas Press, 2003), 73.

5. Robert D. Bullard, "Dumping on Houston's Black Neighborhoods," in Martin V. Melosi and Joseph A. Pratt, *Energy Metropolis: An Environmental History of Houston and the Gulf Coast* (Pittsburgh: University of Pittsburgh Press, 2007), 207.

6. Wood, *Down in Houston*, 72.

7. Barbara Strauch, "Time Is Running Out: History-Rich Fourth Ward Threatened by Urban Growth, *Houston Chronicle*, February 13, 1983, section 2, p. 13.

8. Rives Taylor, "Fourth Ward and the Siege of Allen Parkway Village," *Cite*, Spring 1991, 21.

9. Jan Lin, "Ethnic Places, Postmodernism, and Urban Change in Houston," *Sociological Quarterly* 36, no. 4 (1995), 634.

10. Bullard, "Dumping on Houston's," 207.

11. Richard F. Babcock, "Houston: Unzoned, Unfettered, and Mostly Unrepentant," *Planning* 48, no. 3 (March 1982), 23.

12. Wood, *Down in Houston*, 73.

13. Ibid., 75.

14. Ibid., 85.

15. Robert Farris Thompson, "John Biggers's Shotguns of 1987: An American Classic," in Alvia Wardlaw, ed., *The Art of John Biggers: View from the Upper Room* (New York: Harry N. Abrams: 1995), 108.

16. Alan Govenar, *Texas Blues: The Rise of a Contemporary Sound* (College Station: Texas A&M University, 2008), 245.

17. Horace Tapscott, *Songs of the Unsung* (Durham: Duke University Press, 2001), 1–4.

18. Ibid., 4.

19. Robert Farris Thompson, "Bighearted Power: Kongo Presence in the Landscape and Art of Black America," in Grey Gundaker, ed., *Keep Your Head to the Sky: Interpreting African American Home Ground* (Charlottesville: University Press of Virginia, 1998), 45.

20. Thompson, "John Biggers's Shotguns," 111.

21. Alvia Wardlaw, "Metamorphosis: The Life and Art of John Biggers," in Wardlaw, *Art of John Biggers*, 22.

22. Ibid., 39.

23. Ibid., 39, 40, 43.

24. Thomas R. Cole, *No Color Is My Kind: The Life of Eldrewey Stearns and the Integration of Houston* (Austin: University of Texas Press, 1997), 60–80. Yolanda Braxton, "Bricks without Straw: The Almost Forgotten 40 Year History of the Tigerwalk," *The Herald*, August 31, 2007, www.tsuherald.com/home/index.cfm?event+displayArticlePrint (accessed February 8, 2010).

25. Bullard, "Dumping on Houston's," 218–219.

26. "Texas: Hate in Houston," *Time*, May 26, 1967, http://www.time.com/time/magazine/article/0,9171,843792,00.html (accessed February 8, 2010).

27. Olivia Flores Alvarez, "Houston 101: An Earlier Time When Shots Rang Out at TSU," *Houston Press News Blog*, July 29, 2009, http://blogs.houstonpress.com/hairballs/2009/07/houston_101_tsu-sh . . . (accessed February 8, 2010).

28. Wardlaw, "Metamorphosis," 53. Alvarez, "Houston 101." Braxton, "Bricks without Straw."

29. Wardlaw, "Metamorphosis," 58.

30. Thompson, "John Biggers's Shotguns," 110.

31. Sheryl G. Tucker, "Reinnovating the African-American Shotgun House," *Places* 10, no. 1 (1995), 64.

32. Wardlaw, "Metamorphosis," 63. Thompson, "John Biggers's Shotguns," 110.

33. Edmund Barry Gaither, "John Biggers: A Perspective," in Wardlaw, *Art of John Biggers*, 91.

34. Thompson, "John Biggers's Shotguns," 108.

35. Rick Lowe, "Project Row Houses," Salzburg Global Seminar, Session 446, October 2007, http://www.salzbergglobal.org?2009/includes/FacultyPopup.cfm?I . . . (accessed February 8, 2010).

36. Houston Arts Hound, "El Dorado Ballroom," www.artshound.com/venue/detail/58 (accessed February 9, 2010).

37. Babcock, "Houston," 21.

38. James Peters, "Houston Gets Religion," *Planning* 51, no. 8 (August 1985), 4.

39. *Third Ward TX*, Welcome Home Productions, directed by Andrew Garrison, New Day Films, 2007.

40. Bullard, "Dumping on Houston's," 211–212.

41. Shanna Smith and Cathy Cloud, "Welcome to the Neighborhood? The Persistence of Discrimination and Segregation," in Chester Hartman and Geoffrey Squires, eds., *The Integration Debate: Competing Futures for American Cities* (New York: Routledge, 2010), 16.

42. *Third Ward TX*.

43. Ibid.

44. Ibid.

45. Michael Kimmelman, "In Houston: Art Is Where the Home Is," *New York Times*, December 17, 2006, http://www.nytimes.com/200612/17/arts/design/17kimm.html?_r=1 . . . (accessed February 10, 2010).

46. Ibid.

47. *Third Ward TX*.

48. Thompson, "John Biggers's Shotguns," 110.

49. Sophie Sartain, "Why, Shoot, Who Doesn't Have a Favorite among Houston's . . . Big, Ugly, Lovable Signs?" *Houston Post*, December 28, 1989, D1.

50. Wood, *Down in Houston*, 87, 95.

51. Rubac, "Activists Honor Hampton."

52. Ernesto Aguilar, "Remember Carl Hampton Sunday," http:///ernestoaguilar.org/carl-hampton/ (accessed February 10, 2010).

53. Project Row Houses "Black Panther Exhibition and Auction," http://projectrowhouses.org/2010/07/events-by-the-carl-hampton-commemoration-committee (accessed October 18, 2010). Workers World Party, Facebook, "Houston: Carl Hampton 40th anniversary commemoration of slain Panther leader," http://www.facebook.com/topic.php?uid=20419221992%topic=1627 (accessed October 18, 2010).

CHAPTER 7

Epigraph: Arthur Brittan and Mary Maynard, *Sexism, Racism, and Oppression* (Oxford, UK: Basil Blackwell, 1984), 7.

1. Horace Tapscott, *Songs of the Unsung: The Musical and Social Journey of Horace Tapscott* (Durham, NC: Duke University Press, 2001), 3, 5, 13, 15.

2. Steve L. Isoardi, *The Dark Tree: Jazz and the Community Arts in Los Angeles* (Berkeley: University of California Press, 2006), 145.

3. Tapscott, *Songs of the Unsung*, 15.

4. Isoardi, *Dark Tree*, 52.

5. Ibid., 57.

6. Ibid., 58.

7. The phrase "something left to love" comes from Lorraine Hansberry's *A Raisin in the Sun*, discussed in Chapter 8. I thank Tricia Rose for calling the importance of this concept to the world's attention in her splendid book *Longing to Tell: Black Women Talk about Sexuality* (New York: Picador, 2003), 259–261.

8. Daniel Widener, *Black Arts West: Culture and Struggle in Postwar Los Angeles* (Durham, NC: Duke University Press, 2010), 175.

9. Theophus Smith, *Conjuring Culture: Biblical Formations of Black America* (New York: Oxford University Press, 1994), 31.

10. I am grateful to Paula Ioanide for educating me about the importance of ethical witnessing.

11. Laura Mulvey, "Changes: Thoughts on Myth, Narrative, and Historical Experience," *History Workshop* no. 23 (Spring 1987), 11.

12. Celeste-Marie Bernier, *African American Visual Arts: From Slavery to the Present* (Chapel Hill: University of North Carolina Press, 2008), 186.

13. Quoted in Bernier, *African American Visual Arts*, 188.

14. James Christen Steward, "'Lest We Forget': The Liberating Art of Betye Saar," in University of Michigan Museum of Art, *Betye Saar: Extending the Frozen Moment* (Ann Arbor and Berkeley: University of Michigan Museum of Art and University of California Press, 2005), 16.

15. Bernier, *African American Visual Arts*, 184.

16. University of Michigan Museum of Art, *Betye Saar*, 160.

17. Conversation with Betye Saar, April 23, 2010. Los Angeles, California.

18. Kellie Jones, "To/From Los Angeles with Betye Saar," in University of Michigan Museum of Art, *Betye Saar*, 31–32.

19. Noah Purifoy interview, African American Artists of Los Angeles. UCLA Oral History Program, 100.

20. Steward, "'Lest We Forget,'" 10.

21. Bernier, *African American Visual Arts*, 186.

22. George P. Rawick, *From Sundown to Sunup: The Making of the Black Community* (Westport, CT: Greenwood Press, 1972), 95–96.

23. Betye Saar interview, African American Artists of Los Angeles, UCLA Oral History Program, 112.

24. Richard Candida Smith, "Reverencing the Mortal: Assemblage Art as Prophetic Protest in Post–World War II California," in University of Michigan Museum of Art, *Betye Saar*, 46.

25. Heather Hathaway, *Caribbean Waves: Relocating Claude McKay and Paule Marshall* (Bloomington: Indiana University Press, 1999), 106.

26. Ibid.

27. James C. Hall, *Mercy, Mercy, Me: African American Culture and the American Sixties* (New York: Oxford, 2001), 86.

28. Paule Marshall, *Reena and Other Stories* (New York: Feminist Press at the City University of New York, 1983), 4.

29. Ibid., 7.

30. Ula Taylor, *The Veiled Garvey: The Life and Times of Amy Jacques Garvey* (Chapel Hill: University of North Carolina Press), 2002. Marshall, *Reena*, 5.

31. Stelamaris Coser, *Bridging the Americas: The Literature of Toni Morrison, Paule Marshal, and Gayl Jones* (Philadelphia: Temple University Press, 1994), 60.

32. Hathaway, *Caribbean Waves*, 86.

33. Quoted in Hall, *Mercy, Mercy Me*, 85.

34. Ibid., 94.

35. Paule Marshall, *Brown Girl, Brownstones* (New York: Feminist Press at the City University of New York, 1981), 4.

36. Ibid., 213, 13, 27, 56.

37. Ibid., 13.

38. Ibid., 3. Hathaway, *Caribbean Waves*, 90. Hathaway notes that Barbara Christian first noted that the houses in the novel have the qualities of characters.

39. Marshall, *Brown Girl, Brownstones*, 4.

40. Paule Marshall, "Shaping the World of My Art," *New Letters* 40 (Autumn 1973), 108.

41. Marshall, *Brown Girl, Brownstones*, 134.

42. Coser, *Bridging the Americas*, 60.

43. Barbara Christian, *Black Women Novelists: The Development of a Tradition, 1892–1976* (Westport, CT: Greenwood Press, 1980), 82.

44. I take the phrase "twice Black" from M. Jacqui Alexander's excellent work on the Abner Louima police brutality case and Haitian immigrants.

45. Marshall, *Brown Girl, Brownstones*, 39.

46. Ibid., 17.

47. Marshall, *Reena*, 90.

48. Marshall, *Brown Girl, Brownstones*, 4.

49. The sore that compels Miss Thompson to limp leaves her with the gait of nineteenth-century abolitionist Henry Highland Garnet, well known for his claim that Black people in the United States faced worse obstacles than the Hebrew people in the book of Exodus, because for U.S. Blacks the armies of Pharaoh were "on both sides of the blood red waters."

50. There are other significant differences between Silla and Deighton Boyce: his aimless joy versus her determined joylessness, his sensuality versus her asceticism, and his attachments to nature versus her attachment to possessions. These are significant in the novel, but only accents to the oppositions central to my analysis of it here.

51. Marshall, *Brown Girl, Brownstones*, 46.

52. One reason for the hedonism of Suggie, a boarder in the brownstone, is that she derives no pleasure from her weeklong labor as a live-in maid. Marshall advances this same theme in the story "Reena." See Marshall, *Reena*, 77. This theme also appears in Ann Petry, *The Street* (New York: Houghton Mifflin, 1946).

53. Marshall, *Brown Girl, Brownstones*, 5.

54. Ibid., 211.

55. Ibid., 215, 142–143. Part of Silla's frustration with Deighton's inheritance comes from his irresponsibility, from his frivolous approach to work and money that forces her to work harder. But from her working-class perspective, inheritance is an injustice in itself. On p. 29, "What is it . . . ," she asks, "that does give what little luck there is to fools . . . ? Not a soul ever give me nothing a-tall, a-tall. I always had to make my own luck. And look at he! Somebody dead so and he got ground so. Got land now!"

56. Ibid., 216.

57. Ibid., 222.

58. Hathaway, *Caribbean Waves*, 86, 88.

59. See Kevin Gaines, *Uplifting the Race: Black Leadership, Politics, and Culture* (Chapel Hill: University of North Carolina Press, 1996). Clyde Woods, *Development Arrested: The Blues and Plantation Power in Mississippi* (New York: Verso, 2000).

60. Marshall, *Brown Girl, Brownstones*, 214.

61. Ibid., 70.

62. Ibid., 292.

63. Ibid., 292–293.

64. Ibid., 225.

65. Ibid., 308.

66. Federally assisted urban renewal projects during the 1950s and 1960s eliminated 20 percent of the central-city housing units occupied by Blacks. Nearly two-thirds of those displaced by urban renewal during those years were African Americans or Latinos. John R. Logan and Harvey Molotch, *Urban Fortunes: The Political Economy of Place* (Berkeley: University of California Press, 1987), 114. Arlene Zarembka, *The Urban Housing Crisis: Social, Economic, and Legal Issues and Proposals* (Westport, CT: Greenwood, 1990), 104. For the effects of this dislocation see Mindy Thompson Fullilove, *Root Shock: How Tearing Up City Neighborhoods Hurts America and What We Can Do About It* (New York: Ballantine, 2004).

67. Marshall, *Brown Girl, Brownstones*, 220.

68. Ibid., 310.

69. Ibid., 310.

70. Marshall, *Reena*, 72.

71. Marshall, *Brown Girl, Brownstones*, 308.

CHAPTER 8

Epigraph: Kristin Ross, *The Emergence of Social Space* (Minneapolis: University of Minnesota Press, 1989), 8.

1. Reebee Garofalo, *Rockin' Out: Popular Music in the USA* (Boston: Allyn and Bacon, 1997), 158–160. George Lipsitz, *Rainbow at Midnight: Labor and Culture in the 1940s* (Urbana: University of Illinois Press, 1994), 303–333.

2. Carmen Teresa Whalen, *From Puerto Rico to Philadelphia: Puerto Rican Workers and Postwar Economies* (Philadelphia: Temple University Press, 2001).

3. Garofalo, *Rockin' Out*, 159.

4. Charles de Ledesma and Simon Broughton, "Out of the Orchid House: Calypso and Soca from Trinidad and Beyond," in Simon Broughton, Mark Ellingham, David Muddyman, and Richard Trillo, *World Music: The Rough Guide* (London: Rough Guides, 1994), 507–508. Garofalo, *Rockin' Out*, 158.

5. Joel Whitburn, *Top Pop Singles, 1955–1986* (Menomonee Falls, WI: Record Research, 1987), 42, 324. A cover version of this "cover" came from pop singer Eddie Fisher, making the charts the same week.

6. Burt D'Lugoff later co-owned the Village Gate nightclub in Greenwich Village with his brother Art, a former public relations staffer and organizer for the United Electrical Workers union. See Ingrid Monson, *Freedom Sounds: Civil Rights Call Out to Jazz and Africa* (New York: Oxford, 2007), 165.

7. Dave Samuelson, "The Tarriers," Folk Era Records, 2001, www.folkera.com, 2.

8. Whitburn, *Top Pop Singles*, 497. Samuelson, "Tarriers," 2, 3. The Tarriers had initially been introduced to Philip Rose by Burt D'Lugoff's brother Art, and their manager, Pete Kameron, had managed the Weavers.

9. Lorraine Hansberry, *To Be Young Gifted and Black* (adapted by Robert Nemiroff) (New York: Vintage, 1995), 77.

10. Ben Keppel, *The Work of Democracy: Ralph Bunche, Kenneth B. Clark, Lorraine Hansberry and the Cultural Politics of Race* (Cambridge, MA: Harvard University Press, 1995), 24.

11. Ibid., 23, 24.

12. George Lewis, *A Power Stronger Than Itself: The AACM and American Experimental Music* (Chicago: University of Chicago Press, 2008), 51.

13. Thomas J. Sugrue, *The Origins of the Urban Crisis: Race and Inequality in Postwar Detroit* (Princeton, NJ: Princeton University Press, 1996). Arnold Hirsch, *Making the Second Ghetto: Race and Housing in Chicago* (Cambridge, MA: Cambridge University Press, 1983), 53.

14. Lewis, *A Power Stronger Than Itself*, 51. For a fictionalized account of one of these riots see Frank London Brown, *Trumbull Park* (Boston: Northeastern University Press), 2005.

15. Mary Helen Washington, foreword to Brown, *Trumbull Park*, ix.

16. Arnold Hirsch, "Massive Resistance in the Urban North: Trumbull Park, Chicago, 1953–1966," *Journal of American History* 82, no. 2 (September 1995): 538.

17. Washington, foreword to Brown, *Trumbull Park*, ix. Hirsch, "Massive Resistance," 533.

18. Washington, foreword to Brown, *Trumbull Park*, xvii.

19. Lewis, *A Power Stronger Than Itself*, 5.

20. James Baldwin, "Sweet Lorraine," introduction to Hansberry, *To Be Young*, xviii.

21. Amiri Baraka, "A Critical Reevaluation: *A Raisin in the Sun*'s Enduring Passion," in Lorraine Hansberry, *A Raisin in the Sun and the Sign in Sidney Brustein's Window* (New York: Vintage, 1995), 9.

22. Ibid., 10.

23. See Thomas Shapiro, *The Hidden Cost of Being African American: How Wealth Perpetuates Inequality* (New York: Oxford), 2004.

24. Robert Nemiroff, introduction to Lorraine Hansberry, *A Raisin in the Sun* (New York: Vintage, 1994), 8.

25. See George Lipsitz, *A Life in the Struggle: Ivory Perry and the Culture of Opposition* (Philadelphia: Temple University Press, 1995), 81–82. *New York Times*, April 17, 1964, 1; April 22, 1964, 1, 5.

26. Hansberry, *To Be Young*, 20, 21.

27. Ibid., 17.

28. Ibid., 35.

29. Ibid., 25.

30. Lorraine Hansberry, *A Raisin in the Sun* (New York: Vintage, 988), 106.

31. Keppel, *The Work of Democracy*, 25.

32. Ibid., 209.

33. Baraka. "A Critical Reevaluation," 15.

34. Baldwin, "Sweet Lorraine," xx.

35. Loraine Hansberry, "Quo Vadis?" *Mademoiselle*, January 17, 1960, 34. Quoted in Keppel, *The Work of Democracy*, 203.

36. Nemiroff, introduction to Hansberry, *A Raisin in the Sun*, 7.

37. Hansberry, *A Raisin in the Sun*, 100. Keppel, *The Work of Democracy*, 211.

38. Keppel, *The Work of Democracy*, 201.

39. Robert Nemiroff, "The 101 'Final' Performances of Sidney Brustein," in Hansberry, *A Raisin in the Sun*, 181.

40. Alan B. Anderson and George Pickering, *Confronting the Color Line: The Broken Promise of the Civil Rights Movement in Chicago* (Athens: University of Georgia Press, 1986), 218.

41. Ibid., 220–221.

42. Ibid., 223–224.

43. Ibid., 224.

44. Beryl Satter, *Family Properties: Race, Real Estate, and the Exploitation of Black Urban America* (New York: Metropolitan Books, 2009), 199.

45. Anderson and Pickering, *Confronting the Color Line*, 228.

46. Ibid., 232.

47. Satter, *Family Properties*, 202–203.

48. Linda Bryant-Hall in the film *Eyes on the Prize II: America at the Racial Crossroads—1965 to 1985, Two Societies* (1965–1968).

49. Nancy Jefferson in the film *Eyes on the Prize II*.

50. Satter, *Family Properties*, 210.

CHAPTER 9

Epigraph: Caroline Senter quoting Kalamu ya Salaam, *Hofi Ni Kwenu: My Fear Is for You*, in Caroline Senter, "Beware of Premature Autopsies" (MA thesis, Department of Literature, University of California, San Diego, 1991), 37.

1. Lori Rodriguez and Zeke Minaya, "New Orleans' Racial Makeup in the Air," *Houston Chronicle*, September 29, 2005, 1. George Lipsitz, *The Possessive Investment in Whiteness* (Philadelphia: Temple University Press, 2006), 237–248.

2. Sunni Patterson, "We Know This Place," *American Quarterly* 61, no. 3 (September 2009): 719–721.

3. John Blassingame, *Black New Orleans, 1880–1860* (Chicago: University of Chicago Press, 1976), 5. Benjamin Latrobe, *Impressions Respecting New Orleans: Diary and Sketches, 1818–1820* (New York: Columbia University Press), 1951. Willie Lee Rose, *A Documentary History of Slavery in North America* (Athens: University of Georgia Press, 1999), 514.

4. Dena Epstein, *Sinful Tunes and Spirituals: Black Folk Music to the Civil War* (Urbana: University of Illinois Press, 2003), 85.

5. Sidney Bechet, *Treat It Gentle: An Autobiography* (New York: Da Capo Press, 2002), 7.

6. Alan Lomax, "Jazz Parades: Feet Don't Fail Me Now," *American Patchwork* series, Public Broadcasting System, episode 2.

7. Gwendolyn Midlo Hall, "The Formation of Afro-Creole Culture," in Arnold R. Hirsch and Joseph Logsdon, eds., *Creole New Orleans: Race and Americanization* (Baton Rouge: Louisiana State University Press, 1992), 59.

8. Marina Estrella Espina, "Filipinos in New Orleans," *Proceedings of Louisiana Academy of Sciences*, no. 37 (1974), 117–121. Marina Estrella Espina, *Filipinos in Louisiana* (New Orleans: A. F. Laborde), 1988.

9. Rachel Buff, *Immigration and the Political Economy of Home: West Indian Brooklyn and American Indian Minneapolis, 1945–1992* (Minneapolis: University of Minnesota Press, 2001), 31.

10. Robert Farris Thompson, *The Flash of the Spirit: African and Afro-American Art and Philosophy* (New York: Random House, 1984). Theophus Smith, *Conjuring Culture: Biblical Formations of Black America* (New York: Oxford, 1995).

11. Charles Joyner, *Down by the Riverside: A South Carolina Slave Community* (Urbana: University of Illinois Press, 1986), xxi.

12. Barbara Eckstein, *Sustaining New Orleans: Literature, Local Memory, and the Fate of a City* (New York: Routledge, 2006), 48–49, 100.

13. Clyde Woods, *Development Arrested: The Blues and Plantation Power in the Mississippi Delta* (New York: Verso), 1998.

14. David C. Estes, "The Neo-African Vatican: Zora Neale Hurston's New Orleans," in Richard S. Kennedy, ed., *Literary New Orleans in the Modern World* (Baton Rouge: Louisiana State University Press, 1998), 75.

15. Jane Rhodes, *Mary Ann Shadd Cary: The Black Press and Protest in the Nineteenth Century* (Bloomington: Indiana University Press, 1999), 100–134.

16. William McFeely, *Frederick Douglass* (New York: Touchstone Books, 1992), 124–125, 136.

17. Quintard Taylor, *In Search of the Racial Frontier: African Americans in the American West, 1528–1990* (New York: Touchstone Books, 1998), 46, 49, 60.

18. Anna Julia Cooper, *A Voice from the South*, edited by Mary Helen Washington (New York: Oxford University Press, 1998), 12.

19. Brenda Gayle Plummer, *Rising Wind: Black Americans and U.S. Foreign Affairs* (Chapel Hill: University of North Carolina Press), 1996. Nikhil Pal Singh, *Black Is a Country: Race and the Unfinished Struggle for Democracy* (Cambridge, MA: Harvard University Press, 2005). Cynthia Young, *Soul Power: Culture, Radicalism, and the Making of the U.S. Third World Left* (Durham, NC: Duke University Press), 2006.

20. George Fredrickson, *Black Liberation: A Comparative History of Black Ideologies in the United States and South Africa* (New York: Oxford, 1996). Robin D. G. Kelley, *Race Rebels: Culture, Politics, and the Black Working Class* (New York: Free Press, 1996). Michael Robinson and Frank N. Schubert, "David Fagen: An Afro-American Rebel in the Philippines, 1899–1901," *Pacific Historical Review* 64, no. 1 (February 1975): 68–83. Cedric Johnson, *From Revolutionaries to Race Leaders* (Minneapolis:

University of Minnesota Press, 2007), 131–172. Ula Yvette Taylor, *The Veiled Garvey: The Life and Times of Amy Jacques Garvey* (Chapel Hill: University of North Carolina Press), 2002.

21. Etienne Balibar, *We, the People of Europe? Reflections on Transnational Citizenship* (Princeton, NJ: Princeton University Press, 2003), 9–10.

22. Woods, *Development Arrested*, 37.

23. Dr. John (Mac Rebennack), *Under a Hoodoo Moon: The Life of the Night Tripper* (New York: St. Martin's, 1994), 250.

24. Michael A. Gomez, *Exchanging Our Country Marks: The Transformation of African Identities in the Colonial and Antebellum South* (Chapel Hill: University of North Carolina Press), 1998. Hall, "Formation of Afro-Creole Culture." Ned Sublette, *The World That Made New Orleans: From Spanish Silver to Congo Square* (Chicago: Lawrence Hill Books), 2008.

25. Thompson, *Flash of the Spirit*, 207–8.

26. Quoted in Steven L. Isoardi, *The Dark Tree: Jazz and the Community Arts in Los Angeles* (Berkeley: University of California Press, 2006), 6.

27. Thompson, *Flash of the Spirit*, 93.

28. Daniel Rosenberg, *New Orleans Dock Workers: Race, Labor, Unionism, 1890–1923* (Albany, NY: SUNY Press, 1988), 27. William Ivy Hair, *Carnival of Fury: Robert Charles and the New Orleans Race Riot of 1900* (Baton Rouge: Louisiana State University Press, 1986), 106.

29. Kim Lacy Rogers, *Righteous Lives: Narratives of the New Orleans Civil Rights Movement* (New York: New York University Press, 1994), 20.

30. Ibid., 156. W. E. B. Du Bois, *Black Reconstruction in America, 1860–1880* (New York: Free Press, 1992), 451–486. Miguel Laguerre, *Diasporic Citizenship: Haitian Americans in Transnational America* (New York: St. Martin's Press, 1998), 64–70.

31. Jason Berry, Jonathan Foose, and Tad Jones, *Up from the Cradle of Jazz* (Athens: University of Georgia Press, 1986), 232.

32. Claude F. Jacobs and Andrew J. Kaslow, *The Spiritual Churches of New Orleans: Origins, Rituals, Beliefs of an African American Religion* (Knoxville: University of Tennessee Press, 1991), 9.

33. Jeff Hannusch, *The Soul of New Orleans: A Legacy of Rhythm and Blues* (Ville Platte, LA: Swallow Publications, 2001), 211.

34. Art Neville and Aaron Neville, Charles Neville, and Cyril Neville (with David Ritz), *The Brothers Neville* (New York: Da Capo), 6.

35. Ibid., 233.

36. Ibid.

37. Ibid., 293, 312.

38. Blassingame, *Black New Orleans*, 13. Lester Sullivan, "Composers of Color of Nineteenth Century New Orleans: The History Behind the Music," *Black Music Research Journal* 8, no. 1 (1988): 54–57.

39. Hannusch, *Soul of New Orleans*, 23.

40. Ibid., 5.

41. Michael Bakan, "Way Out West on Central Avenue: Jazz in the African American Community of Los Angeles before 1930," in Jacqueline Cogdell DjeDje and Eddie S. Meadows, eds., *California Soul: Music of African Americans in the West* (Berkeley:

University of California Press, 1988), 27, 38. Rex Harris, *The Story of Jazz* (New York: Grossett and Dunlap, 1955), 70.

42. Burton Peretti, *The Creation of Jazz: Music, Race, and Culture in Urban America* (Urbana: University of Illinois Press, 1994), 22, 41. Harris, *Story of Jazz*, 70–71.

43. Harris, *Story of Jazz*, 151–152.

44. Peretti, *Creation of Jazz*, 22, 41. Bakan, "Way Out West," 24.

45. Clora Bryant and Buddy Collette, William Green, Steven Isoardi, Jack Kelson, Horace Tapscott, Gerald Wilson, and Marl Young: Central Avenue Sounds Editorial Committee, *Central Avenue Sounds: Jazz in Los Angeles* (Berkeley: University of California Press, 1988), 226.

46. Neville et al., *Brothers Neville*, 105.

47. Estes, "Neo-African Vatican," 77.

48. Dr. John, *Under a Hoodoo Moon*, 44–45, 104–105.

49. Douglas Henry Daniels, "Vodun and Jazz: 'Jelly Roll' Morton and Lester 'Pres' Young: Substance and Shadow," *Journal of Haitian Studies* 9, no. 1 (Spring 2003), 116, 118.

50. Jerah Johnson, "Colonial New Orleans: A Fragment of the Eighteenth Century French Ethos," in Hirsch and Logsdon, *Creole New Orleans*, 34, 40.

51. Raul Fernandez, *Latin Jazz: The Perfect Combination* (San Francisco: Chronicle Books, 2002), 18.

52. Sublette, *World That Made New Orleans*, 7.

53. Arthe Agnes Anthony, "The Negro Creole Community in New Orleans, 1880–1920: An Oral History" (PhD dissertation, University of California, Irvine, 1978).

54. Rick Coleman, *Blue Monday: Fats Domino and the Lost Dawn of Rock 'n' Roll* (New York: Da Capo, 2006), 202, 16.

55. Kalamu ya Salaam, "Banana Republic," *Cultural Vistas* 4, no. 3 (1993), 1.

56. Boyd Raeburn, personal communication, 2009. Raeburn served as a reader on a draft of this piece for *Black Music Research Journal* and provided facts like this one and many different kinds of wise counsel on the article. I am most grateful for his help.

57. Rogers, *Righteous Lives*, 6.

58. Beverly H. Wright, "New Orleans Neighborhoods under Siege," in Robert D. Bullard and Glenn S. Johnson, *Just Transportation: Dismantling Race and Class Barriers to Mobility* (Gabriola Island, BC: New Society Publishers, 1997), 132–133.

59. Nayita Wilson, "Housing Discrimination Is Significant in New Orleans," *Louisiana Weekly* 79, no. 3 (March 7–13, 2006), 1A–8A.

60. Tony Scherman, *Backbeat: Earl Palmer's Story* (New York: Da Capo, 2000), 165–166. Hannusch, *Soul of New Orleans*, 47.

61. Hannusch, *Soul of New Orleans*, 61.

62. Jeff Hannusch, *I Hear You Knockin': The Sound of New Orleans Rhythm and Blues* (Ville Platte, LA: Swallow Publications, 1985), 189. Boyd Raeburn, personal communication, 2009.

63. Berry et al., *Up from the Cradle*, 60.

64. Hannusch, *Soul of New Orleans*, 145.

65. Berry et al., *Up from the Cradle*, 4.

66. Ibid., 5.

67. Hannusch, *I Hear You Knockin'*, 89.

68. Ibid., 222.

69. Jim DeKoster, "Wardell Quezergue," *Living Blues*, no. 174, vol. 35, no. 5 (October 2004), 78.

70. Hannusch, *Soul of New Orleans*, 94.

71. Ibid., 122.

72. Neville et al., *Brothers Neville*, 33.

73. Ibid., 59. Hannusch, *Soul of New Orleans*, 129.

74. Kenneth Bilby, *True-Born Maroons* (Gainesville: University Press of Florida, 2005), 140, 452–453.

75. Karla Holloway, *Passed On: African American Mourning Stories: A Memorial* (Durham, NC: Duke University Press, 2003), 181. Thanks to Lisa Cacho for calling this interpretation to my attention.

76. Neville et al., *Brothers Neville*, 52.

77. Hannusch, *I Hear You Knockin'*, 20.

78. Berry et al., *Up from the Cradle*, 4, 64.

79. Ibid., 84.

80. Dr. John, *Under a Hoodoo Moon*, 56, 84.

81. Hannusch, *Soul of New Orleans*, 339.

82. Neville et al., *Brothers Neville*, 188.

83. Berry et al., *Up from the Cradle*, 60.

84. Rick Koster, *Louisiana Music* (New York: Da Capo, 2002), 79.

85. Dr. John, *Under a Hoodoo Moon*, 54.

86. Berry et al., *Up from the Cradle*, 48.

87. Rogers, *Righteous Lives*, 5.

88. Ibid., 6.

89. Ibid.

90. George Guida, "Las Vegas Jubilee: Louis Prima's 1950s Stage Act as Multicultural Pageant," *Journal of Popular Culture* 38, no. 4 (2005), 681. Will Friedwald, "Louis Prima: He's So Delightfully Low," *Oxford American*, Spring, 1997, 55–59. Boyd Raeburn, personal communication, 2009.

91. Hannusch, *Soul of New Orleans*, 135–138.

92. Ibid., 136.

93. Ibid., 130.

94. Hannusch, *I Hear You Knockin'*, 306.

95. Dr. John, *Under a Hoodoo Moon*, 159.

96. Eckstein, *Sustaining New Orleans*, 22.

97. Dr. John, *Under a Hoodoo Moon*, 141–143.

98. Eckstein, *Sustaining New Orleans*, 24. Boyd Raeburn, personal communication, 2009.

99. Hall, "Formation of Afro-Creole Culture," 63.

100. Estes, "Neo-African Vatican," 80.

101. Ibid., 68.

102. Smith, *Conjuring Culture*. Martin Luther King, Jr., *Strength to Love* (Philadelphia: Fortress Press), 1981.

103. Woods, *Development Arrested*. Lipsitz, *Possessive Investment*, 237–248.

104. Woods, *Development Arrested*. Mindy Thompson Fullilove, *Root Shock: How Tearing Up City Neighborhoods Hurts America and What We Can Do About It* (New

York: Ballantine, 2004). John Logan and Harvey Molotch, *Urban Fortunes: The Political Economy of Place* (Berkeley: University of California Press, 1987).

105. Clyde Woods, "Do You Know What It Means to Miss New Orleans? Katrina, Trap Economics and the Rebirth of the Blues," *American Quarterly* 57, no. 4 (2005): 1012.

106. Catherine Michna, "Stories at the Center: Story Circles, Educational Organizing, and Fate of Neighborhood Public Schools in New Orleans," *American Quarterly* 61, no. 3 (September 2009): 529–550, ya Salaam quote on p. 550.

107. Woods, *Development Arrested*.

CHAPTER 10

Epigraph: W. E. B. Du Bois, *Black Reconstruction in America, 1860–1880* (New York: Free Press, 1992), 705–706.

1. Don Cusic, "The Development of Gospel Music," in Allan Moore, ed., *The Cambridge Companion to Blues and Gospel Music* (Cambridge, UK: Cambridge University Press, 2003), 58.

2. Anthony Heilbut, *The Gospel Sound: Good News and Bad Times* (New York: Limelight, 1997), 206–207.

3. Bill Carpenter, *Uncloudy Days: The Gospel Music Encyclopedia* (San Francisco: Backbeat Books, 2005), 87–91.

4. Don Cusic, *The Sound of Light: The History of Gospel and Christian Music* (Milwaukee: Hal Leonard Corporation, 2002), 322.

5. Thomas Brothers, *Louis Armstrong's New Orleans* (New York: W. W. Norton, 2006), 47.

6. Theophus Smith, *Conjuring Culture: Biblical Formations of Black America* (New York: Oxford University Press, 1994), 161.

7. Robert L. Hall, "African Religious Retentions in Florida," in Joseph E. Holloway, ed., *Africanisms in American Culture* (Bloomington: Indiana University Press, 1991), 98–118. James S. Tinney, "A Theoretical and Historical Comparison of Black Political and Religious Movements" (Howard University PhD dissertation), cited by Cheryl Sanders in *Saints in Exile: The Holiness-Pentecostal Experience in African American Religion and Popular Culture* (New York: Oxford University Press, 1999), 9.

8. George P. Rawick, *From Sundown to Sunup: The Making of the Black Community* (Westport, CT: Greenwood, 1972). Smith, *Conjuring Culture*.

9. Quoted in Sanders, *Saints in Exile*, 128.

10. Vincent Harding, *There Is a River: The Black Struggle for Freedom in America* (San Diego: Harcourt Brace, 1981), 150.

11. Sanders, *Saints in Exile*, 149.

12. Harvey Cox, *Fire from Heaven: The Rise of Pentecostal Spirituality and the Reshaping of Religion in the 21st Century* (New York: Da Capo, 2001), 82, 95.

13. Barbara Ransby, *Ella Baker and the Black Freedom Movement: A Radical Democratic Vision* (Chapel Hill: University of North Carolina Press, 2003). Aldon Morris, *The Origins of the Civil Rights Movement: Black Communities Organizing for Change* (New York; Free Press, 1984). Belinda Robnett, *How Long? How Long? African American Women in the Struggle for Civil Rights* (New York: Oxford University Press, 1997).

14. Sanders, *Saints in Exile*, 134.

15. Heilbut, *Gospel Sound*, 206.

16. Paule Marshall, *Brown Girl, Brownstones* (New York: Feminist Press at the City University of New York, 1981), 70.

17. Martin Luther King, Jr., *Where Do We Go from Here: Chaos or Community?* (Boston: Beacon, 2010), 126.

18. Catharine A. MacKinnon, "MacKinnon J., Concurring with the Judgment," in Jack M. Balkin, ed., *What "Brown v. Board of Education" Should Have Said* (New York: NYU Press, 2002), 155.

19. I take this formulation from former Texas agriculture commissioner Jim Hightower.

20. Allison Morantz, "Money and Choice in Kansas City: Major Investments with Modest Returns," in Gary Orfield, Susan E. Eaton, and the Harvard Project on School Desegregation, eds., *Dismantling Desegregation* (New York: New Press, 1996), 241–263.

21. Theodore M. Shaw, "Equality and Educational Excellence: Legal Challenges in the 1990s," in john a. powell, Gavin Kearney, and Vina Kay, eds., *In Pursuit of a Dream Deferred: Linking Housing and Education Policy* (New York: Peter Lang, 2001), 263.

22. Ruth Bader Ginsburg, "J. dissenting," Missouri et al., Petitioners v. Kalima Jenkins et al., Certiorari to the United States Court of Appeals for the Eighth Circuit (No. 93-1821, 1995), 53.

23. Jesus Hernandez, "Redlining Revisited: Mortgage Lending Patterns in Sacramento 1930–2004," *International Journal of Urban and Regional Research* 33 (June 2009): 291–313.

24. James H. Carr and Nandinee K. Kutty, "Attaining a Just Society," in James H. Carr and Nandinee K. Kutty, *Segregation: The Rising Costs for America* (New York: Routledge, 2008), 329.

25. Ibid., 328.

26. Ibid.

27. Jacob S. Rugh and Douglas S. Massey, "Racial Segregation and the American Foreclosure Crisis," *American Sociological Review* 75, no. 5 (2010): 629–651. Niall Ferguson, *The Ascent of Money: A financial History of the World* (New York: Penguin Books, 2009), 260–275.

28. Amaad Rivera, Brenda Cotto-Escalera, Anisha Desai, Jeannette Huezo, and Dedrick Muhammad, *State of the Dream 2008: Foreclosed* (Boston: United for a Fair Economy, 2008), 12.

29. Bradford DeLong, "Grasping Reality with Both Hands," Weblog, Delong/typepad.com accessed July 22, 2010.

30. Gary A. Dymski, "Racial Exclusion and the Political Economy of the Subprime Crisis," *Historical Materialism* 17 (2009): 149–179.

31. Toni Morrison, *Playing in the Dark: Whiteness and the Literary Imagination* (New York: Random House, 1992), 64.

32. Joe R. Feagin, *The White Racial Frame: Centuries of Racial Framing and Counter-framing* (New York: Routledge, 2010), 2–3.

33. Douglas S. Massey, *Categorically Unequal: The American Stratification System* (New York: Russell Sage, 2007), 66.

34. Ajamu Dillahunt, Brian Miller, Mike Prokosch, Jeanette Huezo, and Dedrick Muhammad, *State of the Dream 2010: Drained, Jobless and Foreclosed in Communities of Color* (Boston: United for a Fair Economy, 2010), v, vi.

35. Douglas A. Blackmon, *Slavery by Another Name" The Re-enslavement of Black Americans from the Civil War to World War II* (New York: Anchor Books, 2008), 390.

36. Deborah L. McKoy and Jeffrey M. Vincent, "Housing and Education: The Inextricable Link," in Carr and Kutty, *Segregation*, 127, 134.

37. See George Lipsitz, *The Possessive Investment in Whiteness: How White People Profit from Identity Politics* (Philadelphia: Temple University Press, 2006), 24–47.

38. Douglas Massey and Nancy Denton, *American Apartheid: Segregation and the Making of the Underclass* (Cambridge, MA: Harvard University Press, 1998), 190.

39. Orville Vernon Burton, "Race Relations in the Rural South Since 1945," in R. Douglas Hurt, ed., *The Rural South since World War II* (Baton Rouge: Louisiana State University Press, 1998), 51.

40. Shanna L. Smith and Cathy Cloud, "Welcome to the Neighborhood? The Persistence of Discrimination and Segregation," in Chester Hartman and Gregory D. Squires, eds., *The Integration Debate: Competing Futures for American Cities* (New York: Routledge, 2010), 10.

41. Michael Seng and F. Willis Caruso, "Achieving Integration through Private Litigation." in Hartman and Squires, *Integration Debate*, 53.

42. Ibid., 54.

43. Ibid., 55–56.

44. Emily Tumpson Molina, "Race, Municipal Underbounding and Coalitional Politics in Modesto, CA and Moore County, NC," *Kalfou* 1, no. 1 (forthcoming).

45. Sam Roberts, "In Desegregation Pact, Westchester Agrees to Add Affordable Housing," *New York Times*, August 11, 2009, http://www.nytimes.com/2009/08/11/nyregion/11settle.html (accessed October 24, 2010).

46. Ransby, *Ella Baker*, 335.

47. Martin Luther King, Jr., *Where Do We Go from Here: Chaos or Community?* in James M. Washington, ed., *A Testament of Hope: The Essential Writings and Speeches of Martin Luther King, Jr.* (New York: HarperCollins, 1991), 567–568.

48. Toni Cade Bambara, *The Salt Eaters* (New York: Vintage, 1992), 107.

Acknowledgments

My friend Ivory Perry used to say that being in the struggle for social justice is like being in love with someone who is not in love with you. You think you see how everything can work out perfectly, but the object of your desire is unmoved by your vision. Perry's metaphor expresses eloquently the hurts and heartbreaks that accompany all serious efforts at social change. Yet despite inevitable defeats and disappointments, a life in the struggle is also a life filled with the love, laughter, joy, and generosity of friends, allies, teachers, and mentors of all kinds. The ideas and arguments that I advance in this book emerged from the lessons that I learned largely from participation in collective, cumulative, and continuing struggles for social justice. In the midst of these battles, I have been fortunate to encounter serious people who believe that there is important work to be done, and that it is up to us to do it. I want to acknowledge some of them by name here.

Ivory Perry, Betye Saar, and Johnny Otis have provided me with crucial lessons about the Black spatial imaginary through their activism and artistry. The many personal kindnesses they extended to me, their patience with my shortcomings, and their faith in my potential to learn and grow have been great and greatly appreciated gifts in my life. I have also been profoundly influenced and inspired by many different freedom fighters in the struggle for fair housing, especially by Mary Scott Knoll, Michele White, and Sharon Kinlaw. My research on race and my writing about it have been aided enormously by advice, criticism, and counsel from superb scholars: Robin Kelley, Tricia Rose, Melvin Oliver, Ramon Gutierrez, David Roediger, Claire Jean

Kim, Chela Sandoval, Diane Fujino, Bennetta Jules-Rosette, George San-
chez, Earl Lewis, and the late Peggy Pascoe. Important parts of my education about racial justice also came from work with Willie Brown, Manuelita
Brown, Philip Raphael, George Lewis, Jonathan Holloway, and Linda Young
in the Campus Black Forum in San Diego; from Porter Thompson, Jan Hill,
Ron Gushleff, and Dave Holmes in the Rank and File Teamsters organization
in St. Louis; from Young Shin and Jennifer Chun and their work with Asian
Immigrant Advocates in Oakland; and from Shana Smith and the superb
staff and board of directors of the National Fair Housing Alliance. Fellowship support from the Center for Comparative Studies in Race and Ethnicity
at Stanford University and participation in the Negril Social Justice Writers
Workshop sponsored by the African American Policy Forum helped me tremendously in completing this book.

Individual sections of *How Racism Takes Place* benefited from helpful advice, criticism, and observations by Juan Logan, Dianne Harris, Johari Jabir,
Nick Browne, Bruce Boyd Raeburn, Gary Dymski, Celeste-Marie Bernier,
Clyde Woods, Josh Kun, and Leela Viswanathan. Two confidential readers
for Temple University Press offered wonderfully wise and generative advice,
while Janet Francendese performed brilliantly (as usual) as the book's editor.
I cannot begin to express sufficiently how much I owe to Janet for her guidance, insight, and friendship over the years.

I am deeply grateful to my colleagues and students at the University of
California, Santa Barbara, for all that they have taught me. It has been a special privilege and pleasure to be part of the Department of Black Studies. It is
an honor to be part of the work that this department does. The Department
of Sociology has also been a wonderful home for me and my work. It is a great
source of inspiration, friendship, and intellectual stimulation. Everything I
write owes a deep debt to Barbara Tomlinson, to the intelligence, integrity
and editorial acumen she brings to the writing process, all of which helps me
see what is at stake at the scene of argument. It has been wonderful to share
this journey with her.

Whenever I write, I try to speak from—and for—the tradition of Abolition Democracy, the egalitarian project forged from the freedom dreams of
an enslaved people. The radical democracy envisioned and enacted by African people in America in the years immediately after the Civil War remains
our best resource in the struggle for social justice. That tradition manifests
itself in my life most powerfully through my work with the African American
Policy Forum and its founders: Kimberle Crenshaw and Luke Harris. It has
been a great honor to be associated with Kim, Luke, and the AAPF. It is to
them, and to the community that they represent and serve so well, that this
book is dedicated.

George Lipsitz is Professor of Black Studies and Sociology at the University of California, Santa Barbara. His previous books include *The Possessive Investment in Whiteness: How White People Profit from Identity Politics* and *A Life in the Struggle: Ivory Perry and the Culture of Opposition* (both published by Temple University Press). Lipsitz serves as President of the Advisory Board of the African American Policy Forum and as a member of the Board of Directors of the National Fair Housing Alliance.